Communication Voices

Third Edition

Myra M. Shird
North Carolina Agricultural & Technical State University

KENDALL/HUNT PUBLISHING COMPANY
4050 Westmark Drive   Dubuque, Iowa 52002

Cover image © Digital Juice

Printed in the United States of America
10 9 8 7 6 5 4 3 2 1

I dedicate this to you Daddy. I will always remember your down home eloquence.

Thank you Omnipotent One for the vision.

Contents

Unit 2   Communication in Context   143

CHAPTER 6   Interpersonal Communication: Moving Beyond Self to Connect with Another   145

Unit 3   Communicating in the Public Sphere   267

CHAPTER 14   Persuasive Presentations: Using What You've Got to Get What You Want   371

CHAPTER 15   Special Occasion Speeches   411

Unit
1

Foundations of Human Communication

Chapter 1

Introduction to Human Communication

Key Terms

Communication
Speech Communication
Intrapersonal Communication

Small Group Communication
Cultural Communication

Introduction

This text is designed to give students an introduction to the field of speech communication. It is arranged differently than most other hybrid texts. This text is about you and what you go through in everyday communication acts. I have chosen to let other people tell their stories so we can experience the theory of communication from multiple and sometimes competing viewpoints. How we see ourselves and others is directly related to this thing we call "speech communication."

In this introductory chapter, I will explain my rationale for this type of text, show how the text works, define communication and its elements, and introduce the concepts of critical thinking and listening.

Telling Stories as a Way of Knowing

Exposure to other people's experiences is essential to more competent communication. It is when the knowing, living, and valuing of "others" is taken into consideration that we fully arrive at understanding that our way is not the only way. Yet, we sometimes give in to our supremacist attitudes and consider our way the only way or at least the best way. This attitude yields such societal ills as racism, sexism, classism, and so on.

Georg Wilhelm Hegel (1807) introduced the concept of *Standpoint Theory* in his discussion of the different standpoints or viewpoints present in the master-slave relationship. In his analysis, he essentially shows that while both slave and master exist in the same society, their viewpoints on that society are extremely different. The ultimate conclusion is that there is no single viewpoint of social life. Our viewpoints are influenced by our position in life. Hence, I have chosen to explore this vast world of communication by introducing essays, stories, and examples that represent multiple viewpoints.

Positivist research, generally, has failed at explicating the viewpoints of marginalized groups. As a Black female academician, I am fed up with the incidental paragraphs that discuss how the theory differs when dealing with African Americans or Hispanics. Usually these paragraphs are plugged in at the end of chapters, which makes me feel like an afterthought. Audre Lorde (1984) explains, "it is axiomatic that if we do not define ourselves for ourselves, we will be defined by others for their use and to our detriment" (p. 45). Therefore, I am assuming the challenge of offering multiple viewpoints about how we as humans communicate, how we are communicated to, and what is communicated to us. Stories are a valuable way of understanding society, people's places within society, and people's viewpoints of that society.

Hence, narrative research is necessary to obtain multiple viewpoints of communication. Kathleen Casey (1995) explains, "story telling is a negotiation of power" (p. 219). She further explains that, "the celebration of ordinary people's heroism in liberal and radical narrative research (a major emphasis of the current trend) undermines the conservative glorification of great White men in the established autobiographical tradition" (p. 215).

Catherine Riessman (1993) further clarifies, "The meaning of a text is always meaning to someone. The truths we have constructed are meaningful to specific interpretive communities" (p. 15). To further this argument, Riessman maintains that, "Western, White, middle-class interviewers seem to expect temporally sequenced plots and have trouble hearing ones that are organized episodically" (p. 17).

Because much of the recognized scholarship is by White male researchers, the candor of Casey and Riessman (both women) is extremely valuable in calling attention to potentially slanted interpretations.

Casey says that narrative research is, "at present, distinctly interdisciplinary, including elements of literary, historical, anthropological, sociological, psychological, and cultural studies" (p. 212). She concludes that, "Whether implicit or elaborated, every study of narrative is based on a particular understanding of the speaker's self" (p. 213). Riessman adds, "A primary way individuals make sense of experience is by casting it in narrative form" (p. 4).

W. Pinar (1988) explains that, "through one's self-understanding one comprehends—from a participant's rather than observer's point of view" (p. 150). He continues, "the function of ideas and texts in one's intellectual life, and the function of one's intellect in one's life," helps one rediscover the self in the other. "Understanding of self is not narcissism; it is a precondition and a concomitant condition to the understanding of others" (p. 150).

So this is why I have included my stories, my friends' stories, my students' stories, stories from people I don't know personally, as well as essays that drive home the major points about communication and its theories. It is also why, to the chagrin of some scholars, that I use the word "I" throughout this text. I, along with many others, are the authors of this text. There is no way around my experiences. My experiences make me, shape my language, and even direct my decision of which elements to include in this text. So, "I" am throughout.

Showing You "Whatcha Workin' Wit"

This textbook is organized in a way that allows for interactive learning. You will read things that, hopefully, you will want to discuss in class and to reflect upon during your daily communication. Each chapter is introduced with an outline to help you navigate through the information. Most chapters include essays or narrative comments regarding the communication theory. These stories are not to be considered as incidental, but should be recognized as an attempt to offer multiple and competing viewpoints. There are numerous activities within and at the end of each chapter that will assist in increasing your communication competence.

You may also notice that some of my subtitles and examples sound similar to lyrics from popular songs, movies, and/or language that are frequently used in pop culture. I figure if we listen to these songs, watch these movies, and use this language in our everyday interactions, then why not incorporate them into our learning models. Some will challenge me on this. But, hey, that is the nature of scholarship.

Looking over the Field

The National Communication Association (2001) explains:

> The importance of communication in human affairs was recognized at the dawn of scholarly inquiry, when Plato, Aristotle, and Socrates undertook major treatises on its role in politics, the courts, and epistemology. Its importance is no less evident today in the renewed attention to communication processes recently undertaken by many social sciences, as they attempt to understand the impact of communication technologies on their own practices, as well as the effects on other individuals, their relationships, institutions, and society.

Communication today is a broad discipline, including scholars from academic departments of Communication, Speech Communication, and Mass Communication, as well as groups in Information Systems, Library Science, Management, and Family Studies. Communication research employs a wide range of methodologies, including all types of quantitative and qualitative social scientific research methods, mathematical modeling, simulation, and rhetorical and discourse analysis. The field has also developed methods uniquely suited to its subject matter, such as content analysis, semantic network analysis, nonverbal communication analyses, and phase mapping for the study of communication processes over time.

Communication inquiries range from the development of general and abstract theories on how communication figures in social change, to middle-range research on topics such as the impact of the Internet on interpersonal relationships, to applied research on questions such as how communication promotes learning in both physical and "virtual" classrooms. Significant areas of communication research include:

- interpersonal communication
- nonverbal communication
- persuasion and social influence
- group communication
- organizational communication
- communication networks
- mediated communication
- communication technology and media studies
- health communication
- family communication
- instructional communication
- legal communication
- communication and public policy

What distinguishes communication research from other, similar approaches to social behavior? Often there is considerable overlap, and there is a healthy exchange between communication research scholarship and that of other disciplines. Yet, while communication outcomes are influenced by a host of psychological and sociological factors that set the stage for interaction (e.g., personality, goals, social skills, contextual, and relational norms), their influences of these factors frequently pale in comparison to actual communication dynamics, once people commence interaction. For example, cognitive factors are likely to exert their strongest influence early in conversations and to diminish in importance as the interaction proceeds, as communicators adjust to ongoing conversational behavior. Thus, a focus on *messages and patterns of messages* is essential to understanding the consequences of human interaction and the relationship between what precedes and follows from it. (p. 5)

National Communication Association (2001). *Communication Ubiquitous, Complex, Consequential* [Brochure]. Washington, D.C.: Author.

What does all of that mean? The study of life and academic disciplines are based primarily in the concept of communication. You CAN NOT NOT communicate; hence, everything is about communication. Our relationships proceed based on the kinds of communications we have with others. Generally, we like or dislike a person because of how they communicate. Some may hastily object and say, "No, I liked her from the very first time I laid eyes on her. She hadn't said a word."

Understand that the communication arena covers much more than verbal communication. Physical appearance, although not verbal, constitutes a version of communication. When we get to nonverbal communication, we will explore this area in further detail.

For now, let us reflect for a moment on life without communication. Think. What would the world look like? How would we instruct, explain, and question? How would we create, sustain and alter culture? Scholars generally argue that communication as a field of study originated with Plato, Aristotle, and Socrates. I don't easily accept this notion simply because some of the world's greatest wonders would not exist without communication. The pyramids would not be as perfect without the plans being carefully communicated from the architect to the workers. Without communication, how would the workers be persuaded to perform such laborious tasks?

My argument is that there were systematic forms of communication prior to Aristotle and the lot; hence, there was some study—formal or informal—of the patterns. When we repeatedly watch Hip Hop videos to learn how to "two-step" or how "to walk it off," we are in fact studying. When we look carefully at something and identify the parts and patterns, we have begun to critically analyze. Nay Sayers might offer that imitation does not require critical analysis. I would argue quite the opposite. You cannot imitate that which you have not figured out how to do. A dancer must critically analyze what it takes to get her body to "pop, lock and drop it." Study, to a great degree, is about identifying steps and patterns. Since there have been obvious patterns of communication since the beginning of time, I propose that the science of communication has been studied as long.

When asked about the historical origins of the communication field, Policy Management Professor, Youichi Ito, responded:

> The question itself seems to include some "Western bias" (probably for the better in this case). It is true that the history of academic disciplines in the West has been the history of "spinning off" from larger or more comprehensive systems of knowledge such philosophy, history, and science. Outside of Western civilization, however, this has not necessarily been the case. As I cannot spare the time to write a long explanation, let me limit the subject to science only. There has existed "scientific knowledge" outside the West since ancient times especially in the fields of astronomy, botany, zoology, natural history, and even economics. However, the situation outside the West (before the Western influence in the 19th century) was like that in Europe before the "scientific revolution in the 17th century. Scientific knowledge outside the West before the 19th century was a servant of some practical or pragmatic purpose such as calendar making, medicine, machinery, or public policy. In other words, although scientific knowledge has existed independently as fragmented knowledge in various fields without being systematized or connected to each other. Therefore, there has not been the "spinning off' process. As for scientific knowledge regarding communication, the oldest would be rhetoric ... Serious studies on these subjects started in Japan as early as in the West.

However, what researchers actually did was to examine successful cases and failed cases and try to acquire insights regarding effective methods for achieving their goals. (Dervin & Song, 2004, p. 19).

Professor Ito later explains that Japanese social scientists did not catch up with the West in the "scientific processing" techniques until after World War II. Much of the study of communication at that time had to do with propaganda, public opinion, rumors, and panic.

Communication—"Why You Wanna Know?"

Competence in oral communication—in speaking and listening—is prerequisite to students' academic, personal, and professional success in life. Indeed, teachers deliver most instruction for classroom procedures orally to students. Students with ineffective listening skills fail to absorb much of the material to which they are exposed. Their problems are intensified when they respond incorrectly or inappropriately because of poor speaking skills. Students who cannot clearly articulate what they know may be wrongly judged as uneducated or poorly informed. Additionally, some speech styles of students can trigger stereotyped expectations of poor ability: expectations that may become self-fulfilling. Of equal concern, students who are unable to effectively ask for help from a teacher will not receive it, and typically reticent students progress more slowly despite what may be a normal level of aptitude.

Beyond the confines of school, oral communication competence can contribute to individuals' social adjustment and participation in satisfying interpersonal relationships. Youngsters with poor communication skills are sometimes viewed as less attractive by their peers and enjoy fewer friendships. Antisocial and violent behavior often accompany or occur with underdeveloped social and conflict management skills. On the positive side, the ability to communicate orally supports sound psychological development. One's self concept is acquired through interaction with others. In psychological terms, achieving self-actualization involves communication activities such as making contributions in groups, exerting influence over others, and using socially acceptable behavior.

As individuals mature and become working adults, communication competence continues to be essential. Communication skills are required in most occupations. Employers identify communication as one of the basic competencies every graduate should have, asserting that the ability to communicate is valuable for obtaining employment and maintaining successful job performance. The communication skills essential in the workplace include basic oral and writing skills, and the ability to communicate in work groups and teams, with persons of diverse background, and when engaged in problem solving and conflict management.

Given the importance of the ability to communicate competently, the communication discipline should be viewed as central on college campuses. Humans are born with the ability to vocalize; but not with the knowledge, attitudes, and skills that define communication competence. The ability to communicate effectively and appropriately is learned and therefore must be taught. **(Morreale, S., Osborne, M. & Pearson, J.,)**

Modeling Communication: We've Come a Long Way Baby!

In the 1940's Claude Shannon and Warren Weaver produced one of the earliest models of the communication process. They proposed that communication was linear; meaning communication flowed from Person A, the source/sender to Person B, destination/receiver. Shannon, a research scientist for Bell Labs, held particular professional concerns about how the communication process takes places. Shannon's work was primarily concerned with communication technology.

Essentially the Shannon/Weaver model proposed that the source creates the message, then sends the message verbally via a transmitting mechanism, i.e., walkie-talkie, phone, microphone, and, etc. The message reaches its destination and is received via the hearing mechanisms within the ear or via some mechanical receiving device. Noise or static in a phone could hinder or interfere with the completion of the communication episode. This linear model of communication is limited. The communication is all going

The Shannon-Weaver Model of Communication

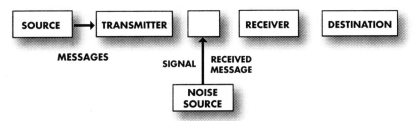

Wood, J. (2004) *Communication Theories in Action: An Introduction.* 3rd. Thompson Wadsworth: United States.

one way. This model assumes if you are the one doing the speaking, then you cannot be the one doing the listening.

Think about the last time your cell phone dropped a call. Wasn't it frustrating? The person on the other end was still talking and had no way of knowing that you were not there. Or what about the last time you were trying to talk to your homeboy on the phone, his music was too loud; he couldn't hear you and you couldn't hear him. The noise frustrated the moment. The sheer frustration of not being able to hear can alter the communication environment. You may no longer feel like talking after you've had to hold the phone, burning up five or six minutes of your daytime minutes, while he argues with his roommate about turning down the music.

The Shannon-Weaver model does not take into consideration that Person B is communicating at the same time as Person A. When you and your friend communicate, don't you send cues to show understanding, confusion, agreement, and, etc.? Person B sends feedback. The Shannon-Weaver model does not account for the continuous cycle of feedback.

There are numerous models and theories of communication. We could cover an entire semester discussing those alone. For your sake, I have limited this discussion to what is widely accepted as the original model, the Shannon-Weaver model and to what is generally accepted as the more comprehensive model, the transactional model.

Communicating by Definition

Now that you are prepared to critically analyze communication, it is important to understand how I am defining this term. **Communication** is a systematic process in which we share ideas and create meaning through human symbolic action. Unfortunately, when some people sign up for a class in speech communication they are under the misconception that the course is just about talking. Talking without thinking or understanding is what gets us in trouble.

Speech Communication is a humanistic and scientific discipline that focuses on how, why, and what effects communication has on people. The discipline is not limited to just talking. It encompasses the entire realm of symbolic interaction. Let me break down the definition of communication into its specific features so that you may get a better grasp of this concept.

Communication is **systematic** in that there are interrelated parts that affect one another. This becomes more evident later in this chapter as we discuss the transactional model of communicating. Communication is a **process** because it is ongoing. You **cannot not** communicate. However, the meaning of our communication relies heavily on the "other's" interpretations of our symbolic actions. **Symbolic action,** in this case, refers to our usage of verbal, as well as nonverbal symbols to create meaning. Thus, the concept of shared meaning arises out of our agreement on the meaning of the symbols. Symbols—verbal and nonverbal—are actually ambiguous, arbitrary, and abstract representations. It is the participants in the communication act that bring meaning to symbols. As we deal more with culture, we will find that symbols vary in meaning from culture to culture.

Communication—"How You Do Dat Dere"?

The transactional model of communication has multiple components. Here, I cover sender/receiver, message, frame of reference, noise, codes, and channels.

In the model of communication, we can see that communication is ongoing. Therefore, the participants in the act change roles frequently. At times, Person A is the sender (source of the message) and at other times, Person A is the receiver (interpreter of the message). In some cases, they are sending messages simultaneously. In any event, the sender of a message must be **stimulated** by either internal or external factors to communicate. Stimulation may come from anything as simple as the desire to communicate to something as severe as the need to communicate, i.e., *HELP.* Internal factors may come from our memory or our feelings on a particular subject. External factors arise out of our surroundings. Although we may be stimulated to send a message, we may lack the motivation. Our **motivation** arises out of the personal benefit we receive from putting our thoughts and feelings out there for public scrutiny.

As the sender of the message, we encode our thoughts so that we might transmit them to others. **Encoding** is the process of putting our messages into a form that can be communicated. We encode by using words as well as nonverbal behaviors. **Decoding,** on the other hand, is the process that the receiver goes through in order to interpret the sender's message. We transport our messages using three different types of **codes:** verbal, vocal, and visual. **Verbal codes** (language) are the means of transporting our messages using the spoken word. **Vocal codes** (paralanguage) are the vocal elements that accompany the spoken word. These codes include the volume, pitch, rate and inflections of the voice. **Visual codes** (nonverbal) are behaviors that we use to communicate messages, such as facial expressions, gestures, posture, appearance, and so on.

Feedback is the receiver's response to the sender's message. It can be intentional, which verbal responses generally are, or unintentional, which is sometimes the case with nonverbal feedback.

Have you ever known by the expression on mom's face that you were not going to get the money you asked for? Then you've experienced nonverbal feedback. With parents, sometimes you never know if their expressions are intentional or unintentional. However, it's a pretty safe bet that they will give feedback one way or another.

Our frame of reference greatly influences how we encode and decode messages. **Frame of reference** refers to our background and our personal experiences. Essentially, this is how we know what we know. It is impossible for two individuals to have the same frame of reference. Just because I am a Black woman, doesn't mean that I have the same frame of reference or viewpoint as Oprah Winfrey.

Unfortunately we sometimes bring negative baggage from previous communication encounters to our present encounters. This can distort the meaning of the sender's message. If you have heard Erykah Badu's song "Bag Lady," you have a clear and creative depiction of how holding on to negativity impacts our frame of reference, hence negatively impacting our communication with others. Take note of this spam e-mail that I received from one of my friends. I acknowledge its original author whomever that might be. It is an excellent analysis . . .

```
--Original_Message-->>>
```

This song is a prime example of the healing powers of music, lessons in lyrics, and a message in the music. It serves as a wake-up call to [people] *sic* everywhere. And none of us are exempt. From the very first verse to fade out, the words resonate. Here are a few key verses we need to remember:

"Bag Lady, you gon' hurt your back draggin' all them bags like that...."

Holding on to pain, hurt, anger and disappointment manifests itself in our bodies. The end result runs the gamut from chronic

illnesses to life-threatening diseases. Sooner or later, our baggage causes our bodies to give out.

"Bag Lady, you gon' miss your bus. You can't hurry up 'cause
you've got too much stuff..."

When we spend our time focusing on negative people and negative
experiences, we end up missing opportunities.... We can't see the
future because we're too busy living in the past. Meanwhile, our
perpetrators go on living their lives, oblivious to the hurt
they've caused. So, who are we really hurting?

"When they see you comin', [men] *sic* take off runnin'...."

How many relationships have come together on crutches? Most [of
us] *sic* know they have no business getting involved when there are
unresolved issues within. Still, due to fear of being alone, or of
'missing out' on a good [mate] *sic,* we cover our wounds, with
tight hairdos, beautiful clothes, and a fake smile. Forging ahead
into an alliance with someone who has no idea we're still hurting
over what that so and so did to us in '95, or over the father that
never came home.

As time passes, the wounds get harder and harder to hide. When
they're finally exposed, [he or she] *sic* is history. In the grand
scheme of things, the only thing stopping us is us. True, we have
no control over what others do or say to us, but we can control
our reactions. And as for our baggage, it's nothing to be ashamed
of. We all have issues. The shame is not in having baggage, it's
in KEEPING it.... Just let it go. Let it go. Let it go. Let it GO!

—->>>

There are other pieces to the communication model that are as important to message encoding and decoding as frame of reference. **Noise** interrupts or interferes with the
intended message. Thus it impacts how we receive the message. Noise stems from external as well as internal factors. **External factors** are those things that exist in our environment. It could be the sound of a lawn mower running outside. The room may be too
cold, so you concentrate more on keeping warm than on the message. **Internal noise**
arises on the inside of us. Have you ever been hungry, tired, or in need of the restroom
and tried listening at the same time? It is virtually impossible—that is unless you have a
strong constitution. Factors such as prejudice, personal problems, sickness and attitude
are certainly considered internal noise.

We must acknowledge **channels** of communication, which are simply the vehicles
that transmit messages from sender to receiver. No, messages are not transmitted or
transported by automobiles. They are, however, transmitted by sound waves (oral communication) and light waves (nonverbal communication). Messages can also be transmitted by written communication (letters, memos, e-mails) or electronic media (radio,
television).

The S.O.U.L. Model of Communications

I offer an extended version of the transactional model to show that multiple and often conflicting social factors greatly impact our communication.

My extended version, the S.O.U.L. (Self Organized Understanding of Language) Model clearly shows that both the sender and receiver are consumed by much more than the message in the moment. Yes, the transactional model shows that the participants bring their own background information to the interactional instance. The S.O.U.L. model, however, helps us to see how each individual's background weighs on his or her organization and understanding of the language.

Remember April 2007; it was right after the Women's NCAA finals. Radio host, Don Imus referred to the Rutger's Women's Basketball team as "Nappy headed ho's." Al Sharpton and Jesse Jackson protested like a literal, not figurative, lynching had taken place. CBS and MSNBC canceled Imus's show. The outrage seemed to be about a white man using this language. Critics immediately fired back at the Imus "haters" by arguing that African American or Black Hip-Hop artist constantly use this language when referring to women. What was the difference?

The S.O.U.L. Model of Communications

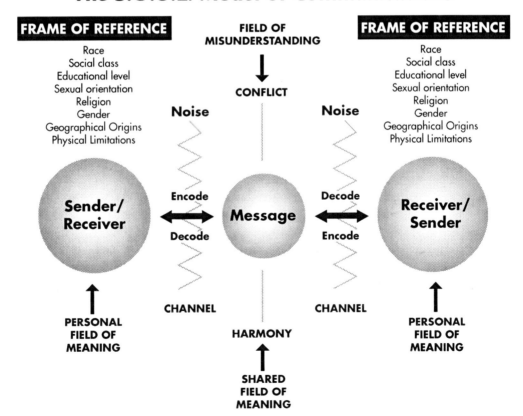

I propose the difference was the memory of the racial conflict between Black and White people in America. Generally, we speak of the frame of reference as our experiences. My race, social class, educational level, sexual orientation, religion, gender, geographical origins, as well as, my physical abilities and limitations influence my Frame of Reference. *Conflict* may be the main dynamic between two people who have bad historical memory. The historical memory is not limited to race. Conflicting memories between gay and straight, rich and poor, or men and women can breed a difference in message reception.

It is important to understand how to handle feedback when there are conflicting memories of a message. The key is to SLAP. No, don't hit the person. Stop, Listen, Analyze, and Prioritize your communication.

Stop. There is no need for a hasty response after you have just heard degrading comments. Surely, you probably want to retaliate. Don't. You need more information before you respond. Take a few breaths and get your head together. Remember, these techniques can be used in any confrontational situation.

Listen. You only exacerbate the situation when you keep talking and fail to listen. I once heard, "A wise man is seldom heard, but a fool talks all of the time." Be economical with your word choices in times of conflict. It is easy to spew out harmful words, but impossible to ingest them again.

Analyze. Think about why the person is saying the things that they are saying to you. What painful memories lead them to use this destructive language? Sometimes people speak out of their own pain. Other times they speak out of their own stupidity.

Prioritize. Determine what is most important to you at that moment. If revenge tops your list, stop. Start the steps all over again. If the most important thing for you at that time is justice, your communication should proceed orderly and cordially. Anger begets anger. Yelling begets yelling. Someone needs to take the high road, let it be you.

Why You So Critical?

It is vogue to be considered "deep." Yet many of us who think that we are deep are only thinking on an epidermal level. This text is designed to provoke deep critical thinking. But, what is critical thinking? According to Drs. Richard Paul and Linda Elder, the authors of *The Miniature Guide to Critical Thinking Concepts & Tools* (2001), "Critical thinking is, in short, self-directed, self-disciplined, self-monitored, and self-corrective thinking. It presupposes assent to rigorous standards of excellence and mindful command of their use. It entails effective communication and problem solving abilities and commitment to overcome our native egocentrism and sociocentrism" (p. 1). Egocentrism and sociocentrism are elements of bigotry. They are the roots of "my way is the only way" thinking. According to Paul and Elder, both professionals in the area of critical thinking, "A well-cultivated critical thinker:

- ▶ Raises vital questions and problems, formulating them clearly and precisely;
- ▶ Gathers and assesses relevant information, using abstract ideas to interpret it effectively;

Elements of Thought

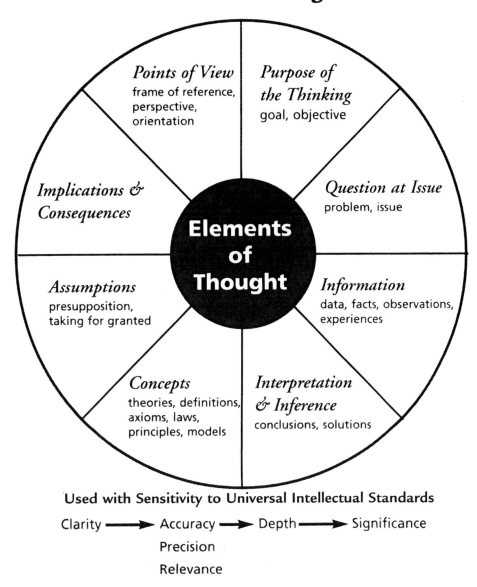

Points of View
frame of reference, perspective, orientation

Purpose of the Thinking
goal, objective

Implications & Consequences

Question at Issue
problem, issue

Elements of Thought

Assumptions
presupposition, taking for granted

Information
data, facts, observations, experiences

Concepts
theories, definitions, axioms, laws, principles, models

Interpretation & Inference
conclusions, solutions

Used with Sensitivity to Universal Intellectual Standards

Clarity ⟶ Accuracy ⟶ Depth ⟶ Significance
Precision
Relevance

From *The Miniature Guide to Critical Thinking: Concepts & Tools.* Copyright © Foundations for Critical Thinking. www.criticalthinking.org, 2001.

▶ Comes to well-reasoned conclusions and solutions, testing them against relevant criteria and standards;

▶ Thinks open-mindedly within alternative systems of thought, recognizing and assessing, as need be, their assumptions, implications, and practical consequences; and

▶ Communicates effectively with others in figuring out solutions complex problems." (p.1)

In order to become more critical in our thinking, we must also become more critical in our listening. Most communication texts of this sort dedicate an entire chapter to listening. This chapter is usually located somewhere in the middle of the text. I, however, want you to understand listening at the very outset. Critical listening is key to your developing improved communication skills. So then what is listening? (See diagram on following page.)

You Hear Me, But Are You Listening?

Supposedly, we listen to speakers with a keen ear. We understand what they are trying to convey. But do we? It is important to listen—not just hear. Hearing is the physiological process that takes place when sound waves hit the tympanic membrane and are transmitted to the site of sensory reception. On the other hand, listening is a cognitive process with six very distinct steps: being mindful, hearing, selecting, interpreting, responding, and remembering.

1. **Being mindful** is the first step. Mindfulness is being present in the moment, being focused on what is going on here and now. Have you ever been so enthralled in thought that you had no clue what your professor had been talking about for the last fifteen minutes? Sure, you have. I'm a professor; we know these things.

2. **Hearing,** the second part of the process, is the physical reception of the message. Hearing takes place when sound waves hit the eardrum. You don't really have to involve yourself extensively to hear, whereas, in listening, you must be present in the moment.

3. We **Select** to entertain or pay attention to certain communication and disregard other communication. We are interested in those things that speak directly to our personal motivations. Why am I listening? What do I expect to get from this communication or message? Once we have selected communication to focus on, we organize that communication based on our own personal "mental" categories. For example, the message we hear may be both what we categorize as "entertaining" and "informing." Based on our personally defined categories, the message may be "political" as well as "motivating."

4. Next, we assign meaning by **Interpreting** the message. What is the speaker saying? What is the speaker not saying?

5. **Responding** to the message is a crucial step in the listening process. Responding allows for clarification; it reinforces the crux of the message.

6. The final step in the listening process is **Remembering**. Essentially, we forget approximately two-thirds of what we ever hear. If you adhere to the first five steps of the listening process, recall will increase and so will the ability to critically analyze what you have heard.

If you are planning a career in the entertainment field, news media, or corporate world, you must refine your listening skills. You must listen for what is said, what is implied, what is not mentioned, what is mentioned, and how it is mentioned. To be a socially responsible citizen, you must listen attentively to the messages that constantly bombard you. The critical listener listens for which arguments are advanced, and how these arguments are substantiated and ordered. Joseph Beatty (1999) explains that a good listener, "focuses her attention on the other's communication in order to understand the other's meaning or experience. The fundamental project is understanding the other and so achieving a kind of fidelity to the meaning or intention of the other. Other projects or purposes must recede, during the listening, to the periphery purposes such as solving the other's problem, morally appraising the other's behavior, counseling the other, gaining the approval of the other, or reducing the other to an emotionally manageable object. If such purposes (which may precede or be activated in the listening situation) do not yield to the intention of understanding, they run the risk of distorting the meaning of the other" (p. 2). Beatty reinforces the notion that good and critical listeners must be mentally present in the moment. All other purposes and prejudices limit our ability to critically listen. Beatty lists the following characteristics of good listeners. The good listener pays attention to:

▶ The other's meaning
▶ How the other expresses her/his thoughts, e.g., "*Barbershop* was a funny movie; *Barbershop* was the funniest movie I have ever seen."
▶ The order in which concerns and themes are expressed
▶ The emphatic and the discounted
▶ The "fitness" of the communication, given existing norms and relationships
▶ The gestures, postures, tones of feeling, and moods
▶ The fit between what is said and the actions that accompany verbal communication. (p. 2)

Why Don't We Listen More Critically?

There are numerous reasons that people fail to listen critically. As Paul and Elder point out, we are natively egocentric, "self deceived animals" (p. 6). Sometimes, we don't listen because we are absorbed in our own thoughts and concerns; we hold prejudices and prejudge others and their communication; and simply, because we do not put forth the effort.

Frequently, we fake listening. There are times that we divert the conversation from the person who is speaking so that the conversation focuses on us. This isn't critical listening because our purpose is to advance our agenda and not pay attention to what is being communicated to us. Sometimes we only focus on a particular piece or part that is being communicated to us. Therefore, we tend to shut out that information that we do not agree with, that is not important to us, or that does not interest us. There are folks that listen only so that they can ambush the speaker. These individuals will distort what you say just so they can argue with you about what you say. I'm sure that you have seen this in the political realm, especially in debates.

Thanks for Listening...

Regina Silverthorne, Ph.D.

"Sydney is someone I can really talk to. I know that she listens to what I have to say!" How can you assure that you are listening and that the speaker feels confident that you are listening also? If it is your desire to listen to what another is saying, then it is probable that you want them to know that you are listening. This can be accomplished simply by employing an ***active listening*** technique. This particular technique is tailored for a small group—specifically, two to five persons that are engaged in conversation.

Active listening is a series of activities performed to ensure a message is transmitted *successfully*. *Successfully* is the key word, because it is my belief that communication is complete only when the message has been decoded at its destination. If the message did not successfully reach its destination, then it was an unsuccessful communiqué. This unsuccessful communiqué is as futile as sending an e-mail to some one who lacks access to a computer. Therefore, active listening is a way of assessing the success of a transmitted message from the receiver's point of view.

When you are the listener, there is a series of activities you will perform to ensure that you are listening and that the speaker knows you are listening. The series of activities involved in active listening tend to be more effective when performed as follows:

a. Provide nonverbal clues that you are interested, i.e., eye contact.
b. Wait for a pause. State to the speaker exactly some of the sentences you heard them say. State the main points.
c. Look for the speaker to express agreement.
d. Give the speaker an opportunity to share more details.

e. Wait for a pause, and then paraphrase what you heard. Be sure to include some of the words from the speaker, but use more of your own words that convey the speakers' message.

f. Look for the speaker to express agreement either verbally or nonverbally, i.e., head nodding as an affirmation.

Example:

Jordan has an idea and begins to tell you about the idea.

1. Provide Jordan with nonverbal clues that you are interested in what she has to say. Some nonverbal clues are eye contact, nodding your head, or leaning in her direction.

2. When Jordan pauses, intently state back to her sentences that she used to describe her idea. Be sure to use many of the same words she used to express herself.

3. Observe her response to you; watch for her to say, "Yes," or watch for her to nod her head in an affirmative manner. [If this does not occur, seek clarification from her, until you agree on what she said.]

4. Give her an opportunity to add to her statement, and wait for her to pause.

5. At this point, paraphrase her statements using some of her words, but more of your own words to describe her idea.

6. Observe her response to you; watch for her to say, "Yes," or watch for her body language to provide affirmation that you understood her idea.

Using the technique of active listening will decrease the noise or interference that takes place during the communication transaction and may develop your ability to understand what another is saying. Active listening also helps the speaker feel as if his/her comments were valued by you, the listener, and that you took the speaker's comments seriously.

Unfortunately, active listening does not seem to be a natural process in our American culture. This is a technique that must be practiced and intentionally, consciously used when listening to another. I believe it is a skill worth practicing. I have heard many individuals who often describe strained relationships with their significant others because one of them did not take the time to listen to the other. I believe that managers and employees as well as parents and their teen-aged children will improve their relationships when they choose to actively listen to one another.

As with most things, there is a caution to active listening if it is performed slightly incorrectly. Do not attempt to "fake listen" by nodding your head and parroting someone's words, without attempting to process meaning for yourself. This is why paraphrasing and restating the speaker's comments in your own words is an essential part of active listening.

The Process of Hearing

Kathryn A. Barrett, Ph.D.

Hearing, an integral part of speech communication, begins every time speech leaves the lips of the speaker and travels to the ear of the listener. The physiologic processes of hearing are extremely complex. Imagine breaking down a cake into its individual ingredients and then putting it back together to make the cake again! "Impossible," you say, yet this is essentially what the ear and brain are able to do with sound. Speech is a complex series of sounds made up of many different frequencies, intensities, and temporal sequences. The ear resolves (breaks down) speech into its individual components and transmits these components to the brain for processing.

Specifically, hearing begins when sound, created by the vibration of an object and propagated across a distance via the oscillation of air molecules, is funneled into the ear canal by the auricle (pinna). The tympanic membrane (eardrum) stretched across the end of the ear canal is sensitive to the pressure variations caused by the oscillation of air molecules. These pressure variations set the tympanic membrane into motion, similar to beating the head of a drum.

On the other side of the tympanic membrane is the middle ear cavity housing the malleus, incus, and stapes (i.e., hammer, anvil, and stirrup), three bones connected to one another and collectively referred to as the ossicular chain. Because the malleus is attached to the tympanic membrane and the stapes is attached to the inner ear via the oval window, the ossicular chain effectively connects the outer ear with the inner ear. Thus, movement of the tympanic membrane results in the rocking movement of the ossicular chain with sound being transduced and transmitted to the inner ear.

The inner ear is a structure that houses both end organs of equilibrium and hearing. The end organ of the inner ear responsible for hearing is the cochlea, a fluid-filled, snail-shaped structure. The rocking of the stapes in and out of the oval window sets the fluid filling the cochlea into a wave-like motion. This motion varies as it represents the changing frequencies (pitches), intensities (loudness), and timing characteristics of the original sound. In a complex fashion, the motion of this wave causes the membranes in the cochlea to bend the cilia located on top of each of the 30,000 hair cells that extend the length of the cochlea. The bending of the cilia enables the hair cells to transmit a neural current to the nerve cells that synapse with each hair cell. This neural current transmits the frequency, intensity, and timing characteristics of the original sound to the brain stem via the VIIIth (Acoustic) Cranial Nerve. The primary auditory neural pathway begins at the level of the brain stem and terminates in the auditory cortex of the temporal lobe of the brain. Along this pathway, neural information is continually processed. Upon arriving at the auditory cortex, the neural information is then sent to other areas of the brain for additional processing. In essence, the brain reassembles the sound so that what is perceived is an accurate representation of the original stimulus.

Critical Thinking: Evaluating Supporting Materials for Your Ideas

Frank E. X. Dance and Carol C. Zak-Dance

Marcus Tullius Cicero (106-43 B.C.), the great Roman orator and statesman, listed five steps to follow in giving voice to one's thoughts in public (Cicero, *De Oratore*). Although there is serious question about whether it was Cicero who first set forth these five steps, they often are referred to as "Cicero's canon." One meaning of *canon* is a set of steps or rules that one should heed when engaged in an activity. Here are the steps:

1. The selection of the idea about which you will be speaking (in Latin, the *inventio*)
2. The arrangement of the parts or elements of your chosen idea (*dispositio*)
3. The choice of words through which you will present your organized thought (*elocutio*)
4. The actual delivery of the speech (*pronuntiatio*)
5. The use of memory to recall your ideas when you present them (*memoria*)

As with all such partitions of experience, Cicero's canon is somewhat artificial. People live their lives with everything going on at once. People don't have the luxury of arranging experience as neatly as formulas would suggest. However, it is still worthwhile to reflect on and analyze your experience for constituent elements and to examine the elements for possible patterns of occurrence. In some instances you may be able to work out a pattern for dealing with life that gives you greater insight into or control over your experiences. In his canon Cicero is suggesting such a pattern that you can use to deal with the public utterance of private thoughts.

Your research and reflection have produced a body of information bearing on the thought or thoughts you wish to present in your speech. At the conclusion of your research you have a collection of data that must be massaged into some kind of order.

You need to think and to think *critically* about the material you have pulled together and how you will use that material to further develop and support your thought. As mentioned in Chapter 1, spoken language is involved in the formation, development, and sharing of your intellect. You need to think critically about what you are going to say, anticipating that the actual "saying" will assist you in the activity of critical thinking. At times just hearing yourself say aloud what you are thinking serves to reinforce your thought or cast doubt on your thought.

You have done some research. You have gathered supporting materials for your ideas. Now you need to think carefully about those ideas, about how the supporting material relates to them, and about how best the supported ideas may be presented to others.

To what conclusions does the material lead you? Are the conclusions correctly drawn from the research? Do the conclusions make sense? *Reasoning* is the process of drawing valid conclusions from your materials.

Some kind of thinking is going on inside of everyone all of the time—images of food, memories of melodies, the sudden focusing of attention on a cramp or of the annoyance caused by a pebble in a shoe, and on and on. This constant flow of random, haphazard, and generally unorganized musings usually consists of recalled or immediately experienced perceptual thoughts.

Perceptual and Conceptual Thought

Perceptual thought is taking into account what is happening around you, what is being presented to your senses—what you see, hear, smell, touch, taste, or experience proprioceptively or kinesthetically. Your memory may also bring back actions, habits, and circumstances that reawaken perceptual experiences from your past.

When you do something as automatic as walking, you take into account things of which you may not be consciously aware—the relative smoothness or roughness of the surface on which you are walking, the evenness or slope of that surface, any breeze or lack of it, the humidity, or the presence of others coming toward you. You take into account all of these stimuli, and based on your analysis of them, you adjust the muscle tension in your limbs, move your shoulders so that someone can pass without knocking into you, or turn up your collar against the breeze. Although often subliminal, such perceptual processing, or perceptual thinking, seems always to be running in the background of human consciousness.

You may even move this relatively automatic type of perceptual thought into your conscious awareness. For example, suppose you are skiing downhill. You are a good skier and most of your skiing behaviors, through long practice, have become automatic. However, you notice some novice skiers below you on the slope so, to avoid colliding with the beginners, you transfer your skiing technique from automatic to conscious control. As another example, you are driving late at night and you are tired. Your driving skills may simply consist of considering the road conditions, the oncoming traffic, your car's positioning on the highway, and, doing all of these things automatically and with little reflection, you are perceptually processing, you are thinking perceptually.

But suppose that while you are simply processing perceptions during this late night drive, your companion (who has been silent for awhile) asks, "What are you thinking about?". Given the fact of your perceptual processing you may well answer, "Nothing."

Your companion next asks, "Are you satisfied with the way your life is going?" Now that is not a trivial question. It is a question which takes some reflection and consideration. It is a question the answer to which relies not on perceptual thought but on conceptual thought. Your perceptual processing moves into the background; it is still going on, but it's on "automatic pilot." You suddenly change from thinking only about things to thinking about ideas, to making judgments.

When you think conceptually, you think about concepts and not percepts; you think about ideas. Perceptual thought deals with the tangible. Conceptual thought deals with the abstract. Theoreticians are often considered to live in a "la-la land" of unreal abstraction. Of course this is not true. Theoretical physicists deal with conceptual structures that are tested in concrete situations. A theoretical physicist for the National Aeronautic and Space Administration (NASA) may be working on the plans for a forthcoming interplanetary exploration. A medical epidemiologist may be engaged in theoretical considerations underlying a possible cure for AIDS. "Justice" is a concept, an abstraction, that finds its grounding in specific acts.

Often you can think perceptually and conceptually at the same time. You walk along a crowded street, weave in and out among the other people, avoid puddles, step off curbs, dodge through traffic, and while doing all of these things that require perceptual thought, you think carefully about a conceptual decision you must make before the day's end. You may even think conceptually about percepts; the best way to arrange your closet; how your wardrobe color choices reflect your mood for the day; or what judgment you make about a person based on how the person dresses. A physician assesses the patient's physical appearance, skin color, redness of eyes, posture, and so forth, to arrive at a judgment about the patient's health status. Architects, engineers, visual artists, and musicians may have conceptual and aesthetic goals in mind as they deal with material objects.

Critical thinking, close thinking, careful thinking, analytical thinking, ratiocination, mentation, exact thinking, accurate thinking, and careful thinking are norms or judgments ordinarily applied to conceptual thought. Critical thinking is not the same as negative, disparaging, or derogatory thinking. Critical thinking takes into consideration both the good and the bad, both the strengths and the weaknesses, of the matter being examined.

People who think critically are not necessarily unpleasant and offensive people. In fact, critical thinkers may be entertaining and delightful. The goal of critical thinking should not be to "put someone down," or to be a "know-it-all," but to get as close to the "truth" of the matter as possible. Contemporary scholars of critical thinking and argumentation have repeatedly pointed out that the presentation of human argument based on critical and analytical thinking should not be a pointless exercise but should be focused on the pursuit of truth and of the devel-opment of individual higher mental processes (Rieke and Sillars, 1984; Trapp, 1981).

Critical Thinking
Truth as the Object of Critical Thinking

Truth is a knotty subject. Many people become wary when the term is mentioned, asking questions such as "Whose truth?" and "What truth?" Arriving at truth, in this context, means getting as close to an unbiased, unprejudiced, unemotional, objective and fully informed understanding of the topic or situation as one can. Truth here refers to what you know you believe. At any given moment you are pretty sure whether you are telling someone what you believe to be true. The philosopher Thomas Aquinas (1225–1274) said, "truth is properly not in things but in the mind" (*Summa Contra Gentiles,* translation by Joseph Rickaby, 1950, p. 44).

The fact that you believe something to be true does not necessarily mean that what you are saying is *actually* true. But it is what you believe to be true. You may be saying what you believe to be true and at the same time, unknown to you, the statement may be false. You may believe that you became ill from eating sweet potatoes and tell someone so, but your illness may have been caused by something else. You may be telling the "truth," meaning that you may be saying exactly what you believe to be true and yet, when you compare your "truth" with the actual thing or event being discussed, you may discover that you are in error. Being in objective error doesn't make you a liar; you have stated what you believe to be true.

It is integral to critical thinking for you to try to measure what you believe to be true against all you can discover about what you are saying. There is an obligation to do all you reasonably can to corroborate what you believe to be true. Such corroboration is the goal of critical thought. The role played by spoken language in the search for truth is discussed in more detail in "Spoken Language and the Genesis of Human Values" (Dance, 1986).

Sir Arthur Conan Doyle's literary creation, the detective Sherlock Holmes, exemplifies a character who combines trained observational skills, highly developed analytic abilities, and critical thinking. *The Adventure of the Dancing Men* gives an example of Holmes' critical thinking skills. This excerpt starts at the beginning of the tale. The narrator is Holmes' companion, Dr. Watson:

> Holmes had been seated for some hours in silence. . . . "So, Watson," said he suddenly, "You do not propose to invest in South African securities?" . . .
>
> "How on earth do you know that?" I asked. . . .
>
> "You see, my dear Watson . . . it is not really difficult to construct a series of inferences, each dependent upon its predecessor and each simple in itself. If, after doing so, one simply knocks out all the central inferences and presents one's audience with the starting-point and the conclusion, one may produce a startling, though possibly a meretricious, effect. Now, it

---

[1]"The Adventure of the Dancing Men, " The Annotated Sherlock Holmes (Clarkson N. Potter, Inc., N.Y.) p. 257.

was not really difficult, by an inspection of the groove between your left fore-finger and thumb, to feel sure that you did *not* propose to invest your small capital in the goldfields."

"I see no connection."

"Very likely not; but I can quickly show you a close connection. Here are the missing links of the very simple chain: 1. You had chalk between your left finger and thumb when you returned from the club last night. 2. You put chalk there when you play billiards to steady the cue. 3. You never play billiards except with Thurston. 4. You told me four weeks ago that Thurston had an option on some South African property which would expire in a month, and which he desired you to share with him. 5. Your cheque-book is locked in my drawer, and you have not asked for the key. 6. You do not propose to invest your money in this manner."

"How absurdly simple," I cried! (Conan Doyle, 1967).

In this example Holmes is reasoning from a number of specific clues to a general conclusion. He is engaged in critical inductive reasoning.

Some Characteristics of Critical Thinking

The concern with critical thinking, although given greater coverage in this chapter, permeates this entire book. Critical thinking is not a trick, something pulled out of a tool bag for special use. Critical thinking is an intellectual posture or habit. Certain characteristics of critical thinking should become intrinsic to your manner of meeting new ideas and testing old ideas. Critical thinkers are always willing to question. They always ask whether any idea makes sense, whether the idea is consistent with things they already know to be based on some factual, authoritative, or experiential source. When considering any idea, new or old, critical thinkers test it against their own experiences.

Critical thinkers inquire about what assumptions or biases underlie an idea. Does the person presenting the idea exhibit stereotyping behaviors ("Well, we all know how *those* kind of people usually behave") that may reflect assumptions that could invalidate the idea presented? Critical thinkers consciously decenter to consciously look at the idea from as many perspectives as possible. Maybe an idea sounds good to someone from your own culture but would be completely offensive to someone from another culture, someone of another gender, or someone with a different sexual orientation.

When considering presenting your thoughts in a public speech, you must bring to bear all of your powers of evidential reasoning. How can you best support your ideas with evidence acceptable and convincing to others who have not had your personal experiences? Reflection on such evidential reasoning is the concern of the next section of this chapter.

Inductive/Deductive Reasoning in Critical Thinking

Reasoning from the specific to the general is called *inductive* reasoning. *Deductive* reasoning, on the other hand, occurs when you reason from a general statement to a specific conclusion that follows from it. When you reason from the general statement that "All humans are mortal," to the specific conclusion that because you are a human, you also are mortal, you are reasoning deductively. The principles of critical thinking apply to inductive reasoning, to deductive reasoning, or to a combination of the two. The development of what has come to be called the *scientific method* has favored the inductive logical process. However, there is some support for the idea that deduction is a more natural and basic human process than induction. Lenneberg states,

> We are discovering a basic process that is reflected in language as well as in many other aspects of behavior. It consists of first grasping a whole that is subsequently further differentiated, each of the specifics arriving at a different time and being subordinated to the whole by a process of temporal integration. In productive behavior a plan for the whole is differentiated into components, the temporal integration results in ordering of movements (or thoughts) (Lenneberg, 1967, p. 296).

Inductive reasoning and deductive reasoning are neither in conflict nor in competition. You can move from the inductive formulation of a concept, based on the observation and grouping of discrete stimuli, to the deductive ordering and application of the concept.

Granted that Sherlock Holmes' clever inductive analysis is the result of Conan Doyle's authorial creativity—doesn't Holmes' reasoning appear quite straightforward and within your own capability when it is explained? Similar conceptual dissections can be found if you consider military campaigns, carefully plotted plays or novels, or reports of ingenious schemes to defraud financial speculators. Note that the only manner by which you have insight into Holmes' powers of critical thinking is through Holmes' expression of these powers in his utterances.

Holmes' analyses are similar to those of an observant diagnostician. What are some other examples of reasoning and critical thinking?

▶ A physician who reasons inductively from the specific physical signs of a patient to what disease that patient may have

▶ Finding that your checking account is unexpectedly overdrawn and then carefully going through the steps to balance your account

▶ Not doing as well on a test as you had expected and recalling your preparation and the places that you could improve your store of information before the next exam

▶ A coroner reaching conclusions about the cause of death after a careful autopsy

As in the Sherlock Holmes example, you can start with a behavior, a set of behaviors, or a situation, then try to critically analyze it. However, rather than starting with a set of behaviors or a situation already in place, you could start with a question, such as "What is the relationship between heredity and criminal behavior?" Or you can pose a problem, such as "What can be done to improve the air quality in our major cities?" The next step is to critically analyze what you would need to know in order to answer the question or solve the problem.

Now consider a specific question. "Does being born deaf affect the development of a baby's self-concept?" An individual's self-concept answers the question "Who am I?" Self-concept is not the same thing as self-esteem. Self-esteem answers the question "Do I like who I am?" Self-concept precedes self-esteem.

Individual self-concept begins to be formed at the instant of birth. Much activity goes on within and around a newborn baby. Along with feeding and crying and many other things, the baby hears the people talking and sees their faces when they talk. It seems logical that the baby's experience would be different if the baby was either blind and couldn't see the faces of those around or was deaf and couldn't hear their voices, or was both blind and deaf.

Experience and your research makes it clear that language plays a major role in the formation and development of self-concept. You reword your question to ask "Does the manner in which a baby acquires language affect the development of the baby's self-concept?" You decide to narrow the problem by focusing on the aspect of congenital deafness and self-concept development. A baby born profoundly deaf cannot use hearing as a means of acquiring language. For the baby born profoundly deaf, sight plays the dominant role in acquiring language. Thus, the question becomes, is there a measurable difference in self concept between a baby born profoundly deaf and a baby born with no sensory deficits?

To answer the question you would probably want to keep as many factors the same as possible so that the only factor (variable) that could account for any difference in the baby's self-concept would be the deafness. Such limitation of cause means taking into account whether the baby lives with a family, whether the baby's parents are alive or dead, whether the parent's are married, whether the parents are themselves deaf or blind, whether the baby has brothers and sisters, the baby's birth order, whether the baby has any other health problems, and on and on. In other words, you try to consider all of the variables that could account for the baby's self-concept in addition to the fact that the baby is profoundly deaf.

This particular question is a singularly difficult one and calls for much more thought than it has been given here. However, even the issues raised so far demonstrate the need to think critically about any question and to analyze closely any problem arising from these contributing factors and the ways to avoid it.

Critical Thinking and Culture

Just as conceptual thought is inextricably intertwined first with spoken language and later with the derivatives of spoken language, so also is culture. Culture is embedded first in spoken language and later in the derivatives of spoken language, such as writing and symbolic gesturing. Among the many ways of defining a culture, one of the oldest is the one suggesting that a culture is formed and carried by a natural spoken language. The culture of Spain is embedded in spoken and written Spanish. The countries colonized by Spain also speak and write languages that reveal their Spanish origin.

In the United States there is such a wonderful mixture of peoples and languages that the tracings of many languages are to be found in American English and the American culture. English, German, French, Spanish, African languages, Native American languages, and oriental languages are part of the mix. This conglomeration of languages and heritages influences what native speakers of American English think about and how they think. Peoples' concepts and how people feel about those concepts are first acquired through the peoples' native language, through the language spoken by those who take care of them as infants and young children. If, through the language spoken around infants and eventually by toddlers, the children learn to think positively about themselves, their gender, their national heritage, and so on, those concepts will be positively weighted. If the people who raise children talk in a demeaning manner about education, or about a specific political orientation, or about certain sexual preferences, then the children will likely become acculturated to a negative set of responses to those things and concepts. As older children they will think about those concepts in a negative manner. Obviously, it's more challenging for older children to think analytically or critically about concepts that are given a negative weight by their culture. Thus, when speakers begin to think about something critically, they need to examine the conceptual predispositions embedded in their natural use of language.

Critical Thinking and Gender

Do women think critically differently than men do? After the authors reviewed a good number of current books dealing with contemporary feminist scholarship and discussed the subject with others interested in and informed on the topic of critical thinking, their conclusion is probably not. There are things that women and men approach differently, feel differently about, or assign different values, hopes, and desires. Such differences, rather than being biological or chemical, are more likely to be culturally derived through the differences in the spoken language of women and men. As Walter Ong points out in *Fighting for Life,* because of their testosterone level, men tend to be more adversarial, more inclined to fight than to reason, and less inclined to reason dispassionately than women. A woman may choose to think about different things or to think about the same things differently than a man does. But whatever the conceptual object of the individual's thought, the individual—male or female—is equally endowed with the capacity for analytical or critical thought about that conceptual object.

Does this mean that you should present an argument or a persuasive speech in exactly the same manner to an audience of women as you would to an audience of men? Not necessarily. A woman does not think critically differently than a man does. However, when she is thinking critically, a woman is different than a man. Gender differences should be considered when making a presentation and such a consideration will be presented later in this book, during the discussion of argumentation and persuasion.

Critical Thinking and Emotion

Excessive emotion damages any effort to be objective and disciplined in thinking. Passion—consisting of the presence of any heightened emotion such as fear, lust, or anger—inhibits a person's ability to take a calm and reasoned approach to recognizing objective reality. In order to think critically and analytically, a person must be able to decenter, to take the conceptual point of view of another person or group.

When you reason with precision, you try and understand the question, problem, or situation from the other person's viewpoint as well as from your own. *Empathy* refers to taking the emotional point of view of someone else. When you learn of a friend's tragedy, such as the death of a family member, and you share in your friend's sorrow (actually feel bad for and with the friend), you experience empathy. *Decentering*, as mentioned earlier, is the process of taking the conceptual, rather than the emotional, point of view of someone else. When you try to understand how a problem looks to someone else or what someone else needs to know to make sense of your point of view, you are decentering. When you try to move your thoughts from inside to outside yourself by means of public speaking, to be successful you need to decenter to audience members. In doing so you consider how your ideas and reasons will be understood by your listeners.

Emotion suppresses decentering. When you are emotionally aroused you are driven back on yourself, permeated with self, and you see and hear everything in terms of yourself. Anger, petulance, lust, fear, and infatuation seem to incapacitate the human logical and critical processes and often forces people to seek what they emotionally desire rather than what logical people would recognize as reasonable, correct, appropriate, or right in the absence of such heightened emotions. Thus, try to accurately assess your emotional state when you embark on a critical thinking venture.

It is also important when you gather evidence and then reason analytically to consider all sides of a question, issue, or problem. A natural human tendency is to find supporting materials for one's own point of view while ignoring the evidence or arguments that support a differing viewpoint. When you speak your thoughts in public it helps an audience accept your position if the audience believes that you understand and have considered opposing ideas. This is especially true when your topic is a highly controversial idea or your audience is hostile.

When you reason critically, keep your mind as open as possible; avoid jumping to conclusions; and avoid the dogmatic view expressed in a statement such as, "I've made up my mind, don't confuse me with the facts!" Being open-minded doesn't mean you lack personal convictions. You will certainly have your own beliefs, but the open-minded individual is able to maintain his or her own beliefs while still trying to understand, if not accept, the beliefs of others. Sometimes people's unwillingness to be open-minded reflects insecurity or ignorance and blinds rather than illuminates their understanding.

Critical Thinking and Economics

Your socioeconomic level can easily affect the manner in which you think about a topic. As with gender issues, someone who teeters on the edge of economic ruin nonetheless has the ability to reason critically as does the individual whose economic level removes all financial concerns. However, if you are seriously concerned about where the next meal will come from, whether you can afford to heat your home, or whether you can afford the doctor's fee for needed medical care, it is not likely you will find the interest, time, or energy to think about where your children will go to college. If you have little, it follows that you have little to risk. If you have little to risk, you will likely rank risks differently than the person who has a great deal of material possessions or position (a lot to risk). At many levels, economics and emotions intersect and, as mentioned earlier, passion suppresses decentering.

There is also evidence that there is a correlation between a person's education level and economic level. People at differing economic levels worry about different things. Obviously, economics and critical thinking have points of convergence, so that it is worthwhile to consider their relationship when you engage in critical thought.

Formal Fallacies and Critical Thinking

Because, for most people, critical thinking is not a natural skill, people can use all of the help they can find to acquire it. The quest to develop and make accessible critical thinking has been pursued for most of human history. Critical thinking is not a genetic trait but an acquired trait. Even though your parents may have been highly developed analytical thinkers, their skills were not genetically transmitted to you. Whatever your heritage, you can individually develop critical thinking skills.

Fortunately, through the centuries, those working to raise the level of critical thought in the human species have codified and set down some tools to help themselves and others in the pursuit of reason. One of these systems designed to help is *formal logic*. The study of formal logic dates back to the Middle Ages; it is defined as the close examination of inferential reasoning.

Inference

When you reason from an already accepted position to another position that seems to follow from the already accepted position, you are using *inference*. Syllogistic reasoning may be considered inferential reasoning. The following syllogism provides an example of inference:

> All humans are mortal.
> Plato is human.
> Therefore, Plato is mortal.

Note that an argument can be correct in terms of the manner or form in which it is presented and yet be false in terms of its inferred conclusion. If the major premise in this example of Plato was changed to "All humans are immortal," and the concluding inference to "Plato is immortal," the form of the syllogism would be correct but the conclusion would obviously be false. There are many rules governing the use of formal syllogistic reasoning. Consult the recommended reading list at the end of this chapter for some references on this form of support.

All people use other, less sophisticated forms of inferential reasoning. When someone says, "If drunk drivers aren't more severely punished there will be a blood bath on our highways," the speaker is using inference. If the inferences you use are well reasoned, they can be a formidable source of support for your specific purpose.

Analogy. Saying that A is to B as X is to Y is using analogical reasoning. *Analogical reasoning* is a form of inferential reasoning that likens something being defined or described to something else that is more familiar or understandable.

For example, if you say that the human brain is like a telephone switchboard or a computer, you are using an analogy. Most models are analogical in nature. A model car is like the real car of which it is a model in some respects, but not in others. When model airplanes are tested in wind tunnels, the testers use analogical reasoning, based on the behavior of the models, which they will then apply to the design of full-size airplanes. Models of human communication are like actual human communication in some respects but not all.

When you reason and then argue that the point you are making is similar to something the audience already supports and that the similarities will generalize to the production of desirable effects, you are using a form of analogical reasoning. For example, you could argue that the problems associated with stage fright are similar to the problems associated with learning any new and fairly complicated skill, like skiing. Your analogy would be, "Stage fright is like skiing." After you stated the analogy, you would develop the analogy further by listing major ways the two are alike.

As other examples, you could say that a college freshman is caught like a rat in a maze or that the college course catalog is like a cafeteria menu. Based on such analogies you could expand the reasoning to make certain inferences about how to successfully pass through the maze or how to make the right choices from the college course "menu." As you can see, analogical reasoning can assist nicely in making a point to support your idea(s) and the specific purposes of your speech.

Faulty Reasoning. As you learn to think critically, it is helpful to consider examples of faulty reasoning. You should then be better prepared to recognize them when they occur in other people's thinking and public speaking and to avoid using them in your own thinking and public speaking. A good number of the classifications of faulty reasoning come from the study of formal logic. Formal logic evolved in Medieval times when the language of learning was Latin. As a result, the examples of faulty reasoning were originally given Latin names. Today the original Latin names are often used to identify instances of fallacious or faulty reasoning. Where appropriate, the Latin names as well as the names in English are included here so that you may recognize the fallacies in other sources that list the names solely by their Latin names:

▶ *After This, Therefore Because of This* (in Latin, *Post hoc, ergo propter hoc*): When you argue that you had a good day because at the beginning of the day you rubbed your lucky rabbit's foot—you are arguing that the day's good fortune occurred because of rubbing the rabbit's foot—you are attributing a consequence to a false cause. This is an example of "after this, therefore because of this."

▶ *Hasty Generalization:* When you argue that because poor communication causes many interpersonal problems, all interpersonal problems result from poor communication, you are guilty of "hasty generalization." Often speakers argue from limited experimental findings to the general applicability of the findings. This circumstance also reflects a hasty generalization.

▶ *Circular Reasoning* (in Latin, *Petitio principii*): When you argue that people are funny because they are so humorous, you are arguing circularly. You are taking your first statement and reasserting it in other words. No real proof is being offered. This is also called "begging the question."

▶ *It Doesn't Follow* (in Latin, *Non sequitur*): When you say that widespread and rampant inflation will be caused by the excessive importation of tomatoes from other countries, you are drawing a conclusion that simply doesn't follow from the first part of the statement.

▶ *Attacking the Person* (in Latin, *Ad hominem*): When, instead of taking issue with someone's idea or someone's reasoning, you attack the character or personality of the person, you are guilty of this reasoning fallacy. This fallacy occurs quite frequently in day-to-day arguments when, for instance, you say "I don't care what reasons she gives, she has that little squeaky, annoying voice; that proves she's dimwitted." Ridicule is a form of attacking the person.

▶ *Appeal to Threat or Force* (in Latin, *Ad baculum*): *Baculum* is the Latin term for "club" or "strong stick." When you stray from the use of reason and logic in your speech and tell your listeners that if they don't support your specific view you are going to severely punish them ("You better agree with me or I'll pound you into the ground with my club") you are guilty of an appeal to threat or force. Appeals to force are found in political statements that demand political allegiance under threat of physical punishment.

▶ *Bombast:* When, by using a loud voice and big words (like a cartoon characterization of a politician), you try to impress your listeners to accept your arguments simply because the arguments flow from such an impressive person, you are using bombast. "Doublespeak" is also bombast.

▶ *Bandwagon* (in Latin, *Ad populum*): When you state that your listeners should support your point of view simply because so many other people support it ("Drink Zippy; everybody is doing it!") and regardless of any logical reasons, you are guilty of using the bandwagon technique. *Argumentum ad populum* literally refers to an "appeal to the people." The underlying idea is that instead of making a rational argument, the speaker simply appeals to the self-interests and passions of the people for their support.

▶ *Appeal to Authority* (in Latin, *Ad verecundiam*): A false appeal to authority is an appeal to your audience to support your idea because it is supported by an authority whose expertise is in some other field. For example, "Thomas Jefferson's favorite wine was a burgundy named *Latriciere Chambertin;* therefore, it should also be your favorite wine." Jefferson was an authority in politics and government, not in wine appreciation. "Einstein believed in God; therefore, we all should believe in God," Einstein was an authority in physics but not a theologian. When you say or imply that your audience should support a view because the chancellor of the university, a popular singer, or a famous actor supports it, your argument is flawed by this fallacy. This fallacy is commonplace during political campaigns, when popular figures from the entertainment industry or sports field endorse candidates.

Numerous books and essays detail how to detect and overcome such logical fallacies. There are also many more types of fallacious thinking than this list presented. The works cited in this chapter often provide more detailed treatments of logical fallacies. Because of the essential link between speech and thought, most of these proofs as well as most fallacies flow from spoken language. Thus their study may prove especially interesting to the student of private thinking and public speaking.

Some Critical Thinking Questions to Ask about Your Research

Following is a list of questions that will probe to what extent you have used critical thinking in your research and speech preparation:

- Have I done adequate research?
- Do my evidence, my research, my speculation, and my critical consideration all bear on the subject under examination?
- Have I gathered evidence that, although forceful, doesn't speak directly to the topic?
- Have I tried to decenter to my audience's viewpoint?
- When I have thought critically about the topic, have I examined all of my research accumulation in terms of my specific purpose? Does my information and my careful thought relate to my specific purpose or is it possible that my effort has become diffused and unfocussed?

Critical Thinking as a Habit

Critical thinking is careful, analytical, precise, and discriminating thinking. Critical thinking almost always begins on a conscious level but may later, through long usage, become habitual. Critical thinking reflects on the ideas under consideration and the presence or absence of support for those ideas, on the consequences of certain ideas, and on the use to which an idea or ideas may be put. Critical thinking may involve the ethical implications of an idea. Critical thinking may explore the artistic or aesthetic properties of a concept.

Every person has analytical ability. Although analytical or critical thinking ability differs among individuals, anyone can optimize his or her personal critical thinking skills and overall critical thinking proficiency. Try to make critical thinking a talent you cultivate not only from time to time but a habit to which your reason naturally gravitates and in which your intellect comfortably resides.

Critical thinking requires self-discipline. The "law of least effort" simply says that given a choice, people usually prefer to do the thing that requires the least effort. The law of least effort certainly applies to the thinking process. It is obviously easier to accept things without questioning them and to deal with ideas without really analyzing them rather than to hold an idea firmly in consciousness and to examine it closely. Much popular advertising relies on lazy thinking for acceptance of product claims. Certainly an attentive examination of many advertising claims likely would raise serious questions about the accuracy and acceptability of those assertions. The precise thinker is a self-disciplined thinker.

Individual critical thinking is integral to the process of creating and recreating a liberated person. The liberated person is free from enslavement to ignorance and free from enslavement to manipulation by others. Someone who is easily bamboozled is at the mercy of every business and political confidence artist around. Critical thinking serves to enlighten human understanding and judgment. Critical thinking, when generalized across a population, creates the base needed for true democracy. In order for citizens to govern themselves they must think critically about the issues facing individuals, society, the nation, and the world. To be free, to be liberated, to be a nation committed to self-governance, the United States must remain a nation in which citizens are informed and critically thoughtful.

Bibliography

Aquinas, Thomas. (1950). *Of God and His Creatures (Summa Contra Gentiles)*. Translated by Joseph Rickaby. Westminster, Md.: The Carroll Press.

Cicero, *De Oratore*. (1942). Translated by E. W. Sutton and H. Rackham. Loeb Classical Library. Nos. 348 and 349. Cambridge, Mass.: Harvard University Press.

Conan Doyle. Arthur. (1967). *The Annotated Sherlock Holmes*, Vol. II. William S. Baring-Gould (ed.). New York: Clarkson N. Potter.

Dance, Frank E. X. (1986). "Spoken language and the genesis of human values" (University of Denver 1986 All University Lecture.) Denver, Colo.: University of Denver.

Lenneberg, Eric H. (1967). *Biological foundations of language*. New York: John Wiley & Sons.

Ong, Walter J. (1981). *Fighting for life*. Ithaca, N.Y.: Cornell University Press. Passim.

Rieke, Richard D., and Sillars, Malcolm O. *Argumentation and the Decision-Making Process*. Second edition. Glenview, Ill.: Scott Foresman, 1984.

Trapp, Robert. (1981). Special report on argumentation. *Western Journal of Speech Communication* 45 (Spring 1981), pp. 111–117.

Where Do We Go from Here?

The study of communication goes back more than 2000 years; there is no way that we can cover the vast amount of information that pertains to communication. However, this text is about to take you to another level of understanding.

We will discuss **intrapersonal communication**—self-talk. It is more than okay to talk to yourself. Self-talk relies on the cognitive process, yet employs language as a means of reflecting on ideas and people.

This text devotes an entire chapter to **interpersonal communication,** which deals with communication between people. Interpersonal can and generally does incorporate aspects of all other branches of communication study except intrapersonal. However, this broad characterization should not lead you to believe that interpersonal communication is a catchall phrase for all the ways we communicate with people. It is not. For example, this text also addresses a more specific type of interpersonal communication called **small group communication.** Studying small group communication allows us to understand how people solve problems, make decisions, and work in the group context. Very closely linked to small group communication is **organizational communication,** which focuses on how we communicate in organizations and corporate entities. In this text, we specifically emphasize leadership within organizations.

The importance of **cultural communication,** the study of how our values, beliefs, and way of life impact our communication, is becoming more and more obvious in our everyday lives. We are living in a global age. Our way is not the only way, and cultural communication allows us to more clearly see this point.

Finally, throughout this text, you will find opportunities to participate in **public communication** or public speaking. This is an area of communication that many people have problems with, because of their lack of experience and their lack of know-how. Hopefully, by the end of this text, you will find yourself more comfortable in the public speaking realm because of your newly gained experience and knowledge.

The model is expanded to show how conflict can influence the meaning of the message. Listening and critical thinking are essential to effective communication.

Wrap It Up

In this chapter, we have discussed how stories give us a better understanding of the "other" in the communication act. We have probed the areas of critical thinking and listening and have discussed them in terms of becoming a more competent communicator. Communication has been defined as a systematic process of sharing ideas and creating meaning through human symbolic action. The transactional model of communication is introduced to show the process in action.

The field and study of speech communication date back more than 2000 years. It is impossible to capture all of the elements of this vast field. In this chapter, however, I introduce several branches of speech communication that we will investigate throughout this text: intrapersonal, interpersonal, small group, organizational, cultural, and finally, public communication.

References

Beatty, J. "Good listening," *Educational Theory*, 49, (1999): 281–299.

Casey, K. (1995). *The New Narrative Research in Education.*

Dervin, B. & Song, M., eds. (2004). Communication as a field—historical origins, diversity as strength/weakness, orientation toward research in the public interest: 54 ruminations from field grandparents, parents, and a few feisty grandchildren. Background paper for the "Strength of our methodological divide: Five navigators, their struggles and success" plenary and post-plenary dialogue, International Communication Association annual meeting, May 27–31, New Orleans, LA © Brenda Dervin & Mei Song, 2004.

Hegel, G. W. F. (1807). *Phenomenology of Mind* (Trans. J. B. Baillie). Germany: Wurzburg & Bamburg, 1807.

Paul, R. & L. Elder. *The Miniature Guide to Critical Thinking: Concepts and Tools.* Dillon Beach, Calif.: Foundation for Critical Thinking, 2001.

Morreale, S., Osborn, M. and Pearson, J. (2000) *Why Communication is Important: A Rationale for the Centrality of a Discipline.* National Communication Association. www.natcom.org/nca/Template2.asp?bid=398

National Communication Association. *Communication Ubiquitous, Complex, Consequential* [Brochure]. Washington, D.C.: Author, 2001.

Nieto, S. *Affirming Diversity: The Sociopolitical Context of Multicultural Education.* White Plains, N.Y.: Longman Publishers, 1996.

One America in the 21st Century: The President's Initiative on Race, (1998). Retrieved April 1, 1999, from the World Wide Web: http://www.whitehouse.gov/Initiatives/OneAmerica/america.html

Pinar, W. (1988). "Whole, Bright, Deep with Understanding: Issues in Qualitative Research and Autobiographical Method. In W. Pinar, (Ed.), *Contemporary Curriculum Discourses* (pp. 134–153). Scottsdale, AZ: Goresuch Scarisbrick, 2001: 134–153.

Riessman, C. K. *Narrative Analysis.* Newbury Park, Calif.: Sage, 1993.

Watzlawick, P., Beavin, J. H., & Jackson, D. D. (1967). Some tentative axioms of communication. *Pragmatics of human communication: A study of interactional patterns, pathologies, and paradoxes* (pp. 48–71). New York, NY: W.W. Norton & Company.

Communication in the Movies

I invite you and a friend or classmates to explore comunication in the movies. Reflect on the communication skills discussed in this chapter. How are they addressed in the movies?

▶ Dream Girls
▶ John Q.
▶ ATL

Name _____ Date _____

Section _____

Think About It → Write About It

Reflect on what you've just read. Now write what you are thinking.

_____

_____

_____

_____

_____

_____

_____

_____

_____

_____

_____

_____

_____

_____

_____

_____

_____

_____

_____

_____

_____

_____

_____

_____

Think About It $\rightarrow$ Write About It

Reflect on what you've just read. Now write what you are thinking.

_____

_____

_____

_____

_____

_____

_____

_____

_____

_____

_____

_____

_____

_____

_____

_____

_____

_____

_____

_____

_____

_____

_____

_____

Activity 1

Airplane (5–10 minutes)

1. Ask the class to write a list of what they believe the components of communication are.

2. While the class is working, ask a volunteer to meet you in the hallway with a sheet of paper.

3. Tell your volunteer to make a paper airplane 'A', in the hallway where no one can see. Explain how they will enter the room and describe in front of the class how to make a paper airplane, without demonstrating. Tell your volunteer: **a) "You cannot *tell* them what they are making!" and b) "You cannot *show* them what they are making!" [Hide Airplane A until the end of the activity.]**

4. Have the student re-introduce herself to the class and then begin giving the class instructions on how to make a paper airplane without telling them what they are making or demonstrating. Class members are not allowed to ask questions.

5. When the student finishes giving the instructions, ask everyone to hold up their finished products.

6. Compare the finished products to the original paper airplane A.

7. Ask why it was difficult/easy to make and difficult/easy to explain.

Activity 2

Journal Prompt:
Observing Human Communication

Consider asking your class to keep a journal. If so, the following instructions may help for the first entry.

Take your notebook and find a place to sit and observe other people at any public place.

Spend at least 30 minutes describing and writing in your notebook

- ▶ features of the communication environment itself,
- ▶ the communicators,
- ▶ the process,
- ▶ the messages,
- ▶ the noise,
- ▶ the emotions,
- ▶ the action,
- ▶ your own decoding of the scene; your perceptual lens

Whatever else appears significant to you about the communication of these people—write it down!

[Consider starting the next class with discussions from journal entries]

Chapter 2

Perception and Social Responsibility

Key Terms

Perception	Culture
Prototyping	Co-Cultures
Mental Yardsticks	Facts
Stereotyping	Inferences

Perception Gone Bad

In the early 1990s, the news media spent millions of dollars to bring to the public the Rodney King story—a story of police brutally beating a Black man. Although the video substantiates a police brutality charge, the policemen are acquitted. The perception of the jury is that no crime has been committed.

I still replay the late February, 2000 newscast report that four New York City policemen had been acquitted of the shooting of Amadou Diallo. Diallo, a West African immigrant, was gunned down at his front door. Four white policemen fired 41 rounds, hitting the unarmed Black man 19 times. The policemen were not convicted of murder, manslaughter, or even criminal negligence. The policemen allegedly perceived that Diallo was pulling a gun from his pocket. The object in Diallo's hand was actually a wallet. Former NBA great, Bill Bradley, who at the time was also a presidential candidate, reportedly commented on the Diallo incident saying, "In America a White man can pull out his wallet, and it looks like a wallet. A Black man can pull out his wallet and it looks like a gun." This is an example of the most socially paralyzing form of perception gone *bad*.

Although definitely not at the same level, I have been privy to my own versions of perception gone bad. One incident I vividly remember. I just purchased my shiny red BMW. Bouncing to the tunes blaring from the Bavarian Motor Works factory stereo and carefully obeying the laws of the road, I drove through the relatively quiet streets of Fayetteville, North Carolina. As I passed one of the city's most recognizable tourist attractions, a well-preserved slave market, a police car pulled in behind me. For no apparent reason, the officer began following me closely. As I turned, he turned. He mirrored my every move. Finally, through my rearview mirror, the police blue lights began dancing to a not-so-friendly beat. Immediately, I pulled into a lighted area. The police car darted in right behind me. Out of my side mirror I could see the officer engage a swagger of authority that mimicked something from a Stephen J. Cannell police drama. He approached the car and asked to see my registration.

In my most polished *Standard English*, I questioned the officer about why I have been pulled over. He replied that my license plate did not match the description of the car. I explained, without hesitation, that the car was a new purchase and that the paperwork I had presented him would corroborate my claim. Politely, I continued to probe into why the officer felt the need to run the plates. I knew it was not common practice for police to run the tags of unsuspecting, law-abiding citizens. I also knew I had not broken any laws.

The officer answered my questions with an almost sheepish voice. I can still hear him saying, "Well Ma'am we just got a report of a stolen Black BMW, so we're just checkin'." He said my car fit the profile of the stolen vehicle. One major problem—my car is RED and the stolen vehicle, if there really is one, is BLACK. This is simply another case of perception gone *bad*.

After reading an earlier version of this text, one of my White colleagues cornered me and argued that I was making too little of my situation and the Diallo case. She commented that by relegating them as mere bad perceptions I was avoiding the reality of racism. As a Black woman, racism is about perception gone *bad*. What do you think? Revisit this question once you've read further.

This chapter is designed to help you understand the role perception plays in our everyday lives. Perception is much more important than most people think. I have heard people say, "that's just his/her perception. No biggie." It is a biggie. Inaccurate perceptions cost Amadou Diallo his life. Perception competency is a social responsibility. Improved perception competency is the major objective of this chapter. The minor objective is to explain the perception process.

Perception as Making Sense of the World

Perception is the complex process of **selecting, organizing,** and **interpreting** information about people, events, activities, and situations. We rely on all of our senses to gather information about our surrounding environment. From the information we gain, we try to make sense of the world around us. Our perceptions, however, are deeply rooted in our personal experiences. **Perception is ultimately about how we select, organize, and interpret information so that we can understand our surroundings.**

Selection as Meeting Our Needs

We select to focus on information that *meets our physiological and psychological needs.* Have you ever been really hungry and food was the only thing you seemed to smell? Probably, there were no more food smells in the air at that moment than there were at any other time. You were simply hungry. Therefore, you selected to focus on something that addressed that need.

We select to focus on information that *interests* us. We are more likely to pay attention to presentations that offer us a benefit or a value. Likewise, we are much more likely to listen to someone we like, to someone who is like us, or to someone whose interests are similar to ours.

Finally, we select to focus on *that which we expect to see.* Seeing what we expect to see instead of what is actually taking place is a cognitive error. The introductory discussion of perception gone wrong is a clear-cut example of how individuals tend to see what they expect to see. I was driving a red BMW. The policeman stopped me because there was a search for a black BMW. The only explanation for the policeman's behavior is that he saw what he expected to see. He made a cognitive error. Do you think it is easy to make this kind of mistake? Quickly, look at the phrases in the triangles below:

Snake
in the
the grass

Once
in a
a lifetime

Bird
in the
the hand

You probably read "Snake in the grass," "Once in a lifetime," "Bird in the hand." Now, go back and reread. Did you have an accurate perception of what was in the triangles, or did you perceive what you expected to see? We easily miss the repeated words, because we don't expect to see them. Seeing what we expect to see rather than seeing what is really there hinders us from seeing change. It hinders our growth as social human beings. These cognitive errors occur without us ever realizing they are taking place. This is the type of cognitive error that costs innocent people their lives and their freedoms.

Check yourself one more time. Read the following.

Busy
as a
a beaver

Paris
in the
the springtime

Snow skiing
in the
the winter

How did you do?

Organizing as a Means of Categorizing

We organize information based on our personal categorizing system. We categorize based on our personal experiences and based on the material and nonmaterial components of our culture. Cognitive psychology suggests that we organize information into *schema* or patterns that are coherent and meaningful. A variety of schemata helps us to organize our impressions: **prototypes, mental yardsticks,** and **stereotypes.**

The Best Example.

One of my students, Angela, was crazy about another student, "Z". Angela constantly told her girlfriend, Regina, "Ooh girl, he is so fine." For Angela, "Z" was the epitome of "fine." He was her prototype or best example of the concept "fine," the best example of male attractiveness. We organize our perceptions by defining a prototype or a best example. The **prototype** is the benchmark for how we categorize a person, object, activity, or situation.

How They Measure Up.

Angela and Regina do a lot of "boy watching." The young women usually categorize a male's attractiveness by measuring him against their prototype, their own best example of attractiveness, "Z." The young women have done what most humans do: they have created their own mental yardsticks for determining attractiveness. Our mental yardsticks provide a bipolar continuum for measuring how close new information measures up to the prototype. Prototypes provide the best example of a concept or phenomena. The mental yardstick allows us to measure new information, using the prototype as the primary basis of comparison.

Just Chatting about the Text

Excerpts from a real chat room session (all names have been deleted):

▶ I have been involved in an interacial marriage for nine years. I remember when my wife's uncle, who is White, made a comment to her about O.J. Simpson. This happened around the same time the trial was going on. Because of the trial he made a perception that we would be in the same boat O.J. was one day. But after getting to know me, his perception changed. We now are great friends and would give the shirt off our backs for each other.

▶ I imagine many interracial couples had to deal with the same types of remarks. It is sad that humans stereotype (many without realizing it). I have a friend who is from Iran. After the 911 bombing, he called me and was very concerned for his family's safety. He had been told to "watch his back." He had lived in the U.S. for 22 years, at that time, but had the "look" of the bombers. My heart broke for him and his family.

▶ Sometimes the people that assume wrong towards you tend to be your best friends. I have a best friend, who tested me like that, and we have been good college friends for the past three years. We are even roommates now.

▶ I think in responding to the uncle that he was just not on you and your wife's level. He did not understand that not every interracial couple will end up in disaster. One should not be judged by someone else's comments or actions.

No Acknowledgment of Uniqueness

In our society stereotypes tend to flourish. When people say things like, "White rappers are just acting Black," or "female basketball players are lesbians," they are stereotyping. **Stereotyping** is the categorizing of people, situations, and objects, without acknowledging unique individual characteristics. Stereotypes stem from our broad generalizations about phenomena. Communication professors William Seiler and Melissa Beall (2002) find that:

> Stereotyping is pervasive because of the human psychological need to categorize and classify information. Through stereotyping we pigeonhole people. This tendency may hamper our communication, because it may cause us to overlook individual characteristics. Also, stereotypes often oversimplify, overgeneralize, or exaggerate traits or qualities, and thus are based on half-truths, distortions, and false premises—hardly fertile ground for successful communication. Finally, stereotypes repeat and reinforce beliefs until they come to be taken as the truth. Stereotypes ultimately perpetuate inaccuracies about people, and thus impede communication. (p. 44)

How we organize our perceptions is inextricably linked to our past experiences. Past experiences may cloud or distort perceptions. It is a social responsibility to make sure that what we see and/or hear represents reality. If we do not, lives could be lost or negatively altered forever. Generally, stereotypes are negative when they hinder the social, psychological, physical, spiritual, and/or financial welfare of any individual or group.

Just Chatting about the Text

Excerpts from a real chat room session (all names have been deleted):

▶ I had been in a situation once where perception was gone bad. Me and some of my friends were downtown in his car. It was around 3 something in the morning and we were just driving back from the club. Out of nowhere 2 cop cars came out and had their lights flashing. We didn't know what we did wrong because we were doing the speed limit.

Once the cop came to the door he asked for the license and registration. Then he came and gave the license and registration back. I was sitting in the front and had a book bag near my feet. He asked me what was in the book bag? And I told him just clothes and make up. After that we didn't know what happened but he told the other cop to come there and asked us to get out of the car, and put our hands on top of the car. We kept asking what did we do wrong? But they wouldn't give us an answer and told us to just put the hands up and not to move. One of the cops had a gun pointing to us, and the other one went to look in the car. He looked near the drivers seat and into the book bag.

In the end it turns out that the cop thought there was a gun in the space near the drivers seat. There was a knob that sticks out from his car but it was the knob for this system in the car. After almost 1 hour the cops apologized to us.

▶ Wow! That must have been very scary. It's amazing how some cops use bad judgement but when I stop and think about all of the danger they are in, I guess they are really just being cautious. That doesn't make it right what they did to you and your friend, but think about all of the dangerous situations the cops must face day after day. Their lives are always in danger. I have a close friend who is a county policeman, and some of the horror stories he tells are so frightening. His wife stays on pins and needles when he works third shift and I can't blame her.

▶ Wanted to just say that I agree that the officers have to be very careful. Sometimes you will find those really hyper ones or the "all-American heroes" or so they think. My husband has been a policeman for eleven years and you would not believe some of the things that have happened to him. He worked in narcotics for 5 years. Many ugly things happen in his line of work!

Boy, you are talking about perception. We had taken my daughter to the park one day and this guy that had his grandchildren there was smoking pot. With his grandchildren! I thought my husband was crazy. I thought he was just happy and having a good time, you know, with a cigarette, not a joint! When he left, my husband had called two on duty officers to stop him and they found a huge stash. He said that he had smoked it at work, while working, etc. for over twenty years. This was the first time he had ever been busted. Go figure. I thought he was just having fun, a lot of fun.

▶ Ya I guess they do have a rough job and just have to be cautious.

Definition of a Redneck

Stephanie Sedberry Carrino

What is a "redneck?" It depends on who you ask. Like many other words, different people define it differently. If you are Black, chances are that you define the term as a White person who is racist. If you are White it is entirely possible that the term refers to the stereotype of "poor white country folk"—uneducated, rural people who live in trailers, smoke, drive pick-up trucks, and have lots of dogs and stuff in their yards. Many white people DO NOT use the term redneck to describe someone who is racist, and do not know that the word is interpreted by some people as racist. Really.

My daughter, Emily, was in a reading class in the third grade that had been divided into reading groups. The kids were asked to name their own groups, and come up with a "cheer" for their group. There were the "Boxing Honey-buns," the "Crunchy Candies," and the "Rednecks." Really. The "cheer" for this group was rubbing their necks whining "I'm so sunburned!" In this group, there were three White children and one Black child. When Emily told me about the reading groups, I almost choked. Although I am White, I spend a great deal of time in a predominately Black environment, so I know that "redneck" is often translated as racist by African-Americans. The next day, I spoke with her teacher, a white woman, who was appalled when I explained to her that to many Black Americans, redneck means racist. She had no idea. The next day, Emily told me that the reading groups had been reassigned, and that they had to come up with new names and cheers. The "Redneck" group was gone. That day, Emily's teacher learned an important lesson about how words can be interpreted differently by different people. I hope you have too!

There's a Redneck in My Backyard, HELP!

A Perspective

Sheila M. Whitley, Ph.D.

When you hear the term *redneck,* maybe many different stereotyped images pop into your head. Maybe you have a definite image and behavior in mind, because your stereotyped image has held true for *every redneck* you ever met.

When I hear *redneck* one stereotyped image pops into my head, southern white male. Let me clarify, I don't think all southern white men are *rednecks,* and not all *rednecks* are the same. My stereotype may differ from your stereotype. Humor me as I label and poke fun at my stereotyped image of a *redneck.*

I place *rednecks* on a continuum. On one side of the continuum is the friendly *redneck.* He is country-talking, gregarious, blue-jean wearing, never met anyone he couldn't get along with, will help anyone, and in general—just a nice guy.

The other side of the *redneck* continuum is the extreme opposite of our friendly *redneck.* He is the guy you don't want living next door. He outcusses a sailor, guzzles beer; favors collecting unemployment money over a job, owns aggressive dogs, scurries off in his mufflerless car, always itching for a good fight—especially in a bar, is overly proud of his race and sees all other races as inferior, had at least one clash with the law before he could legally acquire intoxicating beverages, and in general—someone his friends won't turn their backs on—out of fear or lack of trust. Almost forgot, he picks a woman with the same qualities.

Some guys on both ends of the continuum proudly proclaim their *redneck* status. While others distress if you call them a *redneck.* I know many self-acknowledged and in denial *rednecks.* I adore and appreciate the friendly *redneck.* They are good guys to have as friends and neighbors. But on the other side of the continuum, well . . . I rather only hear stories and be thankful it didn't happen to me.

Sit back, 'cause I'm about to tell you a story that happened to me, and you can be thankful it wasn't you. I need to give you a bit of background so you can fully understand my befuddlement. The names have been changed to protect the guilty.

When I was about 6 years old, Mr. and Mrs. Smith moved into the house on our left side. Karen, their only child, was married and about to have her first baby. Her husband was away in the military, so she moved in with her parents so they could help with the new baby.

Around Thanksgiving, Karen had a baby boy. For satirical emphasis, I'll call him Bubbbbba. His real name doesn't fit the stereotype and he's guilty. Bubbbbba was a cute baby and another neighborhood playmate. I don't remember how long Karen lived with her parents after the baby was born. Eventually, she joined her husband in another town. Bubbbbba visited his grandparents often and some of the visits were for extended periods of time.

All the neighbors grieved when Bubbbbba was about three or four years old and his grandfather was beaten to death in a convenience store robbery. It was about this time, Karen started her marrying and then divorcing spree. Mrs. Smith was financially stable, and paid the bill every time Karen got into a predicament. Karen was engrossed with her life and didn't devote time to raising Bubbbbba. The end result was Bubbbbba lived off and on with his grandmother. Looking back, I wonder if this shuffling back and forth was the birth of what would become his adult value system.

I know Bubbbbba loved his grandfather. It is possible that his grandfather was the only positive male role model in his life. Years after his grandfather's death, Bubbbbba told me he thought his grandfather was the only person who really loved him. Wow! I didn't know what to say then and I still don't know what to say. I think he was wrong. I believe his mother and grandmother loved him. He obviously didn't receive love the way he perceived it should be given. I can only speculate how Bubbbbba's life would have been different if his grandfather lived.

To sum up my relationship with Bubbbbba, we grew up together and had an amicable relationship. I'm told he looked up to me as an older sister. His grandmother affirmed to my mother many times that I was a good influence on Bubbbbba.

I didn't see Bubbbbba much after he reached junior high school. I was away in college and he wasn't spending as much time with his grandmother. His high school years completed his transformation to a new value system. He converted into the type of *redneck* you don't want living beside you.

Bubbbbba didn't try in high school and frequently got into trouble. His grandmother kept us updated on his ins- and outs-of-trouble during this time, mainly traffic violations. My father is a barber, so what wasn't told, he heard through the proverbial barber shop grapevine—gossip.

Throughout high school, Bubbbbba's grandmother bought him several cars. He wrecked, destroyed, or maimed every car. Mrs. Smith bailed him out of trouble every time he drove or walked into it. She lamented many times to my mother about how much it worried her the way Bubbbbba was living his life. I think she believed buying him things and bailing him out of trouble would wake him up. Conversely, it fueled his lifestyle and reinforced an absence of love. He knew her money was available to fix his mess with no parental discipline attached. So he messed and messed and messed.

I saw Bubbbbba for the first time in many years at his grandmother's funeral. He was about twenty-three years old. Noticeably, he wasn't the same person as my childhood friend. We had a pleasant visit and relived some of the good ol' days. It was obvious to both of us that we didn't have any common interests or the necessary foundation for a friendship. Our value systems were too different. Even so, I continued hoping his childhood heart would resurrect. My mother had no doubts. She heard way too much from his grandmother, and knew the type of person he had become. He was someone you didn't want in your neighborhood.

For the first time in two decades, Mrs. Smith's house was vacant. Hopefully, Karen would sell the house. The neighborhood's worst possible nightmare would be for Karen to allow Bubbbbba to move into the house. The neighbors prepared for the worse. I was living at home and would be affected by Karen's decision. I really didn't think Karen would let Bubbbbba move in, because surely she knew the problems he would cause the neighbors. Not to mention, he would probably destroy the house. Karen wasn't like her mother, she wanted all the money for herself. I was sure she would sell the house for the money—if for no other reason.

We all woke up to a nightmare. Bubbbbba moved into the house with several of his friends and his seven-month pregnant soon-to-be wife. Initially, it was difficult to see the intensity of his hostility because it was masked in lightheartedness. It wasn't long before Bubbbbba and I discovered we had nothing in common and no relationship. He no longer respected me as a friend, looked up to me as an older sister, or even talked to me. I won't even talk about how he approached my parents and the rest of the neighbors.

Bubbbbba and his live-in friends worked occasionally, but by far, spent most of their time messing around the house. They competed in front yard cussing episodes in the early morning, mid-morning, noon, night, and late night; drove noisy cars; kept an aggressive pit bull and chow inside the fenced-in backyard; hosted beer guzzling parties that encouraged their propensity for outdoor bladder relief and ended with empty beer cans all over the yard; and performed many other openly defiant behaviors aimed at upsetting the neighborhood old fogies.

One peaceful Sunday afternoon sticks out in my mind and confirmed where Bubbbbba's belief system ended up. I just returned from Baton Rouge and was trying to take a nap since my early morning flight robbed me of a good night's rest. My bedroom was about fifteen feet from Bubbbbba's driveway and the side entrance into his basement. The driveway ran the length of his house and continued beyond the driveway-width chain-linked-fence gate, that wrapped around to the back of the house into the basement garage.

I was awakened from my nap by the jocularity of Bubbbbba and three or four of his friends in the driveway trying to fix his stentorian, but at the moment, broken car. I tried to ignore all the commotion and go back to sleep.

Yeah, right! What was I thinking?

Suddenly, the mood changed. I heard an anguished, "No! . . . NO! . . . BUBBBBBA!"

OK, that didn't sound promising. Could be a problem. Probably not. Drama was commonplace when they were messing around outside.

I'm a bit upset. It's beginning to look a lot like I'm not going to get my nap. I'm soooooo sleepy. Why today Bubbbbba? You planned it this way, didn't you?

Oh my, what's that? Surprise, surprise! The engine started; VAROOM, VAROOMMMMM, VA ROOMMMMM ROOM.

Great! He got the strident engine started. The verdict's in. I lost my nap attempt. Can't sleep with that cacophony. I knew the usual routine. Race the engine in attempt to break the sound barrier or annoy the peace and quiet out of the neighbors.

Success, Bubbbbba! You drove my peace and quiet into the next county. No nap for this very tired gal.

A flash later . . . CRASH, KABOOM! . . . "OH . . . !" Sorry. I didn't quite catch that last part.

Hummmmmm? I wondered what that was all about. Was that a whoops? Sort of sounded like damage. I knew I wasn't dreaming, because I couldn't nap with all that racket!

A split second later, my curiosity mounted beyond restraint. I sprang out of bed—interrupting my insomnia—with an inquiring mind. I was about to take the big risk, and look out the window to see what they destroyed.

Took a deep breath. Held it. Exhaled. Braced for the worse. Prayed. "Please, don't let it be our house."

Looked out the window. Opened my eyes. Sighed with relief—"NOT our house." Sort of chuckled—"HIS house!!!!!"

Based on visual scrutiny and what I heard, I surmised the chain of events. No one was behind the wheel of the car. The boys were all in or near the driveway close to my bedroom window. The hood was up. Bubbbba, and maybe one of his dude's, worked on the engine while the rest joked around and made a lot of needless noise.

Stunner! Bubbbba got the car started. Based on all the joking, I'm guessing his ability to start the engine took his buddies by surprise. After all, Bubbbbba wasn't a mechanic.

Now for the whoops. If you aren't a mechanic, it is in your best interest not to be under the hood trying to fix the engine. Even more so, it really isn't in your best interest to be under the hood with the engine running. You could blow up the engine, electrocute yourself, or accidentally put the car into gear.

What? You think you know where I'm going with this?

For the second time that Sunday afternoon, Bubbbba had success. He didn't blow up the engine or electrocute himself. That's right, he got the car in gear and it took off down the driveway. I'm guessing this evoked the, "No. . . . NO! . . . BUBBBBBA!!"

The car traveled about ten feet, ran through the double gates, busting them off the fence post hinges. It traveled another ten feet and rested after hitting the corner of the free-standing garage. Needless to say, there was a lot—and I mean a superfluity—of cussing. I could only shake my head in bewilderment over his accidental mechanical achievement.

Shoot. This was more entertaining than television. Even my dreams aren't this whacked. Could my afternoon get any more entertaining? Could he appease for terminating my nap? Yea, he could and did!

Bubbbba decided to fix the gates. After all, he needed to keep his pernicious pit bull and chow incarcerated. Resourcefully, he got the necessary supplies to reattach the twisted gates. With twine in hand, he was ready to repair. Luckily, his friends were there for him and willing to help. You know, drink beer and laugh at him . . . I mean . . . laugh with him.

Each gate was half the width of the driveway. The two gates met in the mid-point of the driveway. One gate had a rod that anchored into the driveway. The other gate latched to the anchored gate to ensure the gates closed securely. Anyway, that was the design prior to the "whoops."

Bubbbba diligently worked to secure the mutilated gates back in place—original design in mind. He took his sturdy twine, and wove the twine around each gate, reattaching to its respective fence post. His comrades offered copious encouragement with each weave—laughter.

Wonderful. Beautiful. Most excellent. Finished. Bubbbba had a puff of pride. At last, the gates were shabbily tied to the fence posts.

You ask, "What about the gate with the anchoring rod so the gates close securely?"

Well, let me quote the Rolling Stones, "You can't always get what you want. But if you try sometimes, you just might find you get whatcha need."

Twine was used to hold the two gates closed.

"Securely?" you ask.

Get real. Of course not.

Bubbbba's friends agreed with me. With mockery in their voices, they pronounced their judgement on Bubbbba's workmanship.

Bubbbba retorted, "I ain't no nigger! I'm a white man and don't do no nigger job!"

Ergo, Bubbbba proved beyond a shadow of doubt where he resided on my *redneck* continuum. In addition to exhibiting all the other extreme end criteria (cussing, drinking, loud cars, vicious dogs, no job, police difficulty, and so forth), he announced to the world his racist stance. In doing so, he implied other races can't match his mastery—inferior to his white supremacy.

In reality, race has nothing to do with quality of work. Quality of work is determined by knowledge, ability, skill, and talent. In this case, Bubbbbba was not qualified to fix the gate. Hence, I had to contemplate Bubbbbba's promulgation.

I wondered why the "pride of the race" couldn't process that he didn't have the skill or knowledge to fix the fence. My first thought was, "You goof. You ran the car through the fence and into the side of the garage. The fence shouldn't be broken, and you park the car . . . in the garage." Perhaps, the best solution would have been to call the fence repair man. Needless to say, the gates fell off the "hinges" every time they tried to open the gates. Twine just doesn't work as well as steel bolts and an anchoring rod.

Bubbbba's broken-down repair job kept the dogs inside the fence. We were thankful his dogs weren't smart enough to figure out they could pushed down the gates. He never fixed the garage.

Bubbbbba, his wife (Bubbbbbett), their son (Bubba, Jr.), and friends lived next door to us for many more months. During his remaining time, Bubbbbba continued to do an array of things that reinforced his position on the extreme end of the *redneck* continuum.

Just as he was born with his mother living in that house, his oldest son was born with him living in that house. I only saw his son from a distance. Neither one of us made any attempts to rebuild our previous relationship.

In telling this true story, I've used my *redneck* stereotype satirically. We all have stereotypes and use them daily. Is this fair? How often do you label a person and then judge him by that label? Was Bubbbbba a *redneck*? His attitudes and behaviors fit nicely into my extreme end *redneck* continuum. Our strife had nothing to do with a label. It was all about our opposing value systems.

I can only ponder why our lives took such drastically different paths. I know my family structure and situation was more stable. More importantly, my belief system prohibits me from viewing anyone as inferior or superior. Undoubtedly, our perceptions of a person greatly influences the way we interact with that person. I know attitude and behavior determines the type of relationship I cultivate with anyone. My perceptions and the time I spent with Bubbbbba as a baby and young boy were harmonious. Our opposing adult attitudes and behaviors shattered our childhood relationship.

In spite of the challenges in Bubbbbba's life, he had the opportunity to take a different path. His grandmother was an elementary school teacher. She graduated from college when women were told and expected to stay home and have babies. She would have gratefully paid for him to go to college. What happened, and why did he choose the path of slothfulness instead of opportunity?

In retrospect, I regret I didn't encourage him more when we were growing up. He was six years younger which translated into light years away from my peer group. When I was with my friends, we didn't want him around us all the time—especially when boys entered the picture. It was difficult for twelve-year-old girls to woo the boys with a six-year-old boy hanging around. When I wasn't with my friends, I spent a lot of one-on-one time with him.

Let me tell you the end of the story. Bubbbbba moved out of his grandmother's house about a year after moving in. His sister, Chick, moved in after he vacated. She is six years younger than Bubbbbba and I barely knew her. She was a better neighbor and cared—at least superficially—how the neighbors reacted to her shenanigans. Just like two peas in a pod, Chick had the same belief system. Consequently, she had conflicts with the neighbors. She lived in the house less than a year and moved out.

Karen sold Mrs. Smith's house soon after Chick skedaddled. Once again, my parents have a real neighbor. The new neighbors put up a new gate and tore down the detached garage.

After Bubbbbba moved, we didn't hear much about him, until a neighbor heard his obituary on a local radio station. We found out Bubbbbba committed suicide in his mother's house in Charlotte. He died somewhere around his 30th birthday, the father of three boys, and divorced. His mother buried him in our hometown beside his grandfather and grandmother. I never told my parents, but I visited his grave shortly after he died. I think my parents did too.

After seeing Bubbbbba's lifestyle and attitude when he moved in next door, I'm not surprised he died young. I really thought he would die in a bar room fight or car wreck. He had two serious car accidents—alcohol related—a few years before he moved in next door. I never thought about suicide, because he had a gregarious personality and appeared to have a positive self-image.

Shortly after Bubbbbba moved in next door, my father had his only serious conversation with him. My father asked him if he learned anything from his two near-death experiences. He responded, "Yeah, I'll do the driving next time we are all drunk." My father told him he was headed for a short life if he didn't get it together. He blew off my father's prophetic warning.

I hadn't really thought about the potential reasons Bubbbbba became the person he was until now. I thought writing this essay would be easy, but it wasn't. I've told and laughed about the Sunday afternoon escapade many times.

Bubbbbba was a friend. I remember him fondly as a child and cherish those days. I still think about him around Thanksgiving. As an adult, he became pure misery in our lives for a short period of time. I didn't like or respect him at all. His metamorphosis from friend to nemesis is why writing the complete story wasn't easy. As a matter of fact, it was down right painful.

There is no happy ending for this story. A wasted friendship. A wasted life. After this experience, I hope I never say, "There's a *redneck*—on the unenviable end of the continuum—in my backyard, HELP!"

Accurate Stereotypes, Do They Exist?

We usually develop stereotypes based on our personal experiences or the experiences of those close to us. Stereotypes are linked to our frame of reference. It is sometimes difficult for people to release the baggage of the past and peer progressively towards the future. However, past experiences may prevent us from seeing change, from noticing what we did not expect to see.

Some stereotypes help us to make decisions more efficiently. Say you are at your local bank making a deposit on a warm summer afternoon and in walks a person wearing a ski mask. Do you think, "**BANKROBBER** and instinctively run? Your assessment may be a fair generalization. Some generalizations provide understanding and expectations for how people, situations, and objects should be. Generalizations sometimes provide a basis for us to compare our expectations with reality. In this society, generalizations or stereotypes frequently inform our behaviors, such as your decision to run.

Let's take the bank scenario further. Say you get home that evening and kick back to watch the news. The news anchor reads, "Suspected bank robber, tackled by customers, find out more when the 6:00 o'clock news comes your way." You sit there on the very edge of your seat, waiting to hear about the ski mask assailant from your bank. You say to yourself, "I knew it. I knew that was a robber." Finally, the news comes on. The anchor reads:

> Today, a suspected bank robber was wrestled to the floor by a mob of customers and bank employees. The suspected robber entered the local ABC Bank wearing a ski mask. Two male customers jumped the suspected robber from behind and tussled him to the ground. As the three struggled, one of the customers discovered that the suspected robber was armed. One customer yelled to the others in the bank, "He's armed. We need help." The customers attacked the suspected robber, beating and kicking him until he was unconscious. Once the police and paramedics arrived, the suspected robber was identified as an off-duty police officer who had stopped at the bank after being released from the hospital. It appears the officer was wearing the ski mask for protection. During an attempted arrest, a suspect doused the officer in the face with a lye-based chemical causing major burns to his face and neck. Doctors bandaged the officer and suggested the ski mask as protection from the ultraviolet rays.

You sit back in your chair. You are floored because here is another example of perception gone wrong. Yet, this scenario could have taken a completely different turn. The officer could have truly been a bank robber. Are stereotypes ever accurate?

Not all stereotypes are completely inaccurate. At some time or some place, enough people have experienced a phenomenon in a similar way so that a generalization might be drawn. Hence, there may be a morsel of truth in some stereotypes. And some perceptions are accurate.

I'm a Product of My Environment

We usually assign cause to people's behaviors. I have often heard people justify behavior by claiming, "He's a product of his environment." This claim is a way of attributing cause to behaviors based on an individual's surroundings. **Attribution** is the process of understanding the reasons for our own as well as other's behaviors. We attempt to understand behaviors by attributing cause to either the individual's situation (environment) or the individual's disposition (personality traits). We must remember that the attributions that we make are not always correct.

We make an **attribution error** when we overestimate dispositional causes and underestimate situational causes of others' actions. Research shows that humans are more likely to perceive others as acting the way they do because they are "that kind of person" rather than attributing their behavior to environmental causes (Gilbert & Malone, 1995; Overwalle, 1997; Jones, 1979).

The attributions that we make may influence our relationships with others as well as our relationship with ourselves. Research also concludes that we make attributions that serve our personal interests (Hamachek, 1992; Sypher, 1984). We claim that good things are caused by the power that we have exerted and disclaim responsibility for what we do poorly. This **self-serving bias** distorts our perceptions of our worth in relation to others in the world. We develop an unrealistic image of ourselves and our abilities when we perceive ourselves as invincible and omnipotent—the alpha and omega of any situation.

Factors That Influence Perception

So far, we have discussed the perception process in terms of selection, organizing, and interpreting. Now let's examine factors that impact our perception process. **Physiological, psychological, cultural,** and **gender** factors influence perception. In addition, perception is greatly influenced by the **Media.**

Perceptual Differences Based on Physiology

In the fall of 2002, people living in the D.C., Maryland, and Virginia suburbs were afraid to come outside of their homes to perform simple tasks like pumping gas. They feared they may be the next victims of the beltway sniper. A witness expert commented that it would be extremely difficult to develop a composite drawing of the sniper because witnesses' accounts vary so widely. The expert said that an old person may describe seeing a young person, and a young person may describe seeing an old person. The witnesses' descriptions are relative to their respective ages. An eighty-year-old may perceive a forty-year-old as young; whereas a twenty-year-old may perceive a forty-year-old as old.

Physical factors such as age, weight, height, health, and body shape account for perceptual differences. Think back. As a child, was there someone who you thought was really tall? And now that you are older and taller, do you think of that person as being the same size giant? As age does in this case, other physiological factors may impact perception on multiple levels.

When I was 12 years old, I weighed 204 pounds. Although that was more than twenty-five years ago and although I weigh some fifty to sixty pounds less, I still perceive myself as heavier than I should be. When I tell friends who weigh more than 200 pounds that I need to lose weight, they disagree. They encourage me by saying that if I lose any weight I will look sick. They say you look "fine." What's fine for me and what's fine for them differ based on our weight.

Perceptual Differences Based on State of Mind

Think about when you are happy or sad. Do you perceive situations the same way? State of mind greatly influences perception. Quite frequently, people who suffer from depression are pessimistic about life. Their perceptions are distorted because of their negative state of mind. On the contrary, when we are up and everything is going our way, we perceive possibilities. These are examples of how psychological factors influence perception.

Remember a time when you broke up with a boyfriend or girlfriend? Right after a long-term relationship ends, we are usually fairly vulnerable. We are skeptical of intimate relationships. We sometimes perceive other individuals as being less trustworthy. These perceptions are based on the state of mind caused by the breakup.

Perceptual Differences Based on Culture

Culture is a way of life; it encompasses values, beliefs, and understandings shared by a group of people. The way people live in the "hood" and the way people live in the burbs are quite different. The way people live in the country and the way people live in the city are just as different. The way of life and understanding the assumptions about what is good, right, and worthwhile may vary from group to group. In Afghanistan, it is not right for a woman to go out unveiled. Women are not valued as equal to men. In the United States, although disparities in pay and certain other areas still exist between men and women, they are generally treated as equal. At least that is what is legislated.

Some cultures are very communal. The family is very important to the identity of individuals from these cultures. For example, certain African cultures that strongly value family relationships also greatly value and respect their elders. On the other hand, in the United States, elders are frequently perceived as expendable.

Co-cultures are social communities within a macro or dominant culture. Co-cultures have a system of values and beliefs that may coincide or conflict with those of the dominant culture. People can belong to multiple co-cultures. Members of co-cultures have unique understandings of the world. Our perceptions are influenced by the personal knowledge that comes from our experiences as members of a particular social community. Our perceptions are influenced by our cultural capital. Cultural capital is defined as the personal knowledge and experience that is directly related to membership in a particular social community (Shird, 2001).

Perceptual Differences Based on Gender

Women tend to act as caregivers. They tend to perceive need. Although the maternal instinct may explain part of this proclivity, socialization can explain the other part. In this society, women have been raised to be caring—to take care of the house and the family. Women are the nurturers in this culture.

Men, on the other hand, are less likely to stay at home and care for the ailing child. In this culture, fewer men tend to choose careers in such fields as nursing. Fall 2002 enrollment in the North Carolina Agricultural and Technical State University nursing program was about one male to every twenty females.

Women and men have different socially defined roles. We follow different scripts for how we are to behave. Our cultural capital is different because of our personal knowledge and experience as male or female. Some people tend to defy the norms of the dominant culture. A man, for example, who chooses to wear a dress, makeup, and heels may be perceived as weird, and at the least, different. Simply because a man wears a dress does not make him weird. Gender roles are socially constructed and greatly influence our understanding of the world.

Measuring Objectivity

Dwight Davis, Editor, *High Point Enterprise*

My wife is an ardent fan of N.C. State football. Strangely enough, a comment she made while watching a Wolfpack game on television one day led me to a revelation concerning the concepts of objectivity and subjectivity.

Most of us think of objectivity as a state of mind without bias, and most of us believe we are quite capable of achieving this thought process. I, too, believed that I was an objective thinker. After all, as a longtime journalist I was trained to be objective. I believed this until a close third-down call went against the Wolfpack on this Saturday afternoon.

As State drove down the field, the Wolfpack needed a crucial first down to pull out a victory in the waning minutes. The game hinged on third-and-short yardage situation. This pivotal play required a measurement by the referees. It would determine if State's forward progress had met the required distance, which is ten yards for a first down.

As the chains were stretched on the field to measure the yardage, the referee eyed the situation closely. He then held up two fingers inches apart, indicating my wife's beloved 'Pack had narrowly missed gaining the required yardage for a first down.

My wife, June, was incredulous. She bellowed: "How can they (the referees) place the ball all over the field and then determine they (the Wolfpack) are short (of making a first down) by inches?"

Having covered many football games as a sportswriter, I began to posit an authority's argument. I told my wife that some degree of subjectivity on the part of the referees is a necessary and accepted part of the game. The measurements, though (such as the one made in the State game) are considered an objective standard.

But, June countered: "How can the measurements be objective when the same referees have determined where the ball should have been placed the whole game?"

Ah!

While definitely not an objective observer of N.C. State in any sense of the word, June caused me to realize that objectivity has to be obtained through subjectivity. Therefore, the concept of total objectivity cannot exist.

Let's go back to the game for a moment.

According to the rules, the ball should be spotted at the point where a ball carrier's knee has touched the ground. In many instances, however, it is impossible to determine exactly where a knee has touched, even with the use of slow-motion replays of television cameras. But we leave it to the game officials to determine these spots, and assume they use their best judgment in determining as closely as possible where the ball should be placed. Over the course of any particular game, we can assume placements of the ball could vary by several feet, inches, or yards if compared to the exact spots where the ball should have actually been placed. Often officials or coaches request measurements to determine if indeed a team has moved the ball the required ten yards and should be awarded a first down. A chain attached to two poles measuring ten yards in length is brought on to the field to determine the exact distance a team has moved the ball.

After a measurement, a game official may hold his hands or fingers inches apart, indicating that a team is just shy of attaining the required ten yards to be awarded a first down, when in actuality the team may have exceeded the required distance by several inches, feet, or even by several yards, depending upon the point of the game at which the measurement has taken place—or the team may have fallen short by such margins.

From the accepted subjective notion of maintaining fair play, an accepted objective notion is perceived when a measurement has been made, because when something is measured, this is perceived to be an act of objectivity.

But, this begs the question: How can objectivity be maintained if subjectivity is part of the equation?

The example of spotting a football on the gridiron and subsequent measurements of yards is symbolic of the manner in which the skewed notions of objectivity are perceived.

Subjectivity is defined as "existence in mind only; absorption in one's own mental states or processes; tendency to view things through the medium of one's own individuality" (*The World Book Dictionary*, p. 2085). Objectivity is defined as "intentness on objects external to the mind; external reality" (p. 1432). It could be said, then, that subjectivity is inherent, and objectivity is an attempt to separate ourselves from subjectivity. The latter is not possible.

An objective notion becomes a subjective attempt to separate one's self from preconceived ideologies, which makes the concept of objectivity a slippery one at best.

Defining the concept of objectivity is a multi-dimensional dialectic dilemma within itself because the definition of the term may vary from one individual to another. Hence, defining the term and subsequently applying or attempting to apply the concept reaches to the roots of subjectivity.

Restivo (1994) argues that objectivity is "burdened by a history of interminable and inconclusive discussions and contradictory usages. It has been described as a value and an ideology that embodies and expresses detachment and alienation from self and society" (p. 177).

Philosophers of science, according to Restivo, formulated and systematically developed the social theory of objectivity, conforming to the canons of the sociology of science (p. 177). Objectivity in this regard remains problematic. Even in the sterile, unfettered confines of a laboratory, void of "outside" influences, a subjective tenor remains, which is that of the scientist(s) performing the tests.

If objectivity cannot be fully realized within the concepts of science, it stands to reason objectivity cannot be fully accomplished in the realm of social communication. In this cluttered and complex realm, unbiased thought process—alienation from expressive paradigms in order to interpret the external world with impartiality—becomes layered with subjective issues from which we cannot escape.

In order to become more effective communicators, it is important that we make attempts at objectivity, but realize we will always come up short of the goal.

References

Restivo, Sal P. Science , *Society and Values: Toward a Sociology of Objectivity.* Bethlehem, Penn., Lehigh University Press, 1994.

World Book Dictionary (Eds. Clarence L. Barnhart and Robert K. Barnhart) Chicago: Childcraft International Inc., 1980.

Perception and Media Influence

I can think of no other entity with as much influence on perception as the mass media. The media defines what the public is to perceive as a crisis, what it is to perceive as a scandal, what it is to perceive as newsworthy, what it is to perceive as trendy, what it is to perceive as hot, and what it is to perceive as not. The media translates what our congressional leaders define as national issues.

Look at political advertisements. These ads are designed to alter our perceptions of the candidates. Trashy campaign ads demean the candidates' characters. These ads sometimes go as far as trashing the families and close allies of the candidates, all done with the intention of getting us, the public, to perceive that one candidate is more socially responsible than the other.

Improving Perception Competencies

In the beginning of the chapter, I discussed in great detail how disaster can result when perceptions *go wrong.* To maintain a socially just society, we must understand the impact our perceptions have on ourselves and on others in the world. There are several different ways to improve your perception competency.

Be Mindful

First, we must be mindful in every situation. We must pay attention to what is really taking place. We also must be willing to compare what we think we see to what we really see. This requires that we focus to observe and gain as much understanding as we can about the person, situation, or object in question. Our focus must be centered on the here and now.

Seek More information to Verify Perceptions

Rudolph and Kathleen Verderber (2002) say, "If your perception has been based on only one or two pieces of information, try to collect additional information before you allow yourself to form an impression so that you can increase the accuracy of your perceptions. At least note that your perception is tentative—that is, subject to change. You can then make a conscious effort to collect more data to determine whether the original perception is accurate.

The best way to get information about people is to talk with them. Unfortunately, we tend to avoid people we don't know much about. It's okay to be unsure about how to treat someone from another culture or someone who is disabled. But rather than letting this hold you back, ask the person for the information you need to be more comfortable." (p. 45)

Distinguish Facts from Inferences

We frequently mistake inferences for facts. For instance, you may perceive that Bill Clinton was a better president than George W. Bush. This is not a fact because "better" is a subjective term and at least in this case cannot be proven. A **fact** is a statement that can be demonstrated as true or false, regardless of our own personal beliefs. An **inference** involves personal preferences and opinions.

Table 2.1

Provable	Inferences
Smoking increases a person's chances of contracting lung cancer.	Smoking is relaxing.
The *Los Angeles Times* is the nation's largest newspaper.	The *Los Angeles Times* is better than the News and Record.
Suicide rates among young African American men have risen over the last several years.	Young African American men aren't happy; that's why they are committing suicide at an increased rate.
Students tend to come to class late more often during inclement weather.	Students who come to class late are disrespectful.
The D.C. area sniper(s) shot eight people.	The D.C. sniper(s) should be sentenced to life.

Table 2.1 contrasts provable statements with those that are based on individual preference. It is easy to confuse facts with inferences because we are so confident in our own opinions and preferences. Our preferences may cloud our perceptions so that we cannot see the truth. Let's check your skills.

Fact or Inference

1. Pamela Sue Anderson is the most attractive actress in the world. I or F
2. Men are strong. I or F
3. Reported cases of HIV/AIDS within the co-culture of African American women have risen over the last few years. I or F
4. Children that do not perform well in high school will not perform well in college. I or F
5. Christina Aguilera has won at least one Grammy. I or F
6. In 1986, Run DMC became the first rap act to be featured on the cover of *Rolling Stone* magazine. I or F
7. Children that misbehave deserve to be spanked. I or F
8. Sammy Sosa is the best baseball player of all time. I or F
9. Vanilla Ice paved the way for Eminem. I or F
10. Eleanor has been in five car accidents. I or F
11. Eleanor does not drive well. I or F
12. Seniors are ready to graduate from college. I or F

Answers: Numbers 1, 2, 4, 7, 8, 9, 11, and 12, are Inferences. Numbers 3, 5, 6, and 10 are facts.

It's easy to confuse inferences with facts. After my divorce, I went to a therapist so that I could deal with my feelings. I began explaining to the therapist, "John always . . .". She stopped me in mid-sentence to explain that no one ever always does anything. They may do it sometimes, most of the time, and sometimes they may even do it pretty much close to all of the time. Yet, it is virtually impossible for a person to always be in the act of doing one thing. Humans are much more complex.

From that experience, I learned to use more tentative language, "Tina sometimes arrives late," instead of "Tina is a late person." The latter description is evaluative. It sounds like a character judgment. By saying, "Tina is a late person," I am labeling Tina. Labels are notorious for hindering the progress of certain social communities. We are less likely to perceive change, and our perceptions may be distorted when we label an individual or a group based on our personal preferences. Eliminating evaluative language helps us to distinguish facts from inferences. Distinguishing facts from inferences increases our perception competency, which ultimately increases our interpersonal communication competency.

Perform a Perception Audit

A fourth way of increasing your perception competency is to perform a perception audit. A perception audit is the process of examining your perceptions against reality. As we change, so should our perceptions. As we grow and evolve, so should our perceptions. People, situations, and objects change over time. It is our social responsibility to evaluate our perceptions of those changed people, situations, and objects.

Be Open to New Ways of Experiencing the World

The fifth way to increase perception competency is to be open to new ways of experiencing the world. Try new things. Travel. See how other cultures live. Expand your mind by reading texts from other religions, listening to music from other cultures, seeing movies from other countries, or just spending time with people who are different from yourself. There is a vast ever-changing world around you. Take advantage of the opportunity to experience as much of it as possible.

Wrap It Up

Perception is the complex process of selecting, organizing, and interpreting information about people, events, activities, and situations. Inaccurate perceptions may cost someone his or her life. We select to focus on information that meets our physiological and psychological needs, that interests us, and that satisfies our expectations. A variety of schemata helps us to organize our impressions: prototypes, mental yardsticks, and stereotypes. We attempt to understand behaviors by attributing cause to either the individual's situation (environment) or the individual's disposition.

There are several factors that influence perception. There are the physiological, the psychological, and the cultural and gender factors that influence perception. In addition, perception, is greatly influenced by the media.

To maintain a socially just society, we must understand the impact that our perceptions have on ourselves and others in the world. There are several different ways to improve your perception competencies: be mindful, distinguish facts from inferences, perform a perception audit, and be open to new ways of experiencing the world.

References

Gilbert, D. T. and P. S. Malone. "The Correspondence Bias," *Psychological Bulletin* 117 (1995): 21–28.

Hamachek, D. *Encounters with the Self,* 3rd ed. Fort Worth: Harcourt Brace Jovanovich, 1992.

Jones, E. E. "The Rocky Road from Acts to Dispositions." *American Psychologist* 34, (1979): 107–17.

Overwalle, F. V. "Dispositional Attributions Require the Joint Application of the Methods of Difference and Agreement," *Personality and Social Psychology Bulletin* 23 (1997): 974–980.

Seiler, W. J. and M. L. Beall. *Communication Making Connections.* (5th ed). Boston MA: Allyn & Bacon, 2002.

Shird, M. M. Scars of Struggle, Marks of Strength: Models of Mentoring Black Men. Dissertation Institution: The University of North Carolina at Greensboro; 0154 ISBN: 0-493-19168-2, 2001.

Sypher, B. "Seeing Ourselves As Others See Us." *Communication Research* 11 (1984): 97–115.

Verderber, R. F. and K. S. Verderber. *Communicate.* Belmont, Calif.: Wadsworth Press, 2002.

Communication in the Movies

I invite you and a friend or classmates to explore comunication in the movies. Reflect on the communication skills discussed in this chapter. How are they addressed in the movies?

▶ Deliverance
▶ Driving Mrs. Daisy
▶ Forest Gump
▶ Boys in the Hood

Name _____ Date _____

Section _____

Think About It → **Write About It**

Reflect on what you've just read. Now write what you are thinking.

_____

_____

_____

_____

_____

_____

_____

_____

_____

_____

_____

_____

_____

_____

_____

_____

_____

_____

_____

_____

_____

_____

_____

Activity 1

Reading the Triangles

Reading the Triangles, p. 43 in text (5 min)

1. Ask students to close their textbooks
2. Take one textbook and turn to p. 37.
3. Select one student to quickly read the words in the triangle. (Usually the student misreads the repeated word.)
4. Ask another student to do the same. (Hoping the student misreads the repeated word.)
5. Choose one more student to read it.
6. If any or all three of the students misread, inform them and the class how their perceptions and expectations distorted what they saw in each triangle.

Activity 2

Facts vs. Inferences (5−10 min)

With the class, read each statement on page 63 and determine if it is a fact or an inference and why.

Chapter 3

Culture as Worldview: Individualism and Collectivism in Communication

Veronica J. (Duncan) Walters, Ph.D. and Myra M. Shird, Ph.D.

Key Terms

Culture	Individualistic Cultures
Co-Cultures	Collectivistic Cultures

Culture. We hear the word used regularly in our society. People talk about pop culture, Generation X culture, organizational culture, male culture, female culture, and so on. What then is culture and how does it affect communication? Culture is our thoughts, our beliefs, our attitudes, our values, our behaviors, our look, our clothes, our speech patterns, our language, our notion of gender roles, our valued relationships, our use of time, our management of conflict, our self-disclosure, our acceptance of others' views, and much more. Culture is our way of life. In this chapter we are going to work on getting a better understanding of this notion of culture and explore how it impacts notions of self, others, and communication.

Material and Non-Material Components of Culture

Let's talk about the phenomena we call culture. Simply speaking, culture is a way of life. It is how we live, how we think, what we believe, and how we behave. Our culture is deeply rooted in tradition. We receive our traditions through communication. Ultimately, culture is communicated to us.

I was brought up in a Baptist Church. There we were taught that Jesus is the son of God and that He—Jesus—died on a cross for my sins. Guess what? I believe this because this is what was repeatedly communicated to me. So Christianity is a major part of my belief system. It is not for everyone. Therefore, the Christian community is a co-culture or social community in which I am a member. This concept of co-culture is a way of expressing pieces of our individuality that we have in common with others, but not with the entire populace. I know that sounds deep, but reread it and see if it doesn't start making sense.

In the American culture, most people have had to have their rights legislated for them—except those who resemble the founding fathers. One of my professors, Julia Wood, offers these adjectives when discussing those whom have not had to have their rights legislated: *western, able-bodied, land-owning, heterosexual, Christian males* (Wood, 1999). Think about it. The majority of us who do not fit that description have had to have our rights legislated in some form or another. Thus, we live in a patriarchal society that values material wealth, health, Christianity, and heterosexuality. If this were not so, then there would have been no campaigns for women's rights, civil rights, gay rights, and the Disability Act would have never been needed.

Culture consists of material and nonmaterial components. **Material components of culture** are tangible constructs that impact how we behave and think. These contructs are physically created by humans. Take for example the cell phone. When I purchased my first cell phone back in the early 90s, it was as big as the laptop computer that I am using to type this lecture on. I was, however, on the cutting edge of technology, because not many people owned a cell phone at the time. As we became more and more technologically advanced as a culture, material components such as mobile phones became—or so we thought/think—a necessity. Humans create the material components of culture based on the changing landscape of our daily lives of the culture. Hence, we deduce that culture is constantly changing.

Cultural changes are due to numerous extrinsic scenarios. September 11, 2001, changed the way of life for Americans. Think of different material components of our culture that resulted from the World Trade Center/Pentagon catastrophes. There are all types of surveillance devices that now decorate our nation's airports. Our security systems and abilities resemble something from a 1980s sci-fi flick. Not only have material components been affected by the catastrophic scenario of September 11, but our non-material components have changed as well.

Non-material components of culture are intangible constructions that impact how we behave and think. Let's think of non-material components of culture in terms of beliefs, values, norms, and language.

Beliefs. **Beliefs** are those things that we consider as truth. Truths for most people can be rooted in experience, religion, or science. As I mentioned earlier, I believe that the Christian God and Jesus exist and through them I can have everlasting life. There are many that believe in God, but not in Jesus, and there are many who give other names to God. Beliefs are not always correct, but they do influence how we behave.

Values. **Values,** on the other hand are those things that we believe to be good, right, and worthwhile in life. Americans say they value freedom from terrorism, or at least the government makes this public assertion. As a country, we also say that we value equality. Thomas Jefferson, in the Declaration of Independence, claims that "we hold these truths to be self evident that all men are created equal." I will not editorialize on Jefferson, but he did essentially document this notion of a nation that values equality.

Norms. The third non-material component of culture that I want to discuss is norms. **Norms** are informal rules that govern our social and personal conduct. Norms arise out of tradition, which is communicated to us from generation to generation. Norms characterize that which is appropriate and normal in various situations. For example, as we review media accounts, we find that the nation does not generally accept gay marriages as a norm. This is because the larger culture does not embody the belief in homosexuality or the value of same-sex marriages. On the other hand, we do live in a culture that endorses the marriage of a man and woman.

Language. I am going to conclude by briefly discussing language as a non-material component of culture. **Language molds our perceptions of life, perceptions of ourselves, and our perceptions of ourselves in relation to others in the world.** When I was born, a *web* was the beautiful construction spun by spiders. Now the *Web* connects humans in all corners of the world. When I was five, this country was participating in a *conflict* that we now know as the *Vietnam War*. When my mother was 20 years old, because she was "colored," she could not drink at the same water fountain as those who were "white." Now that she is "African American," she has all the rights of those who are "white." As culture changes, so does language. Language changes to keep up with the extrinsic scenarios or things that happen in the world.

Individualistic and Collectivistic Cultures

Individualistic cultures are those cultures that place greater emphasis on the individual person rather than the group. **Collectivistic cultures** are those cultures that focus on the collective or group rather than the individual person. The dimensions of individualism and collectivism exist on a continuum. However, most cultures are not at either extreme point; rather, they exist somewhere along the continuum. Additionally, as individuals we are a part of multiple cultures which means that there is even greater variability. In this chapter, therefore, when I talk about various cultural groups, understand that I am not saying that every person in a group thinks this way or that way. To the contrary, in the interpersonal chapter I elaborate on how this multiple group affiliation intersects to create the uniqueness of individuals. We will begin by examining the two dimensions on the basis of several characteristics associated with them. However, this list is by no means exclusive.

Table 3.1   Worldview Comparison Chart

Comparison Dimension	Individualistic	Collectivistic
Approach to Knowledge	Objective (Tangible) with Singular "reality"	Subjective (Affective) with Multiple "realities"
Thought/Speech Patterns	Linear/Deductive	Circular/Inductive
Interaction Guiding Principle	Candor/Truth	Courtesy/Harmony
Time	Monochronic	Polychronic

Source: Based on Byrd (1993).

Approach to Knowledge

Approach to knowledge refers to how we come to "know" what is real and what is truth. In individualistic cultures the focus is on the objective or tangible. People from individualistic cultures "know" what they can see, hear, feel, taste, or smell. There is a great reliance on the senses. In order for it to be objective, other people have to be able to see, hear, feel, taste, or smell the same thing. The problem with that approach is that even though someone else may see, hear, feel, taste, or smell the same thing that you do, the way they experience that thing may vary. The differences in perception make objectivity difficult to achieve, which is why in collectivistic cultures the emphasis is on the subjective or affective. Is this why collectivist cultures emphasize the subjective or, do people in collectivist cultures perceive the world based primarily on that which cannot necessarily be verified by the five senses?

Collectivistic cultures focus on the subjective experience of a thing to "know" it. Knowledge comes from the feelings associated with the thing. Because people may experience the same thing differently, the reality of the thing may be different for each person. This approach has led to postmodernism in which there is no objective reality, simply each person's experience of that reality. Let's look at some cultural groups and ways these approaches are demonstrated. Let me reiterate that most cultures are not at one extreme or the other.

We will use gender as our cultural group for this example. In relationships we find ourselves trying to "know" what is really going on with the other person and our relationship. Let's say a female suspects a male of cheating. For many men, cheating can only be declared when there is physical evidence of the act. Women, on the other hand, "know in their bones" that he is cheating. They can just feel it. Upon feeling it, women may approach the man about his cheating even though they have no physical evidence to prove that cheating has occurred. The masculine response to this accusation is often to indicate that she does not have any "proof." This response sets up an interesting scenario and a conflicting situation. Now she must obtain proof by engaging in some detective work which may include "snooping" through his things, checking his messages, questioning his friends, following him, and so on. These behaviors are not desirable and yet, the woman may think that she has to engage in them in order to prove what she feels he is doing. Now we have several relational problems.

First, the woman may not "really" want to know that he is cheating. Second, the man may reject any evidence obtained by those disgusting means, known in police terms as "illegal search and seizure." Third, the relationship is now at risk because trust has been violated or is perceived to have been violated on both sides. Finally, communication between the two has become strained.

From the preceding example, you can see the conflict that can occur based on how we approach knowledge and truth. This may seem extreme, but think about your interactions with the opposite sex to see if you can find any examples of conflict because you approached knowledge differently. Similarly, think of interactions with members of other racial or religious groups or even other majors and see if you might gain some understanding of conflicts you encountered.

Thought/Speech Patterns

How we think affects how we speak. Before we say anything, we have to put our thoughts together. If we are linear thinkers, then we will produce linear or deductive arguments that go from point A to point B. However, if we are circular thinkers, then we will produce inductive arguments that go from specific events, examples, or instances to more general points. Circular thinkers may go from point A to point C to point B to point E and back to point A in making their argument. Circular speakers can be quite frustrating to linear thinkers because the arguments are "too scattered" for them to follow. Similarly, linear speakers can be quite frustrating to circular thinkers because their arguments are "too cut-and-dried" with no room for variation and often lack color or description to keep the listener interested.

For example, imagine an extremely linear thinker, such as a scientist, teaching an English literature class. The teacher gives all of the factual information. However, literature is more than just facts. It is the emotional experience of the writer, characters, and the reader. The linear thinker tends not to value that subjective and affective information and instead adopts an approach of "just the facts."

The text box on Afrocentric Philosophical Foundations provides an explanation of an Afrocentric approach to scholarship. Notice the goals of research, the approach to knowledge, and the room for multiple voices. Which perspective is best illustrated by this approach—individualistic or collectivistic?

Afrocentric Philosophical Foundations

Asante (1990) defines Afrocentric scholarship as research that has as its ultimate goal the humanizing of the world and the creation of space for all voices to be heard. He also contends that this creation of voice and humanizing of the world creates unions between peoples. Thus, Afrocentric scholarship should ultimately seek to build connections that did not exist previously, or support and maintain connections that have already been made. He contends, "The Afrocentric method seeks to transform human reality by ushering in a human openness to cultural pluralism which cannot exist without the unlocking of the minds for acceptance of an expansion of consciousness" (p. v).

Karenga (1993) goes on to explain that there is no one approach to or conception of Afrocentricity. However, scholars do seem to agree that conceptually "Afrocentric means essentially viewing social and human reality from an African perspective or standpoint" (p. 35). This point is important to emphasize because when one says their work is Afrocentric, others begin to immediately think of Afrocentricity as explicated by Asante. Asante's explanation of Afrocentricity is very important; however, other scholars contributed to his understanding and conceptualization of Afrocentricity as noted in his preface to *Kemet, Afrocentricity, and Knowledge.* Similarly, other scholars have since added to and/or further refined the notion of Afrocentricity. Although it is important to give credence and respect to individuals who have made great contributions to our understanding of the experiences of African-descended people throughout the diaspora, we must also be leery that we not view any one person's contribution as "definitive." Once we view one person's work as "definitive," then we stop seeking, which subsequently stunts our intellectual growth. This failure to seek further negates what Asante calls for when he states that " . . . the project of human knowledge is even more, it is a search for a method that will establish a base for further inquiry into the processes and practices of human culture" (p. vi). Thus, further inquiry is a necessary part of the cycle of knowledge and the process of "coming to know."

Another aspect of Afrocentric scholarship is the centering of Africa and the experiences of African-descended people in the research process. This centering of Africa takes place by viewing "the world from the standpoint of the African" (Asante, 1990, p. vi). It is imperative that Africa's experiences, beliefs, values, and approaches to the world be examined both historically and presently. The historical centering often takes place by examining the historical legacy passed on by ancient Kemet and Nubia, both of which were ancient Black civilizations that made phenomenal contributions to Western understandings of politics, medicine, mathematics, geometry, science, communication, architecture, and culture. Some Afrocentric or African-centered scholars have chosen these civilizations as models for current conceptualizations and/or models of African American and African Diasporan relationships with one another, other cultures, nature, and the Divine Creator. These scholars argue that such an approach allows researchers to understand African-descended people from their value system, rather than from the Western, Eurocentric value system that will always lead to African behavior being seen as "deviant" and "pathological." Nobles (1985) describes this use of the Western, Eurocentric worldview as baseline against which to compare African American behaviors as a process of transubstantiation. He defines transubstantiation as the "process wherein the cultural substance of one culture is transformed into the cultural substance of another culture" (p. 42). Therefore, when the African or African American worldview is translated into the European or European American worldview, then transubstantiation has taken place. Anytime people translate the culture, worldview, belief systems, language, etc. of one culture into that of another culture, then they have committed a transubstantive error. This type of mistake results in incomplete and inaccurate understanding of the translated culture. It is very similar to language translation. For example, when one tries to translate a saying or phrase from one language to another, very often there is something that is lost in the translation. For example, among the Navajo, there is no phrase for saying, "I'm sorry." So, if a tanslator wanted to communicate this sentiment, something could get lost in the translation." Translation often results in incomplete and inaccurate understanding of the phrase because the lost piece is critical to the understanding. Here's another example. In English, the term "Maat," means Divine truth, order, balance, harmony, and justice. If we try to reduce Maat to one word, then we would fail to convey the complexity of that one Kemetic word in English. Therefore, as Asante (1990) states we must use many English words to try to provide a definition close to that which is contained in that one word. In order to avoid committing a transubstantive error, one must understand the paradigmatic principle undergirding the African worldview.

Interaction Guiding Principle

What is valued by a particular culture becomes the principle that guides communication. Collective cultures value courtesy, harmony, and peace; therefore, peace and harmony are sought during interaction by being courteous. However, individualistic cultures value candor and honesty more. Therefore, candor is sought by being honest. This honesty is sometimes viewed as brutal by other cultures because it is just too direct.

Often in interactions between Americans and Asians, Americans exhibit too much candor within the communication situation. For example, while in graduate school, I had the opportunity to serve as a mentor for a Japanese student. She came to dinner at our house and brought some Japanese dishes to share with us. My husband tried one of the dishes and said that it was okay, but he really didn't like it. This comment was quite offensive to her, because if she ate anything at our house that she did not like she would not have told us at all for fear of offending us. It is interesting to note that although African Americans are often perceived as more collectivistic than their European-American counterparts, that American core still reveals itself in some people and in some areas. It has been said that there is no more difficult audience than a group of African Americans for an entertainer because if they do not like your performance, they will let you know in no uncertain terms.

Which principle do you find guiding your interactions? Or do you find yourself somewhere in the middle on the continuum? Are there some situations where you find yourself trying to maintain harmony and others where your goal is candor?

Observing Communication Patterns by Examining the Use of Communication Behaviors

African people believed in the powers of observation—observing the stars, nature, people, and behavior. They sought patterns in the universe to use as models of human behavior and experiences. They used these natural models to help explain and understand the world around them (Hilliard, 1986). It is not surprising that these learned Africans introduced the concept of scientific method and rigor.

The same argument can be made when examining communication behaviors. It is by observing the patterns of behaviors that we can begin to understand the relationships between individuals and the relationships of those individuals with the larger society. By starting at the micro-level of the individual, we are able to understand relationships between individuals, for each person is a mirror of the cosmos. All that there is to know can be found within the individual, thus, the origins of the African proverb often attributed to Socrates, "Man (Human) know thyself." It is through this understanding of the self that we as scholars can come to understand the world around us. For without an understanding of ourselves, we will falsely assume that we are obtaining "objectivity" because we have failed to pause long enough to recognize our individual experiences' influence on our scholarship. This influence affects what we study, how we study it, how we interpret what we find, and how the information is distributed within society. Thus, we come to the next point. It is not behavior, in and of itself that is the problem; rather it is people's interpretation of the behaviors.

From the beginning of time, experiences were given meaning through the act of Good Speech (Carruthers, 1995). Thus, meaning is not in the event, behavior, or observations, but rather in the person speaking meaning into existence (Garner, 1998). As scholars, we speak meaning into people's behaviors through our interpretation of those behaviors. Thus, historically the problem has not been the behaviors themselves, rather the meaning attributed to the behaviors and phenomena by individuals using a Eurocentric model of the world. These individuals have been of both European and African descent (ben-Jochannan, 1971/1988). As Asante (1990) states, Afrocentricity is a method that can be applied by anyone who is willing to submit him/herself to the quest for "Truth" using an African holistic worldview. Use of a holistic worldview does not mean that one cannot observe the same communication behaviors. It is important to recognize that if a measure of a communicative behavior is valid (measures what it says it is measuring) and reliable (consistently measures the same phenomenon), then the measure is not inherently "unusable." Although one must examine the scale to see if it functions in the same way in different communities, one does not have to start from scratch in developing a measure. African psychologists have had an understanding of this concept. One has only to look at an issue of the *Journal of Black Psychology* to find the term Afrocentric, Africentric, or African-centered used in an article that may employ quantitative methods.

Noted African and African American scholars such as Delores Aldridge, George G. M. James, Cheik Anta Diop, Joyce Ladner, Theophile Obenga, Molefi Asante, Jacob Carruthers, Linda James Meyers, Wade Nobles, Joseph White (Kobi Kambon), LaFrances Rodgers-Rose and many others have examined the use of different ways of knowing including scientific observation in understanding the experiences of African people throughout the diaspora. In the Kemetic tradition there was no separation or alienation between the ways of knowing. Both scientific observation and intuition (spiritual) were used to gain a holistic view of the past and present. This information was then used to make statements about the future (prediction). However, it is important to note that scholars such as Carruthers (1995) contend that modern science, as we know it, is not an African phenomenon. To truly understand his argument we must examine the basis of scientific knowledge. Greek philosophers, such as Socrates, noted that knowledge is virtue. African Sacred Science would say that the acquiring of truth from knowledge is the first step in achieving virtue that only comes through extensive self-examination.

Time

Time functions in different ways in individualistic and collectivistic cultures. In individualistic cultures, time is viewed as monochronic (singular events occurring at one time). It is valued in its linear form based on the actual time, thus the emphasis on not wasting time. This approach to time is one that values scheduling time and keeping to that schedule. In collectivistic cultures time is polychronic (multiple events occurring simultaneously). Time is not controlled by a schedule but rather by relationships. When monochronic and polychronic cultures come together, there is often misunderstanding. For example, when European or White Americans go to Mexico, frequently there is discomfort at the thought of everything shutting down in the middle of the day for siestas (naps). Mainstream American culture would view taking a nap in the middle of the day as "wasting time and losing money." However, for Mexicans and Mexican Americans, the hustle and bustle of activity carried on by European or White Americans to the point of physical, spiritual, and mental exhaustion is a greater "wasting of life." Even within American cultural groups, there are differences in the use of time with many immigrant groups and people of color functioning more from a polychronic perspective.

In the African American community, for example, the notion of CP time is very real. Growing up I thought CP time was a real time zone because it was talked about so much. I remember telling someone that the event would be on CP time. When they asked me what that was, I told them that it was Central Pacific time. Later I learned that CP time was actually "Colored People's time," which was usually off by an hour or so. I would talk about CP time in my communication classes and especially in my African American communication classes. This talk was extremely important for my European or White American students in their interactions with some of the African American classmates for group projects. If their classmate was fifteen or more minutes late, then the European or White American student would assume that they were not coming or they were disregarding the importance of their time. It was important for me to talk about the necessity for adjusting on both student's part. What the European or White American student did not understand was that fifteen minutes was good for this person who was normally working an hour off the clock time. The differential approaches to time can create problems for polychronic people in a monochronic society; thus, it is crucial that the implications of working on a monochronic schedule be understood. You cannot tell your boss that you are working on CP time and expect to get and keep a job. You cannot say that you have to leave at two for your siesta and expect to get and keep a job.

My use of time has been one of my biggest struggles. I am very much polychronic, but it limits my efficiency and my ability to meet deadlines. Therefore, I have to make adjustments in how I view, schedule, and use my time to compensate. I have to set my clock twenty or so minutes fast, but not know exactly how fast, so that I really don't know what time it is. That sounds extreme, but I have had to find tactics to trick myself into being on time. Now I am working on just gaining the discipline I need to change my use of time, but it is a process.

Let me say once again, not all Americans will view a siesta as an indication of wasting time. Nor does the existence of siestas in Mexico mean that Mexicans or Mexican Americans will ask for a siesta break on their jobs. In fact, the insurgence of Mexican immigrants into the United States has often resulted in other people being moved out of particular jobs because of the willingness of Mexicans to work hard for long hours and minimum pay. I am not saying that it is right to take advantage of people's desire to work hard. However, I am saying that it does happen in individualistic cultures that thrive on capitalism and making the most profit with the smallest investment. We have to work hard to make sure that we don't value our financial resources more than our human resources.

Read the following essay. Embedded in it is information that pertains to a particular social community, as well as information pertinent to public speaking events. From this essay, determine new ways of discussing cultures or social communities that are different from yours.

Connecting Through Experiential Knowing in the Classroom

Amanda M. Gunn, Ph.D.

I have often pondered: if heterosexuals were to truly 'know' homosexuals, would they recognize and come to a deeper understanding of the normalcy of the daily lives, hopes, and dreams of homosexuals? If White people had a deeper connection with a person of color, would they demand that society treat people of color with more dignity? If a wealthy person were to learn about the lives of the poor, would they be more willing to share? If a physically able person were to know the frustration of a disabled person who does not have access to a desired location, would he/she be outraged to the point of action? If there is no longer the separation of "normalcy" between "straights" and "gays," will the heterosexual be moved to emotionally and cognitively recognize the homosexual's rights to social justice? If you come to know me as an individual, will you become active in ensuring the social and political recognition of me? Do you have to know me to fight for me? The answers to these questions may suggest that one, you may not have to know me to fight for me; or two, you may know me and still not act on my behalf. What I am certain of is that if the self and other do not recognize/see/feel the normalness—the humanness of the other—the chances of the continued fear and disconnect that dictate our social and institutional oppressions are much greater. After responding to the question of whether or not you will do right by me if you know me with *perhaps,* I am moved to search for how we might come to know.

The communication classroom offers an opportune site for exploring what we do know about the other and opening up spaces in which we can come to know. In the field of communication we have at our finger tips the theories, methods, and concepts that are about deconstructing the lived realities that surround us, and the reconstruction of meaningful connections. For example, we can use the concept of communication as apprehension to explore notions of voice and silence. When addressing communication apprehension in class we can limit our discussion to an understanding of what is happening physically to people when they feel anxious. We could present some methods of anxiety reduction to increase their skill level with reducing and masking communication apprehension. Or, the discussion could include a critical dimension that engages you and the students, in an exploration of voice and power. The anxiety we experience when placed in a position to share our thoughts and ideas is to some degree cultural. A discussion of fear can be accompanied with a discussion of the pressure we feel to succeed in a competitive culture. Experiences of communication anxiety can be discussed in relation to a culture in which some possess power and others do not. Issues of racism, sexism, and limited access can open up a discussion of why some in our culture feel more silenced than others. Discussions of silence and fear can lead into discussions of the participation that is fundamental to democracy, and therefore, where are we as a democracy if we fear our own voice? We can discuss the relationship between an educational ideology of objectivity and the fear that what we will say is not "right." We can limit our discussion to what people are experiencing physically and how to reduce such a feeling or we can take the discussion further and question what it is about our culture that breeds fear of voice.

It is through the voices of those around us that we come to know. Paulo Freire (1992) writes in the *Pedagogy of Hope* about the dependant relationship between the knowledge that comes from living in the world and the creation of knowledge through a connection to theories that attempt to explain the world. My role as an educator is to nurture an environment in which you can express what you know and then make connections between that knowledge and the knowledge of the "educands." A safe and connected learning environment begins with your lived meaning; a transformational learning environment moves from your lived meaning to a critique of how the world operates. For an educational experience to move you to actually act on behalf of your neighbor, to refuse to live in cultural conditions of alienation and pain, there must be a connection between lived experience and an exploration into the cultural ideologies and the historical and political structures that foster such conditions.

As you, the students, begin to explore and share your lived experiences, the diversity of voices and experiences become learning moments for those that would not otherwise be exposed to differing readings of the world. It is here, in the combined expressions of the variety of your classmates' readings of the world that emerge in a diverse classroom, that moments for connected learning become possible. It is not enough to ask you to immerse yourselves in the texts that explain removed perceptions of the world; we must involve you in challenging, expressing, and listening to the perceptions of life reflected in the members of your classroom. Through hearing your own voices and the voices of your classmates, along with the knowledge of how your experiences reflect and shape larger cultural issues, perhaps you will be moved not only to recognize the other, but to participate in the making of your world outside the classroom in responsibility to the other.

References

Freire, P. *Pedagogy of Hope: Reliving Pedagogy of the Oppressed.* NY: Continuum, 1992.

Wrap It Up

Communication is a complex phenomenon. Culture often confuses the already extremely complicated process by adding additional layers that must be waded through to get to the level of understanding. Culture is our way of life. It is embedded in both material and nonmaterial components.

We must recognize that we belong to many cultural groups, each of which have their own systems. We may function more as a collectivist in one area of our life but more as an individualist in another area. It is important that we recognize that individualism and collectivism are truly on a continuum and our position on that continuum may vary depending on the situation, the other person, and our relationship. Communication across cultures must be viewed through the cultural lens of both participants. As our perspective broadens, our ability to oversimplify begins to decrease and our workload increases. However, the end result is well worth the hard work.

References

Asante, M. K. *Kemet, Afrocentricity, and Knowledge.* Trenton, N.J.: Africa World Press, 1990.

ben-Jochannan, Y. A. A. *Africa: Mother of Civilization.* Baltimore, Md.: Black Classic Press, 1988. (Original work published in 1971)

Byrd, M. L. *The Intracultural Communication Book.* New York: McGraw-Hill, 1993.

Carruthers, J. H. *Mdw Ntr: Divine Speech. A Historiographical Reflection of African Deep Thought from the Time of Pharaohs to the Present.* London: Karnak, 1995.

Duncan, V. J. "Afrocentric Quantitative Approaches to the Study of Relationships including African Americans." In V. J. Duncan (Ed.), *Towards Achieving Maât: Communication Patterns in African American, European American, and Interracial Relationships.* Dubuque, IA: Kendall Hunt, 1998: 11–28.

Garner, T. Understanding Oral Rhetorical Practices in African American Cultural Relationships. In V. J. Duncan (Ed.), *Towards Achieving Maât: Communication Patterns in African American, European American, and Interracial Relationships.* Dubuque, IA: Kendall Hunt, 1998: 29–44.

Karenga, M. *Introduction to Black Studies.* Los Angeles: University of Sankore Press. 1993.

Nobles, W. W. *Africanity and the Black Family: The Development of a Theoretical Model.* Oakland, Calif.: Black Family Institute, 1985.

Wood J. *Communication in our Lives,* 2nd ed. Belmont Calif.: Wadsworth, 1999.

Communication in the Movies

I invite you and a friend or classmates to explore comunication in the movies. Reflect on the communication skills discussed in this chapter. How are they addressed in the movies?

▶   Cool Hand Luke
▶   Saw I, II, III
▶   De Ja Vu
▶   Crank

Think About It → Write About It

Reflect on what you've just read. Now write what you are thinking.

_____

_____

_____

_____

_____

_____

_____

_____

_____

_____

_____

_____

_____

_____

_____

_____

_____

_____

_____

_____

_____

_____

Activity

Gender Perceptions and Stereotypes

1. Ask women to brainstorm a list in response to the following statements:
   a. All men are . . .
   b. Men think women are . . .
2. Ask men to brainstorm a list in response to the following statements:
   a. All women are . . .
   b. Women think men are . . .
3. Ask both groups to prepare to present a short skit to the class based on the following scenarios by switching gender roles (women depict men, and men depict women):
   a. Two friends (of the same gender) meeting each other back at school for the first time this year.
   b. A person flirting with a member of the opposite sex at a party. (Both actors are of the same gender).

Chapter 4

Communication and the "Self"

Key Terms

Sef   Self-Disclosure
Self-Awareness   Self-Fulfilling Prophesies

In *The Politics of Meaning*, Michael Lerner (1997) warns against "surplus powerlessness"—the result of overemphasizing self-negation. Lerner explains that surplus powerlessness arises out of childhood or adult experiences that cause individuals to identify themselves as unworthy of power. He expounds, "most of us have been subjected to a set of experiences in our childhood and adult lives that makes us feel that we do not deserve to have power" (p. 52).

This society is filled with people searching for meaning. They are often searching for a connectedness to each aspect of their lives. The problem is an existential one. It begins as an abstract notion and ends with quantifiable results. This is an overarching problem facing our society. It is the problem of lovelessness. In a society where the main focus is on achieving economic dreams, the preciousness of each individual human being is often minimized. This is especially evident in the numerous reports of youth being killed over something as ridiculous as a pair of name-brand tennis shoes.

In order to create loving relationships between ourselves and others, we often strive to impress those from whom we seek love. Many young people see the street as family, a source of recognition, and a source of love. Often, for these youth, their strategy for recognition may very well entail crime or violence, which are signs of lovelessness. Some children receive recognition from their parents for behavior that is considered commendable and punishment for behavior considered reprehensible. Teachers replicate this process, but in some cases disagree with the children's parents on what is best for the child, and in most cases probably disagree with the "street" on what is best for the child. Lerner (1997) explains:

> Unfortunately, the people who surround us, beginning with our parents, are often
> so emotionally buried within their own painful lives that it is hard for them to see

us clearly. All too often recognition that they give us depends on our willingness and ability to perform within their predetermined categories, responding to their needs for us to fit their already existing picture of the world (p. 33).

Beginning as children we learn to assert a false self so we can receive the recognition or love we desire. This behavior continues throughout adulthood. Repeated assertion of the false self deadens our personal intuitions. We become rote learners and give rote compliance to others' already existing picture of the world. We lose what it means to be who we are, resulting in the emergence of a false self and ensuing internal pain.

Lerner explains in a society where tens of millions of people are in internal pain and are deeply involved in self-blame, there is great potential for the emergence of a series of social crises. "People will act out their pain in a wide variety of ways, depending on their own experiences as children, their own psychological makeup, their economic situation, their cultural assumptions, and the support mechanisms available to them" (p. 40). Anger, depression, drug abuse, drive-by shootings, and much of society's other "crazinesses" can be attributed to individual internal pains, to a loss of meaning, and to the production of a false self. When there is no meaning in a person's life, there is no love for self or others.

Defining Self

There is much discussion of the self, but who is the self? Some people spend all of their lives trying to determine who they are. My college advisor, Julia Wood, says self, "develops over time and, therefore is a process." Virtually all researchers and clinicians who have studied human identity conclude that we are not born with selves, but instead we acquire them. Humans do not come into the world with a clear sense of themselves. Babies literally have no ego boundaries, which define where an individual stops and the rest of the world begins. An infant perceives being held by a father as a unified sensation in which it and the father are blurred. A baby perceives no boundaries between its mouth and nipple or its foot and the tickle by a mother. As infants have a range of experiences and as others respond to them, they gradually begin to see themselves as distinct from the external environment. This is the beginning of a self-concept—the realization that one is a separate entity (p. 73, 1997).

The Self That Is Communicated to Us

From the moment we realize that we are separate entities, we face constant questions of identity. Most often, we get our first definition of self communicated to us by our families, friends, and those who are in our lives on a daily basis. We define ourselves in terms of others' definitions. Our concept of self arises out of the standards of our culture and of our social environment. Our self-concept arises out of the direct definitions and reflected appraisals of others. Thus, self arises out of our communication with others.

Self is the multi-dimensional product that results from the complex process of internalizing and acting from direct definitions that we receive as we communicate. Self is like a completed movie. It is made by the contributions of many. From the moment that we enter this world, someone prescribes how we should behave. Little boys are adorned in blue, while little girls look so pristine in their feminine pink. The little boys get to wear the pants and little girls the dresses. This is step one in the communication of gender to a little one. Parents, educators, and our culture continually communicate gender expectations throughout our lives. Sometimes our parents' own stereotypes bias how and what they communicate to us about gender. When a little boy wants to stay in the house and play with dolls, he is acting like a "girl." When a little girl wants to wrestle, climb trees, and play football, she is a "tomboy." These labels sometimes follow us all of our lives. Labels that define for us who we are and how we are to behave are **direct definitions.** Direct definitions communicate to us who our parents and society see us as.

Limitations of Others' Definitions

When I was 12 years old, I weighed 204 pounds. People referred to me as "fat." Although, I know a lot of people who have suffered immensely from negative weight references, the name-calling didn't bother me too much. At least that is what I professed at the time. Being called "fat" damaged my spirit. According to Webster's dictionary, I was fat. Yet, it was the name-calling that called attention to my physical state and that caused me to internalize the direct definition that was communicated to me. Is that all that I was—fat? Or is that all that I allowed myself to see because of other people's descriptions. This physical description spoke to the American culture's standard for weight, yet it did not speak to the inner being. This description only took into consideration the outward being. This means my wonderful inner qualities such as compassion, intellect, my witty sense of humor, my ability to write poetry, and the thousands of other aspects of my multidimensional self were not taken into consideration.

Too often, I hear parents communicating negative direct definitions and reflected appraisals to their children. John Singleton's movie, *Boyz in the Hood* has a scene that relates exactly to this point. In a roundabout way, the movie portrays Black women defining for Black boys what it means to be a Black man.

The story takes place in South Central Los Angeles. The plot centers around the lives of three young men: Tre, Doughboy, and Ricky. In one of the more telling scenes, Tre has gotten into trouble in school so his mother makes him go live with his father, Furious. On the way, Tre's mother explains that she is taking him to live with his father because she "does not want him hanging out in front of liquor stores, dead, or in jail." Moments later she informs the father, "I can't teach him how to be a man. That's your job."

Tre's first day at his father's house sets the tone for the remainder of the boy's life and the remainder of the movie. He works hard raking leaves until sunset. Tre's friends think Furious is overly strict. But, at the end of the day, Furious explains his behavior to Tre. He says:

> You know, Tre, you may think I'm being hard on you, but I'm not. What I'm doing is I'm trying to teach you how to be responsible. Like your little friends across the street, they don't have anybody to show them how to do that. You're going to see how they end up.

The friends Tre's father is referring to are Doughboy and Ricky, the same ones who think that doing chores is cruel and unusual punishment.

Doughboy and Ricky have the same mother, but different fathers. Throughout the movie, inessential characters notice how the mother treats Ricky better than Doughboy. In one tirade she yells at Doughboy, "You ain't shit. You just like your daddy. You don't do shit. You ain't never gonna amount to shit." She further claims, "I'll knock you into the middle of next week." When Doughboy's mother tells him that he is nothing, just like his daddy, she indirectly contributes to the development of his male identity, of his self-concept.

In the movie, Doughboy goes to prison numerous times and is ultimately gunned down. We internalize others' perspectives. Did Doughboy turn out to be a criminal or "nothing" because that is what his mother continuously communicated to him? Or did he label himself the same way his mother did and acted according to the affixed label?

Prophecies are visions of future actions or expectations. Then, a **self-fulfilling prophecy** is when we act in ways that bring about expectations or judgments of ourselves. Doughboy could very well be an incredibly respectable young man. Yet he may have internalized his mother's description and may have acted accordingly. Essentially, the mother prophesied that Doughboy would be nothing, and Doughboy fulfilled the prophecy.

I often hear my students talk about how people back home expect them to fail or to mess up while they are away at college. The students usually end their tirades by saying, "I'll show 'em. Just wait until I graduate. I'm going to see what they have to say then." These students are focused on not fulfilling the prophecy of failure. Too often, we get trapped by others' labels and continue to communicate in ways that mirror those labels. When we discuss self-talk, we will see the benefits of positive intrapersonal communication.

Sometimes we sabotage ourselves. **Self-sabotage** arises out of negative self-talk. Berko, Wolvin, & Wolvin (2001) say, "We have a choice each time we think, to think positively or negatively. Many of us don't believe it, but that absolutely is our choice. Once we understand that our private thoughts are ours alone to determine, we select to program our brains with empowering, confidence-building thoughts. One method to overcome negative self-talk is: (1) be aware of your negative message; (2) collect your recycled negatives, write them down, and regularly read them to yourself; and (3) replace the negative thoughts with positive ones by flooding your brain with such statements as 'I'm graceful,' 'I'm a people person,' or 'I can pass statistics.' Once you start focusing on the positives, the negatives have to go away. It can't survive if you don't feed it." (Berko, Wolvin, Wolvin, p. 68-9)

Particular and Generalized Others

We have been discussing how self develops through communication with others, yet we have failed to define others. We have already minimally discussed the role our parents play in communicating our direct definitions of self, yet we have barely mentioned the larger society's role. Let's begin with those who are closest to us when we are infants. Mother, father, siblings, aunts, uncles, cousins, and day care providers are our **particular others.** They are the people most important to us when we are infants. These are the people that initially communicate to us who we are and what is expected of us. The Singleton movie is also another good example to explain the significance of communication between a child and a parent. Painfully negative communication or negative direct definitions impact a child's life indefinitely, as was the case with the Doughboy character from *Boyz in the Hood.*

Through their parenting styles, parents also communicate to us who we are and how we are to approach others and relationships. From our early relationships, we learn how our particular others view us, the world, others in the world, and relationships. As with direct definitions, we are likely to internalize these views that are communicated to us through patterns of parenting. Because of how our parents dealt with us, we develop patterns for dealing with others.

If our parents have been consistently positive and consistently loving in our lives, we will tend to have a higher self-esteem and positive view of others. If our parents rejected us and abused us, we are likely to feel bad about ourselves, see others as not loving, and we may fear getting into relationships. When parents are disinterested in us, we tend to become disinterested in others. We may seem cocky; we say, "I don't care about what anybody has to say about me. Don't nobody pay my bills, but me." This is a sign that we have a pretty strong sense of self, but a pretty weak opinion of others. Sometimes we grow up in households where our parents are inconsistent with how they treat us. One day, it may be all hugs and kisses. The next day they may throw a shoe or act as if we do not exist. This type of parenting style yields an individual with low self-esteem. We may find ourselves feeling unlovable and believing that we deserve to be abused. The inconsistency in this pattern of parenting confuses us.

We also must take into account that none of these categories are mutually exclusive. Sometimes parents are disinterested, and sometimes they are positive. One parent may be consistently positive and another abusive. Sometimes it is not the parent that is doing the raising, so the attachment style is learned from an older sibling (who really might not be that much older) or another relative.

Table 4.1

Parent	Self	Others
Consistently Positive (Secure)	Positive View	Positive View
Rejected/Abusive (Fearful)	Feel bad about self, negative view	Not loving, negative view
Disinterested (Dismissive)	Strong sense of self, negative view	Disinterested, negative view
Inconsistent (anxious/resistant)	Feel unlovable and feel we deserve abuse, negative view	More positive about others (comes from confusion brought on by inconsistent treatment).

Adopted from the work of:

Bowlby, J. *Separation: Attachment and Loss (Vol. 2)*. New York: Basic Books, 1973.

Bowlby, J. *A Secure Base: Parent-Child Attachment and Healthy Human Development*. New York: Basic Books, 1988.

The second group to influence us is the **generalized other.** The generalized other is the faceless group of rules and roles accepted by our social community. The generalized other represents society's concerted views. Through communication, we internalize the perspectives of the generalized other and come to accept the perspectives of the generalized others as our own. As students of communication, it is important to understand that the perspectives of the generalized other, as is the case with the particular other, are not always unbiased.

The American culture was built on the premise of freedom. So then, freedom was and is good. But this was not the perspective of the generalized other during the hundreds of years of slavery. Murder, rape, and physical abuse are bad according to American standards. At least, this is the generally accepted viewpoint in our popular culture. This was not the perspective, however, during the period when Europeans were invading the Native Americans' America. Through communication, we learn which aspects of our personal identities are valued or seen as important by the larger society. For example, the American culture tends to emphasize **race, gender, sexual orientation,** and **socioeconomic** class.

Race Does Matter

As the definitions and origins of current racial classifications are explored, it becomes increasingly clear that racial classifications are based on racist generalizations. These broad generalizations have become stereotypes from which the identities of *many "minority" groups* have been socially constructed.

According to sociologist Dr. Sandra Slipp, minorities often internalize the stereotypes of the larger society (quoted in Steen, 2000). If "minority" groups internalize the negative generalizations attached to them because of their race, they act from a negative oppressive race standpoint (Shird, 2001).

In my attempt to explore the term "race," I asked forty-four students who attend a historically Black college their definitions of race. Most of the students define race in terms of skin color and cultural and ethnic backgrounds, while others express a more political perspective on the issue. None of these students give an empowered definition of race.

"I define race as a man-made concept to keep everybody divided and white people on top," comments one Black nineteen-year-old female. A twenty-three-year-old Black male responds, "Race to me is something that someone made up to put people of different colors into categories." "Race is a Caucasian word for people different than them," a twenty-two-year-old Black/Hispanic male claims. Two other students comment specifically on the stereotypical nature of race categorizing. A nineteen-year-old Black female clearly defines race in terms of the negative, "Race is just a way to make distinctions among society that leads to redefining a person . . . and stereotyping." Finally, a twenty-year-old male, who describes his race as "human" explains, "Race is a category given to humans to distinguish color of skin and most of the time it is a form of limitation and [a form of] personality stereotyping."

The students' definitions of race correspond with the oppressive historical origins and purposes for categorizing race by skin color. Windsor (1988) explains that "ancient people did not classify races according to skin color, like the modern nations of Europe and America" (p. 20). Ancient people identified themselves by national or tribal names. "Dividing the world along the color line," according to Windsor, "was an idea that originated with the White supremacists in Europe after the Renaissance" (1988, p. 21).

Johann F. Blumenbach, a German anthropologist living between 1752 and 1840 was the first to divide humanity based upon skin color. Blumenbach classifies humanity into five chief races: Caucasian, Mongolian, Ethiopian, American (American Indians), and Malayan.

By the nineteenth century racial classifications expanded to include psychological values, as well as negative and positive generalizations of an entire group. Botanist Carl von Linne (aka Carolus Linneaus) describes six racial classes:

1. Homo sapiens. Diurnal; varying by education and situation.

2. Wild man. Four-footed, mute, hairy.

3. American. Copper-coloured, choleric, erect. Hair black, straight, thick; nostrils wide, face harsh; beard scanty; obstinate, content, free. Paints himself with fine red lines. Regulated by customs.

4. European. Hair yellow, brown, flowing; eyes blue, gentle, acute; inventive. Covered with close vestments. Governed by law.

5. Asian. Sooty, melancholy, rigid. Hair black, eyes dark, severe, haughty, covetous. Covered with loose garments. Governed by opinions.

6. African. Black, phlegmatic, relaxed. Hair black, frizzled; skin silky; nose flat, lips tumid; crafty, indolent, negligent. Anoints himself with grease. Governed by caprice (quoted in Jones, 1981).

In a work dealing with expressions of white racial identity, Carter (1997) substantiates the impact of racial classifications on nonwhite European-American cultures:

> The emphasis and focus of racial classification systems have mostly been to display both the superiority of White European-American cultural patterns and values (i.e., view of existence, thought patterns, language, temporal focus, social relationships) and how people of color are different from the White norm, where difference is and was thought to be inferior (p. 199).

Transcending oppressive negative images of race becomes a primary responsibility of the "inferior" culture or the nonwhite European-American culture. Race as an empowered philosophy challenges and reconstructs negative or oppressive racial identities.

It's a Gender Thang

As a child, I am mystified as to why Missionary Marie Williams can never become Reverend Williams, or Elder Williams. I never understand why she is not even allowed to sit in the pulpit with the other ministers. Missionary Williams is a Black woman who says God called her to preach. In my denomination, if you say God calls you to preach, that pretty much settles it. Well, not for Missionary Williams. God only calls men or at least that is the way the nine male voting board always rule when they vote on whether Missionary Williams can get her license, or whether she can become a Reverend. This is an obvious and particular slap in the face to Missionary Williams. It speaks volumes about how Black men preachers feel about Black women preachers. To the naïve mind, the ministers' gestures might also speak volumes as to how God feels about women. The Christian God as sexist? Missionary Williams battles the sexist church establishment and becomes an inspiration to numerous female ministers who follow in her footsteps.

Now Eldress (feminine for Elder) Williams, and one of the senior ministers within the conference, has not climbed up the conference hierarchy the way her male counterparts have. She has never pastored her own church. I guess this conference is still saying that it is okay for a woman in the Black church to be a sister, mother, evangelist, missionary, trustee, and even deacon, but pastoring is still off limits. Eldress Williams is now considered "Mother of the Conference," a position developed with her in mind. However, my third-party grapevine research tells me this position still has no clearly defined duties and is fairly symbolic. Knowing Eldress Williams, she will make something out of nothing, which is an empowered race virtue.

The strides of Williams, the demise of some less open-minded ministers, and the leadership of more enlightened men have cut the "Eldress" qualification period to a mere fraction of what it once was. Williams's victories and defeats set precedents for women throughout the local Black female community.

I have also been exposed to trendsetters such as Bishop Richardson, a college educated, Black woman preacher. Instead of fighting the uphill climb in denominational religion, she begins her own church. She incites an individual movement. She sees the possibility of transcending negative conditions. God calls her to preach the gospel, and she is determined to do it from the pulpit, her own.

As the leader of her own church, she defines the role of "her man." As I recall, she makes her husband a deacon. In my church, women become "mothers" or "deaconesses" after their husbands become pastors or deacons. Even in denominational churches where I see women as associate or assistant pastors, their husbands remain laymen until the mens' individual—independent of their wives'—credentials justify hierarchical movement.

Bishop Richardson gives the most insightfully Christian feminist critique I have ever encountered. During a Mother's Day service she preaches "What if Mary would have had an Abortion." The pastor forcefully preaches that had Mary chosen to abort, there would be no Christianity as we know it. Her underlying premise clearly places a woman as the central character in the Christian religion and movement. Her sermon gives voice to a woman's understanding of the Christian story. A simply powerful woman, Bishop Richardson, through her direction from God, rejects the patriarchal model of the church.

The church is not the only example of sexism in the institutional arena. The role of women in social movements is frequently minimized. Many early portrayals of the Civil Rights era *minimize* the major role of women like Rosa Parks or forget Fannie Lou Hamer. Cunningham (1996) analyzes Rosa Park's triumphant refusal to take a back seat as a "new inscription of the body politic. [However] the resulting narrative of Civil Rights is most often understood as authored by men" (p. 132).

While speaking with several Black women students from North Carolina Agricultural & Technical State University and Bennett College who were key players in the 1960s sit-in movement, I find many of these women resent that their contributions are not recognized to the extent of their male counterparts. The women reportedly took class notes for their male counterparts who were incarcerated. They prepared food, and lest we not forget, they sat in.

The sexist society that forces women to minimize their institutional importance must be challenged, but challenging the sexually deviant and institutionally sexist society is not enough. Men and women have to actively work together to change oppressive institutions.

Heterosexism: An American Cultural Reality

Amanda M. Gunn, Ph.D.

We live in an American culture that is not only racist and sexist, it is heterosexist as well. As Sears points out, there is "a belief in the superiority of heterosexuals or heterosexuality evidenced in the exclusion, by omission or design, of nonheterosexual persons in policies, procedures, events, or activities" (1997, p. 16). Heterosexism relies on a relationship between social expectations, both blatant and subtle, and how they are communicated to those members of that society who do not fulfill those expectations. It is also dependent on the assumption that social construction exists as a viable explanation for identity adoption and adaptation. As argued by Sears (1997), heterosexism is ultimately the "belief" that heterosexuality is the "right" orientation. To claim that a society or a culture is largely heterosexist is to claim that its communicated belief system privileges heterosexuality over homosexuality such that the society then communicates its preference through "policies, procedures, events, or activities" (p. 16).

The first heterosexualizing procedures begin during childhood. DPhil (1994) points out:

> From puberty to the end of adolescence, non-gay people are helped along the road to emotional, sexual, and social development by their family and friends, by their schools, by organizations public and private, by the news and entertainment media, and by the society at large (p. 194).

There are common messages that are received through these channels that socialize people to be heterosexual. In school we learn about sex between members of the opposite sex; we learn about where babies come from. As we grow up, we are encouraged to flirt with members of the opposite sex by the comments people around us make—"oh, isn't that cute," or "Susie, do you have any little boyfriends at school?". The songs we grow up listening to champion the wonders and downfalls of love between boys and girls, men and women. Teen magazines focus on heartthrobs and "boy talk;" adult magazines are covered with pictures and articles about how to win a man or assess if you are with a compatible companion. Television shows focus on heterosexual relationships, whether it be through focusing on the union of two single parents and their hardships, or the promiscuity of young adulthood. Our parents represent the model for our own futures: go to college, date a little, get married, and settle down.

If there is any doubt about the subtle heterosexual socialization in American culture, one has only to look at the "events" that are marked as significant in a woman's life. There are several personal and social events that are celebrated in a female's life, all of which are signifiers of the desire for heterosexual unions. A young teenager's first menstrual cycle is viewed as the beginning step towards womanhood. An encouraging mother and envious friends await the first date of a female with excitement and anticipation. The prom becomes a symbol of elegance and romance. Marriage is anxiously awaited and celebrated as the final passage into womanhood. Childbirth fulfills a natural longing that is generally expected for all women. In each of these instances, other than the menstrual cycle, the lesbian is at a disadvantage. A lesbian's first romantic encounter with another female does not begin at the front door with the inclusion of family introductions. A night at the prom might consist of a façade date and glances across the room to observe the desired date from afar. The idea of marriage is loathed for a couple of reasons: for the lesbian who is "closeted," marriage signifies lying to nagging mothers and grandmothers; for the "out" lesbian, marriage is a reminder that her relational preference is not sanctioned legally. Childbirth also presents similar challenges. Lesbians who want children must decide how to approach a discriminatory society; lesbians who do not may fall into the ranks of selfish and are subjected to the comment of "just give it time," and "your clock will start ticking."

The significance of these "events" in a woman's life is based on the assumption that girls like boys and that girls grow up to be women that like men. What does this mean for girls that find they like other girls? In a heterosexist culture it means that the girl will feel strange and alienated. Vivienne Cass (1979) created a "coming out" model that consisted of the six stages a homosexual progresses through while coming to terms with his/her sexual orientation. The girl that recognizes she has attractions that are not represented in the significations she comes in contact with—in the media, school, and family life—experiences what Cass refers to as "identity confusion." She recognizes that what she is feeling is different, which often results in shame.

Perhaps the most significant heterosexist "policy" in American culture is the sanctioning of heterosexual marriage. Marriage in this culture is both a religious commitment and a legal commitment recognized by both federal and state law. It is also a commitment that is a form of relational legitimization denied to homosexuals. Imagine Cindy, a gay woman, living her life with another woman whom she loves and honors. Because Cindy cannot join legally with her partner, Cindy is denied her partner's employment benefits, property rights, and family benefits in local organizations that are afforded heterosexual partners. Cindy can be denied access to her partner in a health facility if her partner becomes sick or is in an accident. Homosexual unions are not recognized in a culture that does not view same-sex relationships as legitimate. Cindy is a member of a group in this society that is denied the same rights as others, based solely on her relational preference.

This privileging of one sexual orientation over another clearly positions heterosexuals as "superior," thus fulfilling Sears' (1997) definition of heterosexism.

References

Cass, V. C. "Homosexual Identity Formation: Testing a Theoretical Model." *Journal of Homosexuality* 4 (1979): 219–236.

DPhil, J. S. "Gay Rights and Affirmative Action." *Journal of Homosexuality* 27 (3/4) (1994): 179–222.

Sears, J. T. Thinking Critically/Intervening Effectively about Heterosexism and Homophobia: A Twenty-Five-Year Research Retrospective. In J. T. Sears & W. C. Williams (Eds.) *Overcoming Heterosexism and Homophobia: Strategies That Work.* NY: Columbia University Press, 1997: pp. 13–47.

Who Are You Comparing Yourself To?

We develop and modify our self-concept when we compare ourselves to others. To whom are you comparing yourself? Why do you compare yourself to that individual? Do you wear a certain brand name because a certain group of people wears that brand? Have you gone out and purchased a pair of Air Force Ones because Nelly's stompin' in his? Who and/or what influences your wardrobe, your vocabulary, your selection of friends, foods, and etc.?

We constantly compare ourselves to someone. When I return papers, students generally scurry to find out each other's grades. They are generally excited to determine how they have performed on the test relative to other students in the class.

"Boy, I wish I had breasts like Pamela Sue Anderson." "I wish I could hit the baseball like Sammy Sosa." Maybe our comparisons are more local. "I want an outfit like Natasha, that girl that lives in Barbie Hall." "I want rims on my truck just like those on T's Escalade."

Check your social comparisons. Determine why it matters that your breasts are not as big as Pamela Sue Anderson's or that your 1988 Escort is not the nicest thing in the student parking lot. Are you concerned because of what someone has said? If your desire to be like or better than someone stems from your need to satisfy someone else's standards or from your need to receive recognition from a particular other, be aware your false self is on the rise. Remember, beginning as children we learn to assert a false self so we can receive the recognition or love we desire. This behavior continues throughout adulthood. Repeated assertion of the false self deadens our personal intuitions. We become rote learners and give rote compliance to others' already existing picture of the world. We lose what it means to be who we are, resulting in the emergence of a false self and ensuing internal pain.

Identity and Sport

Amy Smith, M.A.

In October 2004, the Boston Red Sox won the World Series. It was the first time they had won a World Series since 1918. Fans everywhere rejoiced. Sales of Red Sox merchandise increased tremendously. Newspapers from Boston the following day immediately became collectors items. What was going on here? Put quite simply, people want to identify with a winning team (Eitzen, 2003). Those who were not lifelong Red Sox fans became their supporters, if for no other reason than to root for the underdog. It seems the only people not rooting for the Red Sox were St. Louis Cardinals fans.

Identity is something we consider very important, yet we often have a difficult time realizing that everything we do and say represents our identity. The simple act of wearing a Red Sox hat identifies you to the rest of society as a Red Sox fan. Many people find part of their identity in sports, either through sports they play, or collegiate and professional sporting teams they support. Most often we tend to support collegiate teams from universities that we attended or that are geographically close to where we live or where we grew up. Similarly, professional sports teams support is also based on geographic closeness. Occasionally, we will relocate, and we have to make a choice between supporting our original team or supporting the team that is closest to our new living quarters.

Sport serves many purposes in our society. One of the primary functions it serves is to foster a sense of community among fans. A recent HBO documentary chronicling the 2001 World Series shows how the New York Yankees, playing in those games, were able to help the city of New York heal after the tragic events of September 11. One fan interviewed in *Nine Innings from Ground Zero* (Shapiro, 2004) said "baseball games became communal gathering places for fans to express their emotions. As much of the country turned a sympathetic eye to New York, the city's baseball teams became the objects of affection." The "hated" Yankees suddenly became a favorite team, even in rival cities like Boston. Signs such as "Red Sox fan—I (heart symbol) NY" were seen at Boston home games. "We're the symbol for these people in New York going through this" (Scott Brosius, Yankee).

When thinking about the 2001 New York Yankees, it is important to remember the devastation and loss that New York City experienced only a few weeks before the World Series. Having a local team in the Series gave fans something to focus on other than their grief. It gave them a space to come together and honor their city (Eitzen, 2003). Many games featured moments of silence and inspirational songs such as *New York, New York* and *God Bless America*. These tributes were frequently dedicated to those who lost their lives during the terrorist attacks, particularly members of the NYPD and NYFD.

The real question in this analysis of sport should be "how does sport become representative of individuals?" As I mentioned earlier, people want to identify with a group or organization. Sport gives them a place to do this (Hargreaves, 2000). Whether it is rooting for the local team or the underdog, people find commonality in sport. Prior to 2001, the New York Yankees were one of the most hated teams in baseball outside of those living in New York City. This is because people felt they were too "big" a team, having too much money in salary caps, and always dominating the season. However, American society was able to identify with them during their 2001 attempt to win the World Series because America was rooting for New York City during this time. It was important to our country that New Yorkers were able to survive and recover from their loss, and the Yankees became representative of how they were going to do this.

Similarly, the Boston Red Sox win in 2004 was a great moment in baseball because they were the underdogs. People always want to see the underdog get ahead and succeed. After all, how many of us have felt like there are some days when we are "cursed" and nothing is going to go our way. Thanks to the "curse of the Bambino", the Red Sox suffered for 76 years, never winning a Series championship. Even if they were able to make it to the World Series, it seemed they always suffered a heartbreaking loss in the end. The 2004 victory was special, not only to lifelong Red Sox fans, but to everyone who has thought the deck was stacked against them. The Boston Red Sox proved that the underdog was capable of victory.

Sport and identity go hand in hand. Ever had someone strike up a conversation with you because of the team apparel you were wearing? Being a UCONN Huskies fan who lives in North Carolina basketball country, this happens to me a lot. Often times, the conversations are not exactly pleasant, like the time I accidentally wore my Huskies sweatshirt while walking on the UNC Chapel Hill campus! So next time you get dressed, and you put on that beloved team sweatshirt or jersey, be mindful of what it says about you and your identity. Who do you represent?

References

Eitzen, D. S. *Fair and Foul: Beyond the Myths and Paradoxes of Sport.* New York: Rowman & Littlefield Publishers, Inc., 2003.

Hargreaves, J. *Heroines of sport: The Politics of Difference and Identity.* New York: Routledge, 2000.

Shapiro, O. (Writer). *Nine Innings from Ground Zero* {Motion Picture}. United States: HBO Sports, 2004.

Self That We Communicate to Others

Self disclosure is the process of providing others with information about the self. However, communication theorists have competing views about the "process" of self-disclosure. One view is that "Because self-disclosure is a type of communication, it includes not only overt statements but also, for example, slips of the tongue and unconscious nonverbal signals. It varies from whispering a secret to a best friend to making a public confession on *Oprah Winfrey*.

Self-disclosure concerns you—your thoughts, feelings, and behaviors—or your intimates that have a significant bearing on who you are. Thus, self-disclosure could refer to your own actions or the actions of, say, your parents or children, since these people have a direct relationship to who you are" (DeVito, 1994, p. 48).

Although by definition self-disclosure may be any information about the self, this view of self-disclosure concludes that in practice, self-disclosure is most often used to refer to information that you normally keep hidden rather than simply to information that you have not previously revealed.

Another view is that "self-disclosure is the process of intentionally and voluntarily providing others with information about yourself that you believe is honest and accurate and is unlikely to be discovered elsewhere. To be considered self-disclosure, a message must be intentional rather than accidental or unconscious." (Morreale, Spitzberg & Barge, 2001, p. 74).

In contrast to DeVito's view, Morreale, Spitzberg, and Barge (2001) would say that if Amzi is staring at Angela while she is talking about her vacations, and responds 'What great lips, uh, I mean trips,' Veronica may think he has disclosed something about his thoughts. From this viewpoint, if he, Amzi, had no intention, and his comment were purely accidental, then it is not self-disclosure. Morreale, Spitzberg, and Barge say a "message must be voluntary. This view says that it can hardly be considered self-disclosure if someone is brainwashed, tortured, or coerced to provide information. That we come to know someone not only by what she or he chooses to tell us, but by the fact she or he chooses to tell us at all. The choice to reveal information is as informative as the information itself." (Morreale, Spitzberg, & Barge, 2001, p. 75).

DeVito and Morreale, et al., tend to contradict each other on one very salient point and that is whether self-disclosure can be unintentional. In 2002, at a retirement party for Strom Thurmond, the then-Senate Majority Leader, Trent Lott, celebrated Thurmond's racist, pre-Civil Rights Bill, presidential campaign platform. From a political viewpoint, Lott probably did not mean to disclose personal support for segregation and racial oppression. Yet, the public as well as his fellow senate colleagues demonstrated outrage at his attitude toward this deplorable social ill. Lott was neither brainwashed, tortured, nor coerced to provide information. Yet, he painted a fairly vivid picture of his attitudes and beliefs. Or at least that was the general sentiment of the popular culture.

Generally, these viewpoints on self-disclosure tend to be in agreement on the other two pieces of the self-disclosure model. Self-disclosure provides specific information about who you are and reveals information about the self that others are unlikely to detect by other means.

Self-disclosure provides information about the self. If a person sitting next to you leans over and tells you that he thinks the race is boring, you may not consider this comment revealing about the person next to you. Does his comment say anything about who he is? Certainly it reveals information about his attitudes, which gives you information about him. The guy beside you may not think that he has self-disclosed. He may believe that he is expressing his opinion about the race. Our attitudes, beliefs, and values make up a significant part of our self-concepts. When we disclose information about our attitudes, beliefs, and values, we are essentially revealing something about who we think that we are.

Finally, *self-disclosure reveals information about the self that others are unlikely to detect through other means.* When I come into class and I tell my students that "I'm your professor," it is not self-disclosure. Most students probably already know that I am the professor of this particular class. In this instance, for self-disclosure to occur, I would have to be the sole source of the information being disclosed about me. It is fairly simple to discover who's teaching which class. However, if I tell the students that I am an only child, then I am self-disclosing. "You are not revealing anything about yourself if you tell someone something he or she already knows. In contrast, if you tell someone something that can only be known because you say it, you have truly opened yourself up to that person." (Morreale, Spitzberg, & Barge, 2001, p. 75)

So then self-disclosure is the process of intentionally and unintentionally providing others with information about the self (attitudes, beliefs, values, etc.) that is unlikely to be discovered through other means.

We self-disclose in order to develop relationships. Have you ever tried to get to know someone better? What is one of the first things you do? We usually open up our selves to create an open communication climate. When there is an open climate for communication, others are more comfortable disclosing. Our self-disclosure invites others to self-disclose to us.

TMI: Too Much Information

Have you ever just met someone, say, on the bus, and that person divulged his or her life story to you before you could get off at the next stop—complete with full-blown descriptions of everything from "baby mama drama" to "religious conversions." After the conversation did you find yourself thinking, "Boy, that was simply too much information." Self-disclosure should be monitored for appropriateness. Some people are extremely turned off by hearing too much too soon. In addition, it is not always safe to self-disclose to individuals with whom you are not well-acquainted. It seems like a paradox to say that on the one hand, self-disclosure is necessary for closeness, and to say, on the other hand, that self-disclosure should not take place with individuals that we don't know very well. The question, then, becomes, how do we create closeness? You are encouraged to share information about yourself. Self-disclosure is fundamental to interpersonal closeness. Yet, you are encouraged more strongly to critically analyze those relationships in which you choose to self-disclose. Wait to see if the relationship is developing.

All relationships will not develop to a level where you will feel comfortable or even desire to disclose information about your "self." Know that there is always a risk in the choice to disclose. The person that you choose to disclose your inner being to may not be as accepting of your information as you want them to be. Share a little at a time and make sure you are putting your "self" into good hands. For self-disclosure to continue, both parties must decide to share information. This minimizes risk and of course, increases closeness.

Self That We Communicate to Self

"Do you believe that you have the power to defeat yourself? Have you ever talked yourself out of an "A" by constantly thinking or saying to yourself, "I know I'm not going to pass that Chemistry test?" You do talk to yourself, don't you? Research shows that there is a relationship between what we say to ourselves and what we accomplish. Consequently, **self-talk,** the inner conversations we have with ourselves, greatly influences our emotional well-being.

We are always engaged in intrapersonal communication or self-talk. Sometimes, we talk out loud to ourselves, which usually causes passersby to stare. In other instances, we daydream. We also engage in silent subconscious dialogues that link the multiple voices which create self. Our intrapersonal communication influences our self-concept, self-esteem, and emotional state. How we approach every day is influenced by how we address self. Are you guilty of saying, "Ooh! It's raining this morning. This is surely a good day to stay in bed?" Then you find that you are tired and lethargic for the remainder of that day. All that we do begins with self-talk. Self-talk shapes how we see the world, how we see ourselves in relation to the world, and how we see ourselves in relation to others in the world. Self-talk shapes our attitudes and behaviors. Self-talk can work for or against you" (Berko, Wolvin, Wolvin, 1995, p. 52–3).

Awake or asleep, you are constantly in touch with yourself. You mumble, daydream, dream, fantasize, and feel tension. These are all forms of inner speech.

A process that can allow you to get in touch with your inner voice is to relax, breathe deeply for fifteen minutes, tune out the noise around you, and let your mind wander. This will give you a good appreciation of what you are feeding your mind (Berko, Wolvin, Wolvin, 1995, p. 52–3).

Evolving Self

Change Can Be a Wonderful Thing

Yes. Change can be a wonderful thing. You can handle the uneasiness of the new directions you might decide to take. You are strong enough to transform the course of your life if you take a step each day.

Sometimes we find ourselves in a day-to-day rut spinning our wheels. Although, we work hard at getting somewhere, that day-to-day rut just seems to hold us stuck in the same spot. Sometimes, we find ourselves in relationships that drain us instead of fulfill us. And then there are jobs that we sometimes feel forced to go to because we have to pay bills and provide for our families. You may not have the ability to change how another acts in a relationship, and you may not be able to quit your job at the drop of a hat, but you can change how you respond to these situations. And change can be a wonderful thing.

My trusty old *Webster's New Collegiate Dictionary* says that the word change means "to make different in some particular . . . to make radically different . . . transform . . . to give a different position, course, or direction." Think about your life and this definition. And then ask yourself, "Do I need a change? Are there things in my life that I need to make radically different? Do I need to take a different direction in some particular avenue of my life?" In essence, do you need a change?

We each have the power to control our own lives. For my hat wearing sisters sitting in the amen corner, who are bound to shout, "Whatcha talkin' about? God's got it all in control," I'll make it clear. I am talking about controlling our own behaviors, controlling how we act, and controlling how we respond. Like Michael Jackson says, change starts with the man/woman in the mirror.

Recently, there have been numerous reports claiming that the number of obesity cases has risen. The reports are not quite as clear about the emotional causes as I would like. I think that a lot of weight gain is directly related to unhappiness, to disease in people's lives. Something in our lives causes us disease, and we internalize. What is being internalized is being externalized in the form of weight gain.

My advice for fighting off obesity is to begin an exercise program. No, not the one where you run or walk for 30 minutes each day. Yes, physical exercise is good and necessary. However, the type of exercise that I am referring to is a mental one. Exercise your mind by seeing alternative ways of handling the situations in your life that might be contributing to your weight gain or loss. Is there a bad relationship? Is there financial trouble? Exercise your mind by making a list of things you wish that you could change in your life. Be honest. Once you have completed your list, separate the items into two categories—"Things I Can Change" and "Things I Cannot Change." Don't lie to yourself. Don't put something in a category just because of what you have been taught. Some things you can change that you may have been told you cannot. Prioritize your "can change side." Now, begin a list of "Things I Can Do to Change This" for each of the "can change items." Each day do at least one thing on the "can do" list. You will surely experience change.

Change Can Be a Necessary Thing

Yes, change can be a necessary thing. It beckons for the truth, and truth promotes healing. Change has as its very nature transforming power. When things are not going right, they need to, ultimately, change. When something is causing disease, change and truth help us to reconcile. Understand reconciliation as a way of accepting the unpleasant, of submitting to the truth.

Recently I attended the seating of the Greensboro Truth and Reconciliation Commission. The Greensboro Commission, patterned after the South African model, is the first commission of its kind to form in the United States. The commission seeks to examine, "the context, cause, sequence and consequence of the events of November 3, 1979." If you do not know what happened on that day, check out the Commission's Web page *(www.gtcrp.org)* for historical background. Yet, if you are to understand my point, know that because of those November events, five people were shot to death, ten others were wounded, and a local and global community were changed forever.

When conversations were just beginning about the possibility of such a commission, I was asked whether I thought it would be necessary in our community. The other person's argument was, generally, "let bygones be bygones." At first, I said, "Well maybe?" But then I thought about it and I now see that every continent, country, and community should have a commission like this. Not only should we investigate truths about geographical communities, we should also look at truths about our racial and social communities. Let's look at truths about ourselves. Remember, change starts with the man/woman in the mirror.

We've all made mistakes, but mistakes are only useless if we do not use the knowledge gained from them. Change has as its very nature transforming power. When things are not going right, ultimately, they need to change. When something is causing disease, change and truth help us to reconcile. Understand reconciliation as a way of accepting the unpleasant—of submitting to the truth.

Gotta Do What I Gotta Do

Yes, there are times in our lives where we have to change course. We have to change direction. Some call it "rolling with the punches." When you roll with the punches, you "take lemons and make lemonade." No, this is not an attempt to see how many clichés I can put in this first paragraph. It is an attempt, however, to show you that changing direction is a part of our everyday lives. Many of us change direction and shrug it off with a "Girl, I gotta do what I gotta do."

Like the other day, I found out that a project that I had proposed was approved for a go ahead. Oh, I was floating on the clouds. Within an hour of hearing the fantastic news, I received a phone call with the other party saying, "put everything on hold." I fell hard from my cloud. For a brief moment, it was like someone had hit me right smack dab in the middle of my stomach. You know that feeling you got as a kid when you fell and couldn't catch your breath? That was the feeling I had after the "put everything on hold" call. While slumping with my back against the wall, I had a "eureka" moment. I remembered what my pastor out in San Diego used to say, "It is when your back is against the wall that you can go no further back. There is no where to go but forward." So forward, I went. I found a phone and started making phone calls to put Plan B in place. Oh yeah, I forgot to mention that there was a Plan B.

See, you must always have a Plan B in place in case you have to change direction. One of my friends, D.L., is the queen of the "Plan B." D.L. always says, "Girl, I gotta do what I gotta do. If this one thing here don't work out, then I got a Plan B." Plan B is always an alternate route of sorts. And yes in life, you should probably at least have thought about a Plan B just in case, "this one thing here don't work out."

Sometimes we are forced to change direction, which was initially the case for me. Then, there are other times when a change in direction may be exactly what we need to spark the spirit. I think we need to talk more about completely positive spirit. We need to talk about the spirit that brings forth joy. If you are not experiencing joy in your present situation, you probably need a change of direction. The spirit of the situation isn't good. No matter what it is, if there is no joy in it, I recommend you investigate, "Plan B." No, I am not telling you to leave your girlfriend, boyfriend, husband, or wife because you have no joy in your relationship. I am simply saying you might need to find a way to bring the joy back. Because Plan A isn't working out, don't give up. Go to Plan B. Get the spirit in that relationship right. Somebody might just need to change direction in order to spark the spirit.

I really do believe in having Plans A–Z. But after Plan Z, I'm tired. My energy is low, and I am not giving it my all. One of my professors used to say, "Myra, you can't keep running your head into a brick wall." I'm a headstrong something and I don't give up easily. But I've had to learn that sometimes some people and some situations are just not going to change. After I have tried all that I know, I just have to cut whatever it is a loose and change direction.

Wrap It Up

Who are you? Do you know? We begin this discussion of self by painting a picture of people looking for meaning in their lives. We conclude, definitively, that self is the multidimensional product that results from the complex process of internalizing and acting from direct definitions that we learn as we communicate. Direct definitions are essentially labels. These definitions are communicated to us by our particular and generalized others. The American culture tends to put emphasis on race, gender, sexual orientation, and socioeconomic class.

We use self-disclosure as a way of sharing our thoughts and feelings with others. This can increase or decrease interpersonal closeness. On the other hand, our self-talk greatly influences our emotional well-being. It influences our self-concept and self-esteem.

It the self is ever to evolve, change may be necessary. Change comes through being honest about our current conditions. We must plan for change and always have multiple options.

References

Berko, R., A. Wolvin, and D. Wolvin, *Communicating: A Social and Career Focus.* Boston, Mass: Houghton Mifflin Company, 2001.

Carter, R. T. "Is White a Race? Expressions of White Racial Identity," In M. Fine, L. Weis, L. C. Powell, and L. M. Wong (Eds.), *Off White: Readings on Race, Power, and Society.* New York: Routledge, 1997: 198–209.

Cunningham, G. P. "Body Politics: Race, Gender, and the Captive Body," In M. Blount & G. P. Cunningham (Eds.), *Representing Black Men.* New York: Routledge, 1996, 131–154.

DeVito J. A. *Human Communication: The basic course.* New York: HarperCollins College Publishers, 1994.

Jones, J. M. "The Concept of Racism and Its Changing Reality," In B. P. Bowser and R. G. Hunt (Eds.), *Impacts of Racism on White America.* Beverly Hills: Sage Publications, 1981.

Lerner, M. *The Politics of Meaning: Restoring Hope and Possibility in an Age of Cynicism.* Reading, Mass: Perseus Books, 1997.

Morreale, S., B. Spitzberg, and J. Barge, *Human Communication: Motivation, Knowledge, & Skills.* Stamford, Conn: Wadsworth/Thomson Learning, 2001.

Steen, M. "Learning to Overcome Cultural Barriers in the Workplace," *Greensboro News & Record,* 2000, November 11, F1, F2.

Windsor, R. R. *From Babylon to Timbuktu: A History of Ancient Black Races Including the Black Hebrews.* Philadelphia: Windsor's Gold Series Publications, 1988.

Wood. J. *Communication in Our Lives.* Belmont, Calif: Wadsworth Publishing Company, 1997.

Communication in the Movies

I invite you and a friend or classmates to explore comunication in the movies. Reflect on the communication skills discussed in this chapter. How are they addressed in the movies?

▶ In the Heat of the Night
▶ Do the Right Thing
▶ Pursuit of Happiness
▶ Waterboy

Name _____ Date _____

Section _____

Think About It → Write About It

Reflect on what you've just read. Now write what you are thinking.

_____

_____

_____

_____

_____

_____

_____

_____

_____

_____

_____

_____

_____

_____

_____

_____

_____

_____

_____

_____

_____

_____

_____

_____

_____

Activity 1

"A Display of Self-Perception"

1. Use small poster boards, markers, crayons, magazines, and glue or tape.
2. Creatively use magazine clippings, drawings, and color combinations to represent a pictorial display of how you see your self.
3. After the posters are completed, share your artwork with the class and explain it's representation of self.

Activity 2

Prepare Your Self-Concept Paper

Directions are as follows:

1. Create a unique cover page that reflects you or your personality.
2. Write a 3-page paper, typewritten, double-spaced, 10 or 12 pt font that describes your "self-concept." Use this paper to define who you really are. Be as honest as possible.

Chapter 5

Saying It without Words

Key Terms

Nonverbal Communication
Aesthetics
Artifacts
Body Movements
Chronemics
Environmental Factors
Eye Behavior
Haptics
Kinesics

Oculesics
Paralanguage
Personal Presentation
Physical Appearance
Physical Space
Physical Touch
Proxemics
Personal Objects
Vocal Variations

Nonverbal communication is the process of transporting messages through behaviors, physical characteristics, and objects. As this chapter progresses, it becomes clear that the term "behavior" generally encompasses all that is not verbal. Nonverbal communication is also about how we say things. Do you know someone who is speaking in a low seductive tone on his or her answering machine? Maybe you know someone who yells a lot. Tone and volume are both nonverbal behaviors that communicate messages. Research shows that verbal symbols (words) are not as important to the meaning of a message as nonverbal cues or nonverbal behaviors. Thirty to thirty-five percent of meaning is carried by the words, leaving the other sixty-five to seventy percent being carried by nonverbal cues.

Nonverbal communication has several specific characteristics. It is culturally defined, often unconsciously shows feelings and attitudes, and it may conflict with verbal communication.

Nonverbal Communication Is Culturally Defined

Nonverbal symbols, like verbal symbols, are culturally defined. We receive our meaning for nonverbal symbols from our culture. These meanings are communicated from generation to generation. In America, we are taught that it is polite to make eye contact and shake hands when we greet another. However, some Tibetan hill people greet by protruding their tongues, while people of the Micronesian Islands in the Pacific greet each other by raising their eyebrows or giving a nod.

In the late 1950s, then-Vice President Richard Nixon made a peacekeeping tour of Latin America. As with any move made by public officials and pop icons, the press was right there to cover it all. Nixon stepped from the plane in his famous political posture, smiled and gestured to the crowd by putting his thumb and forefinger in a circle. His nonverbal gesture was what Americans define as the "OK" sign. That day the crowd booed the American Vice President. The next morning, Nixon's picture was painted all over the news. The people were outraged. In Latin America this nonverbal cue meant, "Screw You." Nixon's lack of knowledge about the cultural differences of nonverbal cues could have ruined the United States' relationship with Latin America.

Area/Region	Behavior	Meaning
United States	The thumb-and-forefinger-in-a-circle gesture	OK sign
Greece, Turkey	The thumb-and-forefinger-in-a-circle gesture	Sexual invitation (vulgar)
France, Belgium	The thumb-and-forefinger-in-a-circle gesture	Nothing or 0
Japan	The thumb-and-forefinger-in-a-circle gesture	Money

Within the same culture, the nonverbal behaviors of females usually differ from the nonverbal behaviors of males. Deborah Tannen (Tannen, 1995) watched videotapes of males and females interacting. She discovered that girls and women sit closer together and tend to look each other directly in the eye. Boys and men, however, tend to sit at angles and rarely make eye contact with each other. Men sit in an open relaxed manner when they are with other men as well as when they are in the company of women. Women, on the other hand, tend to sit in "ladylike" positions when they are in mixed groups. Yet, when women are chillin' with other women, they sit in the same open relaxed manner as men do.

Nonverbal Differences Exist Between Women and Men

Although men and women may share a common culture, their nonverbal behaviors tend to differ. Research concludes that gender differences exist between the nonverbal behaviors of men and women. Each statement below characterizes the differences between the nonverbal behaviors of American men and women. Check yourself! Make the statement true by circling the correct gender.

1. Women/Men are less likely to return a smile than women/men.
2. Women/Men use fewer gestures than women/men.
3. Women/Men use fewer one-handed gestures and arm movements.
4. Women/Men are not more attracted to others who smile.
5. Women/Men exhibit greater leg and foot movement, including tapping their feet.
6. Women/Men more frequently use sweeping hand gestures, stretching the hands, cracking the knuckles, pointing and using arms to lift the body from a chair or table.
7. Women/Men establish more eye contact than women/men.
8. Women/Men use more facial expressions and are more expressive than women/men.
9. Women/Men do not convey their emotions through their faces.
10. Women/Men smile more than women/men.
11. Women/Men tend to keep their hands down on the arms of a chair more than women/men.
12. Women/Men do not appear to be disturbed by people who do not watch them.

Answers
1. Men/Women   2. Women/Men   3. Women   4. Men   5. Men
6. Men   7. Women/Men   8. Women/Men   9. Men   10. Women/ Men
11. Women/Men   12. Men.

Adapted from Judy Cornelia Pearson, Lynn H. Turner, and William Todd-Mancillas, *Gender and Communication,* 2nd ed. Dubuque: Wm. C. Brown Publishers, 1991. As in Wilson, Gerald L. Groups in Context: Leadership and Participation in Small Groups 5th ed. Boston: McGraw-Hill College, 1999: 123–126.

Nonverbal Communication Often Unconsciously Shows Feelings and Attitudes

Have you ever seen *the finest* guy or girl walk your way? You are unaware, but your eyes bulge and your mouth drops. You may even find that you unconsciously make some type of sound—no words, just a sound. That is nonverbal communication. Your unconscious behavior in the presence of the "fine" specimen is an example of how nonverbal communication can occur without thought. *Our feelings and attitudes are often unconsciously transmitted through our nonverbal messages.*

I was in a group interview for a job when I realized how unconscious some people are about the impact of nonverbal messages. Because of the nonverbal cues, or behaviors of the panel, I was pretty sure that I wasn't going to get that job. The interviewers were all members of academe. They were overly prepared to stump me on a number of different items. When I fired back with what I thought were well-thought-out answers, I could tell by the nonverbal behaviors of the group, whether they agreed or disagreed with my responses. Some of the panelists would smile; others would roll their eyes upward. At one point, one of the interviewers turned to the person in front of her, rolled her eyes and threw her head backwards. I knew she wasn't impressed. That group shot me down with their nonverbal communication. The feelings and attitudes of the group were communicated through their collective nonverbal messages. Their nonverbal messages said "You are bombing with us. You will not get this job." Their nonverbal messages were reinforced weeks later when I received a rejection letter in the mail.

Nonverbal Communication May Conflict with Verbal Communication

Have you ever ended a relationship and the other partner said, "I just need some time. I need some space. I don't want to see you anymore." But every time you turned to leave, the individual physically reached out to pull you back. That person was sending you mixed messages. When our nonverbal messages are inconsistent with our verbal messages, we are sending **mixed messages.** It is much easier to manipulate our verbal messages than it is to manipulate our nonverbal ones. Essentially, we may lie with our words, but our nonverbals usually reveal the truth.

Nonverbal and verbal communication are not at odds in all aspects. Nonverbal communication functions to reinforce, substitute for, and regulate verbal communication.

Send in the Reinforcement

There are instances where nonverbal communication functions to reinforce verbal messages. When trying a case, attorneys often instruct witnesses to identify the accused by name and to support their verbal identification by pointing to where that individual is sitting in the courtroom. The nonverbal action of pointing to a specific individual reinforces the verbal identification. Similarly, the act of nodding while saying, "Yes, of course, I want to drive your Escalade!" reinforces your message and complements your words.

Send in the Substitute

Nonverbal messages often substitute for spoken words. A man on the side of the road with his thumb extended toward the roadway is using a nonverbal cue to substitute for, "Yo, I need a ride." Simple gestures such as waving hello or good-bye and "flippin' the bird" are other nonverbal behaviors that substitute for verbal communication. Have you looked at a close friend and could tell by her posture and facial expressions that something was wrong? Without saying a word, your friend communicated that there was a problem.

Time for the Regulator

Nonverbal communication can manage our verbal interactions with others. Nonverbal behaviors can regulate the flow of conversation. I've noticed that many professors gaze away or stand to signify the end of a discussion between themselves and students. This is a nonverbal way of regulating communication. Standing and averting eye contact signify the close of the communication event.

Nonverbal Category	Area of Behavioral Emphasis
Aesthetics	Environmental Factors
Artifacts	Personal Objects
Chronemics	Time
Haptics	Physical Touch
Kinesics	Body Movements
Paralanguage	Vocal Variations
Physical Appearance	Personal Presentation
Proxemics	Physical Space
Oculesics	Eye Behavior

Categories of Nonverbal Communication

Nonverbal communication can be broken down into many different categories. Here, we will cover nine different ways we communicate messages through nonverbal means—aesthetics, olfactics, artifacts, chronemics, haptics, kinesics, paralanguage, physical appearance, proxemics, and oculesics.

Turn Down the Lights

Aesthetics refer to environmental factors and how they are manipulated to influence our feelings and emotions. Environmental factors include colors, lighting, spatial arrangement, and sounds. **Olfactics,** more specifically, relates to the perception of scents and smells. Do you burn scented candles or incense? Are the lights low when you are on a date with a special someone? Do you listen to soundscapes CDs to relax? These are all examples of how we manipulate environmental factors to affect mood. We attempt to control or influence the mood by controlling the setting.

Think about the last time you ate at a fast food restaurant. Did your experience go something like this? You walk in and find a guide rope directing you to the cashier. The music is moderately loud and the beat is pretty fast. The lights and colors are bright. The seats look hard. But it doesn't matter; you aren't planning to sit anyway. The cashier quickly takes your order—that is, if he's good at his job. He then yells the order to the back, where a faceless arm slides a pre-pressed, loosely wrapped sandwich down a chute. Your fries, displayed proudly under a heat lamp, have been sitting and waiting hours, just for you. Finally, the "fry girl" recklessly tosses them into your bag. You only receive a cup for your supersize soft drink; it is your responsibility to serve yourself when it comes to securing a beverage. Your meal is complete, so you rush off to consume your *happy meal.* If this sounds like your experience, then the designers of fast-food chains have done their jobs pretty well. The objective of a fast-food restaurant is to feed people *quickly*. The fast-food restaurant environment is not conducive to a long, intimate dinner. Leisurely meals were not the objective of the entrepreneurs who conceived of the fast-food notion. They want to maximize profit by moving bodies in and out of these restaurants. Research on environmental factors shows that fast music in restaurants speeds up the pace of eating, where slow music slows down the pace (Bozzi, 1986; "Did you know?" 1998). When is the last time you heard Maxwell crooning from the sound system at McDonald's?

Artifacts are objects that we use to express our identities. Consider the clothes that we wear; our "bling bling" that "blinds blinds"; the pagers, cell phones, and two-ways that we carry; the 57-inch high definition projection flat screen TV monitors that sit in our living rooms; and even those 22-inch rims on our cars are **artifacts.** These objects announce who we are or at least who we think we are. When we dress ourselves in the mornings, we are making a nonverbal statement. For example, business people adorn themselves in the attire of the corporate world: suits, slacks, skirts, blouses, and other generally conservative gear. Their appearance makes a statement about who they are and what they do. Hip Hop Ballers, on the other hand, usually sport Sean Jean, Phat Farm, Gucci, Prada, and the list goes on. However, as we look at business moguls such as Sean "P-Diddy" Combs and Russell Simmons, the once clearly cut line between business attire and Hip Hop wear has become much less defined. Yet, the general populace still reads something about us by our personal appearance—by the artifacts that we use to announce our identities. Some research says that, "Sociocultural judgments are made about socioeconomic status, residence, occupation, education, and group membership.

Clothing is a symbol of status, and perceptions of success and education are based on dress. A person dressed in a business suit will be perceived as having more status than someone in jeans" (O'Hair, D., Friedrich, G. W., Wiemann, J. M., & Wiemann, M. O., 1995, p. 223).

When young ladies adorn themselves like the scantily dressed girls from the "shake your booty" videos and come to class, they are making a nonverbal statement. I heard one young lady claim, "Just because I show my body doesn't mean that I'm a 'ho'." No, showing one's body does not necessarily speak to the level of one's promiscuity. Yet, we must realize that our personal appearance does make a nonverbal statement. Remember, nonverbal communication is often unconscious. Hence, by our personal appearance, we may unconsciously communicate nonverbal messages that we do not intend to communicate. According to O'Hair, et. al (1995), "Dress and artifacts, whether they be T-shirts or rosary beads, also designate group membership" (p. 223).

Uniforms are artifacts that announce the identities of police officers, firefighters, athletes, priests, military officials, etc. They symbolize specific jobs. Objects that we use in our daily occupations also tend to declare our vocations. For example, the stethoscope, generally, symbolizes a medical occupation just as the hammer, generally, symbolizes carpentry.

Artifacts help us perform gendered roles. Unless he is a member of the transvestite community, we rarely see American men walking down the street in dresses or skirts. These items are generally reserved for women. Men who dress in skirts are going against the socially constructed notion Americans have of what it means to be male. However, from an American viewpoint, Scottish men frequently dress up in skirts, called kilts, and the Scottish are extremely accepting of men in "skirts."

Time Is on My Side

Chronemics is how we use and handle time to communicate messages. As with other nonverbal behaviors, time and its significance are culturally defined. Most Western Europeans, Japanese, and North Americans would probably consider punctuality a sign of good manners. However, Native American Navajo believe that the time to start a ceremony or function is when the preparations for the ceremony are complete—whenever that might be (Hall, 1976). Time is always on the side of the Native American Navajo. Yet, North American industrialists are not as casual about notions of time. Capitalists and industrialists see time as "money" and thus are extremely conscientious about the imprudent use of either.

Power is communicated through the usage of time. Have you ever shown up for your 3:00 PM meeting with your advisor to find that she is not there or that she has five people still waiting to see her? The person in power tends to make you wait. The person in power is that individual whose services you need. Think about it. You usually wait to see your doctor, your hair stylist, your dentist, and your professor. These are all people that you need for one reason or another.

The length of time that we spend engaged in an activity reflects our priorities and preferences. If you spend more time drinking and getting high than you do on your school-work, then you are nonverbally communicating your priorities. If you spend more time with Tiffany than Demetri, you are communicating a preference. Your decision to regularly come to class at 11:00 AM when the class begins at 10:45 AM speaks volumes about your commitment to your education.

A Little Too "Touchy Feely"

Haptics is nonverbal communication that involves physical touch. The research on touch reiterates the importance of touch in our everyday lives. Leathers (1986) says touch is the first of our five senses to develop. Birdwhitsell says that children brought up in dysfunc-tional settings are less likely to be touched than children brought up in healthy homes. Additional research says that premature children who were massaged three times a day for fifteen minutes gained weight 47 percent faster than those who were left alone in their incubators. The massaged infants left the hospital an average of six days earlier than infants treated the usual way. When the children were evaluated eight months later, their weight was constant and their mental and motor abilities were better than those of the infants treated by traditional means (Goleman, 1988). The research generally agrees that we need touch to survive.

The use of touch is greatly influenced by our culture and gender. Latin American, Mediterranean, and Eastern European cultures rely heavily on touch as a form of com-munication, whereas North Americans are much less reliant on touch to communicate messages (O'Hair, et. al, 1995). Wood (1994) says that gender differences in touching behaviors also exist. Women are more likely to hug to show support. Men are more likely to touch as a way of showing sexual desires and to exert power. Research also finds that superiors or more powerful people, regardless of gender, touch subordinates more often than subordinates touch superiors (Hall, 1996).

Walk around campus today and observe the nonverbal behaviors of men and women. Do your own independent survey. Are women touching more or are men? Under what conditions are they touching? Who are they touching?

Make Your Body Talk

Kinesics refers to how we use body movements to communicate. Whether it is a twist of the hips or a "John Wayne" swagger, our body movements constantly communicate information about us. We convey the majority of our nonverbal messages through facial expressions. Research estimates that the human face is capable of more than 7,000 different expressions (Jordan, 1986).

Since the September 11, 2001 terrorists' attack on the United States, "The CIA wants to teach computers to watch for detailed facial-language clues. . . . The agency commissioned the Salk Institute and Carnegie Mellon University's Robotics Institute to work up software prototypes" (Lortie, B., 2002, p. 7–8).

Have you ever watched the nonverbals of presidents or any other political figures? Some of their hand gestures appear rehearsed. Just maybe they are. Spiegel and Machotka, P. (1974) say that hand gestures are associated with power. Are political figures interested in power? You bet! Whitehead and Smith (2002) find that presidents use more hand gestures than smiles in their inaugural addresses. In an ancillary finding, Whitehead and Smith also discover that two of the presidents they looked at did not smile at all—Eisenhower and Kennedy. They attribute this behavior to the proliferation of television. They say, Eisenhower and Kennedy's inaugurals were "during the early days of television. Perhaps the types of nonverbal behaviors that presidents use in their inaugural addresses have changed as television has become an increasing part of all of our lives" (Whitehead & Smith, 2002, p. 671).

Windows to the Soul

Oculesics refers to eye behavior. There is a saying that our "eyes are windows to the soul." This statement has some semblance of truth. We can tell a great deal about people because of their eye behavior. I know when students look downward that usually means they don't want me to call on them. Research says that people look up and to the left when they are recalling or remembering, and look up and to the right when they are thinking of the future (Berko, et. al., 1995).

In the wake of the September 11th terrorists' attack on the United States, "Boston's Logan Airport hired Rafi Ron, former chief of security for the Israeli Airport Authority, to train more than 200 state troopers to watch for the darting eyes and trembling hands of would-be terrorists. . . . Ron told Congress that profiling has been 'very successful for the last 32 years' in Israel" (Lortie, 2002, p. 8).

Communication research is not only interested in the oculesics of criminals. Presidential candidates have come under scrutiny as well. During the presidential campaign of 1976, researchers studied the nonverbal behaviors of Jimmy Carter and incumbent Gerald Ford to determine if either candidate were engaging in unusual behavior during presidential debates. "The findings indicated that if Carter [were] in trouble he would look down at the lectern, shift his gaze randomly, and smile inappropriately. Ford looked away from the camera in similar situations" (Berko, et al., 1995, p. 166).

I Didn't Understand a Word: A Perspective

Sheila M. Whitley, Ph.D.

We communicate in many ways. We use words, symbols, body language, and so forth. Can we understand a person if we don't know their language? Yes, messages are also communicated through tone, volume, gestures, facial expressions, and numerous other ways.

I had the opportunity, along with several students and professors, to visit some public schools in several Black townships in Cape Town, South Africa.

Fortunately for this monolingual visitor, many South Africans speak English in addition to their mother language, and many know a third language. English is one of eleven official languages in South Africa. Ndebele, Pedi, Sotho, Swazi, Tsonga, Tswana, Venda, Xhosa, and Zulu are official languages, and each is a mother tongue for the various indigenous groups. Afrikaan is the primary language for White South Africans and the mother language for some Black South Africans.

Consider the potential communication problems in South Africa with 11 official languages compared to one we have in the United States. You would think it might be extremely difficult to communicate in South Africa, a country with land mass about twice the size of Texas.

A little South Africa history may help put language into perspective. South Africa is ten years into democracy. Prior to 1994, South Africans suffered under an oppressive system known as Apartheid. The minority White population subjugated the majority Black population. It was a brutal time for all South Africans.

During the Apartheid era, the Black South Africans could not publicly sing, dances or play music that was African. They were taught ballads and played European music. Soon, speaking the various mother languages in the Black schools became a disputed point.

In 1974, a decree made Afrikaan the language for school instruction in Black schools. This decree contributed to the June 1976 uprising in the Black township of Soweto. The school children marched to protest the Bantu Educational system and the decree. Many seniors were afraid they would fail their exams if they had to write in Afrikaan (not their native language). The march was suppose to be peaceful. The police arrived, and before noon several school children were killed.

Today, the mother languages thrive in the Black schools. Children are required to study their mother language plus an additional language. Many select English as their second language. Therefore, we didn't have a communication problem when we visited the schools. As a matter of fact, many of the children were amazed that Americans typically know just one language.

Our primary reason for visiting the schools was to see how dance and music are taught in the schools. The children would dance and sing for us. Dance is a universal form of communication. You don't need an interpreter. Music is also universal. It isn't difficult to understand the beat or the rhythm.

When you sing, you use a particular language. Can you understand the meaning of song without an interpreter? We heard several school choirs and groups. The children sweetly sang in their mother language for us. Since none of us spoke their languages, we had no idea what the words meant. The children sang with such facial and vocal expression. Without a doubt, many of the songs were praise songs.

We all were moved to tears at the first school where several choirs performed for us. One girl rivaled any recording artist. Her passion exuded from her voice. The emotionally charged expression on her face and body language reinforced her melodious message.

Do you need to understand the language to experience a person's passion? Do you need to understand the language to feel their emotions? Do you need to understand the language to warm your heart? Confidently I say, "No!" I know of a school in the Zimasa Community near Cape Town, South Africa where singing students communicated to and touched several American hearts, and we didn't understand a word.

You Look Marvelous

Physical appearance refers to an individual's physical qualities. The American culture strongly emphasizes physical appearance. That's why we are inundated with infomercials for fat burning powders and drinks, consumed with Billy Blanks and his Tae Bo, and stretching like taffy to Winsor Pilate videos. Beauty is culturally defined.

Some African countries celebrate a more voluptuous-sized woman, while Americans have come to celebrate a thinner frame. However, what is applauded in terms of physical appearance continuously changes. Thick lips, for instance, were once considered a negative feature. I had a beauty makeover in the late 1980s where the beauty consultant showed me how to reduce the size of my lips by drawing my lip liner on in a special way. She explained, "you'll definitely want to downplay the size of your lips." From the late 1990s to the present, more and more women have resorted to collagen injections to get the physical traits that I was directed to downplay in the 1980s—my thick lips.

Skin color, hairstyle, sex and size, are characteristics that we generally notice as soon as we look at a person. Our first impressions are made during those initial moments.

Unfortunately, society has not gotten passed prejudging people based on appearance. Many of my students have been told by hiring professionals to remove cornrows, colorful weaves, and artifacts such as tongue and eye piercings if they want to get hired. One colleague reports that her nursing students were failing to get jobs. They did not rate second interviews. She asked several of the young ladies to remove their *weaved in* braids and try the job market once more. With freshly straightened hair, the young ladies hit the pavement once again. Each was successful in acquiring employment on the first go-round. Physical appearance can influence hiring decisions, pay raises, and even trial verdicts. Famous trial attorney, Clarence Darrow, once explained that jury members rarely convict people they like or acquit ones they dislike (The Eyes Have It, 1973).

Why Dread Having Locs?

Marrissa R. Dick

Transference of Perceived Hair Ideology

Black women passed their understandings of how to best present themselves to society in terms of their hairstyles, generation after generation. The principal ideology seemed to be the assimilation of their hair to mimic that of dominant culture. There were periods of time where black men straightened their hair as well, following the trends of renowned singers like Little Richard and James Brown. In fact, very briefly, during the civil rights movement of the late sixties and early seventies, black people embraced their natural hair in the form of Afros and Corn Rolls. Unfortunately, for multiple reasons, such as survival, respect, and acceptance, black women have made hairstyle choices that sent strong non-verbal messages of how they see themselves in society, whether they admit or are even aware they are making profound statements or not. For example, the Angela Davis Afro suggests a *natural radical,* while the Susan Taylor Braids promoted the *faux natural.* The Whoopie Goldberg's dreads embraced the *free spirited self image,* while the Tyra Banks Weave supports the achievement of the black *"Barbie Doll"* look. The majority of contemporary black women today predominantly straighten their hair with chemical relaxers and straightening combs because of a general belief that it is most complimentary and accepted in dominant society. My focus is on dreadlocs because it seemed to be the most controversial natural hairstyle for women and men today. Several women were asked to share their hair stories.

"My grandmother discouraged me from getting dreadlocs the day I turned nineteen. I will never forget what she said to me 'Well whatever [hairstyle] you get I'm sure it will be beautiful just so long as you don't come back with those dreadlocs. I read in the paper where they fired a girl for wearing them. If you do that you'll never ever be able to get a job.' I stopped in my tracks and did not start my dreads until I was thirty-seven years old. She went on to say, 'Oh, the shame, everyone is going to think *my* granddaughter, *my* granddaughter is a drug dealer,' she said. Her word was the final word. She gently reminded me that I was about to start a secretarial program for the State of New York and I would probably have difficulty being placed in a "decent" working environment if I had locs. Society had cleverly constructed an unacceptable picture of beauty, drugs, employment, and social status into my grandmother's perception of locs. It was a constructed image that I allowed her to transfer to me.' "

After considering the narrative above, I interviewed Dr. Teresa Jo Styles, Associate Professor at North Carolina A&T State University,

"I think the real key is to research the company that you want to work with and see how that company has acted upon personal appearance in the past. If you can do any kind of study research wise on the number of people that have been hired with locs then you have a good shot at expressing your hair. But if you have not done that and you are really looking and searching for employment you've got to go with what the traditional style is. What am I trying to say is if you really need employment and you don't have the wherewithal to pick and choose companies it's just in your best interest to wear a traditional hair style."

During this research I have discovered that there can be some good transferences of ideology that embrace the African American culture from childhood. Kareem McKelvey, a journalism student at North Carolina A&T State University, Kareem states that,

"I had my hair locked since I was a freshman, going into my freshman year and I'm a senior now. So that was in 2003 since I have had it locked and I decided to get it locked because my family has always felt strongly about having our heritage represented. So my family, especially my mother, sees every dreadlock as apart of your blackness as being part of your ethnicity and everything. Yea so she's always viewed it as if you have dreadlocs you really love who you are as a black person and my oldest brother he has had dreadlocs since he was in high school and he's now 28. My second oldest brother he's had dreadlocs when he was in middle school and high school now he started losing some hair he went to the fade and my little brother he has dreadlocs and my father his father is from the Caribbean so that had a little bit of influence in it too. I'm also from Buffalo NY and most black people up North have dreadlocks. It's not uncommon at all."

In speaking with others about their social experiences with locs I seemed to be the only person that allowed a negative transference of perception to stop them from locking their hair. I spoke with Minister Gregory Drumwright. He explained that having locs did not hinder him with employment.

Today, locs are worn by many cultural groups as a fashion statement or trend while others wear locs for self-awareness, spiritual meaning or for religious beliefs. For many African Americans the wearing of locs is a bold acceptance of who they are and of embracing the hair that God has given to us. Styles believes that

> "locking is a generation that came after me. They are more into locking. I will just explain that I came from a generation of militant folks. You know when I talk about militants I mean during my time in college militancy was really coming on the heels of the civil rights movement under Dr. Martin Luther King. So Rap Brown, Stokley Carmichael, Black Power and so we were basically the generation who truly believed in King supported King. With that came the understanding that we had to say who we are and who we were and that meant freeing ourselves of chemicals, freeing ourselves of straightening combs, women I'm speaking of and therefore we were the generation to bring about life is beautiful and hair is beautiful naturally. But when you are talking about locs women did not understand locs the way they do now. They understood the Afro. I think the generation now of which you are apart understand more the locs because back to the natural then it just became the natural progression to go into the locs. So, if you were to ask me why I do not have locs its because I never had locs but I've had really large fro's and very short fro's. And you know I think the locs are beautiful. I don't know why I don't do them now. I just really think I'm just an older woman who prefers a shorter cut then doing anything longer or just letting it be as it is."

It is not uncommon for a black woman to continue to relax her hair knowing this is not what she wants. She thinks in her mind, "I know this is what society wants. A relaxed head of hair is the look that society can tolerate." She sits with her hairstylist, feeling him base her scalp and edges with a significant amount of grease then applies the lye. In her mind she tells herself, "yep, it's burning already, but I won't say anything. I'll just sit here and press through it." After the wash/dry/style process, she looks outside and thinks, "Why does it always seem to rain when I get my hair done?" as she runs to her car, puts on the air conditioner so she does not ruin her hairstyle. Although she could feel her hair flattening upon her head like pancake batter. What was the point; the hairstyle was ruined. If she were natural, this reoccurring problem would not exist. So why not go natural? Why dread having locs?

Learning to be natural requires an appreciation of self-image. This is something that many women lack. Kareem McKelvey, a journalism student at North Carolina A&T State University states,

> "I felt more attractive because I got compliments. People liked me with the locs more than they liked me with the fro. So definitely I felt more attractive. I felt more in tune with being a black person. I really felt like no one would look at me and say I didn't want to be black or something like that. There are people that do the locks just simply for the look but you know. But being that my father was in the Black Panthers he's basically a revolutionary mind thinking lawyer. I've always had it in the back of my head you should do anything that you can for yourself and other people to help with blackness. That's why I'm at A & T and I know that more women are attracted to me with my locs."

From my personal experience, I discovered the value and the impact of black women encouraging each other with personal testimonies as we transition from assimilated hair to wearing natural hair. I had a dear friend to take me to dinner in celebration of me finally embracing who I was ready to become; finally embracing my journey.

I am a Christian to the marrow of my bone though I am by far not perfect nor do I ever claim to be. What I do claim is my personal Lord and Savior, Jesus Christ. I think if more of that was done the world would be more harmonious instead of filled with so much bitterness and strife. In saying all of that, the church world is full of judgmental people even though no one is perfect from the pulpit to the back door. There is nothing more devastating than church hurt. It's a feeling that people sometimes never get over. I am so glad that I have a personal relationship with God so my church hurt was turned into a ministry that actually drew me closer to God. A great many women in my church had the traditional chemically relaxed hair, wore braids, or had weaves. I had a meeting with my pastor who is a very nontraditional preacher when it comes to preaching the Word of God, but is very traditional or maybe I should say conservative when it comes to outward appearance. I serve this awesome man of God. This is a very prestigious position in most churches because you are directly serving the pastor. Most of you may find it difficult to understand that I asked him for permission to loc my hair. Yes, I did it because he is my leader and I needed to know that locking my hair would not threaten my position. Needless to say he was not pleased. He didn't understand why I would want to do something so drastic. I told him that I had been reading the Bible and discovered that there were many people with locs such as Samson and others who were told specifically not to let razors touch their heads which naturally would lead to locs. Samson even says that he has seven locs. He put his head down and closed his eyes. In my mind went something like, "Even if he says no I'm going to do it anyway! If he says no, then just accept it. You've been a people pleaser your whole life anyway. I'm a grown woman and I'm sitting here asking him for permission! You need to ask for his permission because you're his servant. Just remain humble." He consented and told me that my locs would not hinder me from serving him. He did however request that I maintain them at all times. I just remember crying and feeling a weight lift off of me. I remember the Sunday that I was brave enough to take off my wig and wear my baby locs for the first time. I mean folks mouths were actually gaped open! I could hear the whispers. I could feel the stares. I could see people trying to stifle their laughter as they looked at me. I prayed that God would pull me through. I prayed that he would give me the strength not to burst into tears and run off of the pulpit. This particular Sunday, my pastor was preaching at an evening service at another church and I was serving him. Usually I would not sit in the pulpit, but this particular evening he called me onto the pulpit to sit directly beside him. I surmised that he did that to let everyone know that he was in full support of my hair style and they had better leave me alone. The smirks were gone and so were the stares. After that, no one said another word about my hair until it started growing longer. It seemed like it grew over night. I cannot tell you how many people in my church commented on my hair being beautiful. It's partly because I feel beautiful inside now. Unfortunately, every church-goer does not receive the confirmation or support from their pastor or church congregation as I was blessed. Many of my brothers and sisters in the Body of Christ have been forced to do away with their locs in order to maintain their position in church and my heart grieves for them.

Black on Black Hair Crime: White People Don't View It the Same

We have all seen white people wearing locs and they seem as though they are an anomaly. It just doesn't seem natural that they would wear locs because they have naturally fine long hair. Why would they want to loc their hair when it is not obviously their natural state? One would wonder why whites would intentionally subject themselves to the cruelty of society. When I interviewed two white people, one white woman who currently has locs and one white man who wore locs for nine years, they described their experience very differently but they did not describe it as being dramatic at all. I didn't understand that the woman did not experience any negativity. Casey Crespo, a graphic and textile design student at the University of North Carolina at Greensboro, actually wanted to know what type of drama was she supposed to have endured. I asked about her family. I wanted to know if she experienced any negativity from her family because she was not wearing her hair in her cultures' locs tradition. Casey explained,

> "Well my mom was a hippie in the 60's and hitch hiked from Illinois to California after she graduated so she was real cool. She didn't have a problem with it so I didn't have any negativity from my family. I found that people just in general come up to me and ask me about them and um start a conversation with me more frequently then when I did not have them."

This was difficult for me to believe because African Americans shun one another because of locs. It's almost as though we are the anomaly because we have chosen to embrace the natural state of our hair. I asked Casey why did she choose to wear locs and she stated,

> "I chose to do it because of what it stands for. To me if I look at a person and they have dreadlocs it tells me that they are probably nonconforming to society, their open minded a friendly person and that's what I wanted to convey to society. And I think it's a pretty general statement but I think that if you walked up to anybody with dreadlocs they would be open minded to you and be willing to talk to you pretty much about anything."

When I told Casey about the negative feedback that African Americans receive from our church and communities she was shocked. I shared with her one of the examples of one of the ministers,

> "The only sector that has denied me the privilege of something because of what was on my head was actually Black people. I did some work for a local business person who was in charge of bringing Al Gore here for the presidential candidacy campaign stop and he allowed me to do all this work to bring in a lot of major artists with whom I had connections with. Then after I had done the work and secured the artists he took me into his board

room and he sat me down and he said now what are we going to do about your hair? I said what you mean I don't really understand and he said well I really can't have you around that day if you're not going to cut your hair. He said I just can't have you seen, you know. And that was the first time that I knew that I was shunned for what was on my head. After they had gotten my expertise gotten what was within me after they had benefited from my knowledge, my expertise, and my intelligence it was still an issue with the outer part of me and that really hurt me. It really scared me you know not because of the opportunity of not being able to participate in the opportunity but the reason why and the possessor of that reason was a black man just like me you know and ah I went on from that experience just using that as motivation to continue to be who I am and its been difficult but it hasn't been that bothersome."

The white male, Tracey Thornton, a musician, on the other hand shared a much different experience when he wore his locs. Tracey states,

"Well I had locs back in the mid 90's. For the most part it was positive but most people that might have a negative prospective might not have approached me so I don't know. It always struck up a conversation. Probably the biggest thing about the whole thing was that you really learn how people judge books by its cover and then when you look at me like one person might think I'm one thing like a drug dealer another person might think I'm you know a African wanna be and the next person might think that I'm just culturally in tuned so I guess there are various projections of what they would think. I would get a little more reaction cause I remember when I cut them I never got looked at twice. I literally felt like I just blended into society which is a change cause I was always used to being in line at the bank and somebody either lookin' or talkin' behind my back fifty good or bad you hear a lot of things and so yeah you can see it coming and that was mainly here like in North Carolina. Like when I would go to New York they wouldn't look at me twice. Trinidad for the most part they just thought I was a 'White Trini' so that really helped me because in Trinidad I was staying in the very worst areas down there. I remember when I cut them. I remember the reactions because I had them for nine years so then when I cut them I remember I never had anything said to me or someone look at me as a foreigner or calling me a Yankee or a red neck or something that had never happened to me until after I got them cut literally the day after I cut them I was mistreated. So that was my Trinidad perspective but up here a lot has changed in the last ten years but up here it was a little bit harder. I think I had them before it kind of became stylish because it didn't really become stylish up here even in the black community of Greensboro anyway until the late 1990's you know the whole hip hop thing. You could go to New York or big cities and see it but I had them even before a lot of African Americans were wearing them you know and it really wasn't a Rasta thing. I was not a Rasta you know I was a heavy metal drummer and I guess just wanted to be different but I really liked them because of the conversation you know kind of like my tattoos. Now you go somewhere and always meet somebody and so most of it was positive. A lot of girls liked it a lot. A lot of African American women loved it. I don't know about the guys because they wouldn't go out of their way to say anything to me you know. At that time I was playing Jim Bay a lot too with some African guys down in Durham and they were all cool and everything but I was never a wanna be you know a lot of people thought that I was just likin' hip hop music and that wasn't it. I was just doin' my thing that's all so I wasn't trying' to be anything other than myself. So a lot of times I remember I would go out with girls and they would think you know with the look and all they thought I was someone else then they found out that I was just a regular guy and they would I dump me you know I wasn't some wild drug taken person you know what I'm sayin' so I guess I didn't attract a lot of girls that I'd want to take home to my mom. I liked them but I wouldn't take them home to my mom."

There is a significant difference between Casey's family embracing her locs and Tracey's family embracing his. According to him,

"Well I started off with braids. I always had long hair and I come from a beaver cleaver type house hold and with that though they were always supportive but they hated my long hair. When are you going to get a real job kind of thing. Then we went on a cruse and I got it all braided on the cruse I was like 20 and my mom was like don't get your hair braided, don't get your hair braided. The second day I got my hair braided and she was like please take them out. So I kept my hair braided for about a year and then when I started lettin' them grow out into dreads she was like I'll give you the money just get it braided again but then after they got used to it they were just fine with it. I'm a musician I didn't have to have a real job or anything. A big lesson that I learned was in '97 when I was playing with Big Mo who passed away a couple of years ago he had arranged through his friend Gary Moore a guitar player up in New Jersey who was friends with George Benson somehow we had two interviews with record companies who were real interested in signing me on and the whole trip was like man we got this cat down here in North Carolina he's young, he plays the hell outta the pans, he's got these dreadlocs to his waist, he's got this look, he's a good lookin' guy you know the whole marketing thing. To my understanding they had two meetings. You when I went to Trinidad you know I cut my hair but I didn't know that I was supposed to meet with them when I returned. So when I came back I had cut my hair and I didn't tell nobody so when I came back they called them and said that I was back and I was comin' but he's cut all his hair off the meetings were canceled I never got a meeting. So for years I've been playing music since I was fifteen I thought I was going to get a record deal finally but when I cut my locs I lost the record deal. I would have waited a couple of weeks man I would have gotten the interview but I didn't so that was the hard part of losing my locs. So that was not like a social thing that's kind of like that's the music business for ya so that was real painful so I was like damn I'm gonna have to keep trudging like I've been doin' so that was '97 so that was a lesson."

It appears that having locs enhanced Tracey's musical endeavors. His locs were a part of the perceived image that the music world was wanting to capitalize upon. As soon as he cut his locs his financial opportunity to go further in his music disappeared along with his locs.

Those of us who have locs know that it takes you through emotionally, physically, and spiritually because this is indeed a journey of life. Robin explain that it is called a journey because,

"Well I'll say the first thing that I recognize in making the transition is that we go through the feeling of you know not being accepted . . ."

The locking process is not as natural for whites. Here they talk about their locking process. Casey states,

> "Well my boyfriend use to have dreadlocs so he told me about knotty boy dreadlocs it's like a hard wax and you can use it for black or white hair and I went on their web site nottyboydreadslocks.com and they teach you how to do it. They have all these pictures. It's just a hard wax that holds fine hair together and they have different colors too, for blonds, brown or black hair. I used a flea comb to do mine. I would just back comb it with a fine tooth comb and twisted it and used that wax and now I don't have to do anything to it,"

and Tracey started his locs by braiding his hair, he states,

> "Well how I grew mine was that I'm kind of a neat freak so I never had those thick master dreads. When I had them braided I had them braided really nice. I had like 144 and when I started letting them grow out in dreads I had to maintain them a lot because my hair is not so nappy so it was a lot of grooming. So it literally grew out into the braid and twist up and how I would do it is I would take it and twist it and get a hot iron on it and wrap it up and within a week if I didn't get my hair wet it would dread you know I had to keep it nice and it was a lot involved. When the dreads just kept coming out and then the braids got down to my shoulders, I just cut the braids off and just let my hair grow. My hair just grew like weeds but it was a lot of grooming man a lot of grooming. It wasn't like you just let it go if you want it to look nice I felt like a woman for a moment because I was always in my hair so there you have it."

Conclusion

In conclusion, I believe that African Americans should be more supportive of those brothers and sisters who enter into the journey of embracing their natural hair texture. We should not be made to feel as though we are an anomaly. In fact we are more in tuned with who we are as individuals, we are more in tuned with our culture, and we are more in tuned with our heritage. It is not necessary for everyone to assimilate into white society. Are we not just as beautiful merely because we are unique in our choices? Does it not stand to reason that everyone will not assimilate into a standardized mode of what is perceived as beauty? Why is it that other cultures can see the beauty and embrace it but our own people feel ashamed? These are questions that really need to be researched and studied. Why are we, those who wear locs, depicted as bad or evil? Just know that everyone wearing locs are not out to harm you. We are simply embracing what God has given us, and doing the best that we can with it.

According to Stewart (1999), the sacred self is the personhood of African Americans that strongly resists the historically crafted notions of Blackness through media, popular culture, and hegemonically propagated stereotypes. The sacred self celebrates an African heritage, applauds the cultural rites of Blackness, and contends against marginalizing descriptions, images, and definitions of Black life. . . . The sacred self has to be connected to a sacred community that believes the stereotypes, definitions, and social constructions of Blackness that have been historically and traditionally crafted are incapable of authentically embracing the essence of what it means to be an African American. Finally, having the courage to crown my head with locs gives affirmation to the acceptance of my Blackness.

I would strongly advise anyone who is considering on locking their hair to think long and hard before doing it because it is simply not a fad. Wearing locs are a way of life. The process that you have to endure is like no other. The prejudices are all too real in fact to deal with at times. Prejudices from your family, friends, society, and church community can take an enormous toll upon you emotionally. Can you take it? Locs will make you or break you emotionally, physically, and spiritually. It takes a special person to wear the lion's mane and that's just what our locs are—a main entrance to whom we are as individuals and as a people.

It's Not What You Say, but How You Say It

Paralanguage, sometimes referred to as vocalics, is how we say what we say. Paralanguage includes sounds such as grunts, groans, moans, and sighs, as well as vocal codes such as volume (loudness), rate (the speed at which you speak), pitch (the highness or lowness of your voice), and inflection (the change in pitch and volume of your voice). When we say, "I love you" to our parents, it usually sounds different than when we say, "I love you," to our romantic partners. Vocal codes tell people how to perceive us. Loud, stern calls usually mean that *mommy* is upset with us. Rapid speech can signify urgency. Notice public speakers and television announcers. They frequently manipulate vocal codes to emphasize their points.

Get Off of My Shoe

Proxemics is the study of how we use space to communicate. Edward T. Hall (1969) said that people maintain space between each other based on their relationship or based on how they feel about each other, their objective at the moment and the situation that they are in at a particular moment. According to Hall, we mentally define our space into four distinct spheres: intimate, personal, social, and public space.

Consider yourself inside the center of a bubble. From your skin to eighteen inches outward is your **intimate space.** This space is usually reserved for those with whom we are intimate. People are usually only allowed in this space in private. However, we do allow certain professionals into our intimate space. My dentist cannot clean my teeth if I do not allow her into my intimate space. Your hair stylist cannot style your hair if you do not let him into your intimate space. We allow people that we know fairly well into our **personal space,** which extends from eighteen inches to four feet. The better we know an individual, the closer we allow that individual into our personal space. People that we don't know as well are usually kept closer to the outer perimeter of our personal space. We conduct formal interactions within our **social space,** which extends from four feet to about twelve feet. When you meet with your advisor, the two of you may sit at this distance to discuss your academic progress. When you apply for car loans, checking accounts, and the like, you probably perform these transactions at a social distance. Finally, there is the area that extends from twelve feet and beyond, the **public space.**

As is with all nonverbal communication, spatial preferences and inclinations are culturally defined. Arabs, Mediterraneans, Latin Americans, Italians, Russians, Spaniards, Middle Easterners, and the French tend to permit closer interactions than North Americans. Northern Europeans and North Americans tend to have a larger zone of personal space and often avoid touching and close contact. A friend once warned the person who stood in front of her in the grocery store line, "if you step on my shoe, you're too close." In our culture, if a person is close enough to step on our shoes, they have invaded our intimate space. This is a cultural violation, a violation of our norms. Yet, there are some densely populated areas where the norm is to be so close to the other person that you could actually step on that person's shoes. The concept of space extends past an individuals public space. It extends to include the environment around us. Recently, the American culture has become fascinated with the ancient art of **Feng Shui** (pronounced fung shway), a 3,000-year-old Chinese method of using space to maximize the flow of energy. Feng Shui expert, Master Lam Kam Chuen (1998), says that Feng Shui, "draws together a range of closely interconnected systems for examining and interpreting the relationship between the energies of the earth, the energies of the galaxies, and the energy patterns of each individual human being" (p. 9).

My former boss, H. L. "Bud" Goodall, says that he used the principles of Feng Shui to choose his new office space. Goodall says, "When I assumed the headship of the Department of Communication at the University of North Carolina at Greensboro, I selected for my office a corner space diametrically catty-corner from the doors that open into our end of the hall. The office space—formerly used to house graduate students—was also just off the main corridors where faculty offices typically are situated, almost hidden from view and located next to an exit. . . . I had located my office in the wealth and prosperity area as indicated by placement of the Ba-Gua, which would mean that 'abundance' in these resources would follow. Given my new job as department head and the current low numbers of majors, budgetary dollars, and faculty I had inherited, this seemed to me and to my Feng Shui master to be initial challenges I was being given. Channeling the available energies, or chi, in the building would facilitate a remedy for these organizational, curricular, and financial problems. The selection of my office space was, according to this ancient wisdom, central to these challenges and key to organizing the energies required to for productive change" (Goodall, 2001, p. 3-4). Goodall is not alone in his quest to channel available energies for prosperity. Trump Plaza is also built on the principles of Feng Shui.

Wrap It Up

Nonverbal communication is the process of transporting messages through behaviors, physical characteristics, and objects. Nonverbal communication has several specific characteristics. It is culturally defined, often unconsciously shows feelings and attitudes, and it may conflict with verbal communication. Nonverbal communication functions to reinforce, substitute for, and regulate verbal communication. In this chapter, we cover nine different ways that we communicate messages through nonverbal means—aesthetics, artifacts, chronemics, haptics, kinesics, paralanguage, physical appearance, proxemics, and oculesics.

References

Axtell, R. E. *Gestures: The Do's and Taboos of Body Language around the World.* New York: Wiley, 1991.

Berko, R., A. Wolvin, and D. Wolvin, *Communicating: A Social and Career Focus.* Boston, Mass: Houghton Mifflin Company, 1995.

Birdwhitsell, R. L. *Kinesics and Context: Essays on Body Motion Communication.* Philadelphia: University of Pennsylvania Press, 1970.

Bozzi, V. "Eat to the Beat." *Psychology Today.* (1986, February): 16.

"Did you know?" *Raleigh News & Observer,* (1998, September 30): F1.

Goleman, D. "The Experience of Touch: Research Points to a Critical Role." *The New York Times* (1988, Feb. 2): C1.

Goodall, H. L. "Writing the American Ineffable, or the Mystery and Practice of Feng Shui in Everyday Life." *Qualitative Inquiry,* 7 (1), (2001) 3–20.

Hall, E. T. *The Hidden Dmension.* Garden City, NY: Doubleday, 1969.

Hall, E. T. *Beyond Culture.* Garden City, N.Y.: Doubleday. 1976.

Hall, J. A. Touch Status, and Gender at Professional Meetings." *Journal of Nonverbal Behavior,* 20 (1), (1996): 23–44.

Leathers, D. G. Successful Nonverbal Communication. Principles and Applications. New York: Macmillan, 1986.

Lortie, B. Your Lying Eyes. *Bulletin of the Atomic Scientists,* 2002: p. 7–8.

Jordan, N. "The face of feeling." *Psychology Today,* 1986: 8.

Master Lam Kam Chuen. *The Personal Feng Shui Manual: How to Develop a Healthy and Harmonious Lifestyle.* New York: Henry Holt and Company, Inc., 1998.

O'Hair D., G. Friedrich, J. Wiemann, and M. Wiemann, *Competent Communication.* New York: St. Martin's Press, 1995.

Pearson J. C., L.H. Turner and W. Todd-Mancillas. *Gender and Communication,* 2ed., Dubuque: Wm. C. Brown Publishers, 1991. As in Wilson, Gerald L. *Groups in Context: Leadership and Participation in Small Groups,* 5th ed. Boston. McGraw-Hill College 1999: 123–126.

"The Eyes Have It," *Newsweek*. (1973, December 3), p. 85.

Spiegel, J. and P. Machotka, *Messages of the Body*. New York: Free Press, 1974.

Tannen, D. *You Just Don't Understand: Women and Men in Conversation*. New York: Morrow, 1990.

Whitehead, G. I. and S. H Smith. "The Use of Hand Gestures and Smiles in the Inaugural Addresses of Presidents of the United States," *The Journal of Social Psychology*, 142 (5), (2002): 670–672.

Wood, J. T. *Gendered Lives: Communication, Gender, and Culture*. Belmont, CA: Wadsworth, 1994.

Communication in the Movies

I invite you and a friend or classmates to explore comunication in the movies. Reflect on the communication skills discussed in this chapter. How are they addressed in the movies?

▶ Halloween
▶ Helen Keller
▶ Puppet Master
▶ Meet the Fockers

Think About It → Write About It

Reflect on what you've just read. Now write what you are thinking.

_____

_____

_____

_____

_____

_____

_____

_____

_____

_____

_____

_____

_____

_____

_____

_____

_____

_____

_____

_____

_____

_____

_____

ACTIVITY

Nonverbal Awareness Exercise

a. Work in small groups

b. Each group will make a list of symbols used in our culture.

c. Some examples may be:

    i.   greeting someone by tapping the top of the other's head

    ii. Turning your back to the audience during a speech

d. Each group will share some of their gestures.

e. Discuss how some of these strange gestures may be appropriate in other countries and cultures and inappropriate in others.

Unit Two

Communication in Context

Chapter 6

Interpersonal Communication: Moving Beyond Self to Connect with Another

Veronica J. (Duncan) Walters, Ph.D. and Myra M. Shird, Ph.D.

Key Terms

Egocentrism	Strategy Language
Ethnocentrism	Spontaneity Language
Worldview	Neutrality Language
Intrapersonal Communication	Empathy Language
Evaluative Language	Superiority Language
Descriptive Language	Equality Language
Control Language	Certainty Language
Problem Orientation Language	Provisionalism Languag

Interpersonal Communication Across Relationship Types

Interpersonal communication is the interaction between at least two individuals within a social and historical context, which is affected by each person's environment, experiences, self-concept, general worldview, and previous interactions with each other. But what is beyond the technical terms used in this definition? Well, in layman's terms, **interpersonal communication** is simply moving beyond yourself to consider another person's needs, perspectives, and interpretations of your words and actions in the context of your relationship. I'm convinced that many of society's ills are a result of us not knowing how to go beyond self. In a society where most people are out for self and what they can get for self, from someone else, this definition may be uncomfortable because it defies the values of a self-centered, competitive, and individualistic American worldview. Thus, this definition suggests movement from an individualistic worldview to a collectivistic worldview that recognizes that each person is an individual and yet he/she is also an inseparable part of multiple wholes. This movement changes the perspective from which one views one's self, the other person, the interaction, and the world. Let's begin with a self-examination activity. Complete Activity 1 "Who Am I, and Why Am I Like This?" prior to reading the remainder of this chapter.

Activity 1

Who Am I, and Why Am I Like This?

This activity will give you an opportunity to explore the messages you received about communication, relationships, and yourself. Please be honest in your responses to the following questions. Do not worry about value judgments others may make based on your responses.

Family Interaction

Family is becoming increasingly more complex. In this section, the word "parents" refers to the people who raised you, whether it was your biological parents, a biological parent and a step-parent, adopted parents, grandparents, guardians, and so on, unless otherwise noted by referring to "biological" parents. The word "siblings" refers to brothers and sisters. These may include half brothers, half sisters, step-brothers, step-sisters, officially adopted brothers and sisters, and unofficially adopted brothers and sisters. Because family is socially defined, answer questions based on whom you consider your family. Some questions may not apply to your family situation; if not, move on to the next question.

1. Were your biological parents together when you were growing up?   Yes   No   Don't Know

2. Were you raised by both of your biological parents?   Yes   No   Sometimes

3. If no, who raised you? In the remainder of the questions, use this person or these people as your parents.

4. Did you see your parent(s) talking out problems?   Yes   No   Sometimes

5. Did you see your parent(s) argue a lot?   Yes   No   Sometimes

6. Were your parents violent with one another?   Yes   No   Sometimes

7. Did your parent(s) openly display affection towards one another?   Yes   No   Sometimes

8. Did your parent(s) openly display affection towards you?   Yes   No   Sometimes

9. Did you openly display affection towards your parent(s) and siblings?   Yes   No   Sometimes

10. Did you feel comfortable talking to your parent(s) about your feelings?	Yes	No	Sometimes
11. Did you see a lot of positive romantic relationships in your family?	Yes	No	Sometimes
12. Do you get along well with your mother?	Yes	No	Sometimes
13. Do you get along well with your father?	Yes	No	Sometimes
14. Do you have any siblings (brothers and/ or sisters)?	Yes	No	
15. If you have siblings, do you get along well with them?	Yes	No	Sometimes

16. How many siblings do you have? What child are you (oldest, middle, youngest)?

17. What was the gender breakdown of your siblings (for example, 3 brothers and 2 sisters)?

18. What was it like for you growing up with your siblings? For example, what responsibilities and privileges did you have as a result of your position (oldest, middle, youngest) and your gender (only girl)?

19. What messages (verbal and/or nonverbal) did you receive from your parents about who you are (type of person, work ethic, intelligence, looks, personality, success)? Provide examples of messages that you received.

Peer Interactions

1. Do you have same-sex friends?   Yes   No   Sometimes
2. Do you have opposite-sex friends?   Yes   No   Sometimes
3. Do you communicate well with members   Yes   No   Sometimes
    of the same sex?
4. Do you communicate well with members   Yes   No   Sometimes
    of the opposite sex?
5. Do you prefer to interact with members of the same or opposite sex? Why?

6. When you have problems with a relationship, do you prefer to talk to same-
    or opposite-sex friends? Why?

7. What does communicating well with someone mean to you? Provide a specific
    example of a time when you communicated well.

8. What behaviors of yours make communicating well different from not com-
    municating well? Please be specific.

9. When you communicate well, how does the experience differ from the experi-
    ence you have when you do not communicate well?

Romantic Interactions

1. What things were you told about the opposite sex by parents? Provide examples of messages that you received.

2. What things were you told about the opposite sex by other family members (grandparents, aunts, uncles, siblings, cousins)? Provide examples of messages that you received.

3. What things were you told about the opposite sex by same-sex friends? Provide examples of messages that you received.

4. What things were you told about the opposite sex by opposite-sex friends? Provide examples of messages that you received.

5. Are you currently in a relationship?

6. If you are in a relationship, how long have you been in your current relationship? If not, how long were you in your previous relationship?

7. What are the rules of your relationship when it comes to interaction with the opposite sex? For example, we do not see other people. We spend a lot of time together but we are not exclusive. We do not slow dance with other people. We each do what feels good, and so on.

8. Do you like the way your relationship is now, or would you like more or less commitment? Why or why not?

9. What messages (verbal and/or nonverbal) did you receive from your partners (current and past) about who you are (type of person, work ethic, intelligence, looks, personality, success)? Provide examples of messages that you received.

10. How do you make your partner feel about him or herself? Provide specific examples.

11. Do you and your partner talk out problems?	Yes	No	Sometimes
12. Do you and your partner argue a lot?	Yes	No	Sometimes
13. Are you and your partner ever violent with one another?	Yes	No	Sometimes
14. Do you and your partner openly display affection towards one another?	Yes	No	Sometimes
15. Does your partner openly display affection towards you?	Yes	No	Sometimes
16. Do you openly display affection towards your partner?	Yes	No	Sometimes
17. Do you feel comfortable talking to your partner about your feelings?	Yes	No	Sometimes

18. Does your partner feel comfortable talking   Yes   No   Sometimes
to you about his/her feelings?

19. Do you get along well with your partner?   Yes   No   Sometimes

20. Is communication effective in your   Yes   No   Sometimes
relationship?

Self-Evaluation

1. If you had to describe yourself to someone who had never met you, what would you say?

You need to read back over your answers to the questions in this exercise to complete the rest of this section.

2. What role, if any, do you think your interaction with your family has had in shaping who you are and how you interact with others? Please provide specific examples.

3. What role, if any, do you think your interaction with your peers has had in shaping who you are and how you interact with others? Please provide specific examples.

4. What role, if any, do you think your interaction with your romantic partner or previous partners has had in shaping who you are and how you interact with others? Please provide specific examples.

5. Do you like who you are? If so, why? If not, why not? Please be specific.

6. What did you learn from this exercise?

Perspective

Did the activity help you to gain a better understanding of your perspective? Did you find yourself remembering things that impacted you without you really realizing it? Or were you afraid to really look at your interactions with the important people in your life? No matter how you answered these questions, you just began to articulate your perspective. The great thing about perspective is it will be there whether you verbalize or acknowledge it or not. However, there is power in getting to know who you are, what your point of view is, when it came to be what it is, where your perspective comes from, how it came to be, and why it is what it is.

Although it is important that we understand our perspective, we often think that we are the world and everything centers on us, our desires, our needs, our feelings, our concerns, our fears, and so on. We must understand the impact of **ethnocentrism,** the belief that everything centers around our culture's way of doing and being, on our interpersonal relationships. Likewise, we must understand the impact of **egocentrism,** the belief that everything centers around "me" and my way of doing and being. These forms of self-centering (putting yourself in the center of the universe) create the individualistic world-view that has come to characterize America and Americans. However, when we look deeper into America and across the world, we begin to see more collectivistic worldviews in operation. Because our worldview shapes our beliefs, morals, values, and communication, it is crucial that we understand these two perspectives in order to understand ourselves and our choices.

Worldview

Your **worldview** is basically how you see the world—your vantage point. Imagine standing in front of a statue looking directly at it. Now imagine standing behind that same statue. Does your perspective and perception of that statue change with your change in position? If you change your position but you do not change your perspective, then something will seem wrong with the picture. The same is true of the importance of worldview in understanding interpersonal relationships. If you believe that in a marriage the woman should stay at home and take care of the children, then a career woman who wants to have children but has no desire to be a stay-at-home mom is not going to be an appealing prospect for you. However, if you believe that in a marriage both partners should work to complement one another and help each other fulfill their needs, then that career woman who wants to have children but has no desire to be a stay-at-home mom can be a very appealing prospect for you. Her career combined with yours means that you both will be able to achieve your home-ownership goals in a shorter time period. What is appealing is all a matter of perspective and worldview.

Previously, I discussed two worldviews: individualistic and collectivistic. The **individualistic worldview** is one in which the focus is on the individual advancing regardless of the cost to the collective. In the example of the career woman, the individualistic worldview would say that the man is right and the woman is right. Both should pursue their individual goals. The downside to that approach is that they may actually be perfect for each other but neither person can see it because of their perspectives. The **collectivistic worldview** is one in which the focus is on the good of the collective regardless of the expense to the individual. In that example, the collectivistic worldview would say that both people should be willing to sacrifice for the good of the family. There is recognition of the importance of working together to achieve goals, which opens the mind to the possibilities, advantages, and disadvantages of a particular approach. The reality is that there are few societies, cultural groups, racial groups, gender groups, and so on who function totally from one worldview or the other. Rather, these worldviews may be considered a continuum on which most people lie somewhere in between the two extremes.

Remember the worldview chart from the chapter on culture? Imagine a setting where you, a more circular thinker, are observing a group of people who are totally linear in their thought and speech patterns. It could make for a pretty boring scene for you, but the group members would not be bored because they are accustomed to the linear mode of thought. In much the same way, a linear thinker in a roomful of circular thinkers would go crazy trying to sift through all of the details to get to the point. In actuality it is that person in the middle who has the best potential to reach both the linear thinker and the circular thinker. I used to be more of a circular thinker who gave lots of details with a great deal of flavor but could wind up in a totally different destination from the one I had planned. There is a time when that is perfectly fine. However, if our goal is not just talking at people, then we need to understand the importance of adjusting to maximize the effectiveness of our communication. Additionally, most of us do not lie at one extreme or the other, so the adjustment is really only a matter of degrees. This notion led me to conclude that we are really individuals within a collective or collectives, which gives us more communicative latitude than being either individualistic or collectivistic. In the next section, I will explore myself as an individual within a collective of collectives.

Individuals within a Collective

Let's talk about what it means to be an individual in a collective. In the previous paragraph, I ended with the notion of being an individual and an inseparable part of multiple wholes. Let me elaborate on what that means. Each of us is a part of multiple groups, all of which are a part of the larger world system in which we exist. For example, I am a Christian, African American, woman, wife, mother, daughter, sister, minister, Ph.D., teacher, Mary Kay consultant, and sorority member. All of these groups affect who I am and how I see the world. In our society we are taught that certain characteristics or group affiliations should receive more attention than others. Then, we have to decide the level of importance we will place on our group memberships and the role they will play in shaping our identities.

Initially, when I wrote the list of groups to which I belong, I placed African American first because that's what society says most defines me. I came to believe that race was most important in defining me. However, within the past two years, my Christianity has come to be more important than my race. I am still African American, but I have chosen not to let my race be my most defining characteristic or group. After making this decision, I had to reevaluate several areas of my life because those areas had been governed by race. For example, I was a Democrat because that was the party for African Americans. Yet, when I began to examine the moral stances and values of the Democratic Party, I had to question some of the policy decisions and the effectiveness of policies affecting African Americans. There were also issues such as abortion, which conflicted strongly with my religious beliefs. Although I am currently still a Democrat, I refuse to vote Democratic simply because that's what African Americans do. Now, I vote for the person that I believe will best represent my views and the Word of God. You can see that the importance you place on the groups to which you belong can significantly affect your beliefs, thought patterns, and behaviors.

The combination of groups, environment, and personal experiences create a unique and dynamic ME. The same is true of each of us individually. That's the individual portion of the equation. However, we still are a part of multiple collectives, which are the groups to which we belong and the larger group of society as a whole. The "individual within a collective" approach is not one in which the rights of the individual are denied. Those individual rights still exist; however, they are tempered with our responsibility to others and society. My views cannot represent the views of all African Americans, but my actions can affect how other African Americans are perceived and treated. We do similar things with gender. If women get "dogged out," mistreated, cheated on, swindled, and disrespected by a few men, then there is a tendency and temptation to expect all or even most men to be that way. However, if a few women take men for their money, dress like "hoochies," and have a house full of children, then we don't want to be lumped into the category with them. It is crucial that we begin to allow for the complexities of human beings. Generalizations don't work when we are dealing with specific individuals within a collective or collectives. Many factors will influence those individual choices including acceptance of the responsibilities that come along with freedom and rights.

My twelve-year-old son asked me an interesting question recently. He wanted to know why African Americans sit in the back of the bus if people fought for us to be able to sit in the front of the bus. Before I could answer he said, "I guess we just like sittin' in the back. But I sit in the middle. People can think what they wanna think about me." In his response, he demonstrated the complexity of human nature. Although he said "we" just like sittin' in the back,' he followed it up with the fact that *"he"* likes to sit in the middle. He was stating the notion behind the "individual within the collective," because "we" liked one thing while "he" liked something else and yet they coexist within the same space. This complexity is one of the reasons that we tend to reduce things to what we consider the basic level. However, that reduction is problematic because we tend to make the basic level centered on us as individuals. This complexity is reflected in our communication in our families, our peer relationships and friendships, and in our romantic relationships. The next section will examine how being an individual within a collective affects interpersonal communication across these relationship types.

Interpersonal Communication across Relationship Types

Family Communication

Although anyone can talk to or at another person, it takes work to have effective interpersonal communication, especially within our families. Before we begin, let's explore the question of what is family. As I stated in the directions for the activity, the notion of family has become increasingly complex with changes in demographics and societal approaches to lifestyle. Family means different things to different people. However, the one thing that is consistent regardless of the other trappings is a strong bond that connects individuals to one another. Family does not have to live in the same house, share the same parents or blood, be confined to the nuclear notion of family, or have legal documents that declare that they are related. I grew up with siblings who did not live in the house with me, but they were still my brothers and sisters. I did not live with either of my parents, who did not live with one another, but I am still the daughter of my mother and my father. When my parents married other people, I also became the stepdaughter of my stepfather and my stepmother. When my father divorced one stepmother and more than twenty years later married another woman, I still considered both women a part of my family. When my mother separated from my stepfather, he did not cease to be my step daddy because they were no longer together.

Family is complicated because of the complexity of our society. Divorce, teenage pregnancy, children born out of wedlock, single-parent dating, blended families, gay and lesbian families, surrogate parents, and official and unofficial adoption are some of the factors which make a rigid definition of family difficult to develop. As a result of my experiences with family, it is much easier for me to acknowledge and welcome in a much broader definition of family for the nature of this discussion. Now that we have discussed family and examined its complexities, let's look at some ways communication functions within families.

We'll begin with an example to which most people can relate. In our families, we have rules of some sort. Even in families that say there are no rules, not having rules becomes a rule. In families there are rules for interaction between parents and children. In my family, the rule was that children stayed in their place, which definitely was not disagreeing with or correcting an adult, even if the elders were wrong. In a situation where I found myself disagreeing with an adult, I had two choices: 1. follow the rules and let it go, or 2. speak out and suffer the discipline. Unfortunately, I was not very good with rules, which meant I suffered a great deal of punishment. Although I rarely experienced physical discipline, I knew that it was a possibility. However, more often than not my punishment consisted of getting a "talking to." This "talking to" generally entailed someone telling me all the reasons I was wrong for what I had done. Thus, I learned to be talked to or at and seem like I was listening even when I wasn't. In those instances, communication was taking place, but it was not effective communication. It may have seemed to my mother or grandmother that it was effective because I nodded in the right places and said, "Yes, Ma'am" a number of times (another rule in my family). I only heard ten percent of the message (if that) and shut out the rest. This scenario was definitely not effective communication.

I am now a parent, and in my family there are rules. Like most parents, some of those rules are the ones with which I grew up. "Children should stay in their place" is one of our rules. However, because I have children who happen to be just like me, I have had to modify, in some instances, how I deal with them when they violate a rule. I recognize that blank look of staring off into space with the obligatory "yes, Ma'am" tossed in at just the right time. Therefore, I have a decision to make as a communicator. My child has communicated to me nonverbally that he or she is not really listening to what I am saying. Do I continue to talk to or at this child, or do I try something different? I decide to try something different because I don't want to just talk at them. I want them to clearly understand what I'm saying so I don't have to have the same conversation with the same child fifty times. As a result of that decision, I stop talking. They look up because something strange is going on. The following thoughts are going through their minds.

> What's goin' on? She stopped talkin'. Oh Lord, here we go. She's gettin' ready to try to 'communicate' with me. I don't want to be communicatin'. I just want her to get through so I can get on about my business. I can't stand when she uses that

junk she teaches on me. Oh, well, let me go on and listen or she's gon' keep at it 'til I do.

When it seems that I really have my children's attention, I take the opportunity to point out to them that all the stuff that they are doing, I have done, and I was usually better at it than they are. From there, I begin to try to figure out what is really going on with them. Now some people have accused me of not really being a Black mama. I'm not good at maintaining some of the characteristics of the Black mother that weren't effective with me when I was growing up. If it didn't work with me, then why would I waste my time and my children's time going through all of that? Don't get me wrong; I still give them "THE LOOK" and they know that it means, "Don't mess with me unless you want to die." I still expect them to say "yes, ma'am," "no, ma'am," "yes, sir," and "no, sir." But most importantly, I want to communicate with them in ways that are effective. The importance of effective communication can also be seen in peer interactions and/or friendships.

Argumentativeness and Verbal Aggression in the Sibling Relationship

Sarah E. Symonds, M.A.

It is perhaps inevitable. It is going to reoccur for the rest of your lives. It could be about something as small as who scratched dad's car or as huge as at whose house Thanksgiving dinner will be this year. Fighting—as in the name calling and attacking their character—with our siblings is natural. When mothers and fathers become verbally aggressive and argumentative, the relationship can be terminated. However, when the same situation occurs between siblings, that relationship cannot be terminated.

The sibling relationship is a unique relationship that can exist between sister and sister, brother and brother, or sister and brother. For many, more than one type of this relationship exists. For others, this relationship does not exist at all. Defined as "a nonvoluntary relationship as one in which the actor believes he or she has no viable choice but to maintain, at least at present and in the immediate future" (Hess, 2000, p. 460), the sibling relationship is usually the longest lasting relationship in one's life (Ponzetti & James, 1997).

Because the sibling relationship is filled with unique roles and function, it is necessary to examine the role of argumentativeness and verbal aggression within that relationship. This essay attempts to explores the definitions of argumentativeness and verbal aggression and apply both terms to the sibling relationship.

Before examining the role of verbal aggression and argumentativeness in the sibling relationship, it is important to define both terms. Infante and Wigley (1986) define argumentativeness as "presenting and defending positions on issues while attacking the positions taken by others on the issues" (Infante & Wigley, 1986, p. 62). When one individual argues with another individual, he or she will attack the ideas and not the person. Argumentativeness tends to be a constructive trait, where outcomes are favorable (Infante, Myers, & Buerkel, 1994).

Argumentativeness is a learned behavior: how effective an individual argues depends on how he or she approaches an argument. The motivation to approach argumentative situations and the motivation to avoid conflict all together contribute to a person's level of argumentativeness (Folger, 2001). When an individual has high argument skills, he/she is able to enter social situations with ease and will not resort in violence. When an individual has low argument skills, he/she tends to attack the individual. This type of behavior is referred to as verbal aggression.

Verbal aggression is "attacking the self-concept of, or in addition to, the person's position to inflict psychological pain" (Infante & Wigley, 1986, p. 61). Verbal aggression has a long lasting effect on the relationship because it is a negative and a destructive trait. Verbal aggression is a subset of hostility. That is, all verbal aggression is hostile, but not all hostility involves verbal aggression (Infante & Wigley, 1986). Verbal aggression can appear in many different forms including character attacks, competence attacks, insults, maledictions, teasing, ridicule, profanity, and non-verbal emblems (Infante & Wigley, 1986).

Infante, and Rancer (1996) and Infante and Wigley (1986) explain that there are basically four causes of verbal aggression: frustration, having a goal blocked by someone or having to deal with a disdained other; social learning, when individuals are conditioned to behave aggressively; psychopathology, which involves the transference when the person attacks with verbally aggressive messages those people who symbolize unresolved conflict; and argumentative skill deficiency, when individuals resort to verbal aggression because they lack the verbal skills for dealing with social conflict constructively. Individuals begin to attack the person because they are unable to attack the idea and lack the necessary skills to argue effectively.

The most devastating effect of verbal aggression is damage to one's self-concept. For example, researchers point out that teasing about a physical impediment such as a lisp, weight gain, or scarring can affect a child for their entire life and contributes to the unhappiness or depression that the child will suffer from as an adult (Infante & Wigley, 1986). Moreover, effects of verbal aggression can be temporal in nature. These effects include hurt feelings, anger, embarrassment, and discouragement (Infante & Wigley, 1986). Finally, effects of verbal aggression can also occur in interpersonal relations. Relationships can deteriorate and even terminate (Folger, Poole & Stutman, 2001).

After exploring the concepts of argumentativeness and verbal aggression, it is important to examine how they relate to the sibling relationship. It is also important to note that children tend to mimic the behavior of their parents. Some studies have reported that children who were assertive claimed that their parents were also assertive. Researchers found "when mothers reported having the ability to communicate aggressively without being destructive or attacking the other person involved, their children reported similar abilities. Mothers who reported being verbally aggressive had children who also reported being verbally aggressive" (Martin, Anderson, Burant, & Weber, 1997, p. 302). Researchers have also found that fathers' communication with their sons may influence their sons' communications and satisfaction in interpersonal relationships (Beatty, Dobos, Rudd, & Burant, 1994). This research provides some support for the proposition that parents' communication behaviors may influence their children's communication behaviors (Martin et al., 1997).

Most conflict in families occurs between siblings. This may include, but is by no means limited to, hollering, screaming, and yelling. Most of the time, verbal aggression and teasing takes place outside the immediate realm of the parents. Parents, therefore, underestimate the actual amount of conflict within the family and they are unable to prevent or stop the harsh communication that takes place between siblings (Stormshak, Bellant, & Bierman, 1996). The more conflict that exists between siblings means fewer interactions between that particular set of siblings. As the amount of arguing and verbal aggression takes place between siblings, siblings will have a tendency to be more aggressive with others.

Birth order, age differential, and the amount of contact between siblings also have an impact on the amount of argumentativeness and verbal aggression between siblings. "The birth of a child, whether the first child or a subsequent child, changes the entire family system" (Teven, Martin, & Neupauer, 1998, p. 181). Furthermore, siblings who have been forced to share a bedroom their entire life will have a better relationship then siblings who are born thirteen years apart and have not had a chance to get to know one another (Martin et al., 1997).

Research has shown that siblings tend to be more verbally aggressive than argumentative towards each other. The hostility that takes place between siblings often manifests itself in the way of verbally aggressive messages (Teven, Martin, & Neupauer, 1998). The most common verbally aggressive message used is teasing. Teasing is mainly a destructive trait in the sibling relationship. It creates a lower relational satisfaction and is mainly used to cause embarrassment. Martin and Anderson found that " 'hurting my sibling' might be one of many reasons why siblings tease their brothers and sisters" (Martin et al, 1997, p. 313). "Through teasing, the verbally aggressive person may simply want to be mean toward disdained others" (Infante, Riddle, Horvath, & Tumlin, 1992).

However, there are few instances when the parties involved do not consider teasing hurt-ful. Researchers argue that at times teasing can be constructive (Martin et al., 1997). Teasing is sometimes used as a way of showing affection or immediacy in the relation-ship. For instance, teasing may be used in a humorous way or as a way of attaching another individual's self concept. When teasing is used to attack another, it is considered verbal aggression (Infante, Riddle, Horvath, & Tumlin, 1992).

> Nevertheless, researchers found that "teasing is negatively related to satisfaction and trust in the relationship. When verbal aggressiveness is present in a relationship, there is less sat-isfaction and trust" (Martin et al., 1997, p. 313). Teven, Martin, and Neupauer (1998) found that "the more verbally aggressive messages participants received from their siblings, the less satisfied they were with their sibling relationships" (Teven, Martin, & Neupauer, 1998 p. 181). "People who are in sibling relationships where they are not satisfied seemingly would not be as hurt when those siblings are verbally aggressive; they were not happy with their sibling to begin with so when those siblings are verbally aggressive, possibly that type of destructive communication was expected" (Martin et al., 1997, p. 181).

In most sibling relationships, the gender of the siblings involved influence the extent of the harm in the message. For example, in sibling dyads where both individuals are female sister-sister relationships, there may be less verbally aggressive tone in the message than messages that are present between male-male brother-brother or male-female brother-sister relationships dyads (Martin et al., 1997).

The relationship that exists between siblings is one of the most permanent relationships in one's life; therefore, it is expected that arguments will take place. This essay explored the concepts of argumentativeness and verbal aggression and examined how they are present within the sibling relationship. Verbal aggression, most commonly teasing, is more common in the sibling relationship than argumentativeness. The amount of verbal aggressiveness in the sibling relationship is based on birth order, trust and satisfaction, and the gender of the other sibling.

References

Beatty, M. J., J. R. Zelley., J. A. Dobos, and J. E. Rudd, "Fathers' Trait Verbal Aggressiveness and Argumentativeness as Predictors of Adult Sons' Perceptions of Fathers' Sarcasm, Criticism, and Verbal Aggression," *Communication Quarterly* 42, (1994, Fall): 407–415.

Folger, J. P., M. S. Poole, and R. K. Stutman, *Working Through Conflict,* Boston: Addison Wesley Longman, Inc., 2001: 50–52.

Hess, J. A. Maintaining Nonvoluntary Relationships with Disliked Partners: An Investigation into the Use of Distance Behaviors. *Human Communication Research* 26, (2000): 458–488.

Infante, D. A., S. A., Myers, and R. A. Buerkel, "Argument and Verbal Aggression in Constructive and Destructive Family and Organizational Disagreements" *Western Journal of Communication* 58 (1994, Spring): 73–89.

Infante, D. A. and A. S Rancer, "Argumentativeness and Verbal Aggressiveness: A Review of Recent Theory and Research," *Communication Yearbook* 19 (1996): 319–351.

Infante, D. A., B. L. Riddle, C. L. Horvath, and S. A. Tumlin. "Verbal Aggressiveness: Messages and Reasons," *Communication Quarterly* 40 (1992, Spring): 116–126.

Infante, D. A., and C. J. Wigley, III. "Verbal Aggressiveness: An Interpersonal Model and Measure," *Communication Monographs* 53 (1986): 61–69.

Ponzetti, J. J., Jr. and C. M. James. "Loneliness and Sibling Relationships," *Journal of Social Behavior and Personality* 12 (1997): 103–112.

Martin, M. M. and C. M. Anderson. "Aggressive Communication Traits: How Similar Are Young Adults and Their Parents in Argumentativeness, Assertiveness, and Verbal Aggressiveness," *Western Journal of Communication* 61 (1997, Summer): 299–314.

Martin, M. M., C. M. Anderson, P. A. Burant and K. Weber. "Verbal Aggression in Sibling Relationships." *Communication Quarterly* 45 (1997, Summer): 304–317.

Myers, S. A. "Relational Maintenance Behaviors in the Sibling Relationship" *Communication Quarterly* 49, (2001, Winter) 19–30.

Stormshak, E. A., C. J. Bellanti, and K. L. Bierman. "The Quality of Sibling Relationships and the Development of Social Competence and Behavioral Control in Aggressive Children." *Developmental Psychology* 32 (1996) 79–89.

Teven, J. J., M. M. Martin, and N. C. Neupauer. "Sibling Relationships: Verbally Aggressive Messages and Their Effect on Relational Satisfaction," *Communication Reports* 11, (1998, Summer): 179–186.

Peer Communication and Friendship

Interactions with our peers and developing friendships are an important part of inter-personal communication. It is in our relationships with our peers that we really begin to explore our use of communication strategies. When you watch children interact, you see them employing many different communicative strategies when relating to their friends. My three-year-old daughter is famous for trying to get her way with her friends. When she doesn't get her way, she tells them that "she's not going to be their friend anymore because . . ." of whatever they would not do or give her. If she happens to be the person in power at the time, then the other child may well allow her to have her way to stay in her good graces. I've seen my young daughter really try to work this trick when one of her friends is at our house. They like coming to our house, and she knows this. So she uses the "I'm not going to let you come to my house anymore" strategy. It's amazing, but power plays take place even with children. My youngest son is now nineteen months old. When he was about ten months old, a younger baby came to our house for my daughter's birthday party. My son got in his face, looked at him, and started to scream at the top of his lungs. The poor baby started crying because he didn't know what was going on or why he was being screamed at. These strategies sound so mean, but we use similar ones as adults. For example, when you want something and you are not getting it, you may decide to get in the person's face and raise your voice.

You are in college and you have three classes with a young lady who is very intelligent. You need help studying because you're not doing very well in one of those classes. The young woman's intelligence becomes a power tool that she can use in your interaction should she so choose. However, she's just a nice young woman who says that if you need any help, then she would be more than happy to help you improve your grade. Suppose she were not so nice? Then you might be required to somehow repay her for her help. This repayment is a form of reciprocity. I give to you and you give to me. This relationship is a peer relationship, but not necessarily a friendship. In friendships, there are slightly different rules than the ones used with someone "off the street" or someone to whom you aren't connected.

Friends serve several functions in our lives: 1. identity needs, 2. support and encouragement, 3. companionship, and 4. honest feedback or constructive criticism. These friendship functions can be seen in the following section, "Communicating Friendship across Cultural Lines: From Stereotype to Sacrifice." As you read the essay, think about your friendships with people from your culture and other cultures. Culture always adds a more complex layer to any interaction. Identify some of the ways culture manifested itself. Different friends can serve different functions at different times in our lives; but the bottom line is that we all need friends and real friends are willing to make sacrifices for each other. The acronym below describes some of the characteristics of true friends.

F = FAITHFUL
R = REAL (HONEST)
I = INSPIRING
E = ENCOURAGING
N = NOBLE
D = DEDICATED
S = SACRIFICING

Each of these characteristics is important to have in a friend. You need someone who will be faithful even when the world turns against you. You also need someone who can be real with you by giving you honest feedback and constructive criticism when others are afraid to say anything. Real friends encourage you to press toward your goals, and they inspire you to do what you say. They are noble, moral, upright individuals with whom you are not afraid to be associated. They are dedicated to your friendship and willing to make sacrifices for the success of your friendship and your life. People with these characteristics are hard to find. Therefore, when you find a good friend, it would behoove you to hold on to him or her. Don't let them fall by the wayside. If you have a friend that you haven't talked to in a long time, then take the time today to call them and let them know that you care about them.

My grandmother used to tell me that to have friends, I had to be a friend. Don't expect someone else to have all of those qualities if you don't have any of them. Do an assessment. If all of your friends are shallow, then you might want to check yourself out. The old saying is that we draw to ourselves, what we are. So if you want to have a friend like the one described in the acronym, then you need to become that friend. These same principles apply to romantic relationships. In the next section, we will discuss some characteristics of romantic communication and the dynamics of romantic relationships.

Communicating Friendship across Cultural Lines: From Stereotype to Sacrifice

Friendship is challenging within the same culture. However, as we cross cultural lines in establishing friendships, we increase our level of challenge. This essay addresses three important same-sex cross-cultural friendships in my life from childhood to adulthood. Each relationship played a powerful role in my understanding of self, gender, race, culture, communication, life, and the complex web woven as these things all interact.

When I was growing up in a small town in Kentucky, I often found myself being the only African American in my classes. But even before I reached that point, I remember my best friend and neighbor who lived across the gravel driveway from me. Her name was Donna, but we called her Flootsie. She was my girl. I remember us being in love with Michael Jackson, Leif Garrett, Shaun Cassidy and Parker Stevenson (the Hardy Boys). I remember our concerts singing Michael's rhythm and blues and Leif and Shaun's beach music, our imaginary dates with them, and our conversations about life, love, and friendship. I also remember that she looked out for me and I looked out for her, because we were blood sisters. I remember her wanting me to spend the night at her house and me wanting to go. I also remember the lessons I learned about race through our friendship. My grandmamma, who raised me, told me that I couldn't spend the night with Flootsie. There were several reasons for her decision. As I look back on those reasons, I understand better what my grandmother was trying to say without saying it. She was telling me that I have to be careful because even "good White folks" can be dangerous when allowed too close to "good Black folks." I thought my grandmother was a racist, but she wasn't. She always loved Flootsie and my other White friends and treated them well. However, she saw what I wouldn't really understand and see until many years and many losses later including hers. As you read on, look for the lessons from each relationship.

I had another good friend during graduate school who grew up in the country where there were no Black people. She was often excluded by the other students, but I always took to the people others rejected. It was no different with her. I remember one Thanksgiving I went home with her for Thanksgiving Dinner. Her mother was really cool and the meal was good, but I missed my cornbread dressing. We would often get together. One day she came by my house. My husband, his two brothers, and his cousin were watching the game in the living room. When she walked in, she crossed in front of them. They also had the radio playing with rap music blasting. She asked me how I could listen to that noise because that wasn't music. I asked how could she listen to Rod Stewart because that wasn't music to some people either. Personally, I like a lot of different types of music including Rod Stewart, but that wasn't the point. When we left and got in the car she said that my husband and his male family members were looking at her. Of course, they were; we had to cross in front of the television. I thought of all of the times I had compromised and she had trouble with hearing music from my culture for half an hour, with Black men "looking" at her, and having to adjust to another culture. But I learned a great deal from this interaction as well. Read on for more lessons.

Another good friend of mine came to Kentucky from Wisconsin where she knew few, if any, Black people. She and I were a great deal alike. We were interested in some of the same research and had similar career goals. When she was having relationship problems she would come to me and I would do the same. We both had boyfriends for whom the other did not particularly care, but we supported each other through it all. One day while talking about our career goals, she made the comment that I would have no problem getting a good job because I was a double-minority. I asked why I couldn't get a good job because of my qualifications. She responded that she didn't mean anything by what she said because she thought that I was definitely qualified but being African American and female could open doors for me. One day we went to get Häagen Daz ice-cream in the Student Center. She ordered one scoop and I order two scoops. The final results looked exactly the same but she was charged for one scoop and I was charged for two scoops. She looked at the ice-creams, looked at me, and then looked at the young woman waiting on us. When she looked at me, I gave her a look that said I'm used to it. I looked back at the young lady and asked her about our orders. The young lady's response was that she had gotten carried away on my friend's ice-cream and went on to charge me for two scoops. I suggested that she get carried away on mine or charge me for one scoop. My friend was willing to sacrifice her privilege for our equality during that encounter. That was one of many days to come that my friend would come to get a glimpse into my life as a double-minority. She's grown a lot since then and understands some things that she didn't previously. I believe our relationship has changed her, but it has also changed me. You see, she was a bright student who worked hard and did the things necessary to be successful in the academy, but she didn't get the offers to a Research I institution with a doctoral program in communication. I got those offers. However, I discovered that those schools wanted to count me as a double-minority, but like my friend in the second example they didn't want to accept all that came along with me, which included my culture and my differences. The grass always looks greener on the other side. Through our experiences my friend and I got to see the other side.

All of these young women and our relationships have helped to shape who I am today and my approach to friendship. You see, my grandmother knew that some people would accept me, but others wouldn't. She understood that I would be hurt by that rejection. She realized that I loved people unconditionally regardless of color and popularity because that is what she had taught me. My grandmother also knew that I would have to experience some of the pain of racism. She wanted to protect me and she did as much as she could. Now, I can handle it without becoming bitter and cynical. Now, I can love my friends wisely.

He who trusts in his own heart is a fool, but whoever walks wisely will be delivered. (Prov. 28:26 NKJV)

U.S. Census 2000.

The Double-Edged Sword of Stereotypes

Stephanie Sedberry Carrino

I am a White woman raising two daughters in the southern United States. Race relations among Blacks and Whites continue to be strained in the south, and particularly in my town of Greensboro, NC, the heart of the civil rights movement. "Race," in Greensboro, is defined primarily as Black and White. 38 percent of the population of this town of 224,000 people is Black, 55 percent is White, 4 percent is Hispanic and 3 percent are of other races.*

As an adult, I have struggled with issues of race and race relations, and I've been particularly interested in how my daughters learn about race. To this end, I have ensured that their schools are diverse, and I've worked hard to teach a value system based on equality.

When Emily was three, she attended a church daycare. One afternoon, I picked her up, and before we left, she told me she was mad at Christian for scratching her. When I asked her who Christian was, she looked around the room, pointed, and said "He's the one in the red shirt." At that point, there were only five to six children left, and Christian was the only Black child in the room. Christian was also the only child with a red shirt on. So Emily saw his shirt color as more important than his skin color. I was relieved that race had not yet entered her world.

When Grace was 5 and in kindergarten, she quickly found a new best friend, LaToya. They sat at the same table in the classroom, saved each other a place at the lunch table, and wanted matching everything. Some days they would decide to both wear pink, or both wear black shoes. Grace wanted braids like LaToya's, so I braided her thin, fine blond hair as best I could and sent her to school. They were delighted. If you have not guessed, Grace is White, and LaToya is Black.

One afternoon I saw LaToya's mom at the school, and I introduced myself and told her that Grace talked about her daughter all the time—she said heard about Grace everyday too. So, I asked if LaToya could come over and play one afternoon, and she agreed. On the day that we had arranged, LaToya's mom brought her over to my house, her mom stayed a little while and we talked and split a Coke, then she left, saying she'd be back to pick up her daughter in a few hours. The girls were so excited—they were all giggly and playing in Grace's room.

Fifteen minutes after Latoya's mom left, she called and said she needed to pick up LaToya right away because she forgot they had something to do. I was disappointed, but I understand that things come up, and I got LaToya ready. When her mom got back to my house, she explained that her husband works second shift, and he had just woken up and decided that they had something they had to do, so she had to come and get her. LaToya cried, Grace pouted, and we promised we'd do it again.

I have invited LaToya over again several times, and her mom says how great it would be to allow the girls to play—then she suggests we meet at a park.

Why did her mom pick her up so soon? Did her dad find out she was at a White girl's house, and demand that mom pick her up? Racism is a strange thing—it's hard to define, yet you can "feel" it when it happens. Would her family discourage a five-year-old's friendship because of race? All I know is that I felt hurt that my family was judged as "not worthy" or "racist" because we are White. Racism cuts both ways—I do not deserve to be categorized as "bad people" simply because I am White. So, now in the first grade, Grace's other friends come over to play, and she and LaToya still are best buddies at school. I hope her family's fears and stereotypes about White people don't affect their friendship—though I fear it may already have.

Since then, my daughters and I have had many conversations about race. Emily, now in the fourth grade, is learning about slavery. She is very confused about how people could have been so cruel, and also confused because these people were White, like she is. I've explained to her that many White people were cruel, but that not ALL White people were bad. There were many Whites in the south and north who fought slavery and helped free slaves. Now, even in the midst of a system with white privilege and racism, it is still true that not all White people are racist. "Good White folks" are not dangerous—and rejection can be felt by anyone. Any child can be taught to love others unconditionally regardless of color. We ALL need to examine our stereotypes.

Romantic Communication

I love studying interpersonal communication because of the unique twists that come when you put a male and a female together. Not only do you have to deal with the individual idiosyncrasies of each person, but you also have to deal with two different modes of relating and interpreting. I like to use the following scenario in my classes as I talk about the communication process and gender. To set the stage, the couple has been together long enough for HER to discover something that looks like a problem. She decides to talk to HIM about this "problem." The interaction goes something like this:

HER: I'd like to talk to you about something.
HIM: Okay.
HER: Well, I've noticed something that really bothers me.

(She pauses waiting for him to say something, but he just continues to look at her. She continues.)

Well, it just seems like I'm more concerned about the relationship than you are.
HIM: Why do you say that?
HER: Well, like now you don't seem to be bothered by the fact that something is bothering me. Why aren't you more upset? Or is it that you just don't care?
HIM: No, it's not that I don't care. I just don't see the use of getting all upset.
HER: See, that's exactly what I'm talking about. You don't care. If you cared, you would be upset. Since you aren't upset, then you must not care. So why am I wasting my time with someone who doesn't care about my feelings or our relationship?

(He begins to say something, but she stops him by holding her hand up like a traffic cop to stop him in his tracks.)

No, don't bother answering that question. It doesn't even matter any more. I bet I won't waste any more of my time.

Does this interaction sound familiar to any of you? If it doesn't, then you might be saying to yourself that the dialogue described would only happen with a woman who was a little bit off. Some of you women may be offended because you are saying to yourself that you would never act like that and that it is stereotyping women. I understand both responses, but let me share something with you. As a woman who has had the opportunity to interact with a lot of women of different races, religious backgrounds, and socioeconomic statuses, I have concluded that any of us can "go there" in the right situation. It doesn't mean that you are crazy. It just means that sometimes our logic can be illogical. Reading the previous scenario may have made you see the irrationality of HER responses, but can you see it when you are HER. I had a chance to be HER even as I was writing this chapter.

I became HER when I asked my husband if the interaction sounded real, to which he answered yes. I proceeded to ask him if he had ever had an interaction similar to the one I described, to which he promptly responded, "Yeah, with you." Of course, this answer rubbed me the wrong way. So I had to ask him if I was the only woman he'd had this type of interaction with because in my mind his response seemed to imply that there was something wrong with me. His response was "No, but if I had said yeah, with so and so, and so and so, and so and so, then you would have been upset." Needless to say, I had to laugh because he continued to point out just how real such an interaction is and how easily you can find yourself "going there."

I am a communication scholar with expertise in interpersonal communication. I am not crazy (although I will admit that there have been times that I have engaged in what even I would consider extremely irrational behavior in the name of love). Yet, I found myself responding to things my husband said in much the same way as HER in the example. Why would that be the case? Let's examine some of the factors that influence how we communicate and how we interpret the messages of others.

Research on interpersonal communication is extensive. However, much of this research does not include nor consider people of color. Duncan and colleagues (1998) embarked on a major study of interpersonal variables in African American, European American, and interracial relationships. For a more detailed discussion, see *Towards Achieving Maat: Communication Patterns in African American, European American, and Interracial Relationships* published by Kendall-Hunt. In a summary, Duncan and colleagues discovered that many of the traditional research findings did not hold up when African American relationships were included and considered. For example, the combination of race and gender combined affected the use of several communication variables and the intersection of the two. Although communication competence was positively related to interpersonal solidarity or intimacy for European Americans and African Americans, the relationship was stronger for African Americans. African Americans who perceived themselves to be more competent communicators reported higher levels of intimacy in their relationships.

In this book, differences were also reported on self-disclosure with African American males reporting less positive self-disclosure and less honest self-disclosure than European American males and females and African American females. Additionally, European Americans reported greater amounts of self-disclosure than African Americans. Why might that be the case? What societal factors might affect African American self-disclosure? These trends suggest that race and gender have a greater impact on some aspects of communication than others, but the assumption that there is no impact and no difference should not be made automatically.

Think about your relationships. Has your self-disclosure been positive and honest? How much do you disclose in romantic relationships? Do you disclose more in friendships than you do in romantic relationships? Why or why not? Does it make you feel vulnerable? Does it depend on how much power the other person has in the relationship? There are many factors that can influence whether or not we disclose information to others, allow ourselves to become intimate, and the role our communication competence plays in it all. However, the bottom line is that romantic interaction, like all of the other types of communication, requires that we work on being effective.

Can You Handle the Truth?

Andrea N. Johnson

The media has misled many people when it comes to what is really true concerning relationships between males and females. It is on very rare occasions that we see the media celebrating positive relationships between men and women. What has been celebrated far too often is the sexual exploitation and degradation of human sexuality on television, in the movies, and in music videos. As half-naked women parade around in music videos, the message is being sent that if you want to get the attention of a man, then as a woman you must show him everything that you're working with. On the other hand, men who do not fit the "hood boy" or "ruffneck" stereotype are considered "weak" or "gay." As a result of the mixed signals that society gives, men and women walk around with misconceptions about what the other person truly desires in a healthy relationship. It is not a surprise that many people walk away from relationships feeling frustrated and defeated. In order to have healthy and productive relationships, we must begin to learn, understand and appreciate the differences between males and females.

Truth for the Ladies:
Men are not really looking for sex

Believe it or not and in spite of what the media says, ultimately men are not looking for sex. Now understand, I did not say that men did not want sex, or that they won't go to great lengths to get it, however that is not what will make a man commit. I have had the opportunity to have lengthy conversations with men of various ages. When I ask men what are the qualities that they want in a female, the qualities are as follows: she must have self-confidence, she is not nag, she is someone that will be with him through the good and the bad times, if he opens himself up to her and makes himself vulnerable she will not throw it up in his face later during an argument, she does not tell all of their business to her friends, she does not cling to him, and she is his friend. To my surprise, sex was not mentioned at all on the list, and according to society that is at the top of every man's list. If sex is not top priority on a man's list when it comes to commitment, why do women spend so much time trying to appeal to the sexual part of a man? Let's look at an illustration:

Tim and Shana had been seeing each other for about 3 months. They were both extremely attracted to each other. They had met at an off-campus party. After a couple of weeks of dating they began having sex. Pretty soon their primary activity was sex anytime they were together. Shana developed very strong feelings for Tim and Tim often stated that he cared for Shana. Three months after they began their sexual relationship, Shana noticed that Tim was acting differently. When she questioned him about his behavior he stated he had a lot on his mind with school and all. More time began to pass between Tim's calls and his visits to Shana. Shana would call and leave messages, but Tim rarely returned her calls. When he did return her calls he just stated that he had been really busy. Shana began to wonder what was really going on with Tim. Besides, they had really good sex. As a matter of fact he told her that she was the best he ever had. So what was Tim's problem?

When we look at Shana and Tim's situation, one of the problems was that Shana thought that good sex meant commitment or some other type of obligation to her. Since she had given Tim "the best sex" he said he had ever experienced, she had higher expectations of him. Many times women feel that if they have sex on a regular basis with someone that means that they are in a relationship. In many situations a female may become disappointed when the guy spends less time communicating with her or does not acknowledge her as his "girlfriend." Women are often left feeling misused and abused and will often say they didn't see it coming. This is a classic case of a woman mistaking her interaction with a man as a relationship. Actually what she participated in was a "sexship" and not a relationship. According to Alvis O. Davis, author of *Black Men Not Looking for Sex: Why They Commit Forever* (1995), many women confuse a sexship and a relationship. Davis goes on to say that in a sexship a man basically interacts with a woman primarily for the purposes of having sex. It is important to note that a man may actually take you out to dinner, spend a little money, but this still does not mean that he is in a relationship with you. It just means that he is "putting in work." "Putting in work" means that he is doing whatever he needs to do, nothing more and nothing less, in order to keep the sexual relationship going. For example, if a guy knows that all he has to do is buy a woman a cheeseburger off of the one dollar menu at McDonald's and she'll have sex with him, that's all she'll ever get. On the other hand, he may have to take another woman to Red Lobster in order to get what he wants, because her standards are a little higher. Please understand that I am not suggesting in any way that a woman should trade her body in for a meal. I am simply telling you what goes on inside of many men's minds. A man's respect for a woman is based on how much respect she gives herself.

In the case of Tim and Shana, Tim was probably more committed to her sex versus being committed to her. Understand, a man can be committed to having sex with you and not be committed to you. Unfortunately many females can not tell the difference. So when the guy that they have been sleeping with introduces them as a friend women are often offended and hurt. Now after reading this you are probably wondering how to determine if you are in a sexship. Actually, it is very simple. If a man has not verbally committed to you and you are having sex with him, then you are in a sexship. Knowing the difference will play a huge role in the outcomes of your relationships.

Truth for the Gentleman:
Say What You Mean and Then Do It

I love the male species, however one thing that women find that is most annoying about men is that when it's time to break up or cut ties men may be extremely slow to getting around to it. There are several reasons for this. One may be that some men are just cowards and won't "man up" if they want out. Others sincerely don't want to hurt the woman's feelings. Whatever your reasons are men, understand that either way you may end up hurting her feelings. Now, I suggest that you try the straight to the point approach, it will cause you less drama in the long run. Women need closure. Even if your actions tell them that you no longer want to be with them, you need to verbally say it. I know that you feel that if you just call every once in a while or stop by every now and then it is still ok. However, if you were in a relationship and you know that both of you still have feelings for one another, then it is best to stay away, otherwise you may find yourself in an uncomfortable situation. You are giving a woman false hopes and are leading her around on a string. Now you may say, well I'm over her and I value her as a friend. This may actually be a true statement on your part. However, if a woman is not ready to let go of you and the relationship, you could find yourself in a terrible mess. Understand women hear your words but usually they are watching your actions. So if you say you no longer want to be in a relationship, however, you still come around from time to time, she may feel that you still have a desire be in a relationship with her. In many cases women are not taught to hear your words, but instead they read your actions. So make sure that your words and actions are consistent.

When I meet men of any age one of the questions that I always ask is whether or not they have a girlfriend. In many cases they will say no. I then ask men how many women out there currently think that they are in a relationship with them, and they will ponder for a moment. Some will say none and some will begin to name one or two. I also ask the men why these women feel that they are in relationships with them. Some will innocently say, "I don't know." What I have learned about men over the years is that you must learn how to ask the same questions in different ways. If not, you will only get partial answers. Usually with men, if you don't ask, they don't tell. In order to get to the bottom of the matter I will ask men how they interact with these women. Usually they are treating the woman like they are in a relationship with them. They do things like refer to the woman as "my boo," sweetheart, my baby, or other mushy names reserved for couples. They do special things for her like call her every morning just to let her know that he's thinking of her, cuddle with her, and even have sex with her from time to time, which is the worst thing you can do. Men, if you fall into this category, are you still wondering why certain women may feel that they are in a relationship with you?

Now understand men, even if you tell a woman that you just want to be friends (while you're doing all of this carrying on), she will say with her mouth that she knows that you are "just friends," however in her heart she will see you as her man. Women were made to be emotional creatures. When you stroke the emotional side of a woman she becomes attached. Now some men already know this and they use this to their advantage and to the woman's disadvantage. Some men do this so that they can run their game on a woman, understanding the whole time there is no future with her. If you fall into this category it is important for you to understand that it is not healthy for the woman or women involved, nor is it healthy for you. You must ask yourself what kinds of insecurities would drive you to play games with another person's heart in order to make you feel good about yourself. Always remember you reap what you sow. In his book *Checkmate: The Games Men Play* (2005), Mark D. Crutcher states that he once referred to himself as a "pimp," "player," and gigolo. His life completely changed was when his future wife left him standing at the altar on his wedding day (she left him for another man). He stated that at that very moment every woman he had ever manipulated and mistreated flashed before his very eyes. He had become the victim of the very game he played on others.

On the other hand, maybe you're not a player, you're just an innocent bystander. For example, you may meet a woman and you become friends, however she has a romantic interest in you. What do you do? It is important that you are very careful how you interact with her. You have to be careful because sometimes women will also manipulate a situation. This is the warning, if she frequently wants to buy you nice things, and is ALWAYS there when you need a favor, and often volunteers to do favors for you, BEWARE, particularly if she doesn't have another man in her life. She may even become upset and accuse you of leading her on, particularly if another woman comes into the picture. Have you ever seen court shows where a woman sues a man for something and the guy always says "Well I thought she was just being nice" or "I thought it was a gift, she's always doing nice things for me." I'm sure in most cases the women had some type of romantic interest in him. So be careful, I would really hate to turn on the television and see you on Judge Mathis trying to defend yourself.

The Truth for All

Although many of us have our own personal horror stories about relationships, good men and women do exist. Contrary to popular belief all men are not dogs and all women are not emotional time bombs waiting to explode. The important thing to remember is that sometimes you have to wait to meet the right person. Many times we get involved with the wrong person because we become lonely and impatient. Once a young lady asked me what she should be doing while she was waiting on the right person. My response to her was to continue living your life. Begin to establish your career, build up your income, take trips, meet people, pursue your dreams, just enjoy life. When you begin to do this you never know who you will meet along the way. It is also important during this time that you deal with any emotional hurt and pain from past relationships, whether it is from family, friends, or romantic. I am not suggesting that you have to give up on your desire to have a meaningful relationship. However you must take time out to heal and find out who you are as a person. If you don't you will miss out on a lifetime of happiness, and you won't be able to recognize Mr. or Ms. Right because your judgment will be so cloudy because of your past.

As men and women we must begin to develop relationships on the basis of people's character, and not on how attractive a person is to us. Think about some of your best friends. Did you choose them based on how attractive they were? Or are you friends with them because they add something to your life? One of the biggest mistakes males and females make in relationships, is that we base whether or not we will be friends with the opposite sex on how attractive they are to us. We look at a person and judge them on whether we can see ourselves with them. In order to get the ultimate benefits out of relationships with the opposite sex, we must begin to connect with people on the basis of their character. We must learn how to build the proper foundation for relationships which comes from being friends first. Once we truly grasp this concept we will finally begin to understand one another as well as experience love to the fullest.

References

Crutcher, Mark D. *Checkmate: The Games Men Play.* Washington, D.C.: Literally Speaking, 2005.

Davis, Alvis O. *Black Men Not Looking for Sex: Why They Commit Forever.* San Jose, CA: Zevon Publications, 1995.

Interpersonal Communication Climate

Think about how you communicate with others—family members, peers, superiors, romantic interests. What happens? What type of interpersonal communication climate exists? Think of **interpersonal communication climate** as the way people feel when they interact with each other. Sometimes people will say, "ooh, she seemed really cold didn't she?" You might even hear, "I feel really warm when I talk with her." These feelings are true communication climate barometers. They essentially measure how comfortable we are in communication situations. If we feel threatened or undervalued, we may become extremely defensive.

Communicating on the Internet

Amy Smith, M.A.

Have you ever sent someone an email or an instant message and had them take your intended message the wrong way? This is due, in part, to the lack of nonverbal symbols present in your message. The reader had no eye contact, facial expression, or vocal tone to help them interpret your message. Email and instant messages are examples of computer-mediated communication.

What is computer-mediated communication (CMC)? Like all communication, CMC requires a shared meaning between its participants. Communication is possible only if participants have some common ground for shared beliefs, acknowledge each other's expectations, and accept interactive rules that serve to keep the developing conversation on track (Clark and Schaefer, 1989).

CMC is formulated through two different methods. The first method is synchronous communication, produced when communication occurs simultaneously between two or more people. Examples of this would be instant text messages or chat room discussions. The second method, asynchronous communication, occurs when communication between the participants is not simultaneous. Examples of asynchronous communication are electronic mail messages and discussion boards.

According to Stasser (1992), if CMC is a process of negotiation, then the only way to understand it is by analyzing the individuals involved in it and the environment in which they operate. This means that the social, initial relationship in which CMC occurs plays a crucial role. In addition, new processes and activities will develop that challenge and modify the initial relationship between individual and context. Sproull and Kiesler (1991) state that CMC occurs in a social vacuum where the personal identities of individuals tend to fade and vanish. The most important consequence of this process is that CMC individuals tend to express themselves more openly and freely: "People who interact via computer are isolated from social rules and feel less subject to criticism and control. This sense of privacy makes them feel less inhibited in their relation with others" (Sproull & Kiesler, p. 48). At the same time, however, loss of personal identity may encourage individuals to break social rules (Sproull & Kiesler).

Once CMC is in place, a virtual community may be established. A virtual community is a set of on-going many-sided interactions that occur predominantly in and through computers linked via telecommunication networks (Smith, 1999). Smith goes on to say "virtual communities produce a variety of collective goods. They allow people of like interests to come together with little cost, help them exchange ideas and coordinate their activities, and provide the kind of identification and feeling of membership found in face-to-face interaction" (p. 3).

One aspect of a virtual community is that the members are geographically diverse. In a traditional brick and mortar community, the members of the community are located close to one another, and come together to achieve a like-minded goal. Similarly, virtual community members come together, but in a very different aspect. Virtual communities have no brick and mortar structure, rather a myriad of Internet-based communication methods or CMC.

In order for a community (traditional or virtual) to qualify as such, members must have a **sense of community** (SOC). McMillan and Chavis (1986) define SOC as "a feeling that members (of a group) have of belonging, a feeling that members matter to one another, and to the group, and a shared faith the members' needs will be met through their commitment to be together" (p. 9). McMillan and Chavis' framework of SOC dimensions include feelings of membership, feelings of influence, integration and fulfillment of needs, and shared emotional connection. Blanchard and Markus (2004) take this one step further to create a **sense of virtual community** (SOVC). They state that there are certain things we can expect to see in a SOVC, such as recognition, identification, support, relationship, emotional attachment, and obligation.

Similar research with regard to virtual communities suggest that we should also expect to find: membership, boundaries, belonging and group symbols (Baym, 1995, 1997; Greer, 2000; Herring, 1996; Kollock & Smith, 1994). Other identifying behaviors includes influence (Baym, 1997; Kollock & Smith, 1994; Pliskin & Romm, 1997), exchange of support among members (Baym, 1997; Greer, 2000; Preece, 1999), and shared emotional connections among members (Greer, 2000; Preece, 1999). Members of virtual communities come to feel as though they participate in a community that offers much of the same interaction as a face-to-face community. They discuss, argue, fight, reconcile, amuse, and offend in their virtual communities, as they would in a traditional community. The key difference in this communication is "that text-based communication in the digital environment is the primary formative and shaping force for their evolution, growth, and sustenance" (Bagozzi & Dholakia, 2002, p. 4).

What does all this research mean to you and your communication activities? For starters, it gives you a better sense of the ways in which technology can both benefit and hinder the communication process. It should also help you to understand the invention and necessity of things like "emoticons" and "email symbols." These little smiley-faces (or expressive symbols) help the writer to convey their emotion and intent, as well as help the reader to interpret the writers meaning accordingly. In other words, they are used as symbols of nonverbal communication. Lastly, this research offers you a better understanding of how virtual communities are created, how it is possible to establish relationships with people you've never met. Often times these relationships become as important as relationships with friends you interact with daily. Virtual communities are used for many things, such as support, information exchange, and advice and tips.

So the next time you are online, make sure you check out a virtual community (discussion board or chatroom) and get to know some new people. Note how the community members denote belonging. Do they share a common language or symbol system with one another? And don't forget to use emoticons so that your messages will be interpreted the way you intended them.

References

Babozzi, R. P. and U. M. Dholakia. "Intentional Social Action in Virtual Communities," *Journal of Interactive Marketing* 16, (2002): 2–21.

Baym, N. "The Emergence of Community in Computer Mediated Communication." In S.G. Jones (Ed.) *Cybersociety: Computer Mediated Communication and Community.* Thousand Oaks, Calif. Sage, 1995: 138–163.

Baym, N. "Interpreting Soap Operas and Creating Community: Inside an Electronic Fan Culture. In S. Keisler (Ed.) *Culture of the Internet.* Manhaw, NJ: Lawrence Erlbaum Associates, 1997: 103–120.

Blanchard, A. L., and M. L. Markus. "The Experienced "Sense" of a Virtual Community: Characteristics and Processes," *The DATA BASE for Advances in Information Systems* 35, (2004): 65–78.

Clark, H. H., & E. F. Schaefer. "Contributing to Discourse," *Cognitive Science* 13 (1989): 259–294.

Greer, B. G. "Psychological and Social Functions of an E-mail Mailing List for Persons with Cerebral Palsy." *CyberPsychology,* 3 (2000): 221–233.

Herring, S. C. (Ed.). *Computer-Mediated Communication: Linguistic, Social and Cross-Cultural Perspectives.* Amsterdam: John Benjamins Publishing Company, 1996.

Kollock, P., and M. Smith. "Managing the Virtual Commons: Cooperation and Conflict in Computer Communities." *Computer-Mediated Communication: Linguistic, Social and Cross-Cultural Perspectives* Amsterdam: John Benjamins Publishing Company, 1994: 109–128.

McMillan, D. W. and D. M. Chavis. "Sense of Community. A Definition and Theory," *Journal of Community Psychology* 14, (1986): 6v23.

Pliskin, N., and C. T. Romm. The Impact of E-mail on the Evolution of a Virtual Community during a Strike, *Information and Management* 32 (1997): 245–254.

Preece, J. "Emphatic Communities: Balancing Emotional and Factual Communication," *Interacting with Computers* 12 (1999): 63–77.

Smith, M. A. (1999). "Voices from the WELL: The logic of the Virtual Commons." Retrieved 03/18/04. *http://www.sscnet.ucla.edu/soc/csoc/papers/voices/Voices.htm*

Sproull, L., and S. Kiesler, *Connections: New Ways of working in the Networked Organizations.* Cambridge, Mass: MIT Press, 1991.

Stasser, G. "Pooling of Unshared Information during Group Discussion." In S. Worchell, W. Wood, and J. A. Simpson (Eds.). *Group Processes and Productivity.* Newbury Park, CA: Sage, 1992: 48–67.

*Adapted from *Establishment and Maintenance of Gender in a Virtual Weight-Loss Community,* 2005 Carolinas Communication Annual.

Communication researcher Jack Gibb (1988) studied extensively the idea of defensive communication. Much of this work was in the small group setting, but it is applicable in one-on-one scenarios. He defines what defensive communication is and says it manifests itself in interpersonal relationships in this way:

> Defensive behavior is defined as that behavior which occurs when an individual perceives threat or anticipates threat in the group. The person who behaves defensively, even though he or she also gives some attention to the common task, devotes an appreciable portion of energy to defending himself or herself. Besides talking about the topic, he thinks about how he appears to others, how he may be seen more favorably, how he may win, dominate, impress or escape punishment, and/or how he may avoid or mitigate a perceived attack.

> Such inner feelings and outward acts tend to create similarly defensive postures in others; and, if unchecked, the ensuing circular response becomes increasingly destructive. Defensive behavior, in short, engenders defensive listening, and this in turn produces postural, facial, and verbal cues which raise the defense level of the original communicator. (Gibb, 1988, Definition and Significance section)

The defensive mode prevents a listener from concentrating on the message. Essentially according to Gibb (1988), "as a person becomes more and more defensive, he or she becomes less and less able to perceive accurately the motives, the values, and the emotions of the sender" (Definition and Significance section). Conversely, the more supportive the climate, the less likely the receiver is to distort the messages that she receives.

In an eight-year time frame, Gibb analyzed numerous taped discussions and identified six pairs of supportive and defensive categories: evaluation/ description, control/ problem orientation, strategy/spontaneity, neutrality/ empathy, superiority/equality, and certainty/provisionalism. Based on Gibb's observation, for each defensive way of communicating there is a supportive counterpart. Let's look further into this concept.

Table 6.1   Supportive and Defensive Climates

Defensive Climates	Supportive Climates
Evaluation	Description
Control	Problem Orientation
Strategy	Spontaneity
Superiority	Equality
Certainty	Provisionalism

Evaluation/Description

I absolutely cannot stand it when someone evaluates me. I don't like performance appraisals. I don't like it when someone has to critique my work. Although, I know that is a must, it makes me defensive. I get warm and a little off kilter. Why? Because evaluative language makes us feel defensive. What about you? Say you are communicating with your significant other and that person raises his or her voice. And for the sake of saying, let's say that person's tone becomes sterner. What do you feel? How do you suspect that you will act? If you say that you are going to put up your guard and become defensive, you are not alone. Generally, when we feel that people are evaluating us, we become defensive. **Evaluative language** usually illustrates us as good or bad, right or wrong. As a receiver, we sometimes perceive evaluations based on the tone of voice of the speaker, on the symbols used by the speaker, and/or by the nonverbals of the speaker.

In contrast speech that describes usually solicits a much different behavior from the receiver. A listener is usually much less defensive when she feels that the speaker is genuine and is not asking that she change an attitude or behavior. Think about some of your romantic relationships. When do you become more defensive? Is it when your partner is evaluating you, or when your partner is describing a situation? **Descriptive communication** explains behaviors without evaluating whether they are good or bad, right or wrong.

Defensive
You're getting so big. You eat too much.

Supportive
You seem to have gained weight and I've noticed that you have been eating more.

Control/Problem Orientation

This is not a Janet Jackson oldie, and I am not in the mood for control. Listeners usually resist speech that is used to control them. Whether that speech is overt or covert. Overt speech is more open and would be something like, "it is either my way or the highway." This type of language is sure to cause a defensive response. Covert speech is more subtle and can often be heard in those Sunday morning church services, during those heated political campaigns or even those enticing beer commercials. When you are talking to someone, and you can tell they think that you are—well let's just say it—ignorant, you probably go into defense mode. From Gibb's findings, most people get a little defensive when they feel they are being perceived as unable to make decisions, immature, unwise or holding the wrong values or attitudes. **Control language** attempts to manipulate the listener into accepting the speaker's point of view.

When the focus is on coming up with a solution that is amicable to all parties, the speech is usually problem-oriented, meaning that the speaker focuses on the problem and not on the listener. **Problem-oriented language solicits collaborative decision-making.** Think about this exchange.

Defensive Climate

Jennifer: I want twenty-eight bridesmaids, two flower girls, three ring bearers and I want them to sing only songs by Jaheim. It's my wedding, and that's the way it's going to be.

Supportive Climate

Jason: Look, we can't seem to agree on how this wedding thing should go. Why don't we talk about it and come up with something that we both can live with?

Strategy/Spontaneity

So you have some tricks up your sleeve, and you think that you are going to trick me into thinking what you want me to think or behaving like you want me to behave. Oh you have a strategy, do you? Think again. Listeners usually become very defensive when they think that the speaker has strategized to manipulate them. Speakers who use **strategy language** plan to dupe or manipulate their listeners by keeping their motives hidden.

Spontaneous speech is not contrived. Sure, it may be thought out but it **is not manipulative and does not have a hidden agenda.** Spontaneous speech comes across as natural and sincere. It is speech that results spontaneously from the situation. In contrast to strategized speech that seems preplanned.

Defensive

Juan: After I loaned you all of that money last month, you mean you can't even buy me dinner tonight?

Supportive

Jesus: Man, I'm really broke. Do you think you can cover me at lunch? I'll give it back when I get paid.

Neutrality/Empathy

Speech that is neutral, generally emits no feeling. It is that, "you really don't matter one way or the other" kind of language. **Neutral speech** communicates a lack of concern about the listener. If a listener does not feel valued, he or she is probably going to become defensive. Like many people, I want to feel that I am the object of attention or affection. If I don't feel this, I feel rejected. This is consistent with Gibb's findings.

So now let's say that I'm finally getting the attention and the affection that I have been longing to receive. What kind of communication climate do you think exists now? You're right! It is pretty supportive. **Empathetic speech** communicates to me that I am worthwhile. As the listener, it is important for me to feel that the speaker identifies with me and understands my plight. It really distracts from the conversation when my feelings are not being validated. I'm not looking for a yes man, but an occasional, "yes, I understand. I see how you can feel this way" would certainly be nice. Generally, this is what an empathetic communicator provides.

Defensive

Terrence: I don't care if you think I spend too much time with the fellows. I'm going to do what I want to do.

Supportive

Fran: I can see how you think I spend too much time with my friends. Let's talk about how I can spend time with you and my friends.

Superiority/Equality

Do you know this person? She tends to brag about her money, cars, clothes, parents' jobs, GPA, and about how fine she is. When she starts on her tirade, do you find yourself verbally competing with her? You know how it goes. "Oh yeah, well we have two houses, one at the beach and one in the mountains. And we have three cars. Didn't you say that you only had two?" Now, you know that all of that was not necessary. Yet, you went there simply to do the one-up thing. Maybe instead of competing with her, you simply ignore her. But what if she gets you on bad day? Isn't it possible that you just might become a little jealous? Speakers who communicate their feelings of superiority may create a defensive climate because the listener feels inferior. According to Gibb (1988):

> The person who is perceived as feeling superior communicates that he or she is not willing to enter into a shared problem-solving relationship, that he or she probably does not desire feedback, that he or she does not require help, and/or that he or she will be likely to try to reduce the power, the status, or the worth of the receiver.

As I sit here, I realize that recently I have been guilty of communicating like a true know-it-all. I have been interrupting people when they are talking to me. That definitely communicates that I don't think what they have to say is worthwhile. I don't want advice. I guess that's because I'm not interested in the feedback of others. And trust me, I'm sure that I have tried to make other people feel like they were nothing. Yeah, I know that all sounds pretty bad. But stop for a moment, have you ever communicated superiority? Have you ever let someone know, "hey, I'm not here to work out this problem. I already have the solution because I'm all that." Okay, how about this one? Have you ever tried to make the person that you are talking to feel like they were absolutely worthless? If you answered yes to any of the above, you have probably contributed to a defensive communication climate.

There is nothing like feeling valued in a conversation, nothing like feeling equal to reduce defensiveness. The climate becomes much more supportive when both listener and receiver treat each other as equally valuable contributors. Differences in socio-economic position, attractiveness, or status may occur, but a low defense communicator does not accentuate these differences. **Equality language** communicates congruency.

Defensive
Michele: I know what I'm talking about. I have done this before. You're new. What do you know?

Supportive
Angelique: We've tried several things in the past. If you would like, I can tell you what worked and what didn't.

Certainty/Provisionalism

The old saying "stubborn as a mule" comes to mind when I think of certainty communication. The person who communicates, "I am always right" or "I don't want to hear what you have to say" sets the tone for a very defensive climate.

Certainty/superiority language is absolute and does not allow for further discussion. This kind of communication may make the listener feel inferior. Listeners may perceive certainty speech in the same way that they perceive control speech. Do you get those feelings of grandeur that make you feel like you are always right and like others couldn't possibly have anything to contribute to the conversation or the problem? Did I hear you correctly? Was that a yes? How about this one, do you prefer to win an argument or to solve a problem? "To win an argument," you say. Then it is probable that you, too, are guilty of communicating in certainty mode.

It is never too late. A speaker using **provisional language** communicates a willingness to listen, a willingness to hear other perspectives and criticisms. The speaker's openness to hear other ideas helps the listener feel valued in the conversation. A speaker using provisional language may communicate that she wants to look more closely into the issues. She may investigate, but not necessarily take a stand. Therefore, winning the argument is not that important. Solving the problem is.

Defensive
Luke: My mind is made up. I don't want to discuss it any further.

Supportive
Diamond: I see the problem this way. But I know it's possible that there is another way of looking at this.

Wrap It Up

Interpersonal communication requires us to examine how we function in different types of relationships. Whether it is family, peer/friendship, or romantic communication, the goal of effectiveness depends on a number of factors. However, when we begin to look at the world from the other person's perspective and move closer to a worldview which balances the needs of the individual with the collective, then we are on our way to transforming our interactions. Effective communication is not just knowing the words to say to get your way. It is truly connecting with another person in a way that creates substantive change in each of you. When we begin to view each communication encounter as an opportunity to change someone's life for the better, then we should be more willing to reach a little further, dig a little deeper, and give a little more. One-on-one interaction creating genuine connections and genuine change is what changes the world . . . one person at a time.

Interpersonal communication climate is the way people feel when they interact with each other. Defensive behavior is defined as that behavior which occurs when an individual perceives threat or anticipates threat in the group. The defensive mode prevents a listener from concentrating on the message. Communication researcher Jack Gibb presents six pairs of supportive and defensive categories: evaluation/description, control/problem orientation, strategy/spontaneity, neutrality/empathy, superiority/equality, certainty/provisionalism.

Evaluative language usually illustrates us as good or bad, right or wrong. Descriptive language describes behaviors without evaluating whether they are good or bad, right or wrong.

Control language attempts to manipulate the listener into accepting the speaker's point of view. Problem-oriented language solicits collaborative decision-making.

Strategy communicators attempt to dupe or manipulate their listeners by keeping their motives hidden. Spontaneous speech is not contrived or manipulative, and does not have a hidden agenda.

Neutral speech communicates a lack of concern about the listener, and un-involvement on the part of the speaker. Empathetic speech communicates that the listener is worthwhile.

Superiority language communicates an unwillingness to enter into a shared problem-solving relationship. Equality language communicates congruency.

Certainty language is absolute and does not allow for further discussion. A speaker using provisional language communicates a willingness to listen—a willingness to hear other perspectives and criticisms.

I hope I have raised your consciousness about the power of words to affect communication between the sender and receiver. Most people want to feel valued and appreciated by close friends and even acquaintances. We don't want to feel like we have to be on guard with boxing gloves up to avoid defensive communication. Listen to yourself the next time you interact with a family member, peer, or mate. Is your language causing those around you to run for cover or want to spend more time with you?

References

Duncan, V. J. (Ed.). *Towards Achieving Maat: Communication Patterns in African American, European American, and Interracial Relationships*. Dubuque, Iowa: Kendall Hunt, 1998.

Gibb, J. R. (1988). Defensive communication. Retrieved January 31, 2005 from web site: *http://www.geocities.com/toritrust/defensive_communication.htm*

Communication in the Movies

I invite you and a friend or classmates to explore comunication in the movies. Reflect on the communication skills discussed in this chapter. How are they addressed in the movies?

▶ The Gospel
▶ Norbit
▶ Crash

Name _____   Date _____

Section _____

Think About It → Write About It

Reflect on what you've just read. Now write what you are thinking.

_____

_____

_____

_____

_____

_____

_____

_____

_____

_____

_____

_____

_____

_____

_____

_____

_____

_____

_____

_____

_____

_____

_____

_____

Activity 1

Who Am I and Why Am I Like This?

(p. 147)

Activity 2

Male/Female Communication

[Ask the class to distinguish the characteristics between friendships and romantic relationships.]

Male/Female Interaction (p. 168)

a. Ask for a male and female volunteer to read the script on p. 168.

b. Ask the class if this conversation is realistic and why.

Chapter 7

In Black and White: Race and Communication

Stephanie Sedberry Carrino

Key Terms

Cultural Competence	Communication Patterns

Introduction

There are numerous factors which influence the development of communication patterns: including the family of origin, life experiences, level of education, socioeconomic level, and the communication norms of the communities they belong to. Communication patterns also differ by cultural affiliation and race. What one cultural group defines as acceptable and "normal" may be seen as unacceptable and "strange" by a different cultural group. Cultural groups share speech codes: distinct systems of communication rules, norms, and patterns that guide their communication behaviors with others.

It is easy to identify these systems when we compare cultures from two different countries. For example, most Americans interpret direct eye contact as a display of honesty and respect. Many parents demand direct eye contact from their children (*Look at me when I'm talking to you!*) as do many teachers. Americans tend to think that someone who avoids eye-contact has something to hide.

In Japan, eye contact is interpreted in a very different way. Direct eye contact is considered rude and intimidating, and respect is shown by looking down or averting your eyes when you are speaking.[1] In this example, it is easy to recognize how misunderstandings can result from the different speech codes and patterns cultural groups use.

A **speech code** is a system of communication rules, norms, and patterns which guide communication behaviors with others.

When you start to talk about race within the Unites States, however, it is not so easy to recognize and accept that racial groups who live side by side and share a larger culture maintain distinct communication systems. However, research shows that speech codes differ by race, and that this is the cause of many interracial tensions. This chapter will examine the research related to communication styles and rules in the Black American and White American cultures. Each racial/cultural group in the United States maintains a unique system of communication behaviors and rules. There are many cultural systems in the U.S., however, this chapter focuses specifically on Black people and White people and research on the differences in the ways *some* White people and *some* Black people use and interpret communication. These differences are based on two distinct speech codes: two different sets of communication rules for what is acceptable and normal. This chapter will examine these differences in the hope that understanding these differences will help us all to communicate more effectively with others. Mark Orbe, a scholar who has spent his academic career focused on the relationships among race, culture, and communication states it clearly when he says " The most effective instances of interracial communication are grounded in a working knowledge of the similarities and differences within and between racial and ethnic groups."[2]

The Diversity of Native Americans

Native Americans are a distinct racial group in the United States. However, there are many different tribes in the Native American race. Can we accurately talk about Native Americans as a single, unified group? Each tribe within the Native American race has its own unique cultural customs—different patterns for communicating with others. However, there are some values and beliefs that most Native American communities share, and these commonalities influence their communication patterns. So while there are important differences within the Native American community, there are also some cultural similarities.

In this chapter, I talk about Blacks and Whites as distinct racial groups in the U.S. As you read, remember that there are also many "tribes" within each race. There are many cultural communities within each race, and though there are some similarities, there are also important differences.

Did you know that the government requires Native Americans to prove their racial identity? The U.S. Government requires that an individual prove that he or she has 1/4 "Indian Blood" to be considered eligible for Native American scholarships. What do you think of that?

Definitions: What Is Race?

In this chapter, I choose to use the terms Black and White to refer to African Americans and European Americans in the United States. The ongoing debate about what terms to use shows us just how powerful labels can be. I choose Black and White because I think these terms are more descriptive than African American and European American, and being Black or being White in this country means much more than just what region of the earth your ancestors called home. There are other, more important factors which influence our contemporary definitions of race.

The concept of "race" is defined by people, not by biology. Different cultures define race differently, based on history and tradition. There is no genetic difference among humans that could explain all the attributes we associate with race. Instead, race is a collection of beliefs, values, experiences, history, practices, and social, political, and economic positionality.

In 1795, researchers defined five races of humans. Then in 1950, thirty races of humans were identified. In 1962, one group classified humans into five races (though different from those cited in 1795) and another group claimed that there were thirty-four races. In each instance, the classifications reflected the beliefs of the culture at the time. Communication patterns adopted by groups of people both reflect and create the collective experiences of each cultural group, and provide for shared identity. Within all races, however, there are many different ethnicities and cultural groups. It is problematic to describe all Black people or all White people because the variations within each race are important. Races vary internally, and racial identities can change over time. In fact, the differences within each racial group can be greater than the differences between the races![3] No research can tell us everything about all Black people and White people, particularly since it is difficult to classify people by race. As you read, understand that these findings represent *some* Black and some White communication patterns, and are not intended to represent all people within each racial group. My hope in presenting this information is that you gain some insight into cultural patterns, and learn to see something in a different way. I'm offering you a pair of race-free sunglasses. I'd like you to look at the communication patterns presented in this chapter as systems of communication and interpretation. You do not need to agree with what you see, and you don't have to change your own communication behaviors. However, I do hope that you'll keep these race-free glasses with you, and step outside of your own assumptions about how people should communicate and consider a different system of rules. Maybe by examining some different communication tendencies, we will all choose to wear our race-free glasses more often.

What's in a Name?

■ What should we call Americans of African descent? Afro American, African American, Negro, or Black?

■ What about Americans of European descent? Caucasian, European American, Anglo, or White?

■ How about Americans of Mexican descent? Hispanic, Latino, Chicano, or Mexican American?

■ What should we call the Americans who are native to this country? Indian, American Indian, Native American, or Native People?

■ What about Americans of Asian descent? Orientals, Asians, Asian Americans, Asian/Pacific Islanders, or Asian Pacific Americans?

The power to name yourself, rather than accept a name given to you by others, gives you the power to define yourself. What do you want to be called? Are there other "labels" you can think of?

Guiding Principles

As we begin to explore racial differences in communication patterns and interpretations, consider the following principles:

Different Does Not Equal Wrong

When we identify differences in the communication patterns among different cultural groups, it is not a judgment about which practice is better. Each culture has its own, unique communication system and patterns, and each is valid. Just because two groups are different, does not mean one is better than the other. Also, remember that there is significant difference within groups, as well as among groups. Someone may be different from you, or different from others in his or her own race. Different does not equal wrong.

Cultures Are Dynamic

Racial identities are not static. What it means to be Black or White today is different than what it meant fifty years ago, and fifty years from now it will mean something else. Cultures change as they respond to the world and people around them. In addition, our definitions of race change.

Cultural Competence Is a Process

Cultural competence is the ability to communicate effectively with people from a cultural background that is different from your own. This means that you have an understanding of other cultures as well as your own, and an open mind. Learning to be culturally competent takes some effort, self-discovery, and often a little discomfort, but the rewards go beyond just the personal benefit of becoming a more effective communicator. We each need to be open-minded, because there may be differences we are not aware of, and we need to check our interpretations to make sure we understand.

Learning about Others Helps Self-Understanding

Often, we are not aware of our own assumptions about communication until we are confronted with someone with a different set of assumptions. When we personally encounter another culture, we can begin to understand our own belief systems. For example, when you learn about the ways a different cultural group uses and interprets nonverbal signs, you become more aware of your own nonverbal communication.

Apprehension about Racial Differences Is Normal

It is common when encountering another culture to feel self-conscious, less confident, and even threatened. Much of our self identity is based on race and culture. Our race does not define who we are, but the attitudes, values, and beliefs of our racial culture do influence our communication patterns. It can be uncomfortable to have those assumptions and behaviors thrown into question.

Overcoming Ethnocentrism Is Central

Ethnocentrism is the use of your own culture as the standard to measure others. It assumes that one culture is superior to another. Resisting ethnocentrism means that you are able to stop and consider another person's point of view, based on their cultural or racial norms. It also means that you suspend judgment, and approach others with cultural awareness and an open mind.

Understanding Does Not Mean You Agree

You can understand a system of communication behaviors, and the rules associated with that system, without agreeing or changing your own perspective or behaviors. Acknowledging the validity of a different communication system allows you to better understand another person, and communicate with them more effectively. It does not mean that you need to abandon your own beliefs and values, though you may choose to adopt some new ones along the way.

Patterns Exist, They Don't Define

Communication researchers have been able to define some communication patterns that are different across race. This does not mean that these patterns define people—your race does not define who you are and does not predict your communication behaviors. However, it is still important to identify potential differences so that we can be aware of communication tendencies.

Communication Patterns by Race

The research in the areas of Black and White communication patterns is broad and offers a myriad of voices. Some of the findings presented here are from the scientific community. The scientific perspective looks at behaviors, and tries to predict future interactions. Some of the information presented here is humanistic in nature, meaning that interpretations are provided from a stated point of view to enhance understanding. Both research communities are represented here, and offer a broad introduction to this body of research.

African American Language and Culture: Influences of Sociocultural Factors

Deanna Lacy McQuitty

The basic unit of American culture is the family. There is a dynamic interaction between cultural beliefs, family values, expectations and experiences, and child-rearing practices on the one hand and the language development of young children on the other hand. In particular, the African American family unit has experienced significant structural changes. However, this unique culture's family values continue in the midst of restructuring and play an essential role in the self-identity and personality composition process (Hecht et al., 2003). Children acquire language within the context of the family; therefore, the acquisition of a child's language system is a direct reflection of the expectations within the home environment. "This is true for families from all areas of the globe, from all socioeconomic classes, and from all ethnic groups" (Anderson & Battle, 2002, p. 182).

Over the past decade, scholars have been investigating culturally diverse populations, specifically, African Americans, in an attempt to provide empirical research to understand family and childhood dynamics and their relationships to child development. Deutsch (1964), an early pioneer in developmental studies, investigated the role of social class in language development and cognition. The sample size included African Americans and White Americans from low- and middle-class status. Deutsch recognized that research literature needed to extend beyond single variables such as relationships between social classes and cultural attributes in an attempt to understand the complexity of cognitive-linguistic processes. Rather, the critical researcher must examine cultural dimensions concurrently, which include the social structure of the family unit, economic status, child-rearing practices, and the interaction patterns between the child and the caregiver. Within the cultural dimensions cited, Deutsch acknowledged that there are differences seen when examining multiple variables within the cultural structure that is critical for cognitive and language development.

Although Deutsch's (1964) earlier study provided a preliminary foundation for the development of cognition and language, the investigator failed to recognize the African American culture as a unique entity. As reflected in this study and research conducted by earlier scholars (Dillard, 1972; Hess & Shipman, 1965), most of the research that has been published regarding the relation between families and language development had been guilty of one or both of the following errors:

1. Middle-class families serve as the control subjects or the standard against which working-class families are judged and compared.

2. Socio-economic status (SES) and ethnicity/race are intermingled; for example, working-class African American families are compared to middle class families (Anderson & Battle, 1993; Wallace, Roberts, & Lodder, 1998).

Furthermore, Anderson and Battle (1993) said, "The conclusions drawn are often erroneous in that differences found are attributed to race rather than to SES" (p. 194).

Although Anderson and Battle (1993; 2002) recognized there has been limited nonbiased ethnographic research investigating the influence of SES on language development, Young (1969) was a pioneer in this research endeavor. Young provided field data specifically on the social interaction of the family and child uniquely observed in a working-class African American family in the South. Personality formation had been studied through interviews with children and adolescents. Adult interviews concerning childrearing practices had also been conducted. This type of study was important to dispel the belief that was prevalent in the literature at this time concerning African American families.

A study by Heath (1983) provided an ethnographic investigation that examined the interactive behaviors of African American caregivers and their young children from working-class or lower SES families in rural communities in the South. Specifically, a study conducted by Farran and Ramsey (1980) provided information regarding mother-child interactions of sixty children (three- to five-year-olds) from the Southeastern region. Within the subject selection process, all children who were considered high-risk were African Americans of low SES and the remainder of the sample size comprised of both middle-income White and African American children. Interactions between the mother and child were assessed at six, eighteen, and forty-eight month intervals. Farran and Ramsey suggested, "High-risk mothers seemed to withdraw from the interactions whereas middle-class mothers interacted more" (p. 254). Similar findings were identified in another study conducted by Farran (1982) when she revealed that middle-class mothers (White and African American) were considered to be the prime communicant for the child—communicating with the child during routine nurturing activities. They were also the prime caregivers for transmitting cultural norms and linguistic behaviors to the child.

The conclusions of these studies have been supported in more recent writing on the cultural interaction styles of families living in the United States. Hammer and Weiss (1999) took current research findings a step further and examined the play and interactive behaviors of African American mothers and their children who were of low and middle SES and living in an urban area in the South. The investigator examined twelve African American mother-infant dyads. Findings revealed varied language goals, expectations, and communication patterns from the two socioeconomic classes. Interactions between middle-class dyads were characterized with numerous language goals when compared to interactions between dyads from the lower SES. Furthermore, children who vocalized more frequently tended to produce a higher percentage of spontaneous words and phrases, and mothers responded more to their vocalizations. However, Hammer and Weiss reported, "The small sample size employed in this research study results reduced the statistical significance" (p. 365). Nevertheless, detailed descriptions provided by the investigators revealed extensive analysis of specific characteristics of interaction and parenting styles evidenced in low and middle income families.

Wallace et al., (1998) reported on a similar study that investigated the interaction of African American infants and their mothers at one-year of age. This study focused on "the patterns of mother-infant interaction in African American mother-child dyads and the relationship between those patterns and the development of cognitive and communication skills during the first year of the child's life" (p. 902). The participants included ninety-two one-year-old African American infants and their mothers. These infants were part of a longitudinal study. The investigators of this study administered the Weschler Adult Intelligence Scales (Weschler, 1981) to each caregiver. Findings of the study revealed mothers who elaborated on their child's verbal and nonverbal behaviors and who provided more optimal cognitive and linguistic stimulation had children who scored higher on the measurement of expressive and receptive communication skills. These results suggested a strong relationship between mother-child interaction behaviors and children's expressive and receptive communication skills. Furthermore, this study contributed to previous research concerning the relationship among socioeconomic factors, parental interaction, and children's developmental skills.

The findings of Wallace et al. (1998) were similar to those found in samples of White mother-child dyads (Hoff-Ginsburg, 1991) and in other African American mother-child dyads (Kamii & Radin, 1967). The authors recognized specific limitations within this subject design. Wallace et al. stated, "They were unable to discuss whether there were long-term relationships between early intervention and later communication and cognitive skills, nor did they examine more specific language skills of words or imitation" (p. 910).

Ethnographic examinations of the diversity across families as they interact with young children who are learning language, as depicted in the studies mentioned, are important in that they examine differences in communication in natural family environments. Scholars have supported the principle that each family has its own cultural norm of behavior in child rearing, which influences the normal development of language (Anderson & Battle, 1993, 2002; Hecht et al., 2003; Hill, 2001; Rickford & Rickford, 2000).

The distribution and use of language functions by African American children suggest a socioeconomic orientation in language use. During the language learning process, children simultaneously learn the social system of their respective culture. The social system refers to concepts such as the values, expectations, rules and regulations of a culture. The interactions provider within the social unit are a critical foundation for language acquisition.

According to Battle (1996), these cultural variables are transmitted within the microculture of the mother and child through daily interaction in a variety of situations. The interactions form the basis and are influential in the quantity and type of communication patterns children acquire. Realizing this phenomenon, many prominent authors (Anderson & Battle, 1993; 2002; Battle, 1996; Bleile, McGowan & Bernthal, 1997) have suggested further studies examining how parenting styles and interactions affect African American children's acquisition of morphological, phonological, and semantic structures over time. Furthermore, research has advocated that scholars should provide additional studies within this area using larger sample sizes to obtain statistical significance, providing studies that are consistent in cultural sample selection, and examining children from varied communities across the United States.

References

Anderson, N., and D. Battle, "Cultural diversity in the development of language." In D. Battle (Ed.), *Communication Disorders in Multicultural Populations.* Boston: Andover Medical, 1993: 158–182.

Anderson, N., and D. Battle, "Cultural diversity in the development of language." In D. Battle (2nd ed.), *Communication Disorders in Multicultural Populations* Boston: Andover Medical, 2002: 160–203.

Battle, D. "Language Learning and Use by African American Children." *Topics in Language Disorders,* 16 (4) (1996): 22–37.

Bleile, K. M., J. S. McGowan, and J. E. Bernthal, "Professional Judgments about the Relationship Between Speech and Intelligibility in African American Preschoolers," *Journal of Communication Disorders,* 30 (5), (1997): 367–383.

Deutsch, M. The Role of Social Class in Language Development and Cognition. *American Journal of Orthopsychiatry,* 35 (2) (1967): 78–88.

Dillard, J. *On the Social Significance of a Lexicon for the Black English Vernacular: Lexicon of Black English.* New York: The Seabury Press, 1972.

Farran, D. C., and C. T. Ramsey, "Social Class Differences in Dyadic Involvement During Infancy, *Child Development,* 51 (1) (1980): 254–257.

Farran, D. C. "Mother-Child Interaction, Language Development and the School Performance of Poverty Children." In L. Feagans & D. Farran (Eds.), *The Language of Children Reared in Poverty: Implications for Evaluation and Intervention* New York: Academic Press, 1982: 183–256.

Hammer, C. S., and A. L. Weiss, "Guiding Language Development: How African American Mothers and Their Infants' Structure Play Interactions," *Journal of Speech, Language, and Hearing Research,* 42 (5), (1999): 1219-1233 .

Hecht, M. L., R. L. Jackson, and S. A. Ribeau, *African American Communication: Exploring Identity and Culture* (2nd ed.). Mahwah, NJ: Lawrence Erlbaum Associates, 2003.

Heath, S. B. *Sociocultural Contexts of Language Development: In Beyond Language.* Los Angeles: Evaluation, Dissemination, and Assessment Center, 1983.

Hess, R., and V. Shipman, "Early Experience and the Socialization of Cognitive Modes in Children," *Child Development,* 36 (1965): 869–886.

Hill, S. A. "Class, Race, and Gender Dimensions of Child-Rearing in African American Families," *Journal of Black Studies,* 31 (4) (2001): 494–508.

Hoff-Ginsberg, E. "Mother-Child Conversation in Different Social Classes and Communicative Settings," *Child Development,* 62(4) (1991): 782–796.

Kamii, C. K., and N. L. Radin. "Class Differences in the Socialization Practices of Negro Mothers," *Journal of Marriage and the Family,* 29 (1967): 302–310.

Rickford, J., and R. Rickford. *Spoken Soul: The Story of Black English.* New York: Wiley, 2000.

Wallace, I. F., J. E. Roberts, and D. E. Lodder. "Interaction of African American Infants and Their Mothers: Relations with Development at 1 Year of Age," *Journal of Speech, Language, and Hearing Research,* 41 (4) (1998): 900–912.

Weschler, D. *Manual for the Weschler Adult Intelligence Scales* (Rev. ed.). San Antonio, TX: Psychological Corporation, 1981.

Young, V. H. "Family and Childhood in a Southern Negro Community," *American Anthropologist,* 72 (1969): 269–288.

Language Use

In 1996, the Oakland County School Board in Oakland, California, declared that "Ebonics" was the language of the Black people in their school district. A year later, they declared that "Ebonics" was a dialect of English, not a separate language. These declarations caused a national debate about the words, phrases, and grammar used by many Black people. Whether you consider Ebonics to be a language or a dialect, it is still a unique system of language usage, and is distinct from the language system used by many White Americans.

Black people tend to be creative with language and use words and sayings that have specific meanings to members of the group: a shared code that reinforces shared identity. White people tend to use language literally, which is the use of words that have a specific, dictionary definition.[4]

Possible Interpretations:

1. Black people may think that White people are stiff and formal, and White people may think Black people are not using correct English.

2. We all recognize that language usage is cultural and that people use and interpret language in different ways.

3. We realize that shared code is a way to create and reinforce a shared identity, and many groups, both Black and White, use this as a tool to maintain close ties.

Case in Point

A friend (Black) and I (White) took our young daughters to see a show. In the middle of the show, the girls started bouncing in their chairs and kicking the chairs in front of them. My friend and I turned, at the same time, to say something to them. I said, "Emily, I need you to sit with your bottom in the chair and keep your feet to yourself!" My friend looked at her daughter and said, "Vee, I'm not playin'!" We sent the same message to our daughters, but we chose different words. I used literal language to communicate with my daughter, and my friend used shared code. It took me a lot longer to say the same thing! Was our communication different because of different parenting styles? Different speech patterns? What do you think?

Sequencing

Many Black people organize and present their ideas in a web-like or circular fashion, and rely on examples to communicate an idea. This style of thinking and communicating has been identified in a number of cultures, not just in Black culture. Many White people organize their thoughts in a linear fashion, usually in time sequence. An idea is communicated by presenting it from beginning to end, and staying directly on the topic.[5]

Possible interpretations:

1. Black people may think that White people are boring and dry, or too narrow-minded to see how examples are inter-connected, and White people may think that Black people are disorganized.

2. We all recognize that people may organize and communicate their thoughts in different, and valid, ways.

Case in Point

In a faculty meeting at my previous college, we met to discuss the attendance policy. All the faculty members were Black except for me. In the course of the conversation, we talked about textbooks, graduating seniors, and the new curriculum, and each of these topics was tied back into the attendance policy. Initially, I found myself agitated that we did not get right to the point. I had evaluated the conversation from my own perspective. I later realized that we had a rich discussion, and we did get to the point—just in a different way. Understanding cultural differences is essential to good interracial communication.

Eye Contact

Eye contact is an important part of face-to-face communication, and so is the absence of eye contact. Many Black people and White people share some cultural beliefs about the interpretation of eye contact: mainly that direct eye contact indicates honesty and respect, and the lack of it may mean someone is lying or hiding something. There are, however, some differences in the way eye contact is used in conversations. Some Black people maintain direct eye contact while they are speaking, and look away while listening. Some White people are the opposite: they maintain direct eye contact while they are listening, and avert their eyes when speaking.[6]

Possible interpretations:

1. Black people may think they are being stared down by White people when they are talking, or looked down on, and White people may think Black people are showing disrespect or aren't paying attention when they are talking.

2. We all recognize that people learn eye contact behaviors from their families and communities, and have different ideas about when eye contact is appropriate.

Case in Point

I had a conference with a student about a grade. The student thought I had been unfair, and I thought the grade she earned was appropriate for the work. While I was talking to her, she was looking around my office—I felt like she was not listening to me. Yet when she spoke, it was evident that she had paid attention to what I said. I had misinterpreted her eye contact.

Emotional Expressiveness

Emotional expressiveness is the use of inflection, vocal range, rhythm, emphasis, and tone when speaking. Blacks tend to be emotionally expressive in their speech, and value authentic displays of emotion in public. Whites tend to be more reserved in their speech, and value self-control when displaying emotions in public.[7]

Possible Interpretations:

1. Black people could think White people are cold-hearted or not authentic, and White people could think Black people are dramatic.

2. We could all recognize that our rules for what is and is not acceptable in public communication are cultural, and that we should not use our own cultural communication practices to evaluate others.

3. We should be aware that emotional expressiveness can be influenced by many factors in addition to race.

Case in Point

The middle school that my daughters are supposed to attend has been in the news this year, a lot. Headlines scream that the school is full of aggressive students who have no respect for their teachers, and that some teachers are concerned about their safety. However, they do not give any specific examples. What do they mean by aggressive? Could different definitions of aggression be part of the problem? Many White teachers and Black students do not have the same definition of aggression. If a student disagrees with a teacher, and passionately defends his or her position, is that aggressive? Could White, middle-class teachers feel threatened by a raised voice, or emotional defense of an idea? This type of communication is generally accepted in Black culture, and is not considered to be a challenge to authority. Or, are the students physically hitting the teachers? I plan to go look at the school and make my own decision based on my own observation. I'm not sure if I will send my girls to that middle school, but my decision will not be based on the news reports.

Emotional Expressiveness: How Do Americans Compare?

Expressive ————————— X ————————— X ——————————— X ————————— Reserved

                Latinos   Americans   Asians

Taking Turns

Turn-taking refers to who speaks (and when) and who listens (and when) in a one-on-one or group conversation. How we decide who has the floor depends on a cultural norm for communication. Many Whites follow a rule of taking turns. You should wait until the other person is finished speaking before you speak. Many Blacks give the floor to the most vocal person, and an interruption is generally acceptable.[8]

Possible interpretations:

1. Blacks may perceive Whites as passive or not interested, and Whites may perceive Blacks as rude or aggressive.

2. We all recognize that turn-taking is a practice which results from cultural communication patterns.

Case in Point

It has been said that the most segregated hours in the United States are on Sunday mornings. Many churches are predominately Black or predominately White. One way to observe communication patterns by race is to attend two services—at both a Black and White church. At a Black church, you are likely to hear people in the congregation responding to the minister while he or she is talking, a behavior known as *Call and Response*. This tells the minister that the congregation is involved in the service, and that the message is being received. At the White church, you are likely to hear the minister speaking, with a quiet congregation who responds only when directed to by the minister. Is speaking out in church considered rude and disruptive? Is silence during a sermon a sign that the congregation is asleep? Who talks and when is determined by the communication norms of the church and the cultural practices of its members.

Assertive Language

Some Black people tend to use assertive, powerful language when they speak, and some White people tend to use language that is less assertive, by either softening word choice or tone.[9]

Possible interpretations:

1. White people may think Black people are aggressive or threatening, and Black people may think White people are weak or fearful.

2. We all recognize that Black people and White people follow the communications rules of their cultural group, and we should consider speech codes when we interpret others communication.

3. Assertive communication is not necessarily an act of aggression and less assertive communication is not necessarily a sign of weakness.

Case in Point

I use Mary Kay cosmetic products. My representative used to be a White woman my sister introduced to me at a Mary Kay party. Since we lived in different towns, I usually ordered products over the phone. I would call her and place an order, she would mail it to me with an invoice, and I would send her a check. When I started teaching at a new University, I discovered that a co-worker, a Black female, was a Mary Kay representative and I switched to her. With my old representative, I would receive a note with my products telling me she hoped I enjoyed them, and asking me to send her a check when I got the chance. My new representative would say something like, "Your Mary Kay is in, and it came to 32.25. I need your money." What I realized was that both women were asking me for money, each in their own, culturally appropriate way. Was the White woman wishy-washy? No, she was being polite. Was the Black woman being rude? No, she was being direct. They both wanted their money, but asked in different ways.

Topics of Conversation

Many White people believe that asking another person about jobs, family, or other personal topics is a way to make a friendly introduction, even when they meet someone for the first time. Many Black people regard personal topics inappropriate in initial conversations with people they do not know.[10] For example, what conversations do you hear in an elevator or at a bus stop? About what?

Possible interpretations:

1. Black people may think that White people are asking something that is too personal, and Whites may think that Blacks are unfriendly.

2. We all recognize that different cultural groups have different ideas about what topics are acceptable and which are intrusive.

Case in Point

I used to share an office with other faculty members in the department. The office was open, no cubicles, and everyone could hear others' conversations. One day, a textbook representative came around to show faculty some new texts and materials the company had to offer. This is a fairly common practice, and at least once a semester, a textbook representative hangs around trying to talk faculty into using their company's textbooks. This representative, a young, White male, was probably new to the job. He approached a co-worker, a Black woman, with a hello and a comment about a cute baby picture on her desk. My co-worker replied with, "Can I help you with something?" The salesman was attempting to establish a friendly, positive relationship with my co-worker by engaging her in a conversation about her child. My co-worker thought that a stranger was getting too personal, and wondered what he was doing standing in front of her desk looking at her pictures. It is probable that the salesman felt rejected, and my colleague felt invaded.

Similarities

In this chapter, we have focused on the differences in the ways Black and White people tend to communicate in America. Our focus on differences is important, because cultural understanding broadens our cultural competence, and we become more effective communicators.

However, this focus on difference also obscures the reality of our similarity. Black people and White people share 99.9 percent of genetic make-up.[11] There can be more variation within Black groups and White groups than there are between Black and White people! Many factors influence communication styles, including how someone was raised, in what community, socioeconomic level, gender, and age among others. Race does not tell the whole story. Although there are some speech code differences, we are more the same than we are different.

Remember that our racial identities as Black or White come from our culture—not from our genes. Race is learned, and racial communication systems are also learned. If we can consider the possibility that another person may be operating out of a different speech code, it may reduce some interracial misunderstandings, and help us to discover more of these similarities.

Wrap It Up

We should understand the potential differences in communication patterns of Black people and White people in this country. We should make an effort to learn about other cultures, to check our understanding before jumping to conclusions, and be open-minded when communicating with others. If we do, we will be more effective in our personal, social, and professional relationships.

Notes

1. Imai, G. T. (1997). Gestures: Body Language and Non-Verbal Communication, Common Asian Gestures, *Teachers' Asian Studies Summer Institute,* California State Polytechnic University, www.lntranet.csupomona.edu/tassi.htm, 5–11.

2. Orbe, M. P., and T. M. Harris. *Interracial Communication: Theory into Practice.* Belmont, Calif: Wadsworth/Thompson, 2001: 141.

3. King, J. *The Biology of Race.* New York: Harcourt Brace Jovanovich, 1971: 158–165.

4. Asante, M. K. *In Defense of my First Language.* http://www.asu.edu/, search Asante.

5. Watkins, W. H. "Black Curriculum Orientations: A Preliminary Inquiry," *Harvard Educational Review,* 63 (3) (1993): 331–332.

See also

Adkins, K. C. (2002). "The Real Dirt: Gossip and Feminist Epistemology," *Social Epistemology,* 16 (3) (2002): 215–232.

See also

Spring, J. "Deculturalization and the Claim of Racial Superiority by Anglo-Americans," In J. Spring, *Deculturalization and the Struggle for Equality: A Brief History of the Education of the Dominated Cultures in the U.S.* MA: McGraw Hill, 2004: 1–16.

6. Johnson, K. R. Black Kinesics: Some Nonverbal Communication Patterns in the Black Culture (L. A. Samovar and R. E. Porter, Eds.). *Intercultural Communication: A Reader,* Belmont, Calif.: Wadsworth Publishing Company, 1976: 259–268.

7. Orbe, M. P., and T. M. Harris. *Interracial Communication: Theory into Practice.* Belmont, Calif.: Wadsworth/Thompson, 2001: 65.

See also

Ribeau, S. A., J. R. Baldwin, and M. L. Hecht, M. L., "An African American Communication Perspective." In L. A. Samovar and R. E. Porter (Eds.), *Intercultural Communication: A Reader,* Belmont: Calif: Wadsworth, 1997: 147–154.

See Also

Garner, T. "Oral Rhetorical Practice in African American Culture." In A. Gonzalez, M. Houston, and V. Chen (Eds.), *Our Voices. Essays in Culture, Ethnicity, and Communication* Los Angeles: Roxbury, 1994: 81–91.

See Also

Ribeau, S. A., J. R. Baldwin, and M. L. Hecht, "An African American Communication Perspective." In L. Samovar & R. Porter (Eds.), *Intercultural Communication: A Reader* 7th ed. Belmont, Calif.: Wadsworth, 1994: 140–147.

8. Orbe, M. P., and T. M. Harris. *Interracial Communication: Theory into Practice.* Belmont, Calif.: Wadsworth/Thompson, 2001: 65.

See also

Houston, M., and J. Wood, "Difficult Dialogues, Expanded Horizons: Communicating Across Race and Class." In J. Wood (Ed.). *Gendered Relationships.* Mountain View, Calif.: Mayfield, 1996: 35–56.

9. Orbe, M. P., and T. M. Harris. *Interracial Communication: Theory into Practice.* Belmont, Calif.: Wadsworth/Thompson, 2001: 65.

See Also

Orbuch, T., and Veroff, J. "A Programmatic Review: Building a Two-Way Bridge Between Social Psychology and the Study of the Early Years of Marriage," *Journal of Social and Personal Relationships,* 19, 2002: 549–568. (from wood)

10. NW Regional Educational Laboratory. *Cross-Cultural Communication: An Essential Dimension of Effective Education, Table IV: Examples of Verbal and Nonverbal Communication Contrasts among Some African Americans and Some Anglo Americans,* at www.nwrel.org/cnorse/booklets/ccc/table4.html

11. King, J. *The Biology of Race.* New York: Harcourt Brace Jovanovich, 1971.

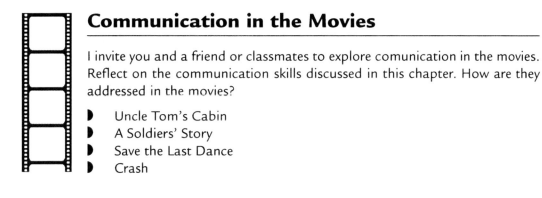

Communication in the Movies

I invite you and a friend or classmates to explore comunication in the movies. Reflect on the communication skills discussed in this chapter. How are they addressed in the movies?

- Uncle Tom's Cabin
- A Soldiers' Story
- Save the Last Dance
- Crash

Think About It → Write About It

Reflect on what you've just read. Now write what you are thinking.

_____

_____

_____

_____

_____

_____

_____

_____

_____

_____

_____

_____

_____

_____

_____

_____

_____

_____

_____

_____

_____

_____

_____

_____

Activity

"Is All That Passion Necessary?"

A. Ask the class if they have any examples of the differences in the way black people speak, compared to white people?

    1.   (There are differences in their posture and passion.)

    2.   i.e., Black people often tend to

        a.   use religious/spiritual terminology,

        b.   sound 'preachy',

        c.   be animated,

        d.   get confrontational,

        e.   be assertive, and

        f.   raise their voices.

    3.   i.e., White people seem less passionate, softer spoken, matter-of-fact and appear to be practical.

B. How can you as a public speaker use this information?

Chapter 8

Small Group Communication as a Social Concern

Key Terms

Small Groups	Group Cohesion
Group Norms	Homogeneous Groups
Explicit Norms	Heterogeneus Group
Implicit Norms	Roles
Group Dynamics	

Each semester, I have students work in small groups. Some groups work wonderfully together. Others fall apart before semester break. One spring, a young man named Ricky and several of his friends formed a group. Ricky was amazed at how his relationship with his friends changed when they became an organized working group. Ricky's journal entry, which follows, is an open letter to future students who find themselves communicating in small group scenarios. This is Ricky's viewpoint. As we go through the chapter on Small Group Communication, you will find useful tools to help you navigate through your small group experiences. And, hopefully, you never find yourself in Ricky's shoes.

Ricky's Story

This past semester I had the opportunity to work with a group named the Five Stars, which was later changed to the "Six Stars." At first, I found it a pleasure to work with those five individuals. The group appeared to be a very functional and well-organized group. When we were assigned a chapter to teach to the class, I knew that we would do our best to present the material in a fashionable manner. I knew everyone in the group, and I also knew that each person brought something unique and beneficial to the table.

Therefore, I knew that the presentation would be a success. Liza and I wrote most of the lines for the skit that our group performed as part of our chapter presentation. The other members of the group also contributed in their own special way. From my perspective, we still appeared to be a functional, well-organized group. But after the presentation, we became the "Six Slackers." At least that is what I thought. In actuality, it was like the Five Stars again and I was the Sun.

When it was time for us to do the group analysis that our professor assigned us, I was left behind like night leaves day when the sun sets. Like the sun the next morning, I am about to rise. So now I am rising to accept the fact that I really can't trust or rely on fellow classmates because they are all about self. I have learned something from each individual person in the group that will leave an impression in my head for a long time.

Starting with Freda, in the first group project, she was the one who always made suggestions when doing the project. She made sure that she was not left out and that everyone was comfortable with the presentation. On the second presentation things changed. She became about self and felt that there was no reason to keep group members informed. Being that I have three classes with her, I don't understand how she could tell our professor that she could never get in touch with me. She sees me at least three days out of the week. When I approached her about the presentation, she said, "we haven't met yet. But I'll let you know." I did not find out until the DUE date that the paper was due. And what makes it so bad, I still did not find out from my group. So I guess I was a bad judge of character. Hey, experience is a good teacher.

Roc, I really don't know what to say about him. I really did not know him before this class. After working in this group, I still don't know him. I really don't care to know him. Roc is a good worker, and he is the type of person that is willing to go the extra mile for the group. He is a good person to work with, because you know that he will get the job done.

Suez is the group member that was open-minded. She goes with the flow. She never had any complaints, but she made some very useful suggestions that kept the first presentation interesting.

Armani is a good worker who likes to have everything in order. Like Freda, she sometimes cares more for self than for the group. But, she is the first to apologize or to offer suggestions so that everyone in the group feels comfortable and included.

When we all started working together, Liza was a good group member. She was open for suggestions and she, like the rest, contributed valuable ideas. After the first presentation, things really changed with her. Every time I approached her about the upcoming project, she also said that she would call me to let me know what was going on with the meetings and everything. The last time I approached her about it, she said that the group had decided to **BS** the entire paper and presentation. She never told me what we were **BS**'ing about.

The remaining group members turned in the group analysis paper. But guess what? They did not put my name or Liza's name on the paper. Liza was outraged. She took matters into her own hands. She immediately went to our professor to plead her case. It was cool how she handled everything, because she also talked to our professor on my behalf.

When our professor agreed to give us an extension, Liza suggested that we each draft three pages and then combine those ideas so that we could turn in one paper. So I agreed to do the last three pages, and she would do the first three. That was all good with me. But every time I approached her in class, she said, "I have not done my three yet, but I'll call you today." I never got that phone call either.

The first week of class, our professor told us that by the end of the term some of us would experience major conflict within our groups. I was thinking, "I will not be in one of the groups that that happens to, because I am working with people that I pretty much know. But, only time will tell." And time did tell. I found that it is better to work with people that you don't know than to work with people that at one time you considered your friends. My friends were the first ones to stab me in the back. So for the next class that may be reading this, DO NOT WORK WITH ANYONE THAT YOU CONSIDER A FRIEND, BECAUSE BY THE END OF THE SEMESTER YOU WILL LOOK AT THEM IN A DIFFERENT LIGHT. Therefore resulting in you transforming from "the sixth star" to "The Sun," doing it by yourself for yourself.

"Excerpted from Ricky's Class Journal" Note: Ricky changed the names of his group members to protect the guilty.

Collections Don't Work

Does Ricky's story sound familiar? *What we have here is a failure to communicate.* This failure reaches beyond the interpersonal (one-to-one) level. Ricky's experience is a failure to communicate within a small group context. **Small groups** consist of three to five interdependent individuals who communicate with one another to accomplish a common goal. You and one other person are not a group. Although strong interpersonal skills are key to successfully working in small groups, there are other dynamics at play when three or more people are interacting to accomplish a goal.

In the small group context, members must be committed to accomplishing a shared goal. The members are interdependent in that they depend on each other in order to accomplish their shared goal. As Ricky did, we sometimes find ourselves in situations where people do not want to work together to accomplish the goal. When there is no desire or attempt to work together, the gathering of individuals is considered a **collection** (Wilson, 1999). It is not, by definition, a group.

Although small groups work toward a common goal, there may or may not be other similarities between group members. Small groups whose members have little or no demographic commonalties are **heterogeneous groups.** On the other hand, groups whose members share common interests, attitudes, levels of knowledge and other demographics are **homogeneous groups.**

Sean Jean Breaks the Explicit Norm

Groups have **norms** that regulate how members are expected to communicate and behave within the group context. Some norms are explicit and some are implicit. **Explicit norms** are rules of behavior that are expressed verbally or that may be put in writing. A young man recently explained how he lost money because he did not follow an explicit norm for his work group. The individual was suspended from work because his clothing was inappropriate. His Sean Jean sweat suit did not meet the standard for his work group. The explicit norm or written rule is that employees cannot wear athletic wear at the call center.

Implicit norms, on the other hand, are the understood and expected behaviors of the group. Each semester, my classrooms develop into formal learning groups. On the first day of class, students sit anywhere they want to sit. On the second day, they may or may not sit in the same seats that they sat in on the first day. But by the midterm, students have usually staked out their spaces and have what they call, "my seat." I never assign seats. I don't ever see the students discussing a seating arrangement. No, none of this takes place. Yet, the students expect to sit in their same seats. They respect each other's territories. They have an implied understanding about the seating arrangement.

Multiple Kinds of Groups

Groups vary in characteristics and concerns. In this text, we cover only five different types of groups: social groups, self-help groups, learning groups, service groups, and work groups.

Social groups seek to accomplish a recreational or social end. Essentially these groups want to have fun through sharing a common interest with others. The common interest can be any number of things, including a hobby, a sport, scholastic aptitude, or a profession. Social groups include fraternities, sororities, athletic teams, car clubs, motorcycle clubs, chess clubs, honors clubs, singing groups, and the list goes on.

Self-help groups provide support to individuals who need help dealing with some aspect of their personal lives. Also readily known as support groups, therapy groups, or encounter groups, self-help groups provide their members with the opportunity to gather and discuss their common problem, issue, or life circumstance. Self-help groups include Alcoholics Anonymous, Weight Watchers, Overeaters Anonymous and etc.

Learning groups enable individuals to enhance their knowledge and skills in a particular area. Members seek or share information. Have you ever participated in a study group? A college study group is a prime example of a group organized to provide members the opportunity to advance their knowledge. In addition to the college setting, learning groups can exist as faith-based study groups, groups of new employees in an orientation session, or seasoned employees in a training seminar.

Service groups provide their members with the opportunity to show goodwill. Like social groups, the members find satisfaction in helping each other as well as nonmembers. Like self-help groups, service groups may focus on one particular type of issue or problem. Service organizations such as the Lions Club often provide needy individuals with eyeglasses, hearing aids, and other supplies that will increase their quality of life. The National Organization of Women (NOW) and the National Association for the Advancement of Colored People (NAACP) are groups that provide services and a formal lobby for *marginalized* individuals.

Work groups focus on accomplishing specific goals or tasks for associations, companies, organizations, faith groups, and institutions. These groups may be established to perform their tasks routinely, or on an as needed basis. At some times in our lives, most of us will participate in some type of work group. I bet you already have. Have you ever served on a committee at your school or church? If so, then you have participated in a work group.

Committees are work groups that form as a result of the needs of a larger group or the needs of an individual in power. They function to take action, to report and to investigate. Committees that form and carry out a specific task within a given time are **ad hoc** committees. These committees disband when their business is done. A fraternity might form an ad hoc committee to *take an action* such as planning a car wash. The minister may ask for an ad hoc committee to *report* on the economic feasibility of expanding the mosque's community assistance programs.

In 1998, then-President Bill Clinton appointed a type of ad hoc committee to *investigate* race relations in the United States. Ad hoc committees that are appointed to investigate specific issues and that are expected to make recommendations based upon their findings are called **task forces.** The President's Initiative on Race Task Force determined that, "Our Nation still struggles with the impact of its past policies, practices, and attitudes based on racial differences. Race and ethnicity still have profound impacts on the extent to which a person is fully included in American society and provided the equal opportunity and equal protection promised to all Americans" (1998, p. 2). Ad hoc committees are no longer needed once their specific tasks are completed. Thus, the ad hoc committees disperse. In contrast, some committees remain active.

Standing committees form so that they can routinely carry out a specific function. These committees can exist as long as the institution exists. At my church, for example, there has always been a welcoming committee. The faces and names of the members have changed over time, but there has always been a group of people performing the welcoming function. The members of a standing committee may change, but somebody will always carry out that standing committee's specific function. This is the fundamental characteristic of standing committees.

In addition to committees, **teams** are also considered work groups. Teams are special kinds of work groups whose success is based on the resources contributed by the individual members. Think about your most basic notion of what constitutes a team. My mind immediately goes to athletic teams. If Michael Jordan, Scottie Pippin, Steve Kerr, and Dennis Rodman had been scrubs, the Chicago Bulls would have never accomplished the double-three-peat that they did. Similarly, if Kobe Bryant, Shaquille O'Neal, Rick Fox, Derek Fisher, and Robert Horry were short on athletic ability, there is a strong possibility that the Los Angeles Lakers would not have threatened the Bulls' championship record.

All groups want to be productive. That is the nature of groups—to accomplish a shared goal. Yet, there are dynamics that minimize a group's productivity and that interrupt the closeness of the individual members.

Fallen Star—A Problem with Cohesion

I am always amazed at how fast many pop, hip-hop, and R&B singing groups come and go. Members leave without hesitation. Usually these members lack a commitment to the collective identity of the group. They have a beef with management, and they bounce. Beyonce Knowles and Kelly Rowland should be members of Destiny's Children, not Destiny's Child. I can't count the number of members that Destiny's Child has had since the group's beginning. Most musical groups break up because they lack **cohesion,** a commitment and attraction to the collective identity of the group. When groups lack cohesion, something has interrupted the group's closeness. Members do not speak positively to each other, about each other, or about the group. Members no longer feel unified and proud to be a part of the group. The interruption in closeness that a group experiences may be due, in part, to a member no longer being attracted to the goal, no longer being attracted to other members, or to a member feeling that he is no longer being treated like a part of the group. Working groups that lack cohesion become less productive. Did Ricky's group lack cohesion?

Individual group members must remain attracted to the collective goal of the group so they do not lose the zest needed to accomplish the task. Also, members need to have a certain level of attraction to other members. No, I'm not saying that members must want to *get up* with each other. I am saying that members must be friendly enough that they can cooperate to achieve their end.

Cohesive groups are much more productive. They get more work done, more efficiently. However, too much cohesion in a group is not good. When there is too much closeness, group members may be less likely to see their collective errors. Yale University professor, Irving Janis (1977) developed the theory of **groupthink,** which essentially says that some groups are unable to rationally make decisions because individual group members are too close to each other. Individual members no longer think critically. They conform or choose a course of action because they like each other.

There are several factors that may lead to groupthink. Groups suffer from groupthink when they are *cut off from the larger society.* Cult members are a prime example. Jim Jones, David Koresh, and the Heaven's Gate group were all serrated from the world. The individual members of these groups failed to critically choose their course of action.

In addition, groups may suffer from groupthink when there is a lack of *ethical leadership.* In the cases of the Jonestown followers, the Branch Davidians, and the Heaven's Gate group, their leaders lacked impartial judgment. These authority figures led their members down a path of destruction.

Activity

Small Group Communication Self Reflection

This activity is designed to increase your awareness of small group as well as interpersonal dynamics. It will also help you analyze your own behaviors as you participate in small group interactions.

Reflect on two specific occasions where you have found yourself in group scenarios. One of these occasions should be an example of "a great group" experience. The second should be an example of "a really really poor group" experience. Compare and contrast the two experiences. In each case, discuss the following:

I.   The Interaction/Event
  a. What happened in sequence?
  b. How did the interaction begin?
  c. How did it end?
  d. What time did the interaction/meeting begin?

II.   The Others/People
   a.   Describe the person/people with whom you were interacting.
      i.   Discuss their gender, age, race, height, weight, physical condition, etc.
      ii.   Discuss those who impacted you most positively.
      iii. Discuss those who impacted you most negatively.
   b.   Describe the behaviors of those with whom you interacted.
      i.   Describe their verbal behaviors.
      ii.   Describe their nonverbal behaviors.
III. Your Feelings/Self
   a.   What did you feel?
   b.   What was happening at the time your feelings changed?
   c.   How did your body change (did your breathing change)?
   d.   What, if any, were your nonverbal behaviors during this particular time?
IV.   Why do you think you responded the way you did?
   a.   What experiences from your past may have led to your response to the event?
   b.   Were there obvious value, belief, norms, or language differences between you and those involved in the interaction?

Can't We All Just Get Along?

Conflict arises when the needs, ideas, and/or opinions of one or more group members are incongruent. Some type of conflict is bound to arise in the group context. With that being said, the question then becomes how to handle the conflict. It is important to realize that not all conflict is disruptive. Conflict can fuel some very energetic debates, yielding constructive results. When group members understand that conflict is natural, discussions are much more open. On the other hand, when group members view conflict as competition, discussions become battlegrounds.

In order to minimize conflict within a group, members should keep the discussions focused on the issues and not the individuals. Members should also be flexible enough so that they can see the others' points of view. The next time you encounter conflict within a group, address the needs of each party. Ultimately, you are striving to reach a mutually satisfying resolution.

Basic Problem-Solving

Committees, task forces, and teams must all solve some type of problem. As you know, it is not always easy to come up with a solution when you are communicating in a small group. Think about the last time you and your friends tried to solve the dilemma of which restaurant to eat at or which movie to see. How long did it take you to make your decision? There is a basic problem-solving model that will streamline the time and effort used in group problem-solving.

Basic Problem-Solving Model

I. **Define the problem.**
   A. Determine the impact of the problem. How does this problem effect people? Under what circumstance does this problem occur?
   B. Phrase the problem in the form of a question. Make sure your question solicits a specific answer. Stay away from questions that can be answered with a "yes" or "no" answer. Think of the question as either a question of fact, value, or policy. **Questions of fact** deal with whether something is true, or to what degree something is factual. **Questions of value** assess the worth of an idea, object, or individual. **Questions of policy** deal with how things "ought" to be.
   C. Define all relevant terms. You don't want to deal with semantic misunderstandings. Clear up definitions at the outset.
II. **Research and analyze the problem.**
   A. Determine if there has been prior research conducted on this problem.
   B. List all the topics that should be covered in order to reach the best solution.
   C. Gather needed information.
   D. Discuss the gathered information.
      1. State the topic to be discussed.
      2. Each member should report his or findings on this particular topic. No other topic can be discussed at this time.
      3. Ask for feedback on this topic.
      4. Summarize the relevant points pertaining to this topic.
      5. Move to the next topic and start the process all over again.
III. **Establish guidelines or rules that the group must follow in order to reach a decision.**
   A. Make checklist so that each group member is fully aware of the standards that they must follow. If a proposed solution does not meet the standards, it cannot be the accepted solution.
   B. Rank the standards so group members have a sense of which standard is most important to follow.
IV. **List and evaluate possible alternatives. Brainstorming** is a way to solicit alternatives. Members spontaneously and orally contribute a list of ideas. There is no evaluation of ideas that result from brainstorming. Some members may prefer to create

their list of ideas in a private manner. These members would prefer the Nominal Group Technique (NGT) as means of generating alternatives.

The **Nominal Group Technique** allows members to generate ideas silently and then have their ideas recorded on the board, the overhead, or a flipchart. Again, there is no evaluation of members' ideas, simply a listing. Individual members may vote for their top five choices. If these methods do not generate credible alternatives, the group can opt to try the **Combination Method** of generating alternatives. As its name claims, it is a combination of the oral style of brainstorming and the silent method of recording that is characteristic of the Nominal Group Technique.

A.   Slash and burn those alternatives that do not meet the standards.

B.   Combine like alternatives.

C.   Further reduce the list of alternatives by determining the strengths and weaknesses of each.

D.   Continue this process until the best alternative is reached.

V.   **Select the best alternative and implement it.**

I present this model in this very rough outline format so that it can function as an agenda for a problem-solving meeting. These steps serve to organize and direct the group's discussion, as well as to determine criterion for solving problems.

Problem Solving Case

Working in groups can be a pleasure. Yet, there are times when it can be discouraging. Small groups assigned to a complete task must perform in an organized manner. This means everything should be systematically organized and carried out. In class, you developed guidelines for how your group should carry out its business. That was the beginning of creating a systematic way of doing things.

Small group work is generally about solving some type of problem. A **problem** is simply defined as that which stands between us and our goal or objective. Often folks have problems identifying *the problem*. Frequently, groups waste time solving the spin-off problems, but do not focus on the core problem. I see the core problem like an illness and spin-off problems as symptoms. A student said the other day, "Well if you treat the symptoms, won't that solve the problem?" Another student quickly responded, "No, if you take a throat lozenge and it clears up your sore throat, you still haven't done anything about the bronchitis that caused the sore throat." This is true. Work on defining the problem.

Your task is to brainstorm a list of problems. Then you are to decide which problem is the core problem. Next, you are to research the problem. Find out as much about the potential harm of the problem in this case. After you are clear on the scope of the problem, you are to again brainstorm. This time you must come up with possible solutions to the problem. Are there criteria that these solutions must follow? If so, outline those guidelines or criteria before generating the list of solutions. Your criteria for the solution will help you weed out those proposed solutions that are not viable. Your next to final step in this assignment is to select a solution. Finally, you must come up with a plan to implement your solution.

This is your case.

The PlayHouse

Tony and Sharon are store managers for a trendy clothing franchise called The Playhouse. Estelle, their District Manager, confides in Tony that another manager, Jenny is about to be fired. Tony, Sharon and Jenny are all friends. They have worked together in some capacity for the past several years. After Tony hears that Jenny may be fired, she immediately calls Sharon. Sharon is outraged. Tony and Sharon debate about whether they should tell Jenny or not.

Your group is on the corporate communications team and you, too, hear about this scenario. How do you handle this situation with the information given?

Group Membership and Role Emergence

As we know, groups—whether large or small—are made up of individual group members who have come together around a common purpose. Athletic individuals may join to play sports. Individuals interested in social connections may join a fraternity or sorority. Those with political interests may run for office, hoping to be elected to student council, city council, or Congress. Regardless of the group's purpose, group members are motivated to join based on a variety of individual reasons. The reasons include:

1. **Attraction to Others in the Group**—Individuals may join groups solely because of physical attraction to other group members. They may also be attracted because of similarities in race, socioeconomic status or perceived likeness in attitudes, beliefs or personality traits. Members who are only attracted to a group because of its members are often not focused on the task of the group.

2. **Attraction to the Group's Activities**—People who are attracted to a group's activities may enjoy aspects of the tasks involved, but they may not truly value the group's primary goal. They may enjoy the social aspects of the group but may not wholeheartedly embrace the group's overall mission.

3. **Attraction to the Group's Goals**—Members who are attracted to a group's goals are often more highly committed to achievement and to getting along with other group members. One of the most important predictors of a group's suc-

cess is whether or not its members are attracted to the primary goals of the group.

4. **Attraction to Being Affiliated with the Group**—Some individuals join groups solely because they want to be associated with that group. They do not really care about the tasks or goals of the group, and they do not really want to get involved with the issues or other group members. They may occasionally attend group meetings. Members who join groups solely for reasons of affiliation will often present problems for the group.

5. **Attraction to Needs Outside of the Group**—Some members are attracted to groups for reasons not at all associated with the goals and tasks of the group. They may have no particular interest in the other group members but may join only to bolster their resumes or because it's a socially accepted thing to do. These members are often poor group members. They are often unreliable, may rarely attend meetings and/or may be disruptive if they do attend.

Individuals join groups for a variety of reasons. Therefore, collectively a given group's membership will represent a variety of interests, backgrounds, and personality traits. During the group process—as the group works to accomplish certain tasks and goals—the unique nature of each group member often becomes apparent. During this process, individuals will gravitate toward various **roles.** In the study of group process, the concept of **role** refers to the part that an individual plays within a group.

While experts have identified many different roles that can be played out in a group setting, it helps to understand the concept of role if we look at it in terms of two broad categories. Some roles are said to be formal. **Formal roles** are specifically assigned by the group and often carry a title like president, secretary, or chairperson. Of course, the group member would have to also accept the responsibility that goes along with the role. When a formal role is assigned and accepted by an individual, there is said to be **role stability.** In other words, all parties are clear about what is expected from the role. With a formal role, the role description and duties do not change no matter who fills the position.

Other roles are said to be informal. **Informal roles** are more naturally occurring and are based more on function (accomplishing a specific task) than position (overall governing of the group). For example, a person may attempt to provide **leadership** around working on a certain project—like heading up a car wash fundraiser—without holding a formal position within the organization. Informal roles are not always leadership positions, however. For example, if a group becomes engaged in a heated discussion, the function required may be that of a **tension reliever.** Someone may need to tell a joke or otherwise step in to lighten the mood if needed. Another function might be that a group member volunteer to serve as a **recorder** on occasion, in order to document important ideas that are being discussed. A final example might be when a group member who knows of information that would be of particular interest to the group serves as an **information provider.** While this list is not inclusive of all identified informal roles, know that it is up to the group members to decide whether or not they accept that individual taking on these roles. For example, while it may be important for a person who is funny to use humor when there is a point of high tension, group members will likely not appreciate a member who constantly clowns around and is never on task.

As we previously discussed, groups are most often successful when they are formed based on the members' desire to accomplish a common goal. That goal can be to play on a winning softball team or to raise $100,000 for an alumni fund drive; to tutor school children in order to help them learn to read or to encourage student activism in order to advance student rights on a college campus. Whatever the group's goal, the tactics used to reach it will vary from group to group and will change for each group over time. Using the examples above, a sports team may need to organize extra practices before a big tournament; a tutoring group may form a committee to design special study packages for students; a fund drive committee might require that teams of people organize a telemarketing campaign, or an on-campus student organization might form a task force to work on establishing a speakers' bureau.

Regardless of the group's overall mission, there will always be opportunities for group members to take on both formal and informal roles that can contribute to the group reaching its ultimate goal. Roles **emerge** over time in what has been characterized as a trial and error process. While individuals constantly have opportunities to take on new roles and challenges, it is ultimately up to the group whether or not they will be successful in continuing to play the role. Members will provide **feedback** on whether an individual's behaviors are acceptable.

Group Task Roles—Roles That Help Groups Achieve Their Goals

1. Initiator-contributor—This person initiates ideas and suggestions. This person is the creative thinker in a group. This function is performed by the leader when he or she introduces an issue.

2. Information seeker—This person asks for evidence that will allow judgment of the factual adequacy of ideas, may also seek information beyond what is available to the group.

3. Information giver—This person offers facts that are relevant to the task. This person has research skills, analytical ability and knowledge to provide accurate and concise data.

4. Opinion seeker—This person asks for clarification and input.

5. Opinion giver—This person offers analysis of the information being presented. This means that the person states beliefs or opinions about suggestions being made.

6. Elaboration-clarifier—This person may test understanding by asking questions.

7. Coordinator—This person tries to draw connections between what different members have said.

8. Diagnostician—This person analyzes and identifies task-related problems.

9. Orienter-summarizer—This is the person who brings the group back if they move too far off task.

10. Energizer—This person raises the level of enthusiasm for the group.

11. Procedural Assistant—This person may take on a variety of tasks. He or she assists the leader in making sure that the group has what it needs and that meetings run smoothly.

12. Secretary-recorder—This person serves as the "group memory." This person keeps track of what is going on in the meetings.

13. Evaluator-critic—The "critical thinker." This person critically analyzes ideas and suggests advantages, disadvantages, questions assumptions, etc.

Group Building and Maintenance Roles-Behaviors That Contribute to Group Cohesion

1. Supporter-encourager—This person offers warmth, solidarity, and recognition to the group's members.

2. Harmonizer—This person helps a group manage conflict.

3. Tension releaser—This person helps the group to relax.

4. Compromiser—This person compromises when it is necessary for group progress.

5. Gatekeeper—This person tries to make sure that all communication channels are open.

6. Feeling expresser—This person monitors the feelings, moods, and relationships in the group.

7. Standard setter—This person sets the standard for the group to achieve.

8. Follower—This person goes along with the movement of the group.

Self-Centered Roles—Roles That Focus on the Individual's Personal Agenda.

1. Blocker—This person prevents progress toward the group's goals by raising objections, rejecting others' ideas, or taking a negative stand on issues.

2. Aggressor—This person tries to enhance self by lowering the status of others in the group.

3. Deserter—This person withdraws from the group's deliberation in some way. The person may act indifferent, aloof, and stiffly formal.

4. Dominator—This person takes more than a fair share of the group's time.

5. Recognition seeker—This person attempts to call attention himself or herself in an exaggerated manner.

6. Confessor—This person presents personal difficulties and feelings to the group.

7. Playboy/playgirl-clown—This person is the one that "plays too much." When a person distracts the group from its task, the role becomes self-serving.

8. Special-interest pleader—This person speaks on behalf of an outside group, rather than the group of which he or she is a part, is pleading a special interest.

Adapted from Benne and Sheats in Wilson, G. (2002). Groups in context: Leadership and participation in small groups (6th ed). New York: McGraw-Hill.

Improving the Jury System: Reducing Jury Size

Margo Hunter

Within the last several years there has been increasing concern over the rising costs of California's legal system. Many within and outside of the legal community have focused their attention on the issues of caseload volume, delay and congestion within California courts as a result of the rising number of civil and criminal cases. These mounting concerns have spawned a growing movement for court reform whose aim is to increase efficiency within the legal system, thereby reducing the costs of maintaining the system.

One area targeted for reform is the jury system, and, in particular, the size of civil and criminal juries. Currently, California permits the parties to agree to fewer than twelve jurors in civil cases. In criminal trials, felony trials are heard by a jury composed of twelve members; misdemeanor trials can be heard by fewer than twelve jurors if the parties agree.

The proposal to reduce jury size is aimed at increasing efficiency within the jury system. Many scholars and experts within the legal community believe that a jury composed of fewer members will take less time to deliberate. As a result, trials will take less time and more cases can be heard. However, there is evidence that decreasing jury size may adversely affect jury deliberations and the quality of the verdicts they render.

I.   Background and Function of the Traditional Rule

The twelve-person jury dates to early English common law. Jury size in England was fixed at twelve persons by the middle of the fourteenth century. By the eighteenth century, the same was true of the American colonies. Although many theories have been advanced to explain the origin of the twelve-person jury, it is still unclear how this requirement gained importance.

As the United States Supreme Court made clear in a series of cases beginning in 1970, the federal Constitution does not require juries to have twelve members in all cases. The practice of having twelve jurors was apparently an "historical accident unrelated to the great purposes which gave rise to the jury in the first place."[1] According to the Court, the real test of the constitutionality of jury size is whether jury size affects the essential function of the jury.

That essential function, according to the court, is to ensure that cases are resolved using the common sense judgment of the community through community participation. This means that the jury must be large enough to do the following: 1. Promote deliberation free from outside attempts of intimidation, and 2. Provide a fair possibility for obtaining a representative cross-section of the community.

Thus, states are free to have juries as small as six, so far as the federal Constitution is concerned.[2] Any number below six, however, would be unconstitutional, because the jury would then be too small to meet the requirement that there be a lair chance that a cross-section of the community will be represented on the jury.[3] Moreover, states cannot circumvent this limit by allowing six person juries to deliver non-unanimous verdicts in criminal cases.[4]

II.   Reducing the Size of the Jury

A.   Advantages of Reducing Jury Size

The main advantages of reducing the size of juries are as follows: Smaller juries would cost less to maintain than larger juries.

The amount of time spent on the voir dire[5] process would decrease because fewer jurors would be needed.

Deliberation time would decrease, and as a result, the jury system would become more efficient because more cases could be heard.

B.   Disadvantages of Smaller Juries

Even though it is constitutionally acceptable to reduce the jury's size to any number above six, opponents argue that this would result in the following adverse consequences:

Juries with less than twelve persons are less representative, and thus, fewer voices in the community are represented.

The quality of jury deliberations would be adversely affected by reducing the jury's size.

Jury awards will be more erratic.

C. **Studies of Jury Size**

Most of the empirical research on the effects of reducing jury size was completed during the 1970s. In fact, the Supreme Court relied heavily upon several of these studies in deciding a number of the jury size cases. However, many of these studies have been criticized for their failure to provide evidence about the quality and reliability of decisions by six-person juries.

Despite this, many researchers do agree that a reduction in jury size would reduce the time and expense of conducting jury trials, and therefore make them more efficient in the long run. In support of this conclusion, researchers agree that when all other factors are equal, smaller juries work faster and more efficiently than larger groups. Another positive result of using smaller juries is that they will help cure some the problems concerning large caseloads and backlogs. If jury size is reduced, the same jury pools which are now used to select juries for one trial could theoretically be used to seat juries for two trials. Many proponents also contend that the use of six-person juries would be less burdensome to potential jurors because quicker deliberation means less time taken off work.

Other research has challenged the idea that six-person juries are more efficient and less costly than twelve-person juries. Many studies have concluded that the amount of time used for voir dire for both sized juries is the some. Moreover, a 1971 study estimated that between 1.5 to 3 percent the federal judiciary budget and an infinitely small fraction of the entire United States budget would be saved by reducing jury size to six.

In addition, many researchers argue that despite the possible benefits, six-person juries adversely affect the composition of the jury and the quality of jury deliberations. As a general rule of statistics, the smaller a sample size is, the less representative it will be. By analogy then, one could expect that a six-person jury would be less representative than a twelve-person jury. Therefore, many argue that six-person juries fail to provide a representative cross-section of the community.

A 1974 statistical study found that in a community with a 10 percent minority population, one or more minorities would be represented on 72 percent of the twelve-person juries; however, on a six-person jury, only 47 percent of the juries co be expected to contain one or more minorities.[6] Studies have also own that women may also be less represented on six-person juries. However, the representative cross-section requirement established by the Supreme Court has been held to only apply to the jury panel, and not the actual jury selected from the panel.

Many studies have also examined whether there is a qualitative difference between the jury deliberations of six- and twelve-person juries. First, several studies suggest that twelve-person juries have a better collective memory than six-person juries because a larger group size increases the chances that someone will remember a fact. As a result, the quality of decision-making may be improved. Second, many researchers agree that twelve-person juries communicate more, for longer periods of time, than six-person juries. Third, several researchers argue that a persuasive, uncompromising juror has a greater impact on a six-person jury than a larger jury, and he or she is able to exert more influence on a smaller jury. However, other researchers have found that there is no discernible difference between the influence of such a juror on either sized jury.

Social science researchers have also attempted to document the differences in outcomes and verdicts between six- and twelve-person juries. Most researchers agree that the jury awards of six-person juries are more likely to be erratic because as is true in the field of statistics, the margin of error increases as the sample size decreases. However, there basic agreement ends. There is a lack of consensus on whether the outcomes of verdicts reached by six- and twelve-person juries differ. Several studies have concluded that there is no significant difference in the outcomes reached by six- and twelve-person juries. In contrast, other studies have shown that criminal defendants are more likely to be convicted by a six-person jury than a twelve-person jury.

1. **The Federal Judicial Conference Study**

    On December 13, 1994 the Committee on Rules of Practice and Procedure of the Judicial Conference of the United States issued a report surveying the literature on jury size. The Conference recommended that Congress amend Federal Rule of Civil Procedure 48 which permits federal district courts to use six-person juries in federal civil cases. The Committee mode the following findings:

    Twelve-person juries are more stable and deliberative.

    Larger juries were more representative of the interests of minorities than six-person juries.

    Although the monetary savings of using smaller juries were significant, these savings were small when compared to the overall judiciary budget.

    The reduction in court time from using six-person juries was not that substantial.

    As a result of these findings, the Committee concluded that the savings did not compensate for the decrease in stability and the effects on jury community representation.

2. **National Center for State Courts Study of Los Angeles County**

    In April of 1990, the National Center for State Courts produced a study for the Judicial Council of California comparing the performance of eight- and twelve-person juries based on data from four municipal courts within Los Angeles County. The study examined the effects of jury size on a variety of areas, including: cross-sectional representation of the community; whether verdicts tended to favor plaintiffs or defendants; size of awards; accuracy, consistency and reliability of awards; time required for impanelment, trial and deliberation; and public and private costs of the jury. The following results were found:

Smaller juries were more likely to be less representative of African Americans. Otherwise, all of the juries were very representative of the jury panels from which they were chosen, including Hispanics. That is, 43 percent of the eight-person juries contained no African Americans, or only one, but only 17 percent of the twelve-person juries had none or one African American. Although several causes were examined, the main factors affecting minority representation were jury size and the number of African Americans on the panels from which the jurors were selected. No real difference was found between the verdicts reached by eight- and twelve-person juries. However, the same was not true for jury awards. The awards of eight-person juries were higher than the twelve-person jury awards. The study found several factors, in addition to jury size, that explain this difference. As a result, the study could not verify, that jury size caused this difference in the size of awards. The data revealed no difference in terms of the accuracy of the verdict/award between eight- and twelve-person juries. Accuracy was based on the judge's assessment of the strength of the evidence presented. Moreover, no real difference was found in terms of reliability. Differences were found for the time required for jury impanelment, trial and deliberations; however, with the exception of the amount of time required far jury selection, these differences were the result of case characteristics and not jury size. The use of the eight-person jury did result in savings. These savings are the result of having fewer persons involved. Moreover, the study found that the smaller juries resulted in projected savings of $120 in juror fees per trial. Smaller juries also resulted in employer savings of $2,000 per trial.

III. Jury Size in Other Jurisdictions

Statistics compiled by the Conference of State Court Administrators and the National Center for State Courts based on state court organization reveal that as of 1993, eleven states allow the use of juries composed of less than twelve in felony trials to some extent.

Arizona: Permits its the use of eight-person juries except in capital cases or when the possible sentence is thirty years or more.

Connecticut: Permits the use of six-person juries, except in capital cases which require twelve-person juries unless the defendant agrees otherwise.

Florida: Permits six-person juries to hear felonies, except in capital cases which require a twelve-person jury.

Indiana: Permits six-person juries to hear felonies in municipal and county court, but not at the circuit or superior court levels.

Kansas: Felony trials must start with a twelve-member jury.

Kentucky: Permits six-person juries to hear felonies at the district level, but not the circuit level. Louisiana: Requires the use of twelve-person juries when punishment necessarily is confinement at hard labor, but uses six jurors if the possible punishment may be confinement at hard labor.

Massachusetts: Permits six jurors at the Boston Municipal court and the district court levels.

Utah: Requires eight person juries and makes no exception for capital cases.

Washington: Allow for a jury of less than twelve but with different restrictions: In Washington, a defendant may elect to have the case tried before a six-member jury, except in capital cases.

Wisconsin: In Wisconsin, both parties may agree to any number less than twelve.

The remaining states and the District of Columbia require juries of twelve members for felony trials. In criminal misdemeanor trials and civil trials, more states permit juries of less than twelve members.

References

Abramson, Jeffrey. *We, the Jury: The Jury System and the Ideal of Democracy.* Basic Books, 1994.

Amar, A. R. "Edward L. Barrett, Jr. Lecture on Constitutional Law: Reinventing Juries: 10 Suggested Reforms." 28 *U. C. Davis L. Rev.* 1169 (Summer, 1995).

Augelli, A. T. "Six-Member Juries in Civil Actions in the Federal Judicial System." 3 *Seton Hall L. Rev.* 281 (1972).

Bermant, G. and R. Coppock. "Outcome of Six- and Twelve-Member Jury Trials: An Analysis of 128 Cival Cases in the State of Washington." 48 *Wash. L. Rev.* 593 (1973).

Bogue, A. W. and T. G. Fritz. "The Six-Man Jury." 17 *S. Dak. L. Rev.* 385 (1972).

Bureau of Justice Statistics. State Court Organizations 1993. Washington, D.C.: U. S. Department of Justice, 1995.

Comment, "The Impact of Jury Size on the Court System." Loy. L.A. L. Rev. 1103 (1979).

Committee on Rules of Practice and Procedure of the Judicial Conference of the United States. "Background Materials on Jury Size" (December 13, 1994).

Diamond, Shari Seidman. "What Jurors Think: Expectations and Reactions of Citizens Who Serve as Jurors." In Robert El Litan, ed., Verdict: Assessing the Civil Jury System. Washington, D.C.: The Brookings Institution, 1993.

Eakin, B. A. "An Empirical Study of the Effect of Leadership Influence on Decision Outcome in Different Sized Jury Panels," *Kansas Journal of Sociology* 11 (1975), 109.

Friedman, H. "Trial by Jury: Criteria for Convictions, Jury Size, and Type I and Type II Errors," *The American Statistician* 26 (1972), 21–23.

Gelfand, A. and J. Solomon. "Considerations in Building Jury Behavior Models and in Comparing Jury Schemes: An Argument in Favor of 12-Member Juries," *Jurimetrics Journal* 17 (1977), 292.

Hans, Valerie P. and Neil Vidmar. *Judging the Jury.* New York: Plenum Press, 1986.

Hastie Reid, Steven Penrod and Nancy Pennington. *Inside the Jury.* Cambridge, Mass.: Harvard University Press, 1983.

Institute of Judicial Administration. "A Comparison of Six- and Twelve-Member Juries in New Jersey Superior and County Courts." (1972).

Keele, Lucy M., "An Analysis of Six vs. 12-Person Juries," *Tenn. B. J.,* Jan.–Feb. 1991, at 32, 33.

Kerr, N. L., and R. J. MacCoun. "The Effects of Jury Size and Polling Method on the Process and Product of Jury Deliberations." *Journal of Personality and Social Psychology,* 48 (1985), 349–363.

Lermack, P. "No Right Number—Social Science Research and the Jury Size Cases," 54 *N.Y. Univ. L. Rev.* (1979), 951–976.

Mills, L. R. "Six-Member and Twelve-Member Juries: An Empirical Study of Trial Results," *U of Mich. J. of Law Reform* 6 (1973), 671.

National Center for State Courts. "A Comparison of the Performance of Eight- and Twelve-Person Juries." (April 1990).

Pabst, William R. "Statistical Studies of the Costs of Six-Man Versus Twelve-Man Juries," *Wm. & Mary L. Rev.* 14 (1972), 326.

Pabst, William R. "What Do Six-Member Juries Really Save?" *Judicature* 57 (1973), 6.

Powell, D. M. "Reducing the Size of Juries," *U. of Mich. J. of Law Reform* 5 (1971), 87.

Roper, R. T. "Jury Size—Impact on Verdicts Correctness," *American Politics Quarterly* 7 (1979), 438–452.

Roper, R. T. "Jury Size and Verdict Consistency—A Line Has to Be Drawn Somewhere," *Law & Society Review* 14 (1980), 977–995.

Roper, R. T. "The Effect of a Jury's Size and Decision Rule on the Accuracy of Evidence Recall," *Social Science Quarterly* 62 (2) (1981), 352.

Saks, Michael J. *Jury Verdicts: The Role of Group Size and Social Decision Rule.* Lexington, Mass.: D. C. Heath and Co., 1977.

Saks, Michael J. "If There Be a Crisis, How Shall We Know It?" *Md. L. Rev.* 46 (1986), 63.

Saks, Michael J. "Ignorance of a Science is No Excuse," *Trial,* Nov.–Dec. 1974, at 18.

Scheiber, Harry N. "Innovation, Resistance, & Change: A History of Judicial Reform and the California Courts, 1960–1990," *S. Cal. L. Rev.* 66 (July, 1993), 2049.

Snortum, J. R., et al. "The Impact of an Aggressive Juror in Six- and Twelve-Member Juries." *Crim. Justice & Behavior* 3 (3) (1976), 355.

Tanford, S. and S. Penrod. "Computer Modeling of Influence in the Jury: The Role of the Consistent Juror." *Social Psychology Quarterly* 46 (3) (1983), 200.

Thompson, E. "What Is the Magic of '12'?" 10 Judges Journal 88 (1971).

Van Dyke, Jon M. *Jury Selection Procedures: Our Uncertain Commitment to Representative Juries.* Cambridge, Mass.: Ballinger Publishing, 1977.

Wiehl, L. L. "The Six Man Jury." *Gonzaga L. Rev.* 4 (1968) 35.

Zeisel, Hans. " . . . And Then There Were None: The Diminution of the Federal Jury." *U. Chi. L. Rev.* 38 (1971), 710.

Zeisel, Hans. "The Warning of the American Jury," *A.B.A. J.* 58 (1972), 367.

Notes

1.   Williams v. Florida, 399 U.S. 78 (1970). In 1973, the Court held that juries in civil cases in federal court could also consist of as few as six jurors. Colgrove v. Battin, 413 U.S. 149 (1973).

2.   Williams v. Florida 399 U.S. 78 (1970).

3.   Ballew v. Georgia, 435 U.S. 223 (1978).

4.   Burch v. Louisiana, 441 U.S. 130 (1979).

5.   Voir dire is the process by which the court, or counsel, ask questions of potential jurors in order to determine if the juror is capable of judging the evidence objectively and impartially.

6.   Michael J. Saks, "Ignorance of Science is No Excuse," Trial, Nov.–Dec. 1974, at 19; Hans Zeisel, "The Waning of the American Jury," 58 A.B.A. J. 367, 368 (1972).

References

Janis, I. L. *Victims of Group-Think*. Boston: Houghton-Mifflin, 1977.

One America in the 21st Century: The President's Initiative on Race. (1998). Retrieved April 1, 1999, from the World Wide Web: *http://www.whitehouse.gov/Initiatives/OneAmerica/america.html*

Wilson, G. L. *Groups in Context: Leadership and Participation in Small Groups* 5th ed. Boston. McGraw-Hill College, 1999.

Wilson, G. *Groups in Context: Leadership and Participation in Small Groups,* 6th ed. New York: McGraw-Hill, 2002.

Communication in the Movies

I invite you and a friend or classmates to explore comunication in the movies. Reflect on the communication skills discussed in this chapter. How are they addressed in the movies?

▶   Coach Carter
▶   Mighty Ducks
▶   Remember the Titans
▶   Jackson 5: The American Dream

Name _____   Date _____

Section _____

Think About It → Write About It

Reflect on what you've just read. Now write what you are thinking.

_____

_____

_____

_____

_____

_____

_____

_____

_____

_____

_____

_____

_____

_____

_____

_____

_____

_____

_____

_____

_____

_____

_____

_____

Activity

The "Eggs" a-llent Egg Protector

1. Provide the following materials for each group:
    a. One raw egg
    b. Two paper towels
    c. Two pipe cleaners
    d. One full roll of masking tape
    e. Two index cards
    f. Three tongue depressors
    g. One piece of bubble gum
    h. Two markers
    i. One small poster board
2. Each group is to design a contraption that will protect a raw egg when dropped from approximately eight (8) feet high to the ground, using ONLY the materials provided.
    a. Additionally, each group is to develop a commercial/jingle to advertise their newly created egg contraption.
    b. Each group will perform their commercial/jingle and then demonstrate their product. (Usually a student will stand in a chair and drop the egg, protected in their contraption, from about eight feet high.)
    c. After each group has demonstrated their product, share the experiences working in the small group.

Chapter 9

Leadership Styles: Gender and Cultural Differences

Key Terms

Accomodation

Authoritarian Leaders

Avoidance

Collaboration

Competition

Compromise

Democratic Leaders

Laissez-Faire Leaders

Leadership

Leadership Styles

Gender Traits

This chapter explores research concerning the differences between woman and men leadership styles as well as those of African American women. We explore the similarities and differences that exist with gender in leadership characteristics, styles, and evaluations, and determine how or if these similarities and differences affect or influence the effectiveness of these leaders. Our research shows that women and men differ in the type of leadership roles they undertake within work groups. Men exhibit more overall leadership and task leadership characteristics, while women exhibit more social leadership characteristics. Men and women have various leadership styles. From our research, women in leadership positions receive greater negative evaluations than do men in comparable positions. Using conflict management as a basis for the study of gender differences, men are more competitive than women, and women are more accommodating than men. We pay particular attention to interpersonal communication skills in the area of conflict management. We look at how these leaders reward and reprimand individuals within their organizations. We see that society influences the roles that leaders take, especially when gender is taken into consideration.

Leadership: A Breakdown

Let's look at specific terminology associated with Leadership. A *leader* as defined by Bennis (1989) is a person(s) who shares some, if not all of the following ingredients: 1. *Guiding vision* of what they want to accomplish, 2. *Passion* for promises of life, combined with a very particular passion for a vocation, a profession, a course of action, and 3. *Integrity* which consists of self-knowledge, candor, and maturity.

If you ask five people to define leader and/or leader, you could possibly receive five different answers. Leadership gurus Ken Blanchard and Mark Miller, authors of the New York Best Seller, *The Secret,* say that great leaders SERVE. SERVE is an acronym for:

▶ See the Future
  • A great leader must have vision for the future.

▶ Engage and Develop Others
  • A great leader must have the right people around him- or herself in order to accomplish the goal for the future.

▶ Reinvent Continuously
  • A great leader:
    ■ must constantly learn about self, others and the world;
    ■ must constantly re-evaluate and look for better ways to do current tasks, and finally;
    ■ must not allow "the current what is" to limit "the what can be."

▶ Value Results and Relationships
  • A great leader challenges as well as supports those who he or she leads.

▶ Embody the Values
  • A great leader walks the walk and talks the talk, i.e., the leader models the core values of the culture.

Peter Senge (1990), explains:

"Our traditional views of leaders—as special people who set the direction, make the key decisions, and energize the troops—are deeply rooted in an individualistic and non systemic worldview. Especially in the West, leaders are *heroes*—great men (and occasionally women) who "rise to the fore" in times of crises. Our prevailing leadership myths are still captured by the image of the captain of the cavalry leading the charge to rescue the settlers from the attacking Indians. (p. 340)"

There are multiple versions of leadership that must be considered in our contemporary society. If we look at leaders only as the people sitting behind the executive's desk or only as the people standing behind the political or religious podiums our examples will be limited. Most of us have the capacity to lead.

If you look at the current leadership literature, you will find that there are more definitions written than you have time to read in a semester. I find that everyone wants to get on the "leadership" bandwagon. There are videos, books, and magazines devoted to the topic. There are degrees in leadership. Do these academic programs teach one how to have "guiding vision"? Do they teach integrity?

I asked students in one of my introductory communication classes what they thought about leaders. Specifically, I asked each of them to list five characteristics of a good leader. The students used Blackboard to post their lists and to discuss each others'. Some of their responses are printed here. These entries have been edited only for grammar. Here is what your peers say about leadership. Would your lists resemble those printed here? What would be different and why?

Five Characteristics of a leader:
1. Positive view of life—should not think in a negative way about things
2. Teamwork—should always be willing to work with others and get other points of view
3. Initiative—should be willing to take the first action when it comes to a problem
4. Problem-solving skills—should be able to solve problems that may arise
5. Responsibility—should be responsible enough to lead others so others will look up to them

---

1. A positive attitude
2. Listens, comprehends, then speaks
3. Takes chances and risk when everyone else seems to bashful
4. Goes over and beyond in their own little ways
5. They recognize themselves and others for a job well done when they have done their best whether they win or lose.

Confidence—if a leader is unsure about his/her self then they are most likely incapable of directing others
Goals/Objective—a leader must have some type of cause, vision, or objective
Charisma—able to appeal and persuade others
Decision Maker—able to work through problems
Passionate—Believes in cause

Vision:
A leader must have vision because without vision, you can't see yourself being successful. As a leader you should learn to communicate your vision to the people who you want to follow you.

Passion:
Passion is a key part of becoming a leader because it inspires them take on new challenges.

Decision Maker:
Shows whether a leader is quick, committed, analytical, and thoughtful.

Initiative:
Show a willingness to share opinions and be capable of making changes toward improvements.

Character:
Shows whether a leader has strengths and limitations.

---

1. Someone that can be a good role model for children because they are the future.
2. Someone with a great personality and is able to speak to you in a respectful way.
3. Someone who has book smarts and common sense.
4. Someone who looks presentable (dresses neatly, and try to look their best when out in public).
5. Very knowledgeable about their job and how to handle things.

---

1. **Decision Maker**—a leader should be able to make decisions that will benefit everyone that is involved in the group; they should make the best decisions in difficult circumstances
2. **Listener**—a leader should listen to all input that group members have to offer
3. **Set Goals and Objectives**—a leader should have a plan; he/she should set goals and objectives
4. **Honesty**—a leader should tell the truth at all times and lying just makes situations harder
5. **Self-Control**—leaders should control themselves by being in a high position; they should not get "big headed" because they have some type of authority

---

The five specific character traits I feel a leader should be:

—Confident—They should believe in themselves. Believe that they have what it takes to have a positive impact on someone's or a group of people's lives.

—Intelligent—They should be smart enough to make good decisions and overcome certain obstacles by thinking logically.

—Poise—They should always stay calm and not break under even the most extreme pressure.

—Dependable—They should be easy to reach and always there for their fellow peers. People should be able to count on them for help.

—Hard working—They should do everything to the best of their ability and be relentless towards achieving the goals that they have set for themselves.

5 traits that I think a good leader should have:

1. **Role Model:** I think the person should be a role model, for not just young kids but for all ages. They should be able to motivate people in any form or fashion, to help them and guide them in anyway that the person may need them for.

2. **Great speaker:** The leader should have great speaking skills, so that the persons that they are leading, will know in their mind that they have a good leader and knows what the leader is talking about and will believe them.

3. **Great Character:** The leader should have nothing negative about them or their appearance. They should have great qualities as a person such as being sweet, loving, and caring.

4. **Active:** The leader should go out and do different things for the community to help anyone they can, and stay active as long as they can so that they may lead other people into doing what they are doing to help others in this world.

5. **Appearance:** The leader should have a excellent appearance, meaning they should be presentable to all audiences at all times. No one wants to have a leader that looks like a bum all the time.

---

1. The first characteristic that a leader must have is vision. Leaders must have a clear sense of where they want to go and how they intend to get there. They have to create change.

2. The second characteristic that a leader must have is excellent communication skills. Leaders must be able to convey their ideas to different individuals and adjust their styles to meet the needs of the people they lead.

3. The third characteristic that a leader must have is integrity. Leaders must have integrity so their followers will have trust in them.

4. The fourth characteristic that a leader must have is faith. Leaders must have faith in themselves, as well as in others.

5. The fifth and final characteristic that a leader must have is motivation. Leaders must have motivation, so that they can motivate their followers.

---

1. A leader must be *open-minded*—They have to be open to other people's ideas and thoughts before they can express the voice of others. If they are going to have one voice, it needs to be the voice of the people.

2. *A leader must be strong*—In the face of adversity they cannot back down. They have to stand for what they believe is right even when there are people who doubt their power.

3. A leader must be *persistent*—If there is an issue they are trying to get across they must continuously tell people how they feel. If they give up even when people don't seem like they understand, the leader must help them to understand.

4. A leader must be a *people person* (sociable)—They have to get along with people. People have to be comfortable enough to come and express their problems with the leader.

5. Most importantly a leader must be *CONFIDENT*—The leader has to believe in him/herself. If a person doesn't believe in him/herself no one else will believe in that person.

First of all a person can't lead if there is no one to follow. The first characteristic of a leader is to be a **good communicator.** This means they are able to intelligently communicate with others. They should be able to respond to the harshest criticism with the utmost respect. A leader must also listen to the opinions of others and take them into consideration. By being a good communicator they empower others to take charge the main component of leading, to have influence on followers.

A good leader should have **integrity.** They need to be an honest and trustworthy person. A leader should establish good moral ethics. Leaders lead others and you don't want someone leading you down the wrong path. They should want to help you and not do anything that will hurt you, them or the cause of the organization. People can't follow someone whom they cannot trust.

Passion and commitment motivates a leader to achieve success through all obstacles. People love to follow someone full of passion and are influenced by them. A passionate person can create a good atmosphere. With a good working climate whether on an actual job or for a non-profit organization, workers will work more efficiently, leading to more productivity.

Then there is the **vision.** A concrete plan needs to be made and executed. "Keep your eye on the prize." You need to know the cause, how to obtain it, and then just do it. This includes having good organizational skills.

Lastly but definitely not least, is to **know yourself.** Just to reiterate what I stated earlier the whole point of a leader is to lead others in the right direction. A person can't help others without first being able to help better herself. She should know her strengths and weaknesses. She should be able to work as a team. Her weaknesses are someone else's strength and vice versa. A leader must be confident and have charisma. She should be confident but not cocky.

I go back to one of my original questions and ask, "Can we teach leadership characteristics?" If we can't, someone had better speak up now. Americans have spent billions of dollars trying to learn what it takes to be a good leader. I encourage you to look at the various pieces that cover this area.

Bennis and many of the students mention that a leader should have a vision. I agree; a vision is critical. I think leaders must first have a clear concept of "self as a leader." What kind of leader are you? What type of leadership style do you have?

Leadership styles are like personality types: they differ from individual to individual. **Leadership style** is generally about control and is essentially the manner in which the leader exerts control over the group.

You may be the kind of leader that wants to direct every activity. You may want to micro-manage every detail of planning the sorority car wash. You have to see everyone's list of items and must make sure that the items are completed to your satisfaction. If this sounds like you, you are an authoritarian leader. **Authoritarian leaders** strive to have the greatest control over the group and its members. Authoritarian leaders are prone to hold the "My way or no way attitude." Authoritarian leaders are usually experts in a particular area; at least that would be the expectation of a person who exerts this type of control or power. An authoritarian style may work well when the group is off track or when the group needs to complete a task quickly.

Maybe you are the person who lets everyone speak. You value others' contributions and would not dare make a decision without everyone's input. If this sounds like you, you are probably a democratic leader. **Democratic leaders** value the input of members in the group. These leaders are not pushovers by any means. They keep the meetings moving productively, but build time in for everyone to present their views. They are not egotistical. Democratic leaders see leadership potential in each person in the group; hence, solicit committee chairs and etc., to lead specific projects.

When your group project is assigned, do you take the names and phone numbers of the people in the group? Then do you call the individual members that night and ask, "When can you meet to go over that project for Dr. Silverthorne's class?" You set the meeting. If that is the last time they hear from you until the day of the presentation, you have exhibited laissez-faire leadership traits. **Laissez-faire** leaders don't lead much at all; they sit back and let the group self-direct. This leader may call the group together, but that's about it. The group and individual members are left to set their own direction.

Effective leaders should be strong communicators. As you have learned this semester, communication covers a multitude of areas. That means that an effective leader should be competent in public speaking; should have strong interpersonal skills; should have high intercultural aptitude, should be able to handle conflict and should have a strong understanding of self.

Effective leaders should provide clear direction to the group. If people do not know where you are going, it makes it difficult for them to follow you. Set measurable goals and objectives so you know what you want to achieve. Develop a plan and articulate it to the members of the group. If you are a democratic leader, you will ask for other members' input. Now that others feel valued and feel like they have had a part in developing the plan, they are more likely to be supportive and participative.

Student Voices

G: I believe that one is able and willing to lead with no followers. Jesus, technically, did not have any followers 24 hours before he was crucified. Peter denied him, Judas betrayed him, and the others fell asleep in the garden (read your word it will bless you). Anyways, what I am trying to say is that leading when it seems you have nobody to instruct or lead may make you an even better leader. I demonstrate that a person is so committed to a cause that they are willing to walk alone than to settle for an objective or belief that they do not agree with.

D: Amen to that Bruh! Most excellent leaders start off without followers. Take me for example. I have devoted my life to Christ, I felt alone, like I am the only one who desires to be like him. Slowly but surely I have friends that are changing some of their ways.

Gender Traits: It's a Man/Woman Thang

This chapter moves to a deeper discussion of how men and women differ when each is in the leadership role. This information has social significance because we still live in a country where gender matters. I suppose we must identify and work from the differences if we are to bridge the gaps that exist. The cursory discussion is a beginning to that end. Let's first look at what we define as gender traits. Brookbank (1991) says gender traits are those personal characteristics that have been historically, culturally, and socially analogous with a specific gender. Examples of masculine gender traits include assertiveness, self-confidence, personal courage, organizational loyalty, and discipline, just to name a few. Examples of feminine gender traits include compassion, nurturance, organizational skills, and attention to "housekeeping" details, just to name a few."

How are men and women different with regards to leadership? First, women and men differ in the type of leadership roles they undertake within work groups. Men exhibit more overall leadership and task leadership characteristics. Women, on the other hand, exhibit more social leadership characteristics (Eagly and Karau, 1991 as cited in Kreitner and Kinicki).

Second, men and women have various leadership styles. Women utilize a greater democratic or participative style as opposed to men, who utilize a greater autocratic and directive leadership style (Eagly, Karau, and Johnson, 1992 as cited in Kreitner and Kinicki).

Finally, women in leadership positions received greater negative evaluations than do men in comparable positions. There is a significant difference in the leadership style of a woman and the leadership style of a men (Eagly, et al. 1992 as cited in Kreitner and Kinicki). Society has had an impact on these differences between women and men. The values and traditions of society are still defined by the concepts of "masculine" and "feminine."

Respond to the following?

"It would be futile to attempt to fit women into a masculine pattern of attitudes, skills, and abilities, and disastrous to force them to suppress their specifically woman characteristics and abilities by keeping up the pretense that there are no differences between the sexes?" (Columbia Dictionary of Quotations, Microsoft Bookshelf, 1998, CD-ROM).

The National Women's Law Center Findings

The National Women's Law Center's investigation conclusively demonstrates that pervasive sex segregation in vocational and technical programs—with girls predominantly enrolled in "traditionally woman" programs and boys primarily participating in "traditionally men" courses—exists nationwide. The Center sought data from every state and the District of Columbia and examined in depth the enrollment patterns in vocational programs in 12 states—one for each of the 12 regions where the Department of Education has a civil rights enforcement office. The Center thus evaluated data on the gender breakdown of students in vocational programs in **Arizona; California; Florida; Illinois; Maryland; Massachusetts; Michigan; Mississippi; Missouri; New Jersey; North Carolina; and Washington.**

Summary of Findings

- ▶ Woman students make up 96% of the students enrolled in Cosmetology.
- ▶ Woman students make up 87% of the students enrolled in Child Care Courses.
- ▶ Woman students make up 86% of the students enrolled in courses that prepare them to be Health Assistants.
- ▶ Men students make up 94% of the students enrolled in training programs for plumbers and electricians.
- ▶ Men students make up 93% of the students enrolled in courses that prepare them to be welders or carpenters.
- ▶ Men students make up 92% of the students enrolled in Automotive Technology courses.

The pervasive sex segregation of woman students into traditionally woman programs has a serious adverse impact on their economic well-being. For example, students entering Child Care fields will earn only a median salary of $7.43 per hour, and Cosmetologists will earn a median salary of $8.49 per hour. By contrast, the median salary for students who become Plumbers and Pipefitters is $18.19 per hour, and the top 10% of workers in that field will make $30.06 per hour. Similarly, Electricians have a median salary of $19.29, and are eligible to earn up to $31.71 while progressing in the career tracks created in their field. In no case, moreover, does the amount earned by the top 10% of workers in the predominantly woman fields of cosmetology, child care, or medical assistant even begin to approach the median wages earned by those employed in predominantly men occupations. While the 10 percent of Child Care workers earn $10.71 per hour, for example, that is 41% *lower* than the median amount earned by mechanical drafters. The differences are stark, and the consequences for these students and their families enormous.

Adapted from National Women's Law Center. *Title IX and equal opportunity in vocational and technical education: A promise still owed to the nation's young women.* Washington, D.C.: Author. (2002, June).

Leadership Characteristics: It's Still a Gender Thang

In our society, we are constantly hearing about job related stress. Leaders have very stressful positions. Stressful conditions and positions can lead to hypertension, depression, anxiety, weight gain, and loss. John Gray (1992) explains how leadership characteristics relate to stress. Coping with stress on the job provides an example of perhaps one of the biggest differences between men and women. Men become increasingly focused and withdrawn when confronted with a stressful situation, while women become increasingly overwhelmed and emotionally involved.

Along with these characteristics come the job titles which society views as feminine jobs—those that women should perform—or masculine jobs—those that men should perform. Job titles viewed as high status include lawyer, politician, business executive, doctor, scientist, police officer, professor, and president, to name a few. Society sees these positions as masculine, task-oriented positions. Until recently, men dominated these roles.

Job titles that are viewed as feminine low-status jobs include nurse, secretary, teacher, librarian, retailer, performer, artist, and social worker. Society sees these positions as feminine because of the social-helping skills that go along with the job. Until recently, women have dominated these roles. These positions offer lower pay than the men-dominated positions.

Masculine and feminine images are firmly stereotyped and are socially accepted principles upon which boys and girls are raised. As children mature, they assume the economic and social roles based on these principles. As Kimbrell notes, research from the past is consistent with depicting society's internalized view of what makes a man and what makes a woman (see Appendix A). Surveys show that these opposite gender traits have become an accepted part of our society (Kimbrell, 1995).

Table 9.1

HE	SHE
More self-interested	More other-focused
Very competitive	Less competitive
Needs less intimacy	Needs more intimacy
Needs less approval	Needs more approval
Very active	More passive
Very objective	Very subjective
More independent	Less independent
More logical	More irrational
Often detached	Often emotional
Strong drive for power and money	Power and money are less important
More manipulative	More cooperative
More machine-oriented	Less technically adept
Never cries	Cries easily
Very ambitious	Less ambitious
Talks mostly about things	Talks mostly about people
Takes things literally	Looks for hidden meanings
Engages in put-downs	Engages in back-biting
Less responsive listener	More responsive listener
Less apologetic	More apologetic
Less willing to seek help	Seeks help readily
Less interested in the arts and religion	More interested in the arts and religion
Often intimidates others	Seldom intimidates others
Often seeks conflict	Tends to avoid conflict
Thrives on receiving	Thrives on giving
More polygamous	More monogamous
More sadistic	More masochistic
More sex-oriented	More love-oriented
Worries less about others	Worries more about others
More aggressive	Less aggressive
Initiates war	Does not make war

Kimbrell, (1995). See, for example, Inge Braverman et al., "Sex Role Stereotypes: A Current Appraisal," *Journal of Social Issues* 28, no. 2 (1972): p. 59; Cris Evatt, *He & She: 60 Significant Differences Between Men and Women* (Berkeley: Conari Press, 1992): pp. 150–151; Sam Keen, *Fire in the Belly*. New York: Bantam Books, 1992:, p. 199.

"Genderizing" Leadership Styles

The differences in leadership styles between men and women show that men are self-interested and focused on status, while women are interested in others and focused on connection. Brookbank (1991) concluded that women leaders who achieved leadership positions through personal gain "rose dutifully to the instrumental challenge but maintained their internalized and socially acceptable obligation to provide for the emotional needs of others" (p. 32).

Women used a democratic or participative approach to leadership since they feel a social responsibility, while men used an autocratic and directive leadership style. Men maintained the point of concentration in their leadership positions and did not change their behavior in order to relate to employees because they remained focused on the task of completing the job. Further research suggests that there is an overall preference "of non-directive styles among leaders in general, and especially women" (Brookbank, 1991, p. 35).

Deborah Tannen (1990) reviewed videotapes that presented girls and boys and women and men talking to their friends in a tentative situation and found there was an indication of gender difference pattern. The tapes showed that girls and women worked together to form a connected community, bonded by talking through troubles with personal relationships, and struggled to maintain their individuality when faced with opposition and were challenged to agree (Tannen, 1990). The tapes showed that boys and men worked hard to maintain their independence in a structured business world in order to attain intimacy between themselves and those colleagues who disagreed. Conclusively, men and women have different styles in the way they lead others.

Leadership Evaluations: "You Don't Know Me Like That"

For years men have been responsible for most of the management positions in the workforce. Since the women's movement caused both women and men to adjust to the changing environment; more women managers have emerged. In the 1900s, 20 percent of women were working; in 1990, 48.3 percent were a part of the workforce (Kovach, 1990). In 1996, this number increased to 56.0 percent (U.S. Bureau of the Census, 1997). By 2004, 57.2 percent of white women are working and 58.5 percent of African American women are working (U.S. Bureau of Labor Statistics, 2005).

Affirmative action programs have given women opportunities that they have never had before. Men have had to adjust to women being a part of the workforce. A 1994 study by the National Foundation for Women Business Owners concluded that women entrepreneurs were different from their men counterparts since women were more likely to seek advice from other people. The study also found that men think on premises of hierarchy and of establishing rules, while women think on the premises of professional relationships as networks (Nelton, 1996).

A study of executives published in the Harvard Business Review concluded that women are evaluated with a greater negative attitude as opposed to men. Thirty-three percent of the men surveyed said that women had a "bad" effect on employee morale; 51 percent said women were temperamentally unfit for management jobs; and 81 percent felt that they would be uncomfortable working for a woman (Kovach, 1990). This indicates that women are already starting with a disadvantage if men (81 percent), who have never worked for a woman, feel that they would be uncomfortable working for one. These men also felt that women could not take the pressure and would "cave in" when faced with a rough situation or would try to prove themselves by being overly dogmatic and overprotective. Strong-willed women may try to overcompensate their behavior to prove to their men colleagues that they can handle any situation with which they are faced. Men are facing a challenge by having to adjust their "traditional" ways of doing business in order to accept women into the workforce.

Conflict Management

Gender differences and conflict management are important issues to discuss because conflict tends to be a part of our existence. Because of hierarchical concerns, there may be conflict between coworkers. Because of power issues, there may be conflict between supervisors and subordinates. Conflict may also exist between and within the gender groups: men conflicting with men, women with women, and men with women. To understand how men and women communicate when there is conflict, we must look at the differences between the two and see how each gender resolves conflict.

Men are often seen as having behavior tendencies toward competitiveness, aggression, and problem solving, while women's behavior tends to lean toward passiveness, noncompetitiveness when bargaining and/or displaying interpersonal skills.

Our society sets a certain standard for acceptable behavior, and this standard is labeled masculine. Therefore any behavior that goes against this standard is labeled feminine. Traits such as independence, competitiveness, and ambition are seen as desirable in our Western culture. Women are seen as possessing the opposites of these traits. The culture values, qualities in women like kindness, tolerance, and humanness, and a "real man" cannot have any of these qualities. These qualities are desirable, but not in a business setting. A business setting requires aggressiveness and competitiveness, which are considered "men" qualities. Patience and kindness, on the other hand, have no place in business. Traditional men characteristics are stressed when portraying the ideal democratic leader. These traits include maturity, forcefulness, and intellect superior to women. Women leaders have traits that include open-mindedness, caring for others, and a desire for stability and unity.

Conflict management between men and women is often dictated by what society has established as traditional men and woman roles. Men and women handle conflict in a manner that is prescripted by gender role expectations. Women and men choose behaviors that society deems proper for the respective gender. Traditionally, the expected method for a woman to solve conflict is to "behave nicely." Because of this tradition, women might disregard assertive behavior in dealing with conflict by pursuing other methods.

R. H. Kilman and K. W. Thomas (as cited in Dellinger) published one of the leading studies in 1977 on gender differences in conflict management. They identified two areas of conflict behavior as assertiveness (concern for self) and cooperativeness (concern for others). Out of those two behaviors, they showed five conflict-handling styles: competition, collaboration, avoidance, compromise, and accommodation.

Competition means to win at the expense of others. This strategy is very uncooperative and very assertive, but it is not necessarily hostile or obviously aggressive. It is used to meet one's own goals. **Collaboration** means to meet both parties' needs. It is concerned with finding new options and joint problem solving. This strategy is both very cooperative and very assertive. **Avoidance** means failing to take a position in a conflict. People who use this strategy refuse to discuss the issues, which might be illustrated by leaving the room or attempting to change the subject. It is very uncooperative and very unassertive. **Compromise** means only partially meeting both parties' needs. It is a give-and-take method, and it reaches the middle ground in finding solutions. Both parties get a portion of what they want, but they do not get exactly what they want. This strategy is cooperative and assertive. **Accommodation** means rejecting one's goals for those of the other party. It allows for the satisfaction of others, and it can be either total agreement, without any hostility toward the other party, or it can be surrender. This strategy is very cooperative and not assertive.

Some researchers point to a sixth variable, **differentiation,** which is defined as: raising the conflict issue, spending time and energy clarifying the positions, pursuing reasons behind the positions, and acknowledging the severity of the differences. Differentiation is the process done in substantive conflict. Previous studies show that men are more likely to become assertive in conflict situations because differentiation also involves depersonalizing the issues of the debate. Men tend to blame conflict on the other partner or on other circumstances, while women tend to be critical of themselves in conflict.

Using the six conflict-handling strategies, research shows that men prefer competition more than women do, while women prefer accommodation more than men. Both men and women are almost equal in collaboration, compromise, and avoidance. Since differentiation is associated with assertive behavior, it is shown that men use this strategy significantly more often than women do. Each of the four parts that define differentiation eliminates nonassertive behavior, which is found to be used more by women than men (Delligner, 1991).

In the area of competition, men use the strategy more than women in women supervisor/men subordinate pairings. Women use competition more than men in men superior/women subordinate pairings. This suggests that men might feel they do not need to be competitive in order to gain what they want. Women do use a lot of competition when dealing with equal women coworkers, which might suggest that women are more competitive when they interact with each other than when they interact with men. In addition, men used competition in every pairing except with women subordinates.

Women use the strategy of accommodation when paired with equal men and women coworkers, while men rarely use accommodation. The research tends to support the stereotypes about gender that say women will more often change their own goals to satisfy the other party, even when dealing with men subordinates. Even when women reach a superior job status, they tend to accommodate more than men do.

There is not a significant difference between men and women when it comes to the compromise strategy. Men, however, use the compromise strategy when paired with other men, when paired with equal status people, and in men superior/women subordinate pairings. Because men are seen as highly assertive, this may sound odd. Delligner (1991) proposes that it is possible that men might be using compromise in a manipulative manner; therefore, leaning toward a more competitive strategy. This may be a method used by men to disguise their competitive strategies.

As with the compromise strategy, there is no significant difference between men and women using the collaboration strategy. Both sexes used this strategy often. Women used collaboration when dealing with men and women of equal status, but not when they have men superiors. The study shows that women use collaboration more often than competition, perhaps because collaboration involves satisfying their goals and the goals of the other party, Because women are not socialized to be competitive, they tend to be more creative during conflict.

> Think about a particular situation where there was conflict between a woman and a man. Was this a personal or professional situation? What strategies did the parties use?

Finally, in the strategy of avoidance, there is little significant difference between the genders. When women are paired with men coworkers, they show more avoidance. This may be due to the traditional stereotypes that men are more aggressive than women; therefore, women are forced to act in a submissive role.

What do you have to say about that?

In negotiating business deals, even in the 1980s, it was often necessary for Blacks to hide their race. In the 1950s, already millionaire, John Johnson, attempted to bid on a White-owned building and was refused. So he could get in and inspect the building, Johnson posed as a janitor. He then hired a White person to act as a front so he could bid on the build.

Minority Women

This section of the chapter challenges the existing leadership theories as they lack coverage of the dynamics affecting minorities and more specifically African American women. The previous discussions have relied heavily on traditional leadership theories and have accepted the conclusions offered. "Consequently, leadership theories are rarely generalizable to women and minorities" (Allen, 1997). Black women especially have been virtually ignored as a topic of sociological inquiry. Chemers (1997) concludes that a definition of leadership that would be widely accepted by the majority of theorists and researchers might define leadership as a process of social influence in which one person is able to enlist the aid and support of others in the accomplishment of a common task. The major tenets of this definition are that leadership requires group activity, is based on social influence, and revolves around a common task.

The African American woman leader must sometimes compete against the interpersonal factors of emotions, prejudice, and societal skeletons such as hundreds of years of oppression, when trying to solidify her role as a leader. She may consider herself at a disadvantage when trying to garner support for achieving a common goal. Therefore, she finds herself in the center of conflict for which she is not directly responsible. The premise here in no way implies that African American women leaders are at a disadvantage in leadership positions. It does, however, propose that theorists/researchers when examining the behavior of any co-culture must entertain the impact of significant societal issues facing particular co-cultures.

African American women have traditionally been relegated to subordinate positions in society that have affected the manner in which their leadership has emerged (Collins, 1991). Allen (1997) summarizes that a "lack of access to traditional sources of power and decision making forced Black women to find alternative means of leadership in nontraditional arenas and ways. Black women have for years been the pillar of their communities, churches and families" (Collins, 1991). African American woman leadership emerges from and is shaped by both the external and internal forces that affect African American womans' everyday experience (Allen 1997).

The remainder of this discussion focuses on some areas that pose a challenge for the African American woman simply because of her race and gender. These areas are: 1. lack of mentors; 2. perception of legislation designed to uplift the status of minorities in the United States; and 3. the lack of respect given to African American woman leaders.

Studies have long shown that African American women have the least access to mentors (Hayes, 1998). Whether this shortage of mentors is due to a lack of those serving in what would be considered a mentoring role, or whether it is based on the insecurities of other African American professionals, these women encounter many roadblocks in developing the trust necessary for strong mentoring-type relationships.

> "Joyce, an African American woman, joined a Fortune 500 consumer products firm as a senior product manager. Her hiring caused some consternation among the other Black managers, who saw Joyce as taking a job one of them could have had. Although not much was said, their resentment showed in small ways. They were overly polite when in Joyce's company and were reluctant to share information with her. In addition, while no one said anything derogatory about Joyce, no one said anything positive either. It was as if the Black managers had bought into the general opinion that Joyce was another affirmative action hire." (Randall, 1998, p. 85).

Societal bandages have helped the African American woman in her struggle for leadership roles; however, they have in some cases increased the challenges of succeeding in those roles. The legislative "fixes" have in some ways isolated the African American woman from her own [people] within the professional community so that mentoring relationships are less likely to occur.

Affirmative Action has not only caused Black-on-Black mistrust, but has also drawn White resistance as well. Barbara Anwine, the executive director of the National Lawyers Committee for Civil Rights under Law says, "The White men who is most angry is not 'Bubba.' When you look at the polling data on affirmative action, the group that is angriest about alleged preferences is professional White men. They haven't necessarily lost jobs to women and/or minorities, but corporate downsizing has made them anxious and they believe that they're entitled to keep and dominate the best jobs" (Anwine, 1995). When a group of people do not want you in a leadership role, then it is extremely difficult to lead that particular group. This type of conflict, due to societal forces, is at the center of the African American woman leaders' manners of handling conflict or conflict resolution. From the literature, it is safe to conclude that the very existence of an African American woman in a leadership role is a conflict of the norm, of the accepted, and/or of the desired.

The manner in which subordinates or peers treat the African American woman leader is relevant to how she deals with conflict between these individuals and herself. Dr. Julianne Malveaux, on her syndicated talk show, points to the blatant disrespect that African American woman leaders receive—in this specific case as political leaders. She comments, "African American women leaders are constantly dissed [disrespected]. Jesse Helms had the audacity to sing "Dixie" in the elevator to Illinois Senator Carol Moseley-Braun. Florida Congresswoman Carrie Meek was called out of order for daring to question Newt

Gingrich's book deal on the House floor." Such blatant displays of disrespect have been part of the African American woman experience since her early existence in America.

Collins (1991) discusses African American women and some of the "disrespectful" labels that have followed them for decades, such as *Mammy* and *Jezebel*. If Collins is correct that African American women are traditionally viewed in this vein, then it is necessary to do more sociological inquiries into the historical experience of the African American woman. For example, in order to understand the African American woman's method of addressing conflict, it is important to understand that she is dealing with more than the conflict that exists in the local situation. She is also dealing with the national perception of her as an African American woman. In the co-culture of the African American woman, conflict is central to her existence. The conflict of being considered as a leader after so many years of subjugation bears on her perception of conflict resolution with others.

Further research must investigate leadership perceptions and behaviors as they related to minority co-cultures. The findings may astound us.

Societal Impact

Society has an investment in seeing that people conform to expected sex-role behavior. Assertive women and expressive men are regarded with suspicion in today's society because these traits are moving away from the traditional roles that men and women should portray. Goldberg (1993) reinforces the fact that society plays a part in the roles men and women are expected to play when he says, "in every society women are responsible for the care and rearing of the young, the single most important function in nature. . . . Just as patriarchy, men dominance, and men attainment of high status roles and positions are universal, so the association of nurturance and emotional socialization with the women is universal, and these woman roles are, in some societies, given very high status" (p. 126). It is important that the expectations of society be changed in order for men and women to be seen as equal.

Women and men are different in the leadership roles and traits that they have. Is this because society has influenced men and women and has molded them into what is considered normal?

Why are men and women not viewed as equal?

"But it is clear that until social expectations for men and women are equal, until we provide equal respect for both sexes, an answer to this question will simply reflect our prejudices" (*Columbia Dictionary of Quotations*, Microsoft Bookshelf, 1998, CD-ROM).

How would you answer the question?

Creating an Acceptable Identity in the Workplace: Lesbian Passing

Amanda M. Gunn, Ph.D.

Sally leaves each morning for work following the same ritual day after day. She kisses her lover Karen good-bye, grabs her coffee, walks outside, gets in her Honda Accord, and leaves for an eight- to nine-hour workday as an executive at one of the top soft drink companies in the southeast. As she drives down the freeway she begins her mental transformation into what she assumes is the only identity that is safe to possess in her position; she begins to pretend that she is heterosexual. When Sally arrives at work, Karen will become Keith. Her weekend with women will have the addition of men names, and she will call her friend Mark to see if he will once again be her fill-in boyfriend Keith for the upcoming company golf tournament.

Sally is just one of countless homosexuals who lives a professional life engaged in the phenomenon of "passing." Berger (1992) defines passing for homosexuals as "the process by which he/[she] presents himself/[herself] to the world as heterosexual" (p. 85). Passing relies on the social construction and self-construction of identities that are deemed, or perceived to be, desirable by society. It is dependent on the norms of a society and the subjective interpretations of those norms.

With an increase in diversity awareness and the implementation of programs designed to bridge diversity gaps in the workplace, one might assume that passing, as an alternative for homosexuals, would become obsolete. The current emphasis in organizational scholarship on worker satisfaction, inclusion, and involvement would suggest that organizational leaders would attempt to eradicate behaviors within the organization, such as passing, that inhibit those outcomes (Cheney, 1995). Yet, as Carnevale and Stone (1995) point out, "gay men, lesbians, and bisexual individuals are one of the 'new minorities' in the workplace and among the least understood" (p. 415). The inclusion of sexual orientation in the discussion of organizational diversity is rare, and when it is included it is often mentioned in the listing of diverse groups with an absence of elaboration (Allen, 1995; Chemers, Oskamp, & Costanzo, 1995). The issues that face homosexuals at work are couched in the "erroneous stereotypes" that perpetuate a desire to remain silent and "invisible in the workplace" (Carnevale & Stone, 1995, p. 416). This is a silence that works in direct opposition to ideologies that promote diversity and voice in the organization.

For many homosexuals, passing at work is certainly motivated by the desire to possess an acceptable identity; however, it is driven by more than that. Homosexual passing is about social strategies that are deemed necessary "to survive in a heterosexually dominated society, (and) . . . evade the effects of stigmatization" (Berger, 1975, pp. 9 & 11). It is affected by the expectations of a work environment that exist in a society that often discriminates against differences.

Woods and Harbeck (1992) contend that the "workplace is heterosexist in the sense that it structurally and ideologically promotes a particular model of heterosexuality while penalizing, hiding, or otherwise symbolically annihilating its alternatives" (p. 9). Taken together, these perspectives indicate that the only option for Sally and others like her is to pass to, as DPhil (1994) suggests, "homosexuals daily engage in an elaborate ruse about their private life" (p. 188). This "ruse" is accomplished through conscious communicative practices. The following figure is a summation of how five lesbians that pass in the workplace carry out that ruse through communicative behaviors.

Strategic Self-Presentation by Lesbians that Pass in the Workplace

Gollwitzer's Methods of Strategic Self-Presentation	The Methods Employed by Five Lesbians that Pass as Heterosexual at Work
"Displaying material symbols"	• Placing pictures of male friends on an office desk • Wearing a ring that indicates marriage or an engagement • Wearing feminine clothing that would not be worn otherwise • Maintaining a longer hairstyle to adhere to perceived gender norms • Wearing more makeup that usual to adhere to perceived gender norms
"Performing daily duties associated with a particular identity"	• The addition or substitution of male names and pronouns in conversations • Bringing male dates to company functions • Utilizing traditionally feminine mannerisms such as smiling and crossing legs while sitting • Participating in office flirtations
"Verbal claim to possession of a particular identity"	• Replacing the name of a girlfriend with a male name • Creating stories about nonexistent heterosexual relationships • Discussing intimate relationships with men • Verbalizing attractions for men

This is a summation of the findings. It is not all-inclusive; these examples are representative of the descriptive accounts. (Gunn, 1998).

Sally spends her days at work in fear of being found out. She then returns home to a love that she has denied just one more day out of many. Employee protection based on sexual orientation exists in very few companies and is almost nonexistent at the state and federal levels. Sally can be fired in most employment situations because she loves some-one of the same sex. These behaviors of passing take a great deal of energy, both emo-tional and psychological. The time that it takes to create a heterosexual person is at once demeaning to the individuals passing, the partners at home that they are denying, and unproductive for the task and maintenance agendas of the workplace.

Sally and countless others continue to leave their voice at home. Organizational leaders must be made to see that this practice of passing undermines the goals of an organization. Once a foundational understanding is established of how all the factions of an organization are affected by homosexual passing, we can begin to work toward a true "democratic workplace." Perhaps then Sally will no longer have to lie. She will not live in a reality of continuous stress, and perhaps she can begin to feel the connection with her coworkers that she is missing. Ultimately, Sally will be able to answer "yes" when she is asked if there is someone important in her life.

References

Allen, B. J. (1995). Diversity and organizational communication. *Journal of applied communication research, 23*, 143–155.

Berger, R. M. (1992). Passing and social support among gay men. *Journal of Homosexuality, 23*, 85–97.

Carnevale, A. P., & Stone, S. C. (1995). *The American mosaic: An in-depth report on the future of diver-sity at work.* NY: McGraw-Hill, Inc.

Chemers, M. M., Oskamp, S., & Costanzo, M. A. (Eds.) (1995). *Diversity in organizations: New per-spectives for a changing workplace.* London: SAGE.

Cheney, G. (1995). Democracy in the workplace: Theory and practice from the perspective of communication. *Journal of Applied Communication Research, 23*, 167–200.

DPhil, J. S. (1994). Gay rights and affirmative action. *Journal of homosexuality, 27*, (3/4), 179–222.

Gollwitzer, P. M. (1986). Striving for specific identities: The social reality of self-symbolizing. In R. F. Baumeister (Ed.), *Public self and private self* (pp. 141–159). NY: Springer-Verlag.

Gunn, A. M. (1998). *Lesbian Passing in the Workplace: A Strategy for Negotiating an Absence of Power.* Masters Thesis.

Woods, S. E., & Harbeck, K. M. (1992). Living in two worlds: The identity management strate-gies used by lesbian physical educators. *Journal of Homosexuality, 22*, 141–166.

Kwakami & White (2000) say that although women have progressed greatly in terms of gaining status in the workplace, men still are more likely to become successful leaders. When women emulate men leadership styles and behaviors, they are generally frowned upon or disliked. When women perform their stereotypical nurturing roles, they are liked, but not respected. Kwakami & White report an increased number of women pursuing managerial positions. Women and men, at least for the period that Kwakami & White were considering (1998–2000), were being hired at approximately the same rate. Yet, men were still getting more of the leadership positions.

And yes, since we began working on this chapter, there has been an explosion in the amount of research on leadership in the cross-cultural context (Dickson, et al., 2003). Yet, many marginalized groups in America still lack the attention needed.

Wrap It Up

In conclusion, the data shown from the studies support the traditional stereotypes between men and women. Women and men differed in the type of leadership roles they undertook within work groups. Men exhibited more overall leadership and task leadership characteristics, while women exhibited more social leadership characteristics. Men and women had various leadership styles. Women in leadership positions received greater negative evaluations than men in comparable positions.

Using conflict management as a basis for the study of gender differences, men were more competitive than women, and women were more accommodating than men. Women used assertiveness in conflict by collaboration, which suggests that even if they are not competitive, women will feel more comfortable when thinking about concern for the other party. One of the only areas where women used competition was when they were paired with other women. Men rarely used the accommodation strategy, even if they were paired with other men. The studies suggested that men and women would use different conflict strategies depending on the sex and status of the other party.

We must realize that as a multicultural society, race and gender are complex, inter-related issues. It has become evident that simple solutions to these issues will not work. We must be willing to consider the multiple, specific contexts of various racial genders and classed groups, and we must devise a way to incorporate these realities into our classrooms and workplace. Here, we have simply skimmed the surface of the societal and cultural impact of the experiences of the woman and the African American leader. However, we believe we have questioned enough to substantiate a more substantive inquiry into the leadership behavior of non-white men. Co-cultures deal with many issues relegated solely to their particular communities.

Society has an investment in seeing that people conform to expected sex-role behavior. Assertive women and expressive men are regarded with suspicion in today's society because these traits are moving away from the traditional roles that men and women should portray. It is important that the expectations of society be changed in order for men and women to be seen as equals. Women and men differ in their leadership roles and traits, but this is because society has influenced them and molded them into what is considered normal.

We advocate more studies based on historical experiences, societal influences and increased studies performed by natives of the specified co-cultures. This type of inquiry could minimize many of the misconceptions formed about leaders representing minority communities and could possibly initiate a rethinking of the present barometers that measure the success of those leaders.

References

Allen, B. L. (1997). Re-Articulation of Black Woman Community Leadership: Processes, Networks, and a Culture of Resistance. *African-American Research Perspectives.* pp. 1–4.

Anwine, B. R. (Fall 1995) guest. Transcript from radio program *On the Issues,* Pacifica radio network.

Bennis, W. (1989). *On becoming a leader.* Massachusetts: Addison-Wesley Publishing Company.

Blanchard K. & Miller M. (2007). *The secret.* San Francisco: Berrett-Koehler Publishers, Inc.

Brookbank, P. G. (1991). Gender Differentiation in Leadership Styles among High School Principals in North Carolina. (Doctoral dissertation, The University of North Carolina at Greensboro, 1991). Greensboro: Personal Strengths Publishing, 206.

Chemers, Martin M. (1997). An Integrative Theory of Leadership. 208.

Collins, Patricia Hill. (1991). *Black Feminist Thought: Knowledge, Consciousness, and the Politics of Empowerment.* New York: Routledge, Chapman and Hall, Inc.

Dellinger, C. A. (1987). *Gender differences in conflict management: A study of conflict strategies and differentiation.* Unpublished doctoral dissertation, University of North Carolina at Greensboro.

Dickson, M. W., Den Hartog, D. N., & Mitchelson, J. K. (2003). Research on leadership in a cross-cultural context: Making progress, and raising new questions. *Leadership Quarterly,* 14, 729–769.

Goldberg, S. (1993). *Why Men Rule: A Theory of Men Dominance.* Chicago: Open Court.

Gray, J., Ph.D. (1992). *Men Are from Mars, Women Are from Venus.* New York: Harper Collins Publishers.

Hayes, C. (1998 August). Business Dynamics. *Black Enterprise.* 29(1)1. pp. 58–67.

Kimbrell, A. (1995). *The Masculine Mystique: The politics of masculinity.* New York: Ballantine Books.

Kreitner, R., & Kinicki, A. (1995). *Organizational Behavior.* Chicago: Richard D. Irwin, Inc.

Kovach, B. E. (1990). *Sex Roles and Personal Awareness.* Lanham: University Press of America.

Malveaux, Julianne Ph.D. (1995, Fall). Host: Transcript from radio program *On the Issues,* Pacifica radio network. Microsoft Bookshelf CD-ROM. (1998 ed.). The Columbia Dictionary of Quotations is licensed from Columbia University Press. Copyright 1993, 1995.

Nelton, S. (1996). A coming sea of change in leadership: A gender gap in ownership may be closing, the active shall inherit the firm. *Nation's Business,* 84(4), 50.

Pollard, D. (1996). Perspectives on Gender and Race. In *Educational Leadership.* (Volume 53/no. 3).

Randall, Iris. (1998, January). Black on Black Management. *Black Enterprise,* 28(6) pp. 85–6.

Senge, Peter (1990). *The fifth discipline: The art & practice of the learning organization.* New York: Doubleday.

Stead, B. A. (1985). *Women in Management.* New Jersey: Prentice Hall, Inc.

Taylor, A. and Miller, J. B. (Eds.). (1994). *Conflict and Gender.* Cresskill, N.J.: Hampton.

Tannen, D. (1990). *You Just Don't Understand: Women and Men in Conversation.* New York: William Morrow and Company, Inc.

U.S. Bureau of the Census (1997). *Statistical Abstract of the United States.* (11th ed.). No. 621-Employment status of the Civilian Population: 1970–1996.

U.S. Bureau of Labor Statistics (2005). Labor Statistics from the Current Population Survey. Series Id: LNU02300029-Employment-Population Ratio—20 yrs. & over, White Women: 1995–2005.

U.S. Bureau of Labor Statistics (2005). Labor Statistics from the Current Population Survey. Series Id: LNU02300032-Employment-Population Ratio—20 yrs. & over, Black or African American Women: 1995–2005.

Communication in the Movies

I invite you and a friend or classmates to explore comunication in the movies. Reflect on the communication skills discussed in this chapter. How are they addressed in the movies?

▶ Saving Private Ryan
▶ Coach Carter
▶ Soul Food
▶ New Jack City

Think About It → Write About It

Reflect on what you've just read. Now write what you are thinking.

_____

_____

_____

_____

_____

_____

_____

_____

_____

_____

_____

_____

_____

_____

_____

_____

_____

_____

_____

_____

_____

_____

_____

Activity

What does "Men from Mars and Women are from Venus" mean?

Unit Three

Communicating in the
Public Sphere

Chapter 10

Ethically Speaking

Regina Silverthorne, Ph.D.

Key Terms

Freedom of Speech	Confirmation
Morality	Present-ness
Ethical Audit	Spirit of Mutual Equality
Virtue Ethics	Supportive Climate
Taoist Ethics	Egalitarianism
Dialogic Ethics	Teleology
Authenticity	Deontology
Inclusion	

Have you ever heard that there's always someone waiting to be offended? Often they are offended by something said or done by another. Most of us have a set of standards that we live by—and we tend to expect others to live by our same standards. There are things that you believe with all of your heart are right, and things that you strongly believe are wrong . . . what we have learned growing up in a particular environment . . . society and family are values that become transformed into our *individual ethics* . . . our set of values which guide us in our daily decision-making. We usually (not always) live up to our personal standards and govern ourselves according to our value system. Moreover, it seems to be a natural desire to act in an ethical manner.

A loose definition for **ethics** may be moral principles for living and making decisions. A more comprehensive meaning may include morals, beliefs, norms, and values that societies use to determine right from wrong. Now it gets more complicated because individual ethics may not always be aligned with the ethics of our society. Hence, there are multiple and competing views on what is considered right and what is wrong. Our thought patterns tend to govern our behavior, thusly, what we believe to be true or what we believe to be right will often determine what we will do or say. Since everyone does not share the exact same morals, beliefs, or principled reality, then our actions and expressions may pose potential conflicting views on ethical speech acts.

When I stated earlier that most of us have a set of standards we live by, these standards may be strictly guided by the law, religious beliefs, social group acceptance, or just personal values. It seems like everyone should be able to make the right and ethical choice at all times because of these standards and values we supposedly live by.

Although I believe most of us want to do the right thing, "the right thing to do" becomes convoluted in today's society. Individuals and society are forced to be confronted with challenges of choice and action. This is evident in speech acts on a daily basis. Essentially, when we choose to express ourselves, we may offend another because of this fragmented societal perspective on what is right. Therefore, it may help to quickly perform an ethical audit before acting. But before we develop our ethical audit (which may be slightly different for each one of us), let's look at the highly valued right in our American society to freely express ourselves, the freedom of speech.

The Basics: Freedom of Speech—A Highly Valued American Right

I alluded in the last section that ethics is a gray area in this postmodern era, where it is difficult to find a clear set of rules. However, the very first amendment to our constitution, located under the title of "The Bill of Rights" is the freedom of speech. The first amendment provides that, "Congress shall make no law . . . abridging the freedom of speech or of the press. . . ." This might suggest that you can say whatever you want at any time, in any place. However, there are times when the highest courts intervene with restrictions to the freedom of speech.

Understanding that "speech" includes other mediums of expression, there are four conditions for assessing the degree of the freedom of speech we have. (Fraleigh, 1997)

1. Freedom to communicate without fear of government sanction
2. Freedom from compulsory speech
3. Freedom of access to effective channels of communication
4. Freedom from government domination of the free speech environment

The freedom to communicate without fear of government sanction suggests that the government will not censor information. However, there are times when the government must exercise prior restraint after proving it is justified in doing so for the protection of society. Similarly, the freedom from compulsory speech means that we should not be required to say certain things. But again, there are exceptions to every rule. For example, there are times when students who attended public school were required to salute the flag and recite the pledge of allegiance. The freedom of access to effective channels of communication seems to be restrictive based more on the socioeconomic means than anything else, although the Internet is swiftly becoming an effective channel for most people to access.

The freedom from government domination of the free speech environment is important and is the reason Europeans wanted to make the continent of North America their home. They were fleeing the domination of their government of their time, desiring the freedom to speak of religious doctrine contrary to the dominant theology in their European countries. However, there are messages our government will send that may dominate the free speech environment. Examples may be recruitment for the armed forces, or the "Just say, 'No!'" anti-drug campaign. We will discuss a case later in this chapter that highlights controversy pertaining to this freedom from government domination of the free speech environment.

Why Is Freedom of Speech So Critical?

We defend and substantiate our right to the freedom of speech because it is critical to our system of "self-government" and it promotes "the discovery of truth." (Fraleigh, 1997) Likewise, it encourages free will, independence, and freedom while affirming the premise that one person does not necessarily possess the moral right to stifle or suppress the ideas of another person!

Even though we highly value this freedom in terms of our individual rights, we also value the rights of the collective. There are many times when individual rights and the concern for the good of society may clash. Even our laws cannot guarantee ethical behavior in terms of the freedom of speech. Why? Speech acts are just too complex and situational! There is a popular school of thought that ethics in communication should be thought of in terms of the collective, as opposed to the individual.

When Do the Courts Tend to Control Speech?

When I suggested earlier that you may not say whatever you want at any time, in any place, I wanted to point out that the safety and welfare of our society often takes precedence in the courts when the freedom of speech is in question. If someone were to yell from the top of their lungs, "fire!" in a crowded nightclub, initiating a mass of people running to an exit, causing injuries, they have compromised the safety and welfare for that group of people. This is the classic example of time and place being variables that may restrict freedom of speech, thus, an ethical concern for the collective.

Additionally, there are many questions about the responsibility a speaker has when provoking or encouraging an audience to perform an illegal act. Consider the effects of a Black Panther Leader during the 1960s, a Ku Klux Klan Leader during the 1950s and 60s, or a Communist Politician during the 1940s. Leaders in each of these factions held meetings and gave speeches on a regular basis. There were some gifted speakers in the art of persuasion and incited members of their audience to commit questionable acts or illegal acts of violence. In some of these cases the courts ruled the speaker guilty for inciting the audience. Argumentatively, many psychologists believe that only individuals who are predisposed to wanting to commit such illegal acts would actually follow through. Another argument advocates the concept of "free will." How could a speaker make someone do something wrong if we all possess free will? Of course, these arguments may or may not apply to children.

Communication and Morality

Inevitably, there will be a debate among those who ascribe to a moral absolute and those who recognize moral relativism. The moral absolute determines right and wrong from their perceived absolute truths. This "absolute" is considering only one standard, *yours,* and no one else's; whereas moral relativism is the notion that we may consider that there are other ethical systems that others choose and their choices are equally respected.

Moral relativism, however, brings difficulty to an already complex study of ethics in communications. And if that isn't challenging enough, ethical communication suggests we are simultaneously expected to be able to respect others, affect another's behavior, and maintain our own psychological health. Therefore, you can understand why a study in ethical communication, albeit very interesting, may also promote an ongoing controversy for speech acts.

An Ethical Audit

What are some of the ethical questions in terms of the role and function of communication in society and for individuals? There are many, but the few I generally ask are, "Is it right?", "Is it fair?", "Is it restrictive or deceptive to others?", "Who does it affect?", "Who does it serve?", and my personal favorite, "Is it something one might become ashamed of when it comes to light?" I use these questions when I perform *ethical audits.*

An ethical audit is simply an appraisal of a situation or a potential situation that may challenge the morality of actions. I have noticed with my students that I rarely have an entire class agree on the ethical standing of a case study. What are your thoughts on the following case?

> Recently, the *USA Today* reported that "Armstrong Williams, a prominent Black pundit, was paid $240,000 to promote President Bush's No Child Left Behind Act on his talk show, to provide media access for the Education Secretary, and to persuade other Black journalist to talk about the law as part of a $1 million department contract with the Ketchum public relations firm. The contract required

Williams to comment on President Bush's program on his TV and radio show, to interview Education Secretary Rod Paige, and to produce radio spots that aired on his show." (1/14/2005). A liberal interest group strongly believed that Williams should return the money given to him illegally. Williams was ultimately fired and refused to return the money. This issue became controversial because Williams did not disclose that he was working for the government. It was believed that he was a journalist reporting a human interest story. President Bush stated he was unaware of the situation.

What do you believe the ethical questions are in this situation? How much responsibility does one have with regard to expression or speech acts have toward society?

As I was preparing this chapter, two other cases, similar to the Armstrong Williams situation were reported:

The Department of Health and Human Services (HHS) paid three conservative columnists to assist in promoting a Bush administration policy. Mike McManus said he received $10,000 and Maggie Gallagher says she was paid $21,500 to promote a conservative view of marriage, an initiative promoting that only marriage between a man and a woman can build strong families. The Armstrong Williams case had already been exposed. All three columnists failed to disclose to their readers their relationships with the administration. The new director of HHS has since implemented a rule to prohibit the use of outside consultants or contractors who have any connection with the press in an effort to restore public confidence that taxpayers' money is not being used to pay journalists (columnist or commentators) to use their positions of influence in the media.

Federal law bans the use of public money on propaganda. There are two major ethical questions. 1. Did these journalists violate general ethical standards for not disclosing their relationship with the government, and 2. Is this an illegal use of taxpayer dollars?

Many of my students stated they would have taken the money, not returned it, and just apologize for not disclosing—no harm, no foul! They really could not see much wrong with the actions of these journalists. Even some of my non-traditional students, (those who are over 25 years of age) seem to feel the same way. Living in a tight economy, I suppose there are many people who may relax their ethical standards if they believe it will not cause harm to anyone.

Ethical Communication Theories

I want to highlight just a few communication theories that may shed some light on why we continue to have controversy regarding the choices we make concerning our speech acts. There are three theories in particular that I believe we can use in our ethical audits for communication: virtue ethics, Taoist ethics, and dialogic ethics. (Anderson, 2002)

The first theory, and the most noted historically, is the Aristotlean idea of the management of rhetoric, virtue ethics, which emphasizes the unity of acts and reasons. Virtue ethics advocates that speakers communicate in a way that is not manipulating another. Aristotle was concerned with the advancement of societal virtues like freedom, justice, courage, temperance, fairness, gentleness, and wisdom. In an effort to be true to these values, Aristotle's view would strongly suggest the ethical goal in communication would be to choose to find mutuality, middle ground, or a central point.

The second theory is referred to as Taoist ethics, an ancient philosophy. Taoist ethics is becoming more popular in America as it embraces the vogueness of "organic" culture. The premise in Taoist ethics focuses on a vigorous ecology of values promoting the concept of natural balance. It suggests that nothing exists alone. Everything should exist only in harmony with someone or something else, hence the "yin-yang" concept. Where yin and yang are comparative opposites, interdependent, supportive of each other, and can transform into one another. In this light, the communicators are unique and will clearly define their views, yet require themselves to defy their egos and use empathy to understand the views of the other.

The third communication theory, dialogic ethics, is an understanding of how important it is not to devalue others by avoiding rhetorical manipulation and objectification. Without realizing it, a speaker might begin to think of his/her audience as merely valuable objects. For example, a candidate may not see their audience as human beings as much as they may see them as potential votes. There are six characteristics of dialogue developed by Richard Johannesen (1990) that fit in this dialogic ethical theory: authenticity, inclusion, confirmation, present-ness, spirit of mutual equality, and a supportive climate.

Consideration of all three of these theories can help when creating your own ethical checklist or can become a useful tool to use when auditing communication.

The Basis of Our Ethical Guidelines

We started this chapter discussing the fact that we all have our own ethical standards based on society, family values and what we have learned growing up in a particular environment. However, there are underlying philosophies that have existed across the ages that are the foundations upon which we have built and structured our value system. Three of these philosophies include egalitarianism, teleology, and deontology (Anderson, 2002). Consider the following scenario:

> You are the team leader working on a major project. One of your team members, Terry, is not doing her part, causing concerns for everyone else on the team. You are concerned that Terry is not taking this assignment seriously. You do not want your grade to suffer because of Terry. What do you do?

Egalitarianism is primarily concerned with the goal of social equality, fairness, and justice. In this philosophy, an ethical speaker will be more concerned with fairness and equality than any other goal in their communication efforts. When involved in speech acts, the desire is to know the information communicated did not infringe upon the rights of another, but also that conditions of equality for all are protected. This is to suggest that someone does not commit an act of good just to gain recognition. Using an egalitarian philosophy, what might be your ethical response to the slacker team member scenario?

The teleology philosophy has a focus on the end result. An ethical communicator grounded in a teleological philosophy is governed by the best possible outcome from their choices of speech acts. The communicator will weigh the different outcomes and decide what will be the best of all possibilities and govern their speech act accordingly. Considering a teleological philosophy, what might your ethical response be to the slacker team member scenario?

Deontological philosophy suggests that the ethical speaker will do what his/her individual commitment to a faith or guiding principles will support, and will not deviate. The ethical speaker has pledged to uphold certain principles, and the speech act should be governed by those principles. Ideally, both parties in the communiqué would be guided by the same principles—articles of faith, for example. What would be your ethical response to the slacker team member scenario under the deontological philosophy?

Usually, we can find ourselves considering one of these philosophies when selecting our ethical behavior. However, it is evident that we shift from one philosophy to another depending on the situation; although, we tend to think only about ourselves, often before others. Remember what my students thought about the Armstrong Williams controversy?

My Space

Most of us were taught that we live in a country that was built on the ideals of liberty and the pursuit of happiness; which in essence is the *freedom* to pursuit how we want to live. There are morals and standards that we live by, but the United States is a pluralistic society, in that we tend to live in a moral relativistic manner as opposed to the moral absolute. What I mean is that moral codes and standards have differences from one person to the next, or from one company or organization to the next. Therefore, when we become an employee, we are to be made aware in advance of the company's code of ethics. This code of ethics are the pre-set guidelines (a deontological philosophy) for behavior the employee must submit to in lieu of their own moral code; thus, the employer has a moral responsibility to inform the employee. Read the following ethical dilemma and determine who is right and who is wrong and why.

1. I had been teaching in the Fulton County School System for three years with all satisfactory evaluations and no write-ups when this injustice took place. On Feb 21st, 2007, I went to work as usual and at 8:45 am. Right after I called the roll, my assistant principal entered my room and requested that I turn in my laptop. Of course wondering what the hell was going on, I did as told. I figured maybe they were going to install updates or something. (Wow was I wrong!!). Anyhow, around 12:30 pm, my principal stopped me in the hallway and told me I needed to report to human resources by 3:00 pm. By then I knew it was some drama.

2. I went down to the Human Resources Office and a guy took me into the office and stated that Fulton County had received a phone call from a concerned citizen. They complained that I had an inappropriate My Space page. When the assistant principal picked up my computer, he took it so that they could determine if I had accessed my My Space page from the school laptop.

3. We were required to take our laptops home everyday. From my understanding, there is no policy against using the laptop at home for personal reasons, as long as you are not accessing inappropriate websites. So yes, they would have seen that I accessed My Space and Hotmail and Yahoo, and etc.

4. My My Space page has been up for about a year now and it promotes me as an actress and model. None of the pictures were inappropriate and I didn't think it was a crime to model and act part time. Hell, every teacher I know has a part time job. You would be amazed at what some of them do!!! (But yet they still have a job in the school system.) I was told that I was being terminated because of Code 10, which discusses moral and ethical issues (I have yet to read code 10). Of course, I asked the dude if he were serious.

5. Could it really be that deep because of a phone call? No warning? No simple take the page down?

6. I was given the option to resign. I told them I would come back tomorrow with my decision of whether or not I would resign. I asked if I would be allowed to report back to the school. The answer was, "No, I'll set up a time for you to meet with the principal and collect your classroom items." You know I am looking at him like he lost his mind right? They were treating me like a straight up criminal. I was still in shock from it all. I couldn't even say goodbye to my students. To this day the principal still has not offered an explanation to the students or parents about my whereabouts. That's just tacky and unprofessional! Parents and students are wondering where I am.

7. I immediately left the Human Resources Office and went back to the school to get all my things. It was like 5:30 pm by this time, so no one was there but the janitors. I took four trash bags and cleaned my whole room out in thirty minutes, loaded my car up,

and left the key with my name on it in the principal's mailbox. I wasn't waiting to meet with him about SHIT!!!!! Mission already accomplished. The next day I returned to the Human Resources with my letter of resignation. I have never been terminated from a job and I didn't want that on my record, so I did resign.

8.   The lady I turned the letter of resignation in to had the nerve to tell me, "Next time, don't mix business with pleasure. And make sure you don't discuss this with anyone because it might be bad for your image as an educator."

9.   I laughed in her face. I hadn't done anything wrong and I will back that until the day I die. My image is just fine.

Interpersonal Discussion

1.   Evaluate the interpersonal dynamics in Paragraphs 2 through 4.

2.   After reading paragraphs 3 and 5, what do you believe would bring clarity to this situation?

3.   In paragraph, 6, the teacher was offered an opportunity to setup a time to meet with the principal. How do you think the teacher should have handled this entire situation?

Wrap It Up

In this chapter, we explored the complexity of ethical communication and the fact that it is governed by morals, beliefs, norms, and values that societies use to determine right from wrong; however, individual ethics may not always be aligned with the ethics of our society. Because our thought patterns tend to govern our behavior, what we believe to be true or right will often determine what we will do or say. There are underlying philosophies that are the foundations upon which we have built and structured ethical standards. Three of these philosophies include egalitarianism, teleology, and deontology. Additionally, we discussed three communication theories that have been identified and maybe used to develop a tool for others to use for their own ethical audits in communication.

References

Anderson, R. and V. Ross. Questions of communication, (3rd ed.). Boston, Mass., Bedford/St. Martin's, 2002.

Arnett, R. C. "The Status of Communication Ethics Scholarship in Speech Communication Journals from 1915 to 1985." In K. J. Grenberg (Ed.), *Conversations on Communication Ethics* Norwood, NJ: Ablex, 1991: 55–72.

Buber, M. *I and Thou* (R. G. Smith Translation), New York: Scribner, 1958.

Dewey J., and A. F. Bentley *Knowing and the Known.* Boston: Beacon, 1949.

Fraleigh, D. M. and J. S. Tuman *Freedom of Speech,* Boston, Mass.: Bedford/St. Martin's, 1997.

Friedman, M. *Touchstones of Reality: Existential Trust and the Community of Peace,* New York: Dutton, 1974.

Johannesen, R. L. *Ethics in Human Communication,* (3rd ed.). Prospect Heights, Ill.: Waveland, 1990.

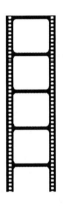

Communication in the Movies

I invite you and a friend or classmates to explore comunication in the movies. Reflect on the communication skills discussed in this chapter. How are they addressed in the movies?

▶ Fighting Temptations
▶ The Challenger
▶ 12 Angry Men
▶ Deliver Us From Eva
▶ The Gospel

Name _____   Date _____

Section _____

Think About It → Write About It

Reflect on what you've just read. Now write what you are thinking.

_____

_____

_____

_____

_____

_____

_____

_____

_____

_____

_____

_____

_____

_____

_____

_____

_____

_____

_____

_____

_____

_____

_____

_____

_____

Ethical Choices and Decisions

Read to your class the following list of activities. Allow them to respond to each one determining if they believe it is ethical or unethical.

a. Purchasing bootlegged movies

b. Taking minor supplies home from work

c. Lying about your age to purchase an alcoholic drink

d. Cheating on your income tax

e. Exaggerating about your work experience in a job interview

f. Flirting your way out of a traffic ticket

g. Surfing the internet during work hours

h. Cheating on a test

i. Splicing cable from your neighbor

j. Exaggerating about yourself to influence someone of the opposite sex

k. Calling in sick when you really are not sick

l. Reporting to your professor about someone else cheating on a test or plagiarizing a paper

m. Telling a child to lie about their age in order to pay the price for a child's ticket or children's meal

n. Telling someone to say you are not home when they call and you do not want to talk to the person on the phone

Chapter 11

Topic Purpose Thesis: The Building Blocks

Key Terms

Thesis   Persuade
Plagiarize

Getting a Topic

What do you know? What are your interests? On what topics could you enlighten others? What controversial issues excite you to the point that you would like to have others agree with your position? These are the kinds of knowledge-appraisal questions that a beginning speaker should ask, and take some thought in answering. It is sad that many inexperienced speakers never make this kind of self-assessment. They ask others, for instance, rather than themselves, what topics they should select. Remember that no one can ever answer the question of topic selection as well as you can. Your instructor may offer some guidance, but you must make the final choice in light of what you know, how you feel, and what you think.

Lack of self-appraisal and self-knowledge makes, for many student speakers, the problem of **"getting a topic"** the most difficult part of a speech assignment. It, therefore, deserves special note here.

Often, a beginning speaker will say, "My life has been so typical, just like the others, and I have nothing really to say." This is, in large part, a "rationalization." Most of us feel challenged and somewhat threatened by a speaking assignment, and generally, we wish that we had greater resources at hand. But actually no one's life is really "typical" and so like another's. We have not all lived in the same places; participated in the same activities; enjoyed the same interests, hobbies, and companions; had the same relatives employed in the same occupations; and so on. What is typical is not the life that each of has led; what is typical is the feeling of inadequacy that each of us experiences in the face of a speaking assignment. The feeling should be recognized for what it is, and it should not be allowed to bring to a frustrated halt our search for a speech topic.

If we take time to assess our accumulation of knowledge about ourselves and our ideas, we will readily recognize those subjects on which we are prepared to speak and those subjects for which additional preparation will be necessary. There is a significant difference between being prepared to speak on a topic and becoming prepared to speak on it. This is the difference between general preparation and specific preparation for speaking. This distinction applies equally to giving a public speech or being interviewed for a job. The speaker's prior experience, reading, and deliberation about a topic constitutes that speaker's general preparation for speaking on that topic. Once the subject is in mind, the additional research, organization, planning, and practice for the event make up the specific preparation.

Try these steps to select a topic for your next assignment. Remember, always look to SELF first for the best topics. Topic lists provided by others stifle your creativity. Think!

List the first five things that come to mind in each category.
I know a lot about:

1. _____
2. _____
3. _____
4. _____
5. _____

I don't know a lot about:

1. _____
2. _____
3. _____
4. _____
5. _____

I really really like:

1. _____
2. _____
3. _____
4. _____
5. _____

I really really dislike:

1. _____
2. _____
3. _____
4. _____
5. _____

I am very interested in:

1. _____
2. _____
3. _____
4. _____
5. _____

I am not very interested in:

1. _____
2. _____
3. _____
4. _____
5. _____

Congratulations, you should now have approximately 30 subjects from which to choose a topic for your next presentation.

Research

Pass the Plate, It's Collection Time

While your memory may have great retentive capacities, you will nevertheless do well to collect and file away information regarding some of your major interests whenever you come across it. Newspaper columns, magazine articles, Web sites, lecture notes (all with citations listing the source, author, and date) should be filed systematically for future reference. Such a procedure will provide both general background and a readily available source of materials for topics of special interest to you. Nothing is so inefficient and frustrating as to spend valuable time intended for specific preparation in searching out vaguely remembered materials, which would now prove useful. While some of this effort may be unavoidable, the systematic practice of collecting and filing reference materials will reduce it to a minimum. Moreover, once you have given a speech or completed a

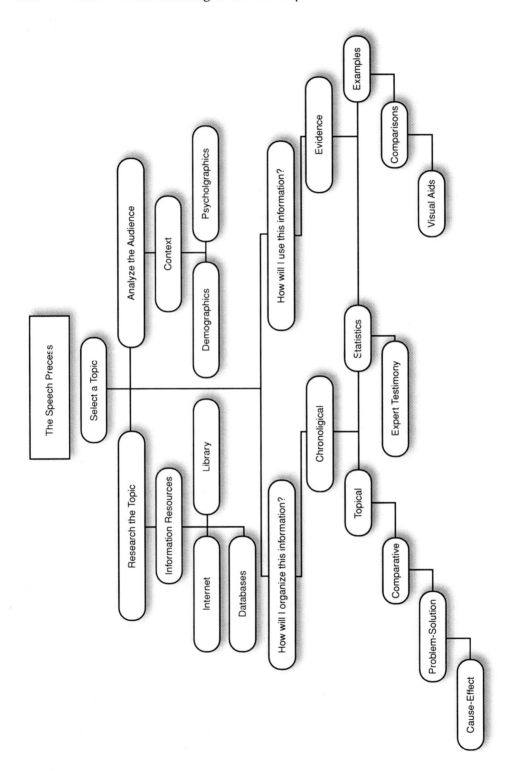

course, do not get rid of your research materials, class papers, and class notes. Hold onto them. Your research, having been completed for an assignment of the moment, is almost certain to have future value and importance to you.

Read through Dr. Whitley's discussion of doing a research paper. This is valuable stuff. You use the same tools to research both speeches and papers. Really look at how to do research. A successful presentation is usually judged by its content, and its content is developed based on the research.

I've Got to Do a Research Paper for this Class? Yuck!

Sheila M. Whitley, Ph.D.

What No College Student Wants to Hear

I hadn't been teaching long when I figured out how to reduce the number of students in my class. I walk into class on the first day with a detailed ten-page syllabus and start going over the course requirements. Not much rustling when I announce exam one, two, three, and so forth. Students may not love the idea of exams, but this is expected and bearable.

Then I get to—gulp—the detestable part that no undergrad wants to hear, "You must write a fifteen-page RESEARCH PAPER with a minimum of SEVEN sources." After a few moments of stifled murmuring, I feel the many silent deleterious thoughts darted at me. Seconds pass, and one student boldly vocalizes, "For real?" I respond sympathetically, "For very real." Before the official drop/add period is over, a few students scurry to the registrar's office and drop my class for a paperless class.

The reality is, as a college student you will write one—let's get real—many research papers during your academic career. You can't avoid researching for a paper or a presentation for long. Why do professor's assign research projects? Maybe you think we want you to suffer through the class. No, that's not the reason. Research papers help you understand and increase your knowledge about the topic (Gibaldi, 1999).

Might as well put on your traveling shoes or fire up the computer. You are destined to physically or virtually go to the library, research a topic, and write or present your findings. Therefore, it is in your best interest to know and use proper research techniques. Yes, there is a correct way to research.

What Do You Fear, the Work?

I think most students fear research papers not because of the amount of work required, but because they don't understand the proper way to research a topic or write the paper. Maybe a past experience proved their techniques created a lot of extra work and the end result didn't get the desired grade.

The lower-than-expected grade may be that the paper was poorly written or lacked substance; the sources were too few, old or not relevant (the student used the first sources they found and stopped researching after reaching the required number of sources); the student turned in the first draft (this is a multi-draft process); the student didn't proof read the paper (always proof your paper many times and read it out loud); the student did the paper at the last minute and had to get something on paper (after all, isn't a "C–" better than a zero?); or the paper was plagiarized (copied someone's paper or got it from one of those Internet sites that faculty also know about—I will discuss this violation in detail). Keep in mind, your paper has a purpose beyond getting a good grade. You are expanding your skills and knowledge. Researching and writing is a calculated and long process. You can't turn in a good paper you wrote in a night or even a week.

Who Am I: Einstein or da Vinci?

Is writing a research paper an art or a science? Some of you are saying an art because a well-written, intellectually stimulating paper is artistry. I agree. I also hear science because there is a method to researching. I agree. Therefore, writing a research paper is an art and a science.

It is an art because you use imagination and creativity throughout the process. In creative writing, the writer tries to awaken feelings in the reader (Goldberg, 1986). How about a boring research paper? Yes, you are trying to awaken feelings and connect with the reader. Some topics easily and quickly engage the reader because they are emotionally charged or highly controversial. What if the topic appears—at least to you—dull and boring? Then, you have more of an artistic challenge. Let me assure you, it is in your best interest to aesthetically and cognitively engage the professor grading your paper. More importantly, part of the idea of assigning a paper is to help you communicate ideas in a clear, logical, concise, and appealing way.

Now for the Einstein part. Every class I assign a research project to must attend . . . the dreaded library orientation lecture. My students openly complain. They inform me they did the library thing their freshman year. Therefore, they already know how to use the library and won't learn anything new. I attend the lecture several times every semester, and I learn something new. Therefore, I know my students will learn something new.

Next, they try to appeal to my sense of productivity and say, "The session is boring." The session is only boring if you go in with the mind set you won't learn anything new. Our library is constantly adding or deleting databases and other research tools. The science part means you are continually perfecting and refining your research technique. Without the knowledge of how to properly use the available library tools, students retreat to what they know and conduct all their research via *Google*. That's a no-no my dear student. That is not the proper way to conduct research.

What Do You Mean A Research Paper?
I Thought She Wanted A Presentation of My Opinion
Before tackling the research process, you must fully understand the assignment and requirements. I know that sounds simplistic. I've had students give me something totally different from what I specified in the syllabus and discussed in class. Don't put yourself in that position. Before you start the research process, know what the professor assigned and the criteria.

Here are some of the questions you need answered to help you understand the assignment. Did the professor assign a paper, presentation, or other? If sources are required, how many and what kind or type? Is there a type of source excluded? Is there a cutoff publication date for the source—for example, no sources before 1998? What is the purpose of the paper or presentation—persuasion or analytical? What is the topic, and are there restrictions? Is the tone of the paper formal or informal? Is anything due before the paper's due date—such as an outline or draft? What is the format—APA, MLA or other? When is the paper due? How many pages?

Let me elaborate about page count; if you are asked to write a fifteen-page paper, that means fifteen pages, and not fourteen pages and one sentence or paragraph on page fifteen. Your job isn't to fill fifteen pages with nonsense or redundancy. Your job is to research and write a fifteen-page meaningful research paper. Be mindful, most professors do not include the title page or works cited page in the page count.

This Is The Way It Is—or—See It My Way
Let's tackle the purpose of your project. Research papers fall into two categories: 1. analytical, or 2. argumentative—persuasive (Hamid, 2004). The professor may assign the purpose, or you might get to choose the purpose.

An analytical approach breaks a topic down and rebuilds it to inform or explain the topic. Therefore, the purpose is to increase your reader's knowledge or update the status of the topic. In this approach, you gather facts, figures, history, current status, and so forth from various sources—articles, books, newspapers, magazine, journals, and so forth. Be aware, in this approach your paper isn't just a regurgitation of the material. In addition to synthesizing the supporting literature, you analyze the topic and add your thoughts and conclusions to the paper (Hamid, 2004).

The analytical approach is similar to what a police detective does when investigating a crime. The detective has no idea who committed the crime. He must investigate and take every piece of evidence and eyewitness testimony into account as he pieces together what happened. As you can see, he breaks down and examines all the pieces, puts them back together in a logical order, analyzes and reports the evidence, and draws a conclusion.

In the argumentative or persuasive paper, you take a position and use evidence from the literature to support your position. As you read the literature, dig deep into the truth or value of the article (Hamid, 2004). Ask questions about the article to determine if it supports your argument. If it does, this is a potential source and supporting evidence for your paper.

This approach is similar to what attorneys do in the courtroom. Our above accused is now on trial. The defense attorney argues and tries to persuade the jury that his client is not guilty. Every person the defense calls to testify in court is proof for the not-guilty argument. Just like the detective in the analytical approach, the defense broke down the evidence and rebuilt it, but is using the rebuilt evidence to prove his argument—not guilty.

In the persuasive approach, there is the other side of the argument. While our defense attorney is arguing not guilty, the prosecution is using the evidence and eyewitness testimony to argue guilty. The jury decides which argument they believe. With a persuasive paper, the reader decides if the arguments prove the point.

Let's Name This Baby

Now it's time to pick a topic. I know you didn't just roll your eyes and say, "Duh, of course I have to choose a topic unless my professor told me exactly what to research." This isn't as simple as you might think, and I'm sure you know this if you have written one research paper. The way you approach the topic is determined by the purpose of the paper. Some topics are more analytical, while others are more persuasive.

If the topic is not assigned and you pick it, find out if there are any restrictions. For example, the psychology professor may give the topic freedom as long as it ties back to the something studied in class, and will not accept a paper explaining Einstein's Theory of Relativity.

What if the professor assigns the topic? More than likely, the topic is very broad. This means you still have some freedom with your topic. You have a general idea, but not the specific idea. I assign very broad topics. For example, one topic I assign is the *First Amendment*. Some students think this is a narrow topic, because I didn't say the entire Constitution of the United States—which is very broad. I'm only asking for one short amendment in the Constitution. The First Amendment may be a relatively short sentence, but ideologically it is extremely complex and is hotly debated in courts around the country. Therefore, it is a topic that needs to be narrowed.

Regardless if you pick the topic or narrow the professor's assigned topic, decide on an aspect of that topic that interests you. If you have no interest in the topic, you will struggle through the entire research and writing process. If the subject interests you, you will want to read and learn about it (Rudestam & Newton, 1992).

Pick a topic that has been researched and published in creditable sources—peer reviewed journals, textbooks, books, professional journals and magazines, and newspapers. You can't do a research paper without supporting literature. Be careful not to pick a topic that has been written about so extensively that your paper serves no purpose (Davis & Parker, 1997). No one wants to read a paper that rehashes an old and worn out topic. There is no science or art in a paper like that. It's just a bad rerun. This is an opportunity for you to add to the body of knowledge by approaching the topic from a different angle or give new insights. Professors love that.

Skinny Up That Topic

It is an art to narrow down your broad topic to a manageable and addressable topic. Let's narrow my topic, the *First Amendment*. Volumes have been written about this amendment—and that is just this past year. There's no way you can effectively cover the entire *First Amendment* in fifteen pages.

Narrowing the topic is a multi-phase process (Hamid, 2004). If you don't know anything about the amendment, you can't narrow the topic and you have no idea what interests you about the *First Amendment*. Before you can proceed, you need to read basic information about this amendment. This will get you to the point where you know something about the amendment, and give you ideas of how to the narrow topic. You also need to read the amendment. The *First Amendment* states:

> "Congress shall make no law respecting an establishment of religion, or prohibiting the free exercise thereof; or abridging the freedom of speech, or of the press; or the right of the people peaceably to assemble, and to petition the government for redress of grievances."

As you can see, the *First Amendment* guarantees five rights. Ask questions to determine how you will narrow it down. What does each right mean? Why did they group together religion, freedom of speech or press, right to assemble, and petition to the government? How are they used today? What is the history of the *First Amendment?* Why is it an amendment and not in the body of the document? How important was this amendment to our forefathers? Was it unanimously supported? What is protected in this amendment? Do we need this amendment today? How many people annually use this amendment to protect their actions or words? Are there any laws prohibiting or restricting these rights? Are they individual or institutional rights?

Let's say you decide the five rights given in the *First Amendment* interest you. This is still a broad topic. Keep asking questions. What do the five rights have in common? Why was it important to the forefathers to give us this many protected ways of express ourselves? Does any right interest you more than the others? What are some of the high-profile court cases for each right? How do rights in the *First Amendment* compare to rights in other countries?

As you narrow the topic, you move to a more specific topic. Let's narrow our broad topic to the right of the people to peaceably assemble. This topic is great for an analytical or persuasive approach.

With the analytical approach, you investigate a research question: "What inhibits a person or group's right to peaceably assemble?" To answer this question, you find court cases or articles that give examples of this right being stifled. An example of a court case is a suit filed by a group of marchers. On March 7, 1965, Martin Luther King, Jr. exercised the Constitutional right to a peaceable march for voting rights of African Americans in Selma, Alabama. Alabama state troopers and sheriff deputies attacked the unarmed marchers. The marchers sued to march to the state capitol without police interference. Judge Frank M. Johnson, Jr. ruled state authorities and police interfered with the marchers' Constitutional right to peaceably assemble and granted the marchers police protection for their march to the state capitol on March 25, 1965 (Freedberg, 2003).

The inhibitors in our court case example were the Alabama state troopers and sheriff deputies. The court confirmed the rights of the marchers were violated. In other cases, you might find that a law inhibited the right. You are looking in the literature to find things or people who have inhibited the right of a person or group to assemble peaceably.

The persuasive approach scans the literature to support a point-of-view, and you investigate a thesis. You can turn our research question into a thesis: "The right to peaceably assemble has been compromised by laws or policies created to combat terrorism." You have taken a side—you think this right has been taken away or compromised because of the growing threat of terrorism. Now you are looking for laws or policies that inhibit peaceable assembly in the name of homeland security.

Put on the Tux

Most research papers are written with a formal tone. This tone is indicative of the research culture and community. Therefore, your audience is not just the professor, but the greater research community. It may be true that the professor is the only one who reads the paper, but you should write for the research community (Sumser, 2001).

The formal style means you follow a specified writing style—American Psychology Association (APA), Modern Language Association (MLA), Chicago Manual Style (CMS), and so forth. The style you use is vital in helping you to communicate your ideas clearly. It helps you organize your material, word usage, grammar, punctuation, and how you cite your sources within the body of the paper—parenthetical citations, footnotes, or endnotes—and how to cite the sources in the bibliography or works cited page (American Psychology Association, 2001).

I require my students to use the style manual of the American Psychology Association (APA). Regardless of the writing style you are required to follow, buy the style book, use the one in the library, or go to the writing center at your university. Don't create your own style.

With all that said, you are ready to search the literature for pertinent information you will consider using in your paper.

The Highway or a Great Garbage Dump

With purpose, topic, and tone in hand, it is time to do the literature search for the paper. Get to a fast computer and kick up the gigahertz. We are going surfing on the Internet. Open up your Internet browser—hold up. Don't load that search engine. No *Google* here. There is a place for *Google,* but it isn't the first stop and may not be a stop at all for your research project. I tell my students *NO* Internet sources for their research projects. Have I confused you? Did it sound like I contradicted myself?

I know I said you are going to use the Internet to do your literature search and you will. If you attend a dreaded library orientation lecture, the librarian talks exclusively about using the Internet to do a literature search. The librarian uses the Internet not as a search engine but as a highway; a way to access on-line search services with databases housing scientific and research-based citations, full articles, and other reputable published material. Therefore, your university's library home page is the first stop for your literature search.

Why don't I allow Internet sources? Some Internet sites are opinion and not based on valid research methodology. An Internet source is something that can only be found on the Internet. Anyone can post on the Internet. There is a lot of garbage on the Internet which may be cleverly disguised as valid research. If it is valid research, it was published in a respected journal.

On the other hand, there are many reputable Internet sites with valid and reliable information. These sites have a place in research. You must be careful when using an Internet source and know how to weed out the bad and determine what is reliable. The Internet address can give you some insight into its reliability. Web addresses end with COM, ORG, EDU, or GOV.

Internet addresses that end with COM are commercial sites. Anyone can get a dot-com site. Therefore, a lot of questionable material appears on dot-com sites. Conversely, there are many dot-com sites with useful information. Banks, automobile manufacturers, pharmaceutical, and virtually every reputable company has a dot-com site. Many professional organizations Web addresses end in dot-com. Get the idea? Know who is posting on the dot-com site. Individuals posting to this type of site may be filled with dubious information, while corporations are likely to have reliable information.

Sites that end in ORG are organizational sites. If your professional organization's Web site does not end with dot-com, it will end with dot-org. Just as with dot-com sites, any organization or individual can post to this type of site. Many of these sites are reputable, and some are questionable. You must weed out the information and look closely at who or what organization is posting the information.

The most reliable Web sites end in GOV or EDU. Web sites for federal, state, and local governments or agencies end in GOV. The government sites post information about their operations, policies, public interest, and etc. Much of this information is also published in hard copy.

Educational institution Web sites end in EDU. Most of the information posted on these sites are highly reputable. A word of caution: many educational institutions allow students to post home pages on their educational sites. This material is not posted or approved by the educational institution and can be very opinionated.

There is a little background on the type of published material you need for a research project. Just as with the Internet—because it is in print doesn't mean it is a creditable piece. You must also evaluate what is in print. Some journals, newspapers, and books are self-published, and filled with all kinds of opinions not backed or supported by research.

Most of the literature used in your research project comes from published works of experts (Gibaldi, 1999). Several types of published works are considered suitable for research projects. The most respected type of publication is a peer-reviewed journal. This type of journal requires the article submitted for publication consideration to be reviewed by a panel of experts (peers) in the field. Most professional organizations publish a peer-reviewed journal and/or professional journal. The professional journals are also highly respected, but the articles are reviewed by an editor instead of a panel of experts. The specific criteria for publication in a peer-review or professional journal varies from organization to organization.

If you are looking for current research, status, or the latest updates on a subject, search for peer-reviewed or professional journal articles. Journals have the latest information because they are published regularly—weekly, monthly, quarterly, etc. Historical information can be found in books, archive journal articles, encyclopedias, and so forth.

On-line search services—such as Lexis/Nexis, ERIC, and GalaNet Group—provide citations, abstracts, and full-text articles from these reputable publications. All university libraries subscribe to a number of on-line search services. As a college student, you are entitled to use your school's electronic resources. Many of the databases can be searched from any computer connected to the Internet by accessing the library's home page. Some of the databases, due to the license agreement, can only be searched from a computer connected to the campus network. Others allow only a few users to access the database at a given time. A few are on CD-ROM and must be checked out at the library's reference desk.

I'm not going into detail on how to access the databases. Every university has a procedure and subscribes to databases that fit within their university's curriculum offerings. The library orientation session explains the search procedure and available databases. If you have any research or search questions, ask the reference librarian. The reference librarian is a specialist in researching, and knows many wonderful tools, shortcuts, and other valuable research tips.

The basic ways to search a database is by keywords, author, and title. For your research project, use a keyword search of your topic in a database catered to that subject matter. If you need court cases, make sure the database has court cases. If you need medical information, make sure the database has medical information, and so forth. A keyword search looks for articles containing those words in the title, abstract, or body of the paper. You may need to try a variety of keyword combinations.

Select the keywords you think best describes what you are trying to find. Let's select the keywords from the research question, "What inhibits a person or group's right to peaceably assemble?" The keywords are *"First Amendment,"* "peaceably assemble," and "inhibitors."

If your keyword is very broad, you will get a lot of hits—hundreds or thousands. For example, a broad keyword search is *"First Amendment."* You will get hits of articles that mentioned the *First Amendment* somewhere in the article. The article could be about the price of eggs in Montana. More than likely, most of the articles will not address the research question. It is a waste of time reading those articles. The broad keyword search needs a qualifier to help narrow the search.

In redefining the search to get more meaningful hits, consider using the keywords "peaceable assembly" instead of the *First Amendment.* You aren't interested in the entire *First Amendment.* You are interested in one right of the amendment, peaceable assembly. Articles about the right to assemble peaceably are addressing a *First Amendment* right. Therefore, peaceable assembly is narrowing the broad keyword *First Amendment.*

If the keyword search is too narrow, or you are using the wrong terminology, you will get only a few, if any, hits. For example, if you search using the keywords, "peaceable assembly and inhibitors" you might not get any or only a few hits. You know more has been written on the topic than a few articles. In this case, you might be using the wrong database, the publication date isn't broad enough, or incorrect terminology.

Make sure you are searching a database that addresses government and/or legal issues. By default, many databases search for articles written within the last six months or year. The publication date may need to be extended to include articles written in the last three or so years. If you are looking for court cases filed during the Civil Rights Movement, extend the search to include that time period.

If you are using the wrong terminology, try synonyms for the keyword and see if you can increase your hits. The keyword "inhibitor" is probably not a good word. Better words might be infringement, violated, ceased, and so forth. You get a feel for the appropriate keywords when you read some articles and see the terminology used in those articles. This is a trial and error method, so write down the keywords and combinations you use. You won't remember and you may need to do a number of combinations of different keywords. This is part of the science of the process.

Check to see what type of language the database understands. Some databases use boolean language. By placing your keywords in quotation marks, you group the keywords together as a phrase. The search will look for the exact phrase "peaceably assemble," and not peaceably in part of the article and/or assemble in another part. Knowing how to group a phrase is also trial and error. Our keyword phrase might appear as "peaceable assembly," "the right to assemble peaceably," "the right of the people peaceably to assemble," or some other combination.

In boolean language, you can use "and, or, not" with the keywords to link or eliminate certain words. For example, if you used the keywords "peaceably assemble" and "infringement" you are looking for articles with the phrase peaceably assemble and the keyword infringement. You guessed it, this is trial and error too. Maybe now it is clearer why researching is such a science and art.

Some databases give you a citation and abstract for an article. Before you can determine if the article is appropriate for your paper, you need to retrieve and read the article. With a citation hit, you must check the library's electronic card catalog to find out if they have the journal, volume, and issue in question. If so, retrieve the journal and read the article. If the article has a potential place in your paper, take excellent notes and don't forget to write down the citation (author, title, journal, volume, issues, page number, date, and so forth).

Some databases offer full-text articles you can print or save to disk. In addition to the full-text article, it also has the necessary citation information. This is NOT an Internet source and is not cited as an Internet source. This article was originally published in a journal, so cite it as a journal article.

When you have the right keyword combination, you will get a manageable number of viable hits of full-text articles and/or citations with abstracts. Print out the appropriate full-text articles. Evaluate the abstracts to determine if those articles are potential sources for your paper. Retrieve a hard copy of the potential journal articles, take excellent notes, include citation information, or copy the article for reference. These are potential sources for your paper. Keep repeating the process until you are satisfied you have more than enough information for your paper. Yes, I said more than enough. You haven't evaluated the articles completely and may reject some. Remember, you do not stop collecting articles when you reach the minimum number of required sources.

Come Together, Right Now

Now it is time to take each article and scrutinize its value and determine if there is a place for it in your paper. Discard inappropriate articles and set aside appropriate articles. Don't be overwhelmed by the notes you took and articles you collected during your literature search. Yes, you should have a lot of information.

Organize the appropriate material by common themes. Word processing is a great tool and can help you organize your notes (Gibaldi, 1999). If you hand wrote the notes, you might want to word process them so you can easily cut and paste. If you don't use a word processor, use the tried and true method of writing your notes on index cards. Put one thought on each note card (Hamid, 2003).

Paper Skeleton

After you group your notes, you are ready to draft an outline. What, an outline? Why can't you just jump in and start typing away? An outline helps you organize your thoughts and prepares you to write the first draft of your paper. Just like your final paper, the outline has several drafts. Why several drafts? It is much easier to make changes at this stage, and you can see if you included all the pieces needed to answer your research question or prove your thesis (Gibaldi, 1999).

Every point in your outline adds information or supports the research question or thesis. I'm not going into great detail about how to create an outline. Your professor may have a specific format. Your style manual goes into great detail on how to develop an outline.

I strongly encourage you to go to your university's writing center for help throughout the writing process. As you know, no one is born a writer and formal writing has a style and guidelines. Writing is a deliberate act and takes practice. Additionally, a critical eye and guidance of people who have mastered the process will help you become a stronger writer. Once again, I stress, go to the writing center.

The way you organize your outline also depends on if your paper is analytical or persuasive. Hamid suggests the classic outline for an analytical paper is as follows:

State the research question.
I.   Introductory
     X   Relevant Background: Anything necessary to set up the research question.
     X   Research Question: Written as a statement in paragraph form.
II. Body of the Paper
     X   Point 1.
     X   Point 2.
     X   Point 3 and so forth.
III. Conclusion
     X   Summary of all the above points.
     X   What other types of research comes from this study?
     X   What are the implications?

Hamid suggests the classic persuasive outline as follows:

State the thesis.
I.   Introduction
     X   Relevant Background: Anything necessary to set up the thesis.
     X   Thesis Statement: Written in paragraph form and includes the various points you will argue.
II. Body of the Paper
     X   Reason 1.
     X   Reason 2.
     X   Reason 3 and so forth.

III. Conclusion
   X   Summary of all the reasons.
   X   What are the implications?

The above outlines are very generic and only are intended to give you an idea.

Put Some Skin on Those Bones

Once you are happy with the outline, you are ready to write the first draft of your paper. Yes, the first draft. Don't write one draft and hand it in. I guarantee you, there will be spelling, grammar, and logic mistakes.

Use your outline as the road map. Take your notes or index cards—arranged by common themes—and start plugging the material into the appropriate place in the outline. At this point, don't be worried about how the paper flows—it won't. Concentrate on matching the literature with the points in the outline. This is a very rough draft.

This is a good time to mention, you are not directly quoting from the articles you collected. Direct quotes are used when the emphasis of the original writer is needed. You are paraphrasing the literature review and writing the introduction, transitions, and conclusion in your voice. A problem with many research papers is the paper does not have one voice. It has the voices of the minimum number of sources. The paper must read like one person wrote it.

After you plug in the literature review into the outline, check for any holes or missing information. Do you need to do more research? Just because you started writing doesn't mean you can't or shouldn't go back to the library for additional or more appropriate material.

Once you are satisfied you have the supporting literature, start the second draft. Write the introduction, transitions, conclusion, and decide if your logic flows. If your logic doesn't flow, rearrange points or paragraphs, add supporting material, and delete material that doesn't support the research question or thesis.

Draft three is the refining draft. Read the paper out loud for the flow, and check the grammar. You can't judge a paper until you read it out loud. When you read a paper silently, you read what you think is there. When you read it out loud, you read what is there. This also helps you hear if you are making sense or not.

In this draft, concentrate on the flow of the paper and the one voice. After this draft, put the paper down for days and don't touch it. The paper needs to get cold in your mind. You are heavily vested in the paper at this point, and everything sounds good and right. While you are waiting for the paper to cool off and for you to become less emotional and detached about it, let's talk about ethics.

Don't Be a Word Thief—Plagiarism and Ethics

Don't skip over this part. Your ethics are your character, and you take it from the classroom into the work world. A major ethical problem at universities is plagiarism. Let's get real—it's a problem in the work world too.

The simple definition of plagiarism is claiming an idea or someone's work—in part or whole—as your work (Attkisson & Vaughan, 2003). A few ways college students plagiarize are by not properly citing sources, copying or paraphrasing in part or whole a source or student's paper (even if given permission to copy), using the same paper for two or more courses, and purchasing a paper from one of those Web sites and placing your name on the work.

In college, plagiarism translates into a zero for the assignment, course, or permanent expulsion from the university. In work world, it can mean losing your job or career. Plagiarism is a serious offense. Take it seriously, your professors and co-workers will. Additionally, liability can be attached to plagiarism. The copyright owner has the right to sue you for plagiarizing his/her material. Is this—what some call a shortcut—worth the consequences? No!

The idea of a research project is to expand your knowledge and understanding. If you are stealing someone's work and claiming it as yours, you've gained nothing and won't be prepared to tackle the forthcoming professional challenges. Keep in mind, your professors will be the ones recommending you for your first job. Do you want your professors to tell—and they will—a prospective employer you are a plagiarizer?

How do you avoid plagiarizing? Within the body of the paper, give a parenthetical citation or footnote every time you use a source. This gives credit to the source, and the reader knows where you got the information. Attaching a works cited page is a must, but not enough (Procter, 2001).

Don't go on-line and buy a research paper. Without question, this is plagiarizing. I did a simple search on *Google* and found a site claiming to sell original, non-plagiarized papers. They claim college professors custom write the paper for you. You aren't buying the same paper other students are buying. Hence, the reason—they labeled it—the papers are non-plagiarized. Carefully, look at the definition for plagiarism. If you didn't do the research and writing but claim you did, you plagiarized even with all the parenthetical citations and works cited page. I don't care how you look at it or what the site claims—purchasing a paper is NOT doing the work. You are placing your name on the paper instead of the rightful author—busted, and you plagiarized.

Incidentally, many professors can tell if the paper is not your work. I'll leave it to you to figure out how we can tell. Keep that in the back of your mind. Think twice before you plagiarize. If you do plagiarize and get caught, don't be surprised at the consequences. You've been warned.

Who Wrote This Thang?

After the paper has cooled off for several days, you are ready to pick it back up for draft number four. Read your paper out loud. You will be amazed at how the paper looks and reads after you've put it down for several days. You might even wonder who wrote that paper—yuck. Time to revise and rewrite.

You get tired of a project after working on it for days or weeks. At that point, you will settle for how it is and you won't have the energy to improve it. After the paper has cooled off, you will have new energy to work on the paper. Start looking for the little things now. Maybe beef up the vocabulary or tighten up the sentence structure.

As a reminder, you can't do any of this if you started working on the paper just days before it's due. Start working on the paper when it is assigned. This approach gives you time to leisurely work on it a little bit every day and not all at once under pressure.

It is difficult to be your own editor. You know what the paper is suppose to communicate. Does it? Maybe the paper only makes sense to you. Get someone with knowledge of grammar and writing skills to read your paper. They can tell you if they understood your points or argument, and point out grammatical errors you didn't catch. You may need to do some final tweaking after you get comments from the other person.

Before you hand in the paper, let's go over the last minute checklist. The paper is properly formatted with parenthetical citations or footnotes according to the specified style manual; clearly printed on white paper; proper margins; appropriate typeface and font size; has the required number of pages; works cited paper is attached; and neatly stabled.

Sigh of Relief–The Due Date Is Here

The due date is here. Hurray! Oh, the pay off is so sweet for planning, using proper research techniques, and starting the process when the paper was assigned.

Sit back and smile as you turn in your research paper. You didn't stay up all night. You didn't have an anxiety attack last week when you realized you had a fifteen-page paper due in one week. You even had time to hang out with your friends while others were sweating and trying to squeeze out a poorly researched and written fifteen pages from nothing.

Logging Off, For Now

Now you are an Einstein and a da Vinci. As you can see, the process isn't difficult, but it is time consuming and takes effort. If you follow the proper research process—you will breeze through your research project because you aren't wasting time looking in all the wrong places for supporting literature. Let's sum up our investigative journey.

First, you need to thoroughly understand the assignment. You won't be successful if the professor wants one thing and you do another. Ask the critical questions. Did the professor assign a paper, presentation, or other? What type and how many sources are required? Is there a type of source excluded? Is there a cutoff publication date—for example, no sources before 1998? What is the purpose of the paper or presentation—persuasion or analytical? Is the tone of the paper formal or informal? When is it due? Is anything due before the paper's due date—such as an outline or draft? What is the format—APA, MLA, or other? What is the page count?

Second step is to determine the purpose or approach of the paper. Is it analytical or persuasive? The analytical approach is similar to what a police detective does when investigating a crime. You find the relevant literature, break it down, put it back together, analyze and report your findings, and draw a conclusion.

In the argumentative or persuasive paper, you take a position and use the evidence from the literature to support your position. This approach is similar to what attorneys do in the courtroom. You take a stance and using supporting literature, and argue your point as you try to persuade the reader to your way of thinking.

The third step is to pick a topic or take the assigned topic and narrow it down to a manageable and reportable size. Make sure you understand any topic restrictions. The topic helps determine your approach. Some topics are better for the analytical approach, while others are better persuasive topics.

The fourth step is to decide on the tone. As discussed, most research projects are formal. Therefore, you write in formal language. Make sure you follow the required style manual (APA, MLA, CMS, etc.)

The fifth step is to search the literature for supporting evidence. Today's technology makes this step easy compared to the old days (ten or so years back). You can sit at your computer and access thousands of databases your university library subscribes to via the Internet. As a reminder, you are not using the search engines like *Google* or *AltaVista* available through your Internet provider. You are accessing specialized vendors like Academic Search Elite, ERIC, Biological Sciences, EBSCOhost, Ethnic NewsWatch, Gale Group, Lexis Nexis Academic, various newspapers, and so forth that are accessible to subscribers like your university library.

In step six, take all your articles and evaluate if they are appropriate for your paper. Group your notes into categories with common themes. Create an outline to help you organize your thoughts and prepare you to write the first draft of your paper.

In step seven, plug the material from the literature search into the outline. Several drafts are required to refine your thoughts and tighten up the paper. Put the paper down for a few days and let it cool off.

In step eight, examine your ethics. Know the definition of plagiarism. If you didn't do the work and claim you did, it's plagiarism even with all the parenthetical citations and works cited page. Don't be guilty of this violation.

In step nine, pick the paper back up after it has cooled off for several days. Read your paper out loud. You will be amazed at how the paper looks and reads when you've put it down for several days. You might even wonder who wrote that paper—yuck. Time to revise and rewrite. Let someone else read your paper.

Step ten: the day is here. Turn your paper in. Hurray! Sit back and smile when you turn in your research paper. You didn't stay up all night.

Step eleven: rest before going onto the next research paper. Enjoy, you know how to properly research. You never need to fear writing a research paper.

Make time your friend. Start on your project as soon as it is assigned. Don't delay. Procrastination is your enemy. The process isn't difficult. As you can see, it takes time and effort. Remember, the goal of a research project is to help you gain a greater under-standing and knowledge of the topic. Make the paper meaningful to your educational process.

In the process, you also enhance your research skills. You might not be asked to write a research paper when you enter your professional career, but you will be asked to gather information, draw conclusions based on the information given, and so forth. Therefore, you will use many skills gained from the research process in the real world.

Don't look at a research paper or project as a bad thing. Don't drop a class because of the paper. Hopefully, you are now saying, *"I've got to do a research paper for this class? No problem!"*

References

American Psychology Association. *Publications Manual of the American Psychology Association,* (5th ed.). Washington, DC: American Psychology Association, 2001.

Attkisson, S. and D. R. Vaughan, *Writing Right for Broadcast and Internet News,* Boston: Allyn and Bacon, 2003.

Davis, G. B. and C. A. Parker, *Writing the Doctoral Dissertation: A Systematic Approach,* (2nd ed.). Hauppauge, New York: Barrons Educational Series, 1997.

Freedberg, R. A. "Rights of Assembly and Protest Are Crucial to Liberty," *The Morning Call* (2003, November 02): A19.

Gibaldi, J. *MLA handbook for writers of research papers,* (5th ed.). New York: The Modern Language Association of America, 1999.

Goldberg, N. *Writing Down the Bones: Freeing the Writer Within.* Boston: Shambhala, 1986.

Hamid, S. (2004). *Artist by Movement: Impressionism* [On-line]. Available: <http://owl.english.purdue.edu/workshops/hypertext/ResearchW/>

Proctor, M. (2001). *How not to plagiarize* [On-line]. Available: <www.utoronto.ca/writing/plagsep.html>

Sumser, J. *A Guide to Empirical Research in Communication: Rules for Looking.* Thousand Oaks, Calif.: Sage, 2001.

Rudestam, K. E. and R. R. Newton, R. R. *Surviving Your Dissertation: A Comprehensive Guide to Content and Process.* Newbury Park, Calif.: Sage, 1992.

What Is My Purpose?

I know you have heard, "speeches are like conversations." Yes, this is true to some degree. Yet, there is one major difference between conversations and speeches. You usually do not prepare as strategically for conversations as you do for speeches. If you are giving a speech, you should, however, have some of the same spontaneity and excitement that you would have in everyday conversations. We will keep with the conversation and public speaking parallel later in this text. Yet here, we will focus more directly on the purpose presentations.

General Purpose

When you are giving a speech, it is your responsibility to determine the general purpose of the speech. Most speeches fall under one of three different purposes: to entertain, to inform, or to persuade. It is easy to determine the purpose of your speech by asking questions like:

1. What do I want my audience to know?
2. What do I want my audience to do?
3. How is the best way to achieve what I want from my audience?
4. Is it feasible what I want to achieve?

The way that you answer these questions determines the general purpose of your speech. General purpose statements should be stated in a single infinitive phrase: to inform, to persuade, to entertain.

General Purpose: To Entertain

If your purpose is to entertain the audience, you are generally the person that inspires the audience. You may welcome them to the occasion, may introduce the speaker, may accept or present an award, or may present a celebratory or eulogistic message. Your purpose will be based on the type of entertainment of special occasion speeches that you present.

General Purpose: To Inform

When the purpose is to inform the audience, you are the teacher, the lecturer, and the one that passes along factual information. If you purpose is to inform, you might give the audience facts on how to do something, like how to bake a cake. In this type of speech, you give information about a process. Likewise if the purpose is to inform, you might tell the audience information about a particular concept, object, or event. **A speaker that informs is responsible for enlightening the audience and providing them with information that they probably did not already know.**

General Purpose: To Persuade

Of course, if your purpose is to persuade the audience, you are an advocate. **Persuasive speeches seek some type of behavioral or attitudinal modification.** Hence, persuasive speakers must ask the audience to believe something or to do something. As the persuasive speaker, you may question facts, values, or policies. Your general purpose is to sway the audience toward your perspective on the facts, values, or policies.

The first step in developing any speech is to know your purpose. If you do not know what you want to achieve with your speech, there is no way that you will achieve your goal. But then, you can't have a goal if you do not have a general purpose. Sit down and figure out the general purpose so that you can move on to the specific purpose.

Specific Purpose

A specific purpose is a general purpose plus one main aspect of your topic. The specific purpose narrows your topic so that you can focus on accomplishing one specific goal. The specific purpose of any speech should be stated concisely and should clearly and specifically state what the speaker wants to achieve. It should also be stated in infinitive form. Again, it should address one main idea and should focus your presentation.

General Purpose: To Inform

Specific Purpose: To inform my audience about the campus policy on reserved parking after six

General Purpose: To Entertain

Specific Purpose: To create a friendly atmosphere and ease anxiety of incoming freshman at the opening Orientation Assembly

General Purpose: To Persuade

Specific Purpose: To persuade my audience that I am a qualified candidate for student government

When you are developing your specific purpose, ask:

1. Is my purpose relevant to my audience?
2. Have I stated my purpose in clear and concise language?
3. Will I be able to achieve this purpose?

Is My Purpose Relevant to My Audience?

You know how hard it can be sometimes to listen to speeches, especially those speeches that have nothing to do with you. We are more likely to listen and to be present mentally during a speech if that speech has something to do with us. As a speaker, your job is to draw the audience into your speech by showing how the topic relates to your audience.

Let's say you decide to inform a group of high school students about the price of long-term care insurance. Most of American high school students are not interested in how much they might have to pay to secure long-term care. You're in college. Do you care? Is that a topic that is high on your list of current priorities? See, I told you. This speech is more geared toward an older group of individuals.

Have I Stated My Purpose in Clear and Concise Language?

Sometimes speakers think that they impress their audiences by using big confusing technical terms. Most times audiences shut down from shear boredom, confusion, or message overload. If your purpose is too complicated for audience members to digest, they simply will not ingest it. They will refuse to listen and will become consumed with internal and/or external noise. Hence, they will completely shut down on you.

Some topics are inherently technical and confusing. Try and find a way to explain the very technical in a way that your audience will understand. As we delve deeper into the how-to's of speech development, we will discuss how to determine what might or might not be too technical for a particular audience. For now, try and restrain from superfluous and technical language.

Will I Be Able to Achieve This Purpose?

You can determine if your purpose is achievable by asking: Do I have time allotted to really provide the information that will lead to my purpose being achieved? If you only have one minute, do you think that you will really get people to take off work to participate in the Carolina Interfaith Task Force on Central America's Pilgrimage for Peace and Justice? Think about it—the average person speaks approximately 150 words per minute. For that one-minute presentation, your purpose must be achievable in 150 words or less. Essentially, you must be able to thoroughly develop and present your topic in 150 words or less.

Will I be able to get the desired results from my audience in this amount of time? Changing a person's attitudes, beliefs, and behaviors can take a lifetime. It sure would be nice to have people come up after your persuasive speech on giving back to the local community and say to you, "Hey, I was so moved by your speech that I want to donate $1,000,000.00." Sometimes, it's just that easy, but most of the time, it is not. So, prepare for limited effects.

Thesis Statement/Preview

The Basic Premise

When I was in high school, my teachers would always yell something about writing a thesis sentence. I always thought that the thesis was the main idea, a sort of abbreviated roadmap of the paper. Somehow, because of lots of different opinions and definitions, I became confused. Here I am resolving that confusion with you. **The thesis statement/preview tells exactly what you plan to do in the speech.** It essentially lays out your main idea and provides a general idea of the evidence that you will use to support that idea. In one declarative statement, you should state your thesis/preview for your speech.

Thesis Statement/Preview

In this speech, I will explain how women's rights have been violated in the Sudan and examine the efforts of the U.N. to protect these women as they attempt to return to their homes.

Sample Thesis

The thesis statement is the result of critical thought. I have included examples of thesis statements my students completed. Notice the thesis sentences are at the top of each students' speech development exercise; however, the students did not decide on the thesis statements until they worked through their own understanding of the topic. These examples show how different students go about developing and organizing their thoughts. Generally, you have an opinion about something. Then you work through your opinion as the students have done. As you see, each student drafted some background information about his or her topic. The depth of the background material varies from student to student. The depth of the thesis statement also varies. Your instructor may prefer very thorough thesis statements like the one in Example 5 or she may be one who prefers a more general statement such as the one in Example 1.

These thesis statements can stand alone, but have more power and give the listener more direction when coupled with your general purpose statement.

Example 1

Thesis: America is the land of the free with a supreme democracy and wealth

Background: America is seen as the greatest nation in the world, as depicted by the media. Everyone says democracy rules and shun any other type of government. I feel that these are false stereotypes and through my paper, I will prove it.

Example 2

Thesis: Powerful and successful black women are charged with being overly independent, lonely without companionship and uptight.

A) Overly Independent
   I.   They don't need anyone, and believe they can do everything by their selves.
   II. They don't ask or receive help from others which may cause a stressful environment.
   III. Lack of trust in other people.

B) Lonely without compassion
   I.   Men seem to be intimidated by women that hold high positions
   II. They don't have children, and if they do then the children are being neglected.
   III. They are too demanding and expect the impossible.

C) Uptight
   I.   They are rude, serious all the time, lack a sense of humor and don't know how to have fun
   II. Lack a sense of humor, and
   III. Unwilling to help others get to there level of superiority because they want to stay on top. (selfish)

*There are findings that prove and disprove all of these stereotypes

Definitions (Webster):

- Power—the capacity or ability to do or accomplish something, strengthen force or might
- Successful—The achievement of something desired, intended, or attempted
- Independent—not dependent, not subject to control by others, not affiliated with a larger controlling unit, not requiring or relying on something else
- Lonely—being without company, cut off from others: SOLITARY: not frequented by human beings: DESOLATE
- Uptight—being tense, nervous, or uneasy: ANGRY, INDIGNANT c: rigidly conventional

Example 3

Thesis: African-American men are classified as low-quality Americans because they lack education, populate the prison system, and are simply good for playing sports and making babies.

Background:
- There are more single Black mothers than White mothers who have offspring with Black fathers
- African-American men have the highest incarceration rate than any other ethnic group in America
- Black men are more likely to participate in sports, such as basketball, football, and track and field—they can run
- Thus they are likely to go to college simply because of athletic ability rather than scholarship
- Frequently drop out of school because:
  - Careless attitude
  - Make a "Quick Dollar"
  - Become incarcerated
  - Get kicked out
  - Not 'cool'—peer pressure

I will likely be conducting a survey and give it to a few black men. This survey will examine if they have ever been faced with these stereotypes. I also have the intentions to survey some Black women and other men of different ethnicities asking them have they witnessed or view Black men by these stereotypes.

I will also be collecting evidence from past experiments and studies conducted by other creditable individuals/groups to prove or disprove these accusations.

Example 4

Thesis: Ministers are superior to other persons.

Ministers are put on a pedestal by the congregations of the churches they serve. The congregation forgets that they are human and have downfalls the same as everyone else. Many congregations see no fault with their ministers until they do something to offend them personally. Some ministers use their status to gain favors from the congregation and the community.

Hypothesis 1: Ministers have a calling to preach the gospel.
  A.   Ministers dedicate their lives to the ministry and helping the less fortunate.
  B.   Ministers truly want to help others through their trials.

Hypothesis 2: Ministers preach for the monetary gain.
 A. Ministers start out with good intentions but it gets out of hand.
 B. Evangelist, mailings, TV shows

Hypothesis 3: Ministers like the power they have with other people.
 A. Ministers place their wants above the wishes of their church,
 B. Can have negative influence over vulnerable members of church.

Example 5

Black Men

Thesis: Three common misconceptions of black men are that they are irresponsible, criminals, and are lazy.

Misconceptions: Black men are often misconceived in every aspect of the lives they live. Without first getting to know the inner self of these men, we, as a society, often think we have them all figured out. With negative connotations and illegitimate conclusions, the souls of many of these black males are the complete opposite. Some of these common misconceptions include the following: black men lazy, black men irresponsible (single moms), black men are "players," black men play football or basketball well, black men have no sensitive side, all black men have been to jail at least once.

Background: Many of the stereotypes that our society has formed today are formed because of what is considered to be normal. This norm has been set by the lives lived by the majority of our black male population. It has been found that in 1990, 61% of all black males lived in single parent homes and the number is steadily rising. 47% of our black male youth lived below the poverty level. This still holds true today and attributes to the actions of black men today. In 1993, black males accounted for 65% of the 6000 juvenile offenders held in adult prisons. It is also stated that the leading cause of black males death is homicide, killing our own kind. There are many other devastating statistics that can be found about black males, these are just a few. It is apparent, however, that this is the reason for such black stereotypes.

Statistics:
www.criminology.fsu.edu/jjclearinghouse/whyblackmales.htm
In 1990,61% of all Black males lived in single-parent homes
In 1992, 47% of Black juveniles lived below the poverty level

Black males compose 19.4% of the special education population while making up 8.2% of the national school enrollment

In 1993, Black males accounted for 65% of the 6,000 juvenile offenders held in adult prisons

It is estimated that 1 in every 4 Black males, 28% of the Black male population, will be incarcerated in a federal or state prison at least once in their lifetime

By the age of 20, an estimated 7.9% of Black males will serve a federal or state prison sentence

During 1992, the national cost of incarcerating 490,000 Black males was $8.9 billion per year

In 1993, 49% of all gunshot victims were Black males ages 15–24

In 1992, there were 3,718 homicides of Black males ages 12–24, which represented 17% of all homicide victims. This was a rate of 114 homicides per 100,000 Black males

In 1992, Black males were 14 times more likely to be homicide victims than any other racial group

THE LEADING CAUSE OF DEATH IN 1990'S FOR BLACK MALES AGES 15–24 IS HOMICIDE

Outline:

Hypothesis #1: All black men are lazy.

Evidence A: Percentage of black men that attend college.
1. Percentage of black men at my university
2. Percentage of black men that graduate from my university
3. Percentage of black men that do something with their degree
4. Personal example

Evidence B: Percentage of black men that graduate from high school on time.
1. Percentage of black men that drop out of high school.

Evidence C: Unemployment rate of black men.

Evidence D: The perception of black men in the classroom today. (high school & college)

Hypothesis #2: All black men are irresponsible.

Evidence A: Percentage of single parent (mother) homes.
1. How many black men actually pay child support.

Evidence B: Personal example / newspaper article / survey / questionnaire

Evidence C: Unemployment rate of black men.

Hypothesis #3: All black men are criminals or gang bangers.

Evidence A: Percentage of black men in prison / percentage of black males that are or have been in a gangs.

Evidence B: When black men go to jail, what are they usually found guilty of?

Evidence C: Survey / Personal Opinion

*Extras:

Hypothesis #4: All black men play basketball and/or football well.

Evidence A: Percentage of NBA players that are black. (repeat analysis for football players)

Evidence B: Percentage of high school/college basket ball players that are black. (repeat analysis for football players)

Discussion/Reflection:

What are my personal stereotypes of black males and why do I have these stereotypes? Should our society have these stereotypes?

What are some ways in which we can end these stereotypes?

Are the majority of black men really this way?

Do I as a black women sell myself short from holding stereotypes against black men? What about other black women?

Opinions of others white and black

Wrap It Up

Choosing a topic is the beginning step in developing a presentation. Always look at what you know and wish you knew, like and dislike, and are interested in or not interested in when you are looking for a topic. Researching your topic is crucial. Your content will be weak if you only go with opinion and have no credible evidence to support your thesis. The thesis previews what you plan to do in the speech.

Name _____   Date _____

Section _____

Think About It $\rightarrow$ Write About It

Reflect on what you've just read. Now write what you are thinking.

_____

_____

_____

_____

_____

_____

_____

_____

_____

_____

_____

_____

_____

_____

_____

_____

_____

_____

_____

_____

_____

_____

_____

Activity

Thesis Preparation

1. Divide the class into small groups.
2. Ask each group to select a topic.
3. Have each group agree on an opinion, an argument, or a concise point of view from their topic.
4. Have a member from each group volunteer to write their topic and their opinion on the topic on the board.
5. Discuss each group's work with the class and determine as a class if the group developed a viable thesis statement.

Chapter 12

Audience Analysis: "Don't Talk to Strangers"

Key Terms

Motivation	Language Adaptation
Audience Analysis	Stasis
Rapport	Feedback

To know your audience is to relate to them based on their background and demographics. How can you know your audience when you've never met them? They're strangers, and mama always said, "Don't talk to strangers." One of the best ways to get to know your audience is to talk with the person who invited you to give the speech. This individual can provide you with background information such as how much the audience will know about the speech topic, for example. Also, finding out such demographics as age, gender, and race of those in the audience will help you tailor your speech to your audience. Conducting audience analysis will mean on speech day you succeed.

As a first requisite for communicating effectively, you must be aware of and sensitive to the major components of the speech process. These are 1. the self, 2. the "other," 3. the communication context.

Understanding How the Self Functions in the Public Speaking Event

"Know thyself," admonishes the ancient adage. It's sound advice. You should try to formulate a clear concept of yourself *as a speaker*. Strive to see yourself *as others see you* in the act of speaking, attempting self-assessment as if you were an impartial, outside observer. As a first step, by systematic and make a careful, objective analysis of your feelings and behaviors in a number of speech communication *situations*.

Understanding the "Other" in the Public Speaking Event

When you are the speaker, the "Others" in the speech communication context will comprise your listeners—your audience. You should, therefore, learn as much about them as possible. That is if you desire to interact with them effectively. The analysis of audiences begins and is inextricably interwoven with the history of rhetorical theory. In his dialogue, *Phaedrus*, Plato asserts that the good speaker must know the nature of his audience—must know their "souls." Aristotle, who also devoted much attention to audience analysis, discusses in the *Rhetoric* what an audience is likely to consider good. He touches upon several human emotions—anger, fear, love, shame, and pity—and examines the effects produced by the various emotions on listeners and the factors which create those effects. His discussion of the generation gap, hardly a new phenomenon, is a useful model of audience analysis and one pertinent for almost any era. Examine it and decide in what respects (if any) you agree, and to what extent.

Young men have strong passions and tend to gratify them indiscriminately. Of the bodily desires, it is the sexual by which they are most swayed and in which they show absence of self-control. They are changeable and fickle in their desires, which are violent while they last, but quickly over; their impulses are keen but not deep-rooted, and like sick people's attacks of hunger and thirst. . . . They look at the good side rather than the bad, not having yet witnessed many instances of wickedness. They trust others readily because they have not yet often been cheated. They are sanguine; nature warms their blood as though with excess of wine; and besides that, they have as yet met with few disappointments.

Their lives are mainly spent not in memory but in expectation; for expectation refers to the future, memory to the past, and youth has a long future before it and a short past behind it: on the first day of one's life one has nothing at all to remember, and can only look forward. They are easily cheated, owing to the sanguine disposition mentioned. Their hot tempers and hopeful dispositions can make them more courageous than older men are; the hot temper prevents fear, and the hopeful disposition creates confidence;

we can not feel fear so long as we are feeling angry, and any expectation of good makes us confident. . . . They have exalted notions, because they have not yet been humbled by life or learned its necessary limitations; moreover, their hopeful disposition makes them think themselves equal to great things—and that means having exalted notions. They would always rather do noble deeds than useful ones. Their lives are regulated more by moral feeling than by reasoning; and whereas reasoning leads us to choose what is useful, moral goodness leads us to choose what is noble. . . . All their mistakes are in the direction of doing things excessively and vehemently. . . . They think they know everything, and are always quite sure about it; this, in fact, is why they overdo everything.

The character of elderly men—men who are past their prime—may be said to be formed for the most part of elements that are the contrary of all these: They have lived many years; they have often been taken in, and often made mistakes; and life on the whole is a bad business. The result is that they are sure about nothing and under-do everything. They "think," but they never "know;" and because of their hesitation they always add a "possibly" or a "perhaps," putting everything this way and nothing positively. They are cynical; that is, they tend to put the worse construction on everything. . . . They are cowardly, and are always anticipating danger; unlike that of the young, who are warm-blooded, their temperament is chilly; old age has paved the way for cowardice; fear is, in fact, a form of chill. They love life; and all the more when their last day has come, because the object of all desire is something we have not got, and also because we desire most strongly that which we need most urgently. They are too fond of themselves; this is one form that small-mindedness takes. Because of this, they guide their lives too much by considerations of what is useful and too little by what is noble—for the useful is what is good for oneself, and the noble what is good absolutely. . . . They live by memory rather than by hope; for what is left to them of life is but little as compared with the long past; and hope is of the future, memory of the past. This, again, is the cause of their loquacity; they are continually talking of the past, because they enjoy remembering it. Their fits of anger are sudden but feeble. . . . Old men may feel pity, as well as young men, but not for the same reason. Young men feel it out of kindness; old men out of weakness, imagining that anything that befalls any one else might easily happen to them (Aristotle, 1941, pp. 1403–1406).

What Is Their Motivation Here?

The analysis of audience behavior is also a central concern in contemporary research in communication. In fact, it has probably received more attention than any other single aspect of the oral interaction process. To know and to study the "subject matter" of an intended message is one thing; to know and analyze the nature, inclinations, and biases of the "others"—the audience members—is quite a different task—and a much more elusive one. And, of course, the larger the number of listeners, the more complex the assessment becomes. Here again, however, you can make certain preparations of both a general and a specific nature.

When preparing to speak with any audience (whether it be one good friend or a thousand strangers), you should try to assess the dominant values and motives which will be operative in the audience at the time of the speaking event. Because you will have to make your assessment well before the time you actually meet your audience face to face, your work will not be easy. To an extent, you will have to rely upon generalizations and speculations. But regardless of how you formulate your audience appraisal, the procedure can assist you in two important ways. First, it will reveal to you the nature of the audience you will face; you will become more aware of the types of personalities represented among your listeners. Second, by discovering the present thought position (and nature) of your audience, you can more knowledgeably determine the directions and emphases your speaking must take in order to move the thinking of that audience to the desired position on the subject.

One means of accomplishing this goal is to ascertain the nature of the groups to which the listener(s) belong. Are they, for instance, predominately members of a single political party, or a church organization, or a certain social group? Do they come from a particular geographical region? Almost always, the individual identifies with one or more groups or collectives. By identifying with a certain group a person places himself in a category: he belongs to X group, she is one of the X. When you identify yourself with a group, you associate yourself with and support the attitudes, values, and motivations of that group. If you can accept the group memberships of your prospective listeners, you can use their associational attitudes, values, and motivations to bridge the communicational gap, to facilitate closer interactions.

In one research study, for example, a questionnaire containing some items opposing norms of the Roman Catholic faith was administered to two groups of Catholic students. Before filling out the questionnaire, group one was informed that they were all Catholics. Group two was not so informed. You can anticipate the results. Subjects in group one answered the questionnaire's critical items in clever accord with the positions prescribed for Catholics than did group two. The awareness of group membership clearly influenced group one to follow more closely the norms of their religious commonality.

A speaker will often wear his Legion cap when addressing the American Legion Convocation, thereby calling attention to the customs of the group and letting his audience know that he, too, is a member of their organization—one of them. Even if a speaker is not a member of the organization or group to whom she is addressing herself, she often tries to create the appearance of oneness with them by wearing a symbol of their organization or trade. A political campaigner, for example, might wear a hard hat when speaking to a group of construction workers. Almost any group can be expected to respond more favorably to one of its own or to one who shows evidence of a willingness to be "one" with them—especially if the speaker emphasizes visibly their common bond.

In analyzing an audience, then, our advice to you as a speaker is that you should seek out all of the information you can about the others who are or will be in the communication setting. Trying to discover their views on the topic at hand, their beliefs and evaluations, their values and motives, the groups and viewpoints with which they associate themselves, and other characteristics or variables such as self-esteem, extremity of view, ego involvement, hostility, aggression, sex, etc.

This, admittedly, is no small task. It requires patience, perseverance, and a degree of ingenuity; but any speaker who hopes to interact effectively must do it. Never address an audience you can conceive of only in vague and general terms. Address a specific audience that you are aware of and that you know. This applies to every communication. Each audience is a different audience. And if you fully realize this, you will readily understand why you may on occasion speak to your father very differently from the way you may speak to your mother, or why you would not use the same speech for a political gathering that you would use when addressing fellow graduates at a commencement, although many of the same people might be in both audiences.

The Feedback Principle

The thermostat is a common example of a mechanical feedback device. It controls the temperature in a room by receiving stimuli, indicating temperature levels, and reacting with electrical connections with the furnace to produce malfunctions in the physical environment. When the temperature falls to a certain level, the furnace is activated; when temperature then rises to a certain level, the furnace is deactivated; when the temperature then rises to a certain level the furnace is turned off. Mechanisms regulating feedback occur and can be observed throughout nature. The human organism itself, for instance, contains numerous feedback mechanisms, which serve homeostatic purposes. They keep body temperature, blood-sugar level, and many other physiological factors within desired ranges.

To pursue our first analogy a bit further, you might ask, "Does the temperature influence the thermostat, or does the thermostat influence the temperature? Which is cause and which is effect? The correct and crucial answer is that each is cause and each is effect; each is influencing, and at the same time, being influenced. The key factors in our analogy are interdependence and interaction of the elements or agents. The people in the speech communication context operate in an analogous situation: both influence and are influenced; both must agree to this joint participation.

From the vantage point of the speaker we need to answer the question: What can be done to gain and maintain the participation of the listening audience? In planning for a speech act, you must think in terms of your listeners and must plan with them in mind. In this preplanning, you will find that the principle of feedback functions in at least two very useful ways: (1) it enables you to allow for "feedforward," and (2) it enables you to adjust more readily and effectively to feedback from your listeners during the actual communication of your message. Actually, prior planning is feedforward, a counterpart of feedback.

Adjusting to Feedback from Your Audience

If, in your initial step in planning for a speech situation and event, you have carefully anticipated the nature of your prospective audience, have assessed their preferences and priorities, have taken into close account the variables of feedforward, and feel confident to carry the resultant adaptation into the speech context itself, you are ready to take a second important step toward effective interaction—adjusting to audience feedback.

This step involves an on-the-spot, face-to-face problem which you can detect and solve only with your actual audience before you. You must correctly interpret your audience members' responses as you are speaking, and you must adapt to that response very quickly. The requisite skill is adaptive readiness.

One of the key differences between planning for feedforward and adjusting to feedback is that in the former, you are, in effect, predicting probabilities, but in the latter you are facing immediate activities. In the former, you can attempt specific preparation; in the latter you have to rely largely upon general preparation and flexibility. In adjusting to feedback, you must "think on your feet," and you must think now. In planning for feedforward, you are making allowances for what you have reason to believe might happen in a possible situation; in adjusting to feedback, you are making allowances for what is happening in and to your audience. You must read reactions accurately, devise and assess possible new and unanticipated courses of action—"instantaneous feedforward"—and select the one that seems best to you at that particular instant.

If the facial expressions of your listener(s) reveal puzzlement, you may adjust by reiterating your point and amplifying it with clarifying materials. If your listener(s) appear bored, you may react by interjecting some humorous or novel material. If your audience is antagonistic or noisy negative, quite probably you will want to react promptly by voicing a pertinent value generally held by the preponderance of the audience members.

As an example of successful adaptation to audience feedback, consider an impromptu statement by Henry Ward Beecher. When an audience in Liverpool, suffering from the embargo during the American Civil War, reacted negatively by heckling a point in his speech, Beecher is reported to have said, "All I ask is simply fair play." Fair play apparently was a value embraced by most of the members of his audience. They allowed the speaker to proceed without further interruptions. Malcolm X, when speaking in favor of Black nationalism to a college audience, sensed a negative audience reaction to his rate and intensity of delivery. He attempted to adjust to this interpreted feedback by saying, "I'm sorry to be talking so fast, but I haven't much time, and I do have a lot to say." If you hope to be effective as a speaker, you must be sensitive to such audience cues, able to interpret them accurately, and able to react to them in ways that facilitate positive interaction.

Audience Rapport

Good rapport, the empathy that one human being has for another, and the relationship it seeks to identify should be one of your guiding goals as you plan and incorporate feedforward. You have no doubt heard the expression "having good vibes" to describe a feeling of natural understanding and sympathy. In the physical world, scientists use the term "sympathetic vibrations." To demonstrate the principle, two tuning forks having equal frequency are placed in fairly close proximity. When one fork is struck and then its vibrations stopped, a similar sound can be heard entering from the second fork; it has been set into sympathetic vibration by a very small amount of sound-wave energy created by the vibrations of the first fork. If the second tuning fork has a vibration frequency different from the first fork, this phenomena will not occur. Sympathetic vibrations can also be produced with piano strings having the same frequency. The necessary condition for sympathetic vibrating is that the two bodies have identical resonant frequencies.

Similarity, if two or more individuals having similar psychological "resonant frequencies" are brought into association in a speech communication context, they seem to have a natural tendency to respond favorably to one another. They apparently have many characteristics in common—backgrounds, beliefs, values, attitudes, experiences, etc.—which seem to cause persons to respond to an event or events similarly. This is not a matter of mere conjecture. In persuasion, of the general findings of behavioral scientists is that a person is most significantly influenced by his close friends and associates, and by family. Voting behavior of the young citizens, for example, appears to be determined to a greater extent by the predisposition of his parents than by the effects of a political candidate's charisma and speeches in particular election campaign. Of course, this parent-induced "sympathetic" behavior is not an instantaneous or automatic response.

Reacting to Absence of Feedback

Adjustment to feedback has, of course, certain advantages; but it also has its pitfalls; and as we will see, the total absence of feedback can produce serious obstacles to human interaction. The able communicator will therefore want to be alert to all of these possibilities.

An early study by Leavitt and Mueller revealed a number of the many positive effects of feedback in communication. In their study, a speaker described geometric pattern to a group of listeners who then tried to reproduce it. Feedback conditions ranged from "zero," in which the speaker could not see his audience and no feedback of any kind was allowed, to "free" in which the instructor could see the audience and in which the audience was permitted to ask questions. The study found, in brief, that the more complete the feedback between speaker and listener, the greater the accuracy with which the given information was communicated. Further, free feedback permitted the participants to learn a mutual language which appreciably reduced or even eliminated the need for further feedback. Leavitt and Mueller found also that free feedback was accompanied by a high degree of mutual confidence and mutual good feelings among speakers and listeners, whereas zero feedback caused low confidence and hostility.

At its worst, the inability to respond to others in real-life situations is a form of mental illness, and under so-called "normal" day-to-day conditions, failure to provide and receive feedback can do inestimable harm. One of the major problems in large organizations is that of "role ambiguity," in which a person feels that she doesn't quite know where she stands, what is expected of her or just how she fits in. She may be uncertain about the "task" elements of her job—the specific ethics—or she may feel insecure about the "socio-emotional" elements of the work—her interpersonal relationships. A frequent cause of this role ambiguity is the lack of communication or feedback from superiors. No matter how unsatisfactory the role itself may be, ambiguity about it is even worse. The deletrious effects of zero feedback doubtless extends to all speech communication settings. Outright heckling, for instance, is in many ways easier for the speaker to take than no reaction or indifference. As a speaker, you must do all you can to sense reaction in your hearers, and your hearers should do all they can reasonably do to provide "readable" reaction. You must learn to look at your audience to see people in it, and to see reaction. You must come to read reactions as "interest," "approval," "antagonism," "skepticism," "boredom," "polite blank stares," and so on.

Overreacting to Feedback

At the same time, both as speakers and listeners, you must be firmly on guard against over reading or over responding to these or any other cues. Inherently, all feedback mechanisms, whether mechanical or human, have in them a tendency to overreact to stimuli. A radar-aimed antiaircraft gun programmed to zero in on a swiftly swerving, expertly maneuvered fighter jet tends to develop a momentum which carries it beyond a correct alignment with the target: it tends to overcorrect itself. The elusive target causes the gun to swing back and forth so rapidly that it has difficulty setting down on a straight line to the plane. Another example of this tendency to overcorrect is the boxer's response to the feinting jab employed by a skilled fighter to draw his opponent off guard and off balance.

Similarly, in the speech communication situation, a speaker may over react and over adjust for feedback and thereby lose sight of her basic purpose. Stated conversely, an audience—or even a small segment of it can provide such a strong or vociferous response as to cause the speaker, in turn, to over correct, distort, or lose sight of his intended message.

Over reaction to audience feedback is by no means exclusively a problem for beginning speakers. Experienced orators and seasoned political campaigners are highly susceptible on occasion. Indeed, there are some speakers, as you no doubt have observed, who are so eager to sense from which directions "the winds of change are blowing"—and to react instantaneously to those currents—that their values and goals seem to come more from their listeners than from themselves. Although they may be public figures and "leaders," they are, in fact, "followers," the epitome of the other-directed person.

Language Adaptation

As a public speaking communicator, you should be aware also that two persons having many experiences in common tend to develop similar categories and strategies for reasoning. You should be alert to the fact that as you plan the phrasing of your ideas, propositions, and arguments—that persons having these similar backgrounds are likely to have similar connotations for language symbols. Individuals with a good rapport or who have worked closely together in a school, business, or profession sometimes speak in a jargon which generally abbreviates their messages into a mutual language which strengthens their communicative bond. Various groups have their own verbal "shorthand"—they can count on the other's ability to fill in a cryptic message with appropriate detail. In Tolstoy's novel *Anna Karenina,* for instance, two lovers communicate by using the initial letter to each word, such as I - L - Y. If, in planning for feedforward you are cognizant of the range of language adaptability, your audience interaction will be much more effective.

Unfortunately, many participants in public speech scenarios do not have the close natural rapport and mutuality that we are describing in this section. Yet your goal as speaker is to try to discover the extent to which these bonds do exist among your listeners, and to strive for the feedforward which can facilitate and broaden their understanding of what you are trying to communicate to them.

To some degree, the functioning of this linguistic commonality is under your direct control as the speaker. Within reasonable bounds, you should adapt and attempt to "speak the language" of your listener. Behavioral research reveals something of the ways in which you as a speaker may effect such adaptation. Speaking to the Methodist Women's club on water pollution, you may, for instance, relate your proposition to family life and social values. If later in the day you speak to the local Junior Chamber of Commerce, you may relate the same proposition in values of economic concern. The important point is that you will obviously be less effective if you attempt to give the identical speech in two different settings. Nor is it enough merely to adjust the introductory material of your speech. The entire message must be fitted to the beliefs and evaluation and values of the audience.

In feedforward, what you are doing, then, in your role as a speaker-to-be is to anticipate audience reactions and prepare for them. And the greater your knowledge of the audience, the more accurately you will be able to predict their responses. In some special cases, as with a televison address, attention to feedforward becomes of utmost importance because your audience is "faceless," and only delayed feedback will be possible. But for most of the other forms of oral communication, including informal conversation, your anticipation of listener judgments and responses can help you achieve the desired interaction.

Stasis

Our study of the facets of feedforward would be incomplete without a consideration of what classical rhetoricians called stasis or the "status of the case." Assuming for the moment that you have ascertained with reasonable accuracy, the beliefs, attitudes, values, and general backgrounds of your listeners, in addition you need to know "where they now are" in their thinking about their ideas or prepositions you intend to advance. At what point in their thinking and believing will you come upon them as you begin to speak? At what point in the oral process can you most efficiently and effectively initiate their consideration and induce their receptivity? At what juncture do you "hook on" to their collective train of thought?

If you assume, for instance, that your listeners have more background knowledge of your topic than they in fact possess, you will "lose" them at the outset; if you assume that they have less than they really have, they may quickly lose interest and become bored.

Cicero and Quintilian taught that the status of a case can be determined by asking certain questions: whether a thing is, what it is, and of what kind it is. Does the case focus on a question of fact, of definition, or of quality? For example, take a hypothetical case in which A is accused of murdering B. The first question (of fact) asks: did A kill B? The second question (of definition) asks: did the killing of B fit our legal definition of murder? The third question (of quality) asks: was the act good or bad; was it justified? We can see that, at any given moment, the focus of the argument might fall on one or the other of these states. The issue might be: did A kill B? If it is proved that A did intend to kill B, then the issue could become: was it an act of murder? If murder is proved—or perhaps, admitted by A—the issue could become: was the murder justifiable (self-defense, for instance), or was it premeditated and in cold blood?

No effective communication will occur if you present an issue and your listener doesn't know enough about what you are talking about to understand your meaning; nor will any real communication take place if you are belaboring an issue already accepted by the listener.

When you are speaking on social issues, you may sometimes find it necessary in demonstrate the existence of a problem and other times necessary to argue the workability of a specific solution to the problem. If the listener already accepts the existence of the problem, you should talk about solutions and not waste time trying to persuade the listener of something he already accepts. On the other hand, there is little value in arguing for a specific solution and a new course of action if the listener doesn't feel that a problem even exists. If you hope to have the listeners respond maximally to your message, you must sense and concentrate upon the particular concerns, needs, and expectations of that listener at that moment. The degree to which you as a speaker are capable of planning this adaptation will determine in large part the degree of your effectiveness. Hence, the importance of stasis to you as a preplanner of speech communication.

Understanding the Context of the Impending Communication

To know your audience is not enough. You must also know the communication context. You must make yourself aware of the specific speaking situation or setting, the particular elements which will be multidimensionally, multidirectionally, and simultaneously operant within it and upon the interactants because:

1. The specific context constrains and directs your choices of materials and approaches.
2. The specific context helps you as the speaker to determine what is expected of you.
3. The specific context helps you to define what is desired of the speaker.
4. The specific context bears importantly upon what is required of the speaker.
5. And, over all, the context strongly influences the outcomes of the communication act.

Context has both physical and psychological dimensions. Those dimensions are significantly influenced by certain social, temporal, and cultural factors. They are the contemporaneous, causative, and circumstantial influences which bear upon an impeding communication event.

Contemporaneous Influences

Time and timing are significant elements of the context. Public speakers must, therefore, be attuned to the tenor and timbre of the times. What are the common topics and issues of the day? What are the prevailing beliefs and practices? The length of speeches, like the length of women's skirts, vary from era to era. Standards for the "ideal" length of a speech change more slowly; however, some ages do go for maxi speeches while others seem to prefer the mini speech. The typical language (an unmistakable dating factor) of one age will appear ornate and artificial in another. You're the speaker—have some sensitivity to the contemporaneity of the context.

Causative Influences

The public speaker should also be aware of the **impetuses or forces which have continued to produce the specific speech situation.** What in this context has brought these particular people together at this particular time? Is the situation one of negotiation, where an antagonist and you—as protagonist—will attempt to arrive at a compromise that will bring to an end some impasse between you? Or does the situational milieu require you to enact the role of arbitrator in which you will attempt to create agitation among others in order to end an impasse between them? The problems may be similar, but there are different contextual requirements if your role is that of negotiator rather than arbitrator.

Or is the situation perhaps, one of debate, where you are contending one person against another person in order to project your view to still other people? If so, design and marshal your arguments so that they will sway those listening to the debate. It is pointless to try to influence your opponent in a structured context of this kind.

Circumstantial Influences

As a speaker, you must know within the specific context not only to whom you are speaking, but also—and this is equally crucial—you must know what your audience expects of you. Are you being called to the specific situation to "present information" in a fairly unbiased manner? In that situation, outright advocacy may be objectionable, out of place, and ineffective. Or the situation might be calling for a polemic before a partisan crowd where you are expected to "pour it on." Is your presence a matter of genuine audience desire, or is it more of a perfunctory appearance? In the latter case you may choose to present "a few fitting and appropriate remarks" however significant, other than a lengthy discourse. Is it a serious interview or social conversation? Audience expectations should, of course, help to shape every communication context.

Clearly, the circumstantial aspects of the occasion dictate significant differences in the content, thought direction, and delivery of a given message. A speaker addressing a routine Rotary Club luncheon on a given topic would not present the identical speech to the same group if they had convened for an evening meeting in a church social hall. As the speaker, you want to know in each instance what else, if anything, is planned for the program: who and what will precede your speech, and who and what will follow it; whether the general atmosphere of the occasion is to be serious or light; whether you will be seated at the head of a long dining table, or whether you will be speaking to the group from an elevation of some kind. If at all possible, you should make it a practice to inspect the physical facilities and arrangement some time before you are to speak. Invariably inquire about the occasion and ascertain the intended order of events—find out what "usually" happens at such a meeting.

Wrap It Up

There are significant implications in this reaction principle for you as a public communicator. Don't let a single negative expression or a frown from a listener disturb you disproportionately, and don't, as a result, become unduly defensive in your presentation of a message. Don't allow a lone heckler to bring you to a halt because you react to him only, rather than to the other people in your much larger audience. While you must indeed look for feedback and react appropriately to it, you should always maintain your self-control in the speaking situation, and try to interpret the feedback in its proper perspective. Rarely, if ever, will all members of an audience react alike and be highly favorable to a speaker. Some will respond negatively, and others not at all; some reactions will be overt and visible; many will not be. What is important above all is that you recognize speech behavior and its potential for influencing and being influenced during human interaction.

References

McKeon, R. *Aristotle, Rhetoric, The Basic Works of Aristotle.* New York: Random House, 1941.

Plato. *Phaedrus.* (W. C. Helmbold, Trans.) New York: The Bobbs-Merrill Company, Inc., 1956.

Name _____   Date _____

Section _____

Think About It → Write About It

Reflect on what you've just read. Now write what you are thinking.

_____

_____

_____

_____

_____

_____

_____

_____

_____

_____

_____

_____

_____

_____

_____

_____

_____

_____

_____

_____

_____

_____

_____

_____

Activity

"Working the Audience" Role-play

1. Place a variety of roles in a container for each student to select without looking at the role in advance.

2. Explain to the students they are to become the role they selected. They should think and act the way they believe that role should act and be offended in the way they believe this person could be offended. For example:

   a. Student selects the following role:

      Single Parent,

      One child

      Male,

      Works two jobs,

      Early thirties

      Lives in an apartment

   b. How would this person feel as an audience member if they were listening to a speech suggesting children without mothers are highly likely to become parents in their teen-aged years?

3. Have a student read the speech written from the Instructor's Manual to the mock audience.

4. Request feedback from the audience based on the roles they are playing.

5. Discuss.

Chapter 13

Making Informative Speaking Sound Conversational

Key Terms

Audience Analysis	Attention-Getter
Feedback Principle	Outlining

Most of us consider ourselves fairly accomplished in the art of conversation—and we should, considering that the average-aged adult spends about 30 percent of his/her waking hours in conversation. Yet, with all of this experiential training in conversational style, we wilt at the notion of giving a public presentation.

Daily conversations and public speaking are very similar. Simply look at how we handle our daily conversations juxtaposed with the techniques of developing an effective presentation. Effective, here, is relative to the purpose of your public speech. Your speech may be designed to inform. Maybe, it is to persuade. Yet, effectiveness should be measured based on how well you accomplish your purpose; i.e., "Do you do what you set out to do?"

There are several issues that you must attend to in order to become more effective in your informational presentations. Among multiple other techniques not discussed here, effective informational presenters perform sound audience analysis, develop a strong introduction, include strong evidence and transitions in a well-organized body, as well as conclude their presentations by reviewing their main points and leaving their audience with a memorable final thought.

Types of Delivery: Ways of Saying It

The last time you heard a dynamic speaker, what made her dynamic? Did she read the speech? Did her speech seem memorized? Did she speak from notes? A speaker's method of delivery can make or break the presentation. There are four basic delivery methods: speaking from a manuscript.

Speaking from a manuscript entails writing out your entire speech on paper and reading it to an audience. Let me tell you; this kind of speech has the potential to be boring. This type of speech, generally, does not allow for you to interact with your audience. In a case such as special occasion speeches, you may read; however, you should strive to sound as conversational as possible. Take a look at newscasters. Their news reports are usually scripted prior to going on air, but they try hard to make it seem as if they are telling the story off the top of their heads. If you must read, please strive to sound conversational.

Although, you may have a manuscript for your speech, you should never try to memorize a speech verbatim. **Speaking from memory** entails writing the speech on paper, memorizing the speech and, from memory, delivery the speech to the audience. Memorized speeches can bore as well. They do not allow you to adjust for audience misinterpretations, questions, or comments. Audience members convey through nonverbals their sense of confusion. As a good speaker, you must clarify. Just remember that a memorized speech is the one that you just might forget. So, just forget about remembering it.

I always ask my students to strive to be as extemporaneous as possible. Speaking from an outline or notes is an example of **extemporaneous speaking.** You are able to adjust to feedback, to interact with the audience, to clarify ambiguities and to just have fun delivering your speech. Extemporaneous speeches are thoroughly planned. There may be memorized moments, as well as manuscripted moments. And still, there are those almost impromptu moments.

Impromptu speaking is free style speaking. It is strictly off the cuff. At any given time, at any given place, you may be asked to speak before a crowd. Give them your bootleg format of introduction, body, and conclusion. A second may be all the time that you have to prepare for your presentation; 'Off gate' (I heard someone use that the other day and it sounded cute so,) Off gate, know the styling. Deliver based on the occasion. Then, sit down because your job is finished. That's the impromptu game.
*Off gate is slang for "from the beginning."

Audience Analysis

Let's say you have some news that you want to share. You know that you have to get this news into just the right hands. So, you think about the characteristics of all your friends. You decide to call your girlfriend, Audience' (pronounced Au de' ensay). You know her. You know how old she is. You know her race and her sex because—why—she is your friend. You also know how she feels about good gossip. And, finally, you know how she feels about you in general.

In public speaking, this is what we call **audience analysis.** You must gather information on the demographics of your audience. That is, you should know, generally, the age of your audience members, their sex, and their race. You must also know the psychological makeup of your audience—that is, know what is meaningful to them, know their attitude toward your topic, know what they know about your topic, and finally, know what they think about you.

You must also know the context of the public speaking engagement. You should know where the presentation is being held; know about the room; and know why the event is taking place. In general, what you learn from the audience analysis is going to influence how you package or organize your message. It will inform the language that you use. Let's face it, we rarely tell our parents about a date in the same manner that we tell our friends about the very same date. We package messages differently based on audience.

Audience analysis even influences our appearance. For instance, as discussed previously, I might wear a patriotic lapel pin when I address the American Legion. If I'm addressing a much older crowd, I will certainly wear more conservative attire. There are some basic tips on dressing for public presentations. Stay away from the too tight, the too loud, the too loose, and the too distracting attire. Remember, your appearance should not distract from your message.

Now, back to the parallel between an informational conversation and an informative public address. Once you complete this first step of audience analysis, you call your friend to give her the information. Note that audience analysis continues throughout the speaking phase, as you must continually monitor the feedback that you receive from your audience.

Introduction

What's the first thing you do when you call your friend on the phone and that friend picks up? Usually you say, "Hey girl, this is Myra." You introduce yourself. This is same thing you do in a good presentation. You want to introduce your topic. But first you have to gain the audience's attention. In conversations, when we call each other, to gain attention we usually say something like, "Girl, guess what?" Your friend, Audience', usually says, "What?" She is drawn in at that time. Then you give her motivation or a reason to listen. "I have some news that is going to blow you away." Now, Audience' wants to make sure that she can believe you. You want to establish your credibility by explaining how you became knowledgeable about what you are discussing. Did you see it with your own eyes? Did someone tell you this information? Establish your credibility by letting Audience' know how you know. So you then explain to her why you are qualified to spread this news. You say, "Girl, this is no hearsay, I saw this with my own two eyes." Now your friend has reason to believe you because you have stated why you are qualified to spread this news. But what is the specific purpose of the call? You establish that by saying, "I just want to tell (inform) you that Phil is cheating on Sabrina." The central theme or thesis of your discussion is the concise statement that explains what you are going to be discussing.

You know that, early on, Audience' is going to want to know what evidence you have to support your claim. So you preview the conversation. You say, "I know he's cheating because I saw him at the party with Chante'. I saw him kiss Necia at the bus stop, and I saw him pick up Chelse' from work." In informational public speaking, just like in conversations, your introduction should address five specific areas. It should gain the attention of the audience; tell the audience why they should listen; establish your credibility; and tell what and how you plan to accomplish what you came to do.

Body

After you have covered the introduction, you tell the story. Your story must have facts, support, or evidence for the story to be believable. There are five forms of evidence that we usually use to support public presentations: statistics, examples, comparisons, quotes/expert testimony, and visual aids.

Forms of Evidence

1. **Statistics** are numbers that summarize or expand the view of the problem. Make sure your statistics are current. In an effort to keep your presentation flowing, you should round numbers off during your delivery.

2. **Examples** can be quick references, detailed examples, hypothetical examples, stories, or extended examples, which include lots of detail.

3. **Comparisons** state associations between two things that are similar in important respects. Remember, similes and metaphors are great ways to compare like and unlike items.

4. **Quotes or expert testimony** are quotations and/or expressions made by individuals whom the audience respects, such as an expert who is qualified to speak on the specific issue.

5. **Visual Aids** reinforce your verbal message. Please spare your audience; keep your visual aids simple, clear, clean, and uncluttered.

Once your evidence has been pulled together, you must decide how you are going to organize the public presentation. There are several ways to organize presentations. However, here, I'm only addressing five different methods of organizing the body of your informational presentation.

Organizational Methods

1. **Chronological Method** allows you to organize your speech based on time relationships. You may consider talking about events in the order in which they have occurred.

2. **Topical Method** allows you to organize your speech into several categories or areas of focus. As the label implies, your speech may progress from subtopic to subtopic.

3. **Comparative Method** allows you to organize your speech by comparing two or more situations so that you can emphasize their differences and similarities.

4. **Problem-Solution Method** allows you to organize your speech into a discussion of a problem and solution.

5. **Cause-Effect** and **Effect-Cause** allows you to organize your speech so that you can argue that one situation is directly caused by another.

Be conservative in the number of main points that you include in your speech. Usually, your audience can comfortably handle three to five main points. In addition, it is important to note that humans generally forget approximately two-thirds of what they hear. This makes it even more important to be economical and precise with the information that you provide to your audience.

Do you know anyone who jumps from topic to topic during your daily conversations with them? Think about how this fragmented discussion makes you feel. I know that I usually become very frustrated. I'm thinking, "where is this going?" That's what your audience feels when you jump from point to point without giving them a "heads up." You must guide your audience through conversations as well as through presentations by using transitions. Transitions can be verbal or nonverbal. **Verbal transitions are words or sentences that connect ideas and the parts of your speech. Nonverbal transitions are physical behaviors that signal to your audience that you are introducing new points or that you are moving on from the present point.** Remember, no matter how well you organize your speech, and no matter how tightly your transitions fit, your speech will not be as effective if each main point is not supported by good solid evidence.

Conclusion

So far, we have developed an introduction and a body to an informational speech. We have done this by comparing a conversation to an informational presentation. Now, we are at the final piece, the conclusion. Your conclusion is the last thing that your friend,

Audience', is going to hear from you. In the conclusion of both conversational and informational speaking, you want to make sure that your audience remembers your purpose and the main points—the highlights of your conversation. In the conversational mode, you might say, "Girl I have to go, but I just wanted to call you and tell you that Phil was cheating on Sabrina. I know he's cheating because, I saw him at the party with Chante', I saw him kiss Necia at the bus stop, and I saw him pick up Chelse' from work." Essentially, you have just reviewed your purpose and your main points. But your conversation does not end there. You put the cherry on top, by saying, "If he's doing that now, can you imagine what he'll do when they get married?" You provide that final emotive, thought-provoking utterance that leaves Audience' thinking about what you have just said.

In informational public speaking, you want to do the same thing. You want to reinforce your purpose and your main points by reviewing them for your audience. You too must put the cherry on top at the end. Give your audience something to think about. Provide them with a final, emotive, thought-provoking saying, i.e., a memorable final thought. Your audience should not leave your presentation wondering what it was about.

Let's see how effective your informational speeches become when you perform sound audience analysis, develop a strong introduction, and include strong evidence and transitions in a well-organized body. Your speech can't end there. You mustn't leave your audience hanging. So, in the end, review your main points for the audience. Leave them with a memorable final thought.

Remember, within twenty-four hours after hearing information, most humans will forget approximately two-thirds of what they've heard. Essentially, that information is dead. You can increase the chances that your audience will retain your information by putting your main points before the audience at least three times. This means you should tell your audience what you are going to tell them (Introduction), tell them (Body), and tell them what you have told them (Conclusion).

If you follow this method, when you hang up, or when you sit down, your information is much more likely to be recalled. That means that your purpose has come to life, and now your information lives within your audience.

Outlining—The Bootleg Version

You might ask what's so important about outlining. Outlining is the way to organize your information. If your information is unorganized, then your presentation will be unorganized. Unorganized presentations are boring and generally useless because the audience cannot follow the logic of the message.

So now, that's what so important about outlining. The following is an overview of outlining order. Remember each letter or numeral should represent only one point. Also note that this is the format for the body. The specific pieces of the introduction and conclusion are covered in the outlines on the next several pages.

Body

I. (Main Point 1) Your first main point should go here.
  A. (Subpoint) You cannot have just one subpoint under a main point.
  B. (Subpoint) There has to be a minimum of two subpoints under a main point.
    1. (sub-subpoint) This subpoint expands on the statement made in Subpoint B.
    2. (sub-subpoint) Again, there has to be a minimum of two sub-subpoints under a mainpoint.
      a. This is the generally accepted format of subpoints.
      b. Here goes the two rule again.
        (1) Yeah, I'm getting tired of writing subpoints, too.
        (2) But, this is what you have to do to get a good working outline.
          i. I know you want to have a good presentation.
          ii. So, follow this format and your outline will catapult your presentation to galactic levels.
II. (Main Point 2) Your second main point should go here.
  A. (Subpoint) And the party starts all over again...

Working Outline	Speaking Outline
State General Purpose	
State Specific Purpose	
State Thesis	
Label each part (introduction, body, conclusion)	Use key words or phrases versus sentences
Establish main points (3–5 recommended)	Write a prompt for each main point
Write out complete sentences	Write out difficult material (stats, phonetic pronunciations, quotes, etc.)
Label and write out transitions	Develop prompts for transitions, visual aids, etc.

Outlines

Cause-Effect

Organize this speech arguing that one situation is directly caused by another.

I.   **Introduction**
   A. **Attention Gaining Device:** *Choose a startling statistic or fact, a powerful example or illustration, or rhetorical question to capture your audience's attention.*
   B. **Audience Motivation:** *Explain to the audience how your subject directly impacts them. Give them a reason why they should listen.*
   C. **Establish Credibility:** *Tell the audience what makes you an expert on the topic.*
   D. **Specific Purpose and Thesis:** *Tell the audience in a concise sentence the overall theme of the speech and your purpose for making the speech. Do you know your purpose? Are you informing, persuading, or entertaining?*
   E. **Preview Main Points:** *Tell the audience the main points of your speech.*

II. **Body** (Present the issues that you talk about in your thesis statement and in your preview.)
   A. **Main Point #1** *(The Cause)*
      1. Supporting Evidence for Main Point #1
         ❏ Statistic
         ❏ Example
         ❏ Illustration
         ❏ Comparison
         ❏ Quote/Expert Testimony
         ❏ Visual Aid
      2. Supporting Evidence for Main Point #1
         ❏ Statistic
         ❏ Example
         ❏ Illustration
         ❏ Comparison
         ❏ Quote/Expert Testimony
         ❏ Visual Aid
      3. Supporting Evidence for Main Point #1
         ❏ Statistic
         ❏ Example
         ❏ Illustration
         ❏ Comparison
         ❏ Quote/Expert Testimony
         ❏ Visual Aid

[Transition]

B. **Main Point #2** *(The Effect.)*
1. Supporting Evidence for Main Point #2
   - ❏ Statistic
   - ❏ Example
   - ❏ Illustration
   - ❏ Comparison
   - ❏ Quote/Expert Testimony
   - ❏ Visual Aid
2. Supporting Evidence for Main Point #2
   - ❏ Statistic
   - ❏ Example
   - ❏ Illustration
   - ❏ Comparison
   - ❏ Quote/Expert Testimony
   - ❏ Visual Aid
3. Supporting Evidence for Main Point #2
   - ❏ Statistic
   - ❏ Example
   - ❏ Illustration
   - ❏ Comparison
   - ❏ Quote/Expert Testimony
   - ❏ Visual Aid

[Transition]

III. **Conclusion**
A. **Review Main Points:** *Remind the audience of the main points that you have just discussed.*
B. **Memorable Statement:** *Put the cherry on top. Choose a startling statistic or fact, a powerful example or illustration, or rhetorical question to conclude your presentation. You may also want to make reference to something that you said in the introduction.*

Chronological

Organize this speech based on time relationships.

I. **Introduction**
A. **Attention Gaining Device:** *Choose a startling statistic or fact, a powerful example or illustration, or rhetorical question to capture your audience's attention.*
B. **Audience Motivation:** *Explain to the audience how your subject directly impacts them. Give them a reason why they should listen.*
C. **Establish Credibility:** *Tell the audience what makes you an expert on the topic.*

D. **Specific Purpose and Thesis:** *Tell the audience in a concise sentence the overall theme of the speech and your purpose for making the speech. Do you know your purpose? Are you informing, persuading, or entertaining?*

E. **Preview Main Points:** *Tell the audience the main points of your speech.*

II. **Body** (Present the issues that you talk about in your thesis statement and in your preview.)

A. **Main Point #1** *(The first or last item of a chronological sequence)*

1. Supporting Evidence for Main Point #1
   - ❏ Statistic
   - ❏ Example
   - ❏ Illustration
   - ❏ Comparison
   - ❏ Quote/Expert Testimony
   - ❏ Visual Aid

2. **Supporting Evidence for Main Point #1**
   - ❏ Statistic
   - ❏ Example
   - ❏ Illustration
   - ❏ Comparison
   - ❏ Quote/Expert Testimony
   - ❏ Visual Aid

3. **Supporting Evidence for Main Point #1**
   - ❏ Statistic
   - ❏ Example
   - ❏ Illustration
   - ❏ Comparison
   - ❏ Quote/Expert Testimony
   - ❏ Visual Aid

[Transition]

B. **Main Point #2** *(The second or next to the last item of a chronological sequence)*

1. Supporting Evidence for Main Point #2
   - ❏ Statistic
   - ❏ Example
   - ❏ Illustration
   - ❏ Comparison
   - ❏ Quote/Expert Testimony
   - ❏ Visual Aid

2. Supporting Evidence for Main Point #2
   - ❏ Statistic
   - ❏ Example

        ❏ Illustration
        ❏ Comparison
        ❏ Quote/Expert Testimony
        ❏ Visual Aid

    3. Supporting Evidence for Main Point #2
        ❏ Statistic
        ❏ Example
        ❏ Illustration
        ❏ Comparison
        ❏ Quote/Expert Testimony
        ❏ Visual Aid

[Transition]

  C. **Main Point # 3** *(The third item of a chronological sequence)*
    1. Supporting Evidence for Main Point #3
        ❏ Statistic
        ❏ Example
        ❏ Illustration
        ❏ Comparison
        ❏ Quote/Expert Testimony
        ❏ Visual Aid

    2. Supporting Evidence for Main Point #3
        ❏ Statistic
        ❏ Example
        ❏ Illustration
        ❏ Comparison
        ❏ Quote/Expert Testimony
        ❏ Visual Aid

    3. Supporting Evidence for Main Point #3
        ❏ Statistic
        ❏ Example
        ❏ Illustration
        ❏ Comparison
        ❏ Quote/Expert Testimony
        ❏ Visual Aid

III. **Conclusion**
  A. **Review Main Points:** *Remind the audience of the main points that you have just discussed.*
  B. **Memorable Statement:** Put the cherry on top. *Choose a startling statistic or fact, a powerful example or illustration, or rhetorical question to conclude your presentation. You may also want to make reference to something that you said in the introduction.*

Comparison

Organize this speech by comparing two or more situations, emphasizing their differences and similarities.

I. **Introduction**
    A. **Attention Gaining Device:** *Choose a startling statistic or fact, a powerful example or illustration, or rhetorical question to capture your audience's attention.*
    B. **Audience Motivation:** *Explain to the audience how your subject directly impacts them. Give them a reason why they should listen.*
    C. **Establish Credibility:** *Tell the audience what makes you an expert on the topic.*
    D. **Specific Purpose and Thesis:** *Tell the audience in a concise sentence the overall theme of the speech and your purpose for making the speech. Do you know your purpose? Are you informing, persuading, or entertaining?*
    E. **Preview Main Points:** *Tell the audience the main points of your speech.*

II. **Body** (Present the issues that you talk about in your thesis statement and in your preview.)
    A. **Main Point #1** *(The first item to be compared)*
        1. Supporting Evidence for Main Point #1
            ❏ Statistic
            ❏ Example
            ❏ Illustration
            ❏ Comparison
            ❏ Quote/Expert Testimony
            ❏ Visual Aid
        2. Supporting Evidence for Main Point #1
            ❏ Statistic
            ❏ Example
            ❏ Illustration
            ❏ Comparison
            ❏ Quote/Expert Testimony
            ❏ Visual Aid
        3. Supporting Evidence for Main Point #1
            ❏ Statistic
            ❏ Example
            ❏ Illustration
            ❏ Comparison
            ❏ Quote/Expert Testimony
            ❏ Visual Aid

[Transition]

- B. **Main Point #2** *(The second item to be compared)*
    1. Supporting Evidence for Main Point #2
        - ❏ Statistic
        - ❏ Example
        - ❏ Illustration
        - ❏ Comparison
        - ❏ Quote/Expert Testimony
        - ❏ Visual Aid
    2. Supporting Evidence for Main Point #2
        - ❏ Statistic
        - ❏ Example
        - ❏ Illustration
        - ❏ Comparison
        - ❏ Quote/Expert Testimony
        - ❏ Visual Aid
    3. Supporting Evidence for Main Point #2
        - ❏ Statistic
        - ❏ Example
        - ❏ Illustration
        - ❏ Comparison
        - ❏ Quote/Expert Testimony
        - ❏ Visual Aid

[Transition]

- C. **Main Point # 3** *(The third item to be compared)*
    1. Supporting Evidence for Main Point #3
        - ❏ Statistic
        - ❏ Example
        - ❏ Illustration
        - ❏ Comparison
        - ❏ Quote/Expert Testimony
        - ❏ Visual Aid
    2. Supporting Evidence for Main Point #3
        - ❏ Statistic
        - ❏ Example
        - ❏ Illustration
        - ❏ Comparison
        - ❏ Quote/Expert Testimony
        - ❏ Visual Aid

3. Supporting Evidence for Main Point #3
    - ❏ Statistic
    - ❏ Example
    - ❏ Illustration
    - ❏ Comparison
    - ❏ Quote/Expert Testimony
    - ❏ Visual Aid

[Transition]

III. **Conclusion**
   A. **Review Main Points:** *Remind the audience of the main points that you have just discussed.*
   B. **Memorable Statement:** Put the cherry on top. *Choose a startling statistic or fact, a powerful example or illustration, or rhetorical question to conclude your presentation. You may also want to make reference to something that you said in the introduction.*

Problem–Solution

Organize this speech into a discussion of a problem and solution.

I. **Introduction**
   A. **Attention Gaining Device:** *Choose a startling statistic or fact, a powerful example or illustration, or rhetorical question to capture your audience's attention.*
   B. **Audience Motivation:** *Explain to the audience how your subject directly impacts them. Give them a reason why they should listen.*
   C. **Establish Credibility:** *Tell the audience what makes you an expert on the topic.*
   D. **Specific Purpose and Thesis:** *Tell the audience in a concise sentence the overall theme of the speech and your purpose for making the speech. Do you know your purpose? Are you informing, persuading, or entertaining?*
   E. **Preview Main Points:** *Tell the audience the main points of your speech.*

II. **Body** (Present the issues that you talk about in your thesis statement and in your preview.)
   A. **Main Point #1** *(The Problem)*
       1. Supporting Evidence for Main Point #1
           - ❏ Statistic
           - ❏ Example
           - ❏ Illustration
           - ❏ Comparison
           - ❏ Quote/Expert Testimony
           - ❏ Visual Aid
       2. Supporting Evidence for Main Point #1
           - ❏ Statistic
           - ❏ Example

❏ Illustration
❏ Comparison
❏ Quote/Expert Testimony
❏ Visual Aid

3. Supporting Evidence for Main Point #1
❏ Statistic
❏ Example
❏ Illustration
❏ Comparison
❏ Quote/Expert Testimony
❏ Visual Aid

[Transition]

B. **Main Point #2** *(The Solution)*
1. Supporting Evidence for Main Point #2
❏ Statistic
❏ Example
❏ Illustration
❏ Comparison
❏ Quote/Expert Testimony
❏ Visual Aid

2. Supporting Evidence for Main Point #2
❏ Statistic
❏ Example
❏ Illustration
❏ Comparison
❏ Quote/Expert Testimony
❏ Visual Aid

3. Supporting Evidence for Main Point #2
❏ Statistic
❏ Example
❏ Illustration
❏ Comparison
❏ Quote/Expert Testimony
❏ Visual Aid

[Transition]

III. **Conclusion**
A. **Review Main Points:** *Remind the audience of the main points that you have just discussed.*
B. **Memorable Statement:** Put the cherry on top. *Choose a startling statistic or fact, a powerful example or illustration, or rhetorical question to conclude your presentation. You may also want to make reference to something that you said in the introduction.*

Topical

Organize this speech into several categories or areas of focus.

I.   **Introduction**
   A. **Attention Gaining Device:** *Choose a startling statistic or fact, a powerful example or illustration, or rhetorical question to capture your audience's attention.*
   B. **Audience Motivation:** *Explain to the audience how your subject directly impacts them. Give them a reason why they should listen.*
   C. **Establish Credibility:** *Tell the audience what makes you an expert on the topic.*
   D. **Specific Purpose and Thesis:** *Tell the audience in a concise sentence the overall theme of the speech and your purpose for making the speech. Do you know your purpose? Are you informing, persuading, or entertaining?*
   E. **Preview Main Points:** *Tell the audience the main points of your speech.*

II. **Body** (Present the issues that you talk about in your thesis statement and in your preview.)
   A. **Main Point #1** *(The first topic to be discussed)*
      1. Supporting Evidence for Main Point #1
         ❑ Statistic
         ❑ Example
         ❑ Illustration
         ❑ Comparison
         ❑ Quote/Expert Testimony
         ❑ Visual Aid
      2. Supporting Evidence for Main Point #1
         ❑ Statistic
         ❑ Example
         ❑ Illustration
         ❑ Comparison
         ❑ Quote/Expert Testimony
         ❑ Visual Aid
      3. Supporting Evidence for Main Point #1
         ❑ Statistic
         ❑ Example
         ❑ Illustration
         ❑ Comparison
         ❑ Quote/Expert Testimony
         ❑ Visual Aid

[Transition]

B. **Main Point #2** *(The second topic to be discussed)*
   1. Supporting Evidence for Main Point #2
      - ❏ Statistic
      - ❏ Example
      - ❏ Illustration
      - ❏ Comparison
      - ❏ Quote/Expert Testimony
      - ❏ Visual Aid
   2. Supporting Evidence for Main Point #2
      - ❏ Statistic
      - ❏ Example
      - ❏ Illustration
      - ❏ Comparison
      - ❏ Quote/Expert Testimony
      - ❏ Visual Aid
   3. Supporting Evidence for Main Point #2
      - ❏ Statistic
      - ❏ Example
      - ❏ Illustration
      - ❏ Comparison
      - ❏ Quote/Expert Testimony
      - ❏ Visual Aid

[Transition]

C. **Main Point # 3** *(The third topic to be discussed)*
   1. Supporting Evidence for Main Point #3
      - ❏ Statistic
      - ❏ Example
      - ❏ Illustration
      - ❏ Comparison
      - ❏ Quote/Expert Testimony
      - ❏ Visual Aid
   2. Supporting Evidence for Main Point #3
      - ❏ Statistic
      - ❏ Example
      - ❏ Illustration
      - ❏ Comparison
      - ❏ Quote/Expert Testimony
      - ❏ Visual Aid

    3. Supporting Evidence for Main Point #3
- ❏ Statistic
- ❏ Example
- ❏ Illustration
- ❏ Comparison
- ❏ Quote/Expert Testimony
- ❏ Visual Aid

[Transition]

III. **Conclusion**
    A. **Review Main Points:** *Remind the audience of the main points that you have just discussed.*
    B. **Memorable Statement:** Put the cherry on top. *Choose a startling statistic or fact, a powerful example or illustration, or rhetorical question to conclude your presentation. You may also want to make reference to something that you said in the introduction.*

Seeing and Hearing the Speech

Many times I have watched students, as well as professional speakers stand like statues in Central Park and deliver their lines with the lackluster of a rock. They appear stiff and uninterested in their own subjects. As you know, boredom is contagious. So, guess what? I, too, am bored with their delivery. I usually think to myself, "Why don't they just loosen up? Why don't they move or make some type of gesture?" Some of my students have said that they simply do not know what to do with themselves when they get in front of a group of people. "Should I let my hands hang down by my side? Should I hold the lectern? Should I move away from the lectern?" These questions have perplexed many. Why? Because many public speakers forget that a public speech event is very similar to an interpersonal speech event. They forget to act natural. When we converse with our friends, we laugh, smile, use various facial expressions to convey messages, use our hands to emphasize main points, and even use our bodies to express an open or closed communication climate.

Speech and Articulatory Strategies to Facilitate Effective Communication

Deana Lacy McQuitty

1. Before conversations, perform the following oral musculature exercises to prepare for the speaking event:

a. Open and close your mouth, extending the buccal (jaw) oral musculature structure. (Repeat 10 times). As you perform this task, complete a yawning sound to ensure full range of motion of the buccal structure.

b. Next, pucker your lips, noting the strength and tension around the mouth. (Repeat 10 times).

c. To assess lingual (tongue) structures, protrude and retract your tongue. It is important to notice how rapidly you can perform this task. Proceed to move your tongue side to side with consistent rate of speed. Move the tongue tip up and down. (Repeat this sequence 10 times).

Once you have completed these oral exercises you are ready to proceed with the speech act. Helpful strategies to remember during this process include:

1. Make sure you overarticulate monosyllabic words. It is important that you place emphasis on the first, middle and last sounds of a word. This strategy will ensure clarity.

2. Pay particular attention to and place emphasis on producing final consonant sounds. Specifically, words ending in -st (such as be*st;* re*st;* lea*st*).

3. Words that include /th/ should be observed closely. This combination is misarticulated with the /f/ sound usually at the end or middle of a word. As a communicator, you should be conscious and pronounce this consonant cluster accurately to improve clarity in speaking.

Gestures

A **gesture is a movement of the body or limbs that expresses or emphasizes an idea.** Gestures are powerful. They create a bond between you and the audience. It is important to remember, however, that your gestures should not draw attention to themselves, but to the correlating message you are trying to emphasize.

When I was in middle school, I competed in numerous oratorical or speaking contests. One contest in particular sticks out in my memory. I was competing for the zone championship. My opponent that evening stepped to the podium with the confidence of the Nellie Olsen character from the "Little House on the Prairie" series. Actually, she reminded me a lot of Nellie, the same old-fashioned dress, the blonde curls, and the same overly dramatic expressions. This young lady had a dazzling speech, but her hands were all over the place. She flailed and flung. She pranced and paraded. She glared and gazed. I thought, "Surely she has wowed the audience with her extremely animated presentation." Not! The judges decided that she overly gesticulated and they awarded me with first place. Sometimes you can overdo it with the gestures. The rule of thumb is to make gestures that are open and, most of all, natural. If it does not feel natural, it probably will not look natural to your audience.

Controlling the One Big Nerve

We know that novice speakers are often confused about what to do with their hands and their bodies. Some rock back and forth, while others shift from one foot to the other. Then there are those who pace the floor like anxious fathers-to-be. Usually, this excessive movement is about nervous energy.

It is important to find a place to direct your nervous energy. You might find that you are more comfortable walking from one side of the lectern to the other side at a controlled pace. Be careful. You do not want your steps to appear too choreographed. Always remember to take deep breaths. Deep breathing works wonders for the nerves. Don't pant, just breathe deeply.

Freedom Exercise

If you can see it, you can believe it.
If you can believe it, you can achieve it.

Often we are held hostage by our own mental chains, are oppressed by our own thoughts, and are powerless because we give up our innate power. These tips for freedom are designed to free you from your own inhibitions. Meanwhile, you will experience a level of relaxation that will enable you to become more in tune to your inner abilities as a professional public speaker.

Find a quiet place, where you feel free from the anxiousness caused by daily life. As you prepare to free your mind, you may find that soft music will help in this relaxation process. Let's get started.

1. Close your eyes.

2. Take several deep breaths by inhaling deeply through your nostrils, holding the breath for 2–3 seconds, and then exhaling slowly through your mouth.

3. As you inhale, mentally isolate a body part. Tighten or squeeze that part. You may want to begin this phase of the exercise by inhaling and then tightening your lower abdominal area. Hold the breath for 2–3 seconds, then release the breath and the body part. Continue this process until your body is completely relaxed.

4. See (visualize) yourself confidently walking to the podium. Continue to breathe.

5. Remember that you are the expert. Take deep breaths.

6. See yourself looking out into the audience. Keep breathing.

7. Feel your body relax as you prepare to speak. Breathe.

---

8. Hear your voice as you begin to address the group. Remember to keep breathing.

9. Hear the enthusiasm in your voice. You are still breathing.

10. Hear the smile in your voice. Take deep breaths.

11. Hear yourself articulate clearly. Continue breathing.

12. See yourself moving from behind the podium. Breathe.

13. See yourself incorporate your hands into your presentation. Continue breathing.

14. Hear your presentation gracefully flow. Take a deep breath.

15. See yourself successfully incorporating your visual aid(s) into your presentation. Continue breathing.

16. See yourself successfully concluding your presentation. Breathe.

17. See yourself backing slowly away from the podium. Take a deep breath.

18. Hear the roar of the applause. Breathe.

19. See yourself confidently returning to your seat. Continue breathing.

20. Remember that the applause is for the expert—that's YOU!

You are free to incorporate any positive vision that you wish into this model. The only requirement is to keep your images positive.

Again, Don't Imitate

I had a student who was mesmerized by the oratory of Dr. Martin Luther King, Jr. When he approached the lectern, he would stand tall, grasp the corners of the lectern the way my old Black southern Baptist preacher used to grab the edges of the pulpit, and then he would commence preaching any speech he gave. Imagine the inconsistency the day he preached his informative speech about "Pimp-Prostitute Relationships." The information was good, but the delivery, imitating Dr. King's cadence, was almost comedic.

Find your own delivery style. Just as with gestures and body movement, you want to appear as natural as possible. If you are funny, then let that come across. Humor is good when appropriate. However, you should not be the only one who thinks that you are funny. Bad humor and humor in poor taste can ostracize you from your audience.

Your delivery style should be appropriate to the context of the speech. My delivery style can get fairly raw at times. However, when I go back home to speak to the members of Prong Chapel Freewill Baptist Church in Whiteville, North Carolina, in the little tiny community of Rose Hill, I tone it down considerably. I respect the context of the speech act.

The average person mentally processes about 600 words per minute. On the other hand, the average person speaks about 150 words per minute. The average person, then, mentally processes four times faster than the average person speaks.

You don't want to lose your audience, so keep them attentive by speaking at a moderate-to-faster pace. Although we advocate a faster pace of speaking, realize you should never speak as rapidly as Crazy Bone of the rap group Bones Thugs N' Harmony unless, however, you are rapping. If you do speak this rapidly, you run the risk of losing your audience because you are going too fast for them to understand.

Country Grammar Won't Work Here

Hopefully, you don't know anyone who has "just got my nails did" or who "like-id" something. Yet, people who make these types of grammatical errors do exist. Poor grammar is an audience turnoff. Most people perceive poor grammar as a sign of ignorance and/or lack of education.

In this hip-hop culture in which we find ourselves, correct grammar is extinct. Aw naw, hell naw, booty shakin', bling bling rap lyrics do not tend to emphasize "good grammar." Many rap stars are actually very articulate; however, they may grant interviews assuming the artist personae, the voice of the rapper. Yet, in their daily business dealings, it's back to a more standardized English. By no means are we advocating that you disavow the language of any co-culture. However, as with any discussion of speech communication, you must know the audience. Most professional audiences will not be impressed by your country-dirty south grammar. Stick to the basics.

I Can't Hear You

How many times have you sat listening to a speaker wishing that he or she would speak up? Think about how much time that speaker put into creating the message. All of that work is essentially down the drain because the speaker is not speaking loudly enough for the audience to hear. Your message is completely lost when people can't hear you.

Approach the speaker's area with confidence. Take a deep breath. Fill your lungs and then exhale. Now go for it. Speak from your diaphragm, that muscle area that separates the chest and the abdominal cavity. Speak with force. Remember, don't yell or over exaggerate the sound of your voice. Audiences generally don't like loud, artificial, dogmatic-sounding speakers. Just make sure that the person in the last row can hear you. Take a deep breath. You can do it.

Vocalized Pauses

Many speakers use some type of silence fillers when they speak. They can't stand the silence. Ah, uh, mm, nata mean (you know what I mean) simply fill the silent moments. We refer to these fillers as vocalized pauses. I mention them here, so that I will not hear them in your presentations.

10 Ways to Increase the Value of Your PowerPoint Presentation

- Focus each slide on a few critical ideas.
- Use no more than five bullets per page and five words per bullet.
- Avoid all caps.
- Avoid changing the "look" from slide to slide, i.e., don't mix horizontal and vertical formats.
- Use a maximum of two transition types.
- Use animations and sound effects sparingly.
- Keep graphs and tables simple.
- Maintain maximum foreground/background contrast.
- Diligently copyedit and proofread.
- Make slide titles read like headlines.

PowerPoint Presentations!

PowerPoint Presentations are the most often misused visual aid on the contemporary market. I almost hate PowerPoint presentations. "Wow! Why is she so put off by the notion of PowerPoint presentations?" you ask. My answer, usually, they are not handled appropriately.

PowerPoint is a visual aid. As with all visual aids, PowerPoint slides should be used to enhance your presentation. They should not be your presentation, meaning you should not read directly from the PowerPoint. Your PowerPoint slides should outline what you want to say, not say it verbatim. One of my biggest problems with this aid is that people generally write too many words on each slide. If you are not a speed-reader, there will be no way you can read all of the information on some of the slides I have seen. If the information is that important to your presentation, pass out handouts at the end of the presentation or before—never during. Passing out handout during a presentation creates noise, which distracts from your presentation.

People argue with me all the time about this one, but I have set rule for PowerPoint presentation. It is the 5-5-5 Rule. No more than five words on each line. No more than five lines on each slide and no more than five slides in each presentation. Some say, that's impossible. No, it is possible. It was possible before the advent of PowerPoint.

It is also important that you are consistent and clean with the look of your slides. The fonts should be consistent and easy readable. Sailing words and flying can frustrate audience members. Yes, animation can be good and so can sound. But, too much is too much. If your animations distract from the meat of the presentation, they should not be used.

Each slide should have a title. The titles should read like headlines. They should reemphasize what you as the speaker discussing at the moment. Make sure that your audience does not have to struggle to read the print on the slide. Your typed words should show up well on the background. Too much color is not good. What is too much color? You gage what you think the audience will categorize as too much. Always think about the audience.

My students often use cutesy animations to transition from one thought to another. This can work if you use a maximum of two animation types as transition markers. My students also use music to enhance their presentations. Sometimes the music is too loud. If your background music is louder than you are, turn it down or off.

Your PowerPoint presentation should reinforce the information that you are discussing. Your slides should be focused and should be straightforward. If you don't remember anything else, keep the 5-5-5 Rule in mind.

Make these statements true for your PowerPoint and you should be in good shape:

▶ The topic is very clear when you first look at it.
▶ The main ideas are appropriate to the topic and are presented correctly.
▶ The drawings and illustrations are purposeful and interesting.
▶ The spacing, colors, fonts, and graphs add visual appeal and concrete information.
▶ There are no grammatical errors.

Speaking as the Expert

by Regina Silverthorne, Ph.D.

The "Welfares" and the "Dangers"

It is highly likely that you will be asked to deliver a speech in your area of expertise. Each occupation or career has unique terms, phrases, concepts, ideas, and jargon that the average audience may not understand. When developing the content of your speech, the burden is placed on the speaker to overcome shortfalls of understanding amongst non-technical audiences, but intensely involved with the subject matter. In fact, sometimes it is more challenging to deliver a technical speech to mixed audiences, which would consist of both your colleagues and people who have no technical education. You, as the speaker, may want to keep the following tips in mind:

The welfares:
1. Address important issues in a thoughtful, caring, and considerate manner.
2. Provide convincing logic and discourse, explaining your thinking process to provide your audience with comfort (appropriate use of metaphors and simile).
3. Identify and prepare to creatively simplify the complexities and idiosyncrasies of your area of expertise in advance.

Also, be aware of the following dangers:

1. Do not weigh your speech down with unnecessary and confusing details.
2. Avoid exuding or conveying arrogance or condescension.
3. Limit your message to no more than three major points to support the purpose of your presentation.

Methodology

Consider the linguistic profile of your audience. Plan pregnant pauses for the audience to reflect on a potentially new concept. Plan to repeat new, unique, and uncommon phrases to prompt your audiences' memory. Avoid professional jargon, acronyms, and excessive new terminology. Note the list of words below to avoid when speaking to lay audiences:

Portfolio	Downsizing
Rightsizing	Prioritizing
Branding	Customer-calibrated
Benchmarking	Value-driven
Debriefing	Reflective modernity
Eeputation management	Per-share growth
Leveraging	Promise management
Sunset clause	Balanced scorecard

List adapted from *Public Speaking: Building Competency in Stages,* (2008) Oxford University Press p. 463.

The "Standards"

When you are asked to deliver a speech in your area of expertise to your colleagues, you must still analyze your audience. Apply all of the public speaking strategies to include graphs, handouts, pictures, and/or a read-ahead to support your purpose. Build in feedback to insure understanding. Remember that rarely is there a homogeneous audience, therefore, you should make very few assumptions. Presenting to executives will be different than presenting to middle managers, supervisors, peers, or employees. Unique terms, phrases, concepts, ideas, and jargon may become more acceptable, but could be overdone.

Business Communication

In business communication, there is traditionally a hierarchical flow of information:

a. Upward Communication
b. Downward Communication
c. Horizontal or Lateral Communication

The content of upward communication generally consists of progress reports telling results and accomplishments, discussing issues and problems, or requesting clarification of an assignment. If the environment is non-threatening, ideas, suggestions, and feelings may be included in this communication. Ethical dilemmas of truth-telling are more prevalent in the content of this communication.

The content of downward communication generally addresses policies and procedures, organizational goals and strategies, work assignments, employee development, constructive criticism, praise and recognition. Ethical dilemmas of scapegoat(ing) become most common in the content of this communication.

The horizontal or lateral communication involves coordination of interrelated activities, problem-solving efforts and family-type relationship building. The most widespread ethical dilemmas we see here involve information-sharing and balance of work- efforts.

Speech presentations for an audience of your colleagues are often impressed with all the bells and whistles technology can provide, as long as it is not overdone and the format is accurate, well-integrated, and not choppy. I heard Donald Trump of the *Apprentice* state to a contestant, "Your presentation was choppy, your couldn't handle your technology, and you printed the wrong phone number on the brochure—YOU'RE FIRED!"

Social and Behavioral Science Communication

If you are the expert in the humanities or the social or behavior sciences, your speech presentation most likely includes historical facts, famous people in history, data comparisons with contemporary studies or information regarding the human condition.

The "standards" for analyzing the audience remain the same, however, your colleagues will be aware of most historical information; therefore, you must double check the accuracy of your information to maintain credibility. Additionally, your audience may have an extensive background in human behavior and will quickly see through mind puzzles or tricks to invoke a particular audience reaction. This necessitates your need to be sincere in your approach toward engaging the audience.

Unlike what appeals to audiences in business communication, these audiences are *more* impressed by well-researched information than the bells and whistles of a PowerPoint presentation or any other technology. How you connect with people is what they are learning from you.

Technical Speaking

The cultivation of the technical mind and the implementation of the technological society have characterized the passage of the eighteenth century, the unfolding of the twentieth century, and the anticipation of the twenty-first century.

The technical mind, in the formation, public expression and refinement of its thoughts, uses all of the elements discussed throughout this volume. In addition to the considerations attendant on the public expression of any private thought, the utterance of the technical mind is also complicated by being expressed in a notational system at least one step removed from natural language.

Technical speaking is defined as the oral presentation of material in a language or notational system at least one step removed from a natural language.

A "natural language" may be characterized as one's native tongue, the language(s) learned as a child, the language(s) spoken by the child's caretakers and peers, the language(s) acquired in the natural process of maturation and development. For a child born into an English-speaking family, English is a natural language; for a child born into a Spanish speaking family Spanish is the child's natural language, and so on. In the process of growing up a child may acquire more than one natural language.

When speakers need to use a language or notational system that has been especially constructed and developed for the representation of a subject, such as medicine, mathematics, chemistry, engineering, or music, the speakers are called on to express the ideas or content of the special subject in a notational system at least one step removed from a natural language. On occasions a notational system can be more than a single step removed from a natural language, as in codes and ciphers.

No one comes to an artificial notational system except through a natural language. Babies are not born speaking mathematics or music. Whatever your native language, you learn the notational system of mathematics, music, and so on through that native tongue. Once you acquire and master the notational system, you may forget the path through natural language that you followed in acquiring the notational system. The physician who is unable to explain to the patient the nature of a procedure in everyday language, such as, "I am going to test your neurological condition by examining how your knee jerks in response to a tap with this mallet, " but can express only the medical terminology, "Now I am going to test your patellar reflex," exemplifies this problem. Some scientists, artists, and others are almost incapable of helping the lay person understand the technical topic.

The person who has acquired a technical language or notational system and is still able to explain in a natural language the content of that technical notational system is much better positioned to express to the uninitiated public the technical content than is the individual who is skilled in the notational system but has forgotten the natural language path he or she followed to acquire that notational skill. Today it is imperative to make scientific and technological subjects as accessible as possible to the general public. It is the responsibility of the technical communicator, whether through spoken or written language, to extend this public accessibility (Buehler, 1983; Menzel, 1992).

Technical speaking is not restricted to the world of science; it is also used within the artistic domain as in music, dance, and other fine arts. A technical notation system may also be specific to a vocational pursuit marked by a vocabulary generally unfamiliar to people outside of the vocation/profession (insurance adjusters, actuaries, accountants, plumbers, physicians, attorneys, computer programmers, and so on).

From all that has gone before in this book it is apparent that the technical speaker is especially challenged by the task of decentering to the anticipated audience. What does the audience already know about the subject, and to what degree is the audience familiar with the subject's special notational system? The term and concept of *shoshin* can prove helpful to all speakers but especially to the technical speaker. Shoshin is a Japanese term that translates as beginner's mind." A speaker, especially an expert speaker, needs to take the point of view of a beginner when looking at the speech's content from the audience's vantage point. The teacher of skiing who takes the first time skier up the chair lift to the top of a black run and says to the beginner "just follow me," is not practicing shoshin. (Suzuki, 1970).

There are two levels of technical speaking:

▶ Level one, where a technical speaker is talking about a technical subject to a technically aware or sophisticated audience—perhaps even an audience of technical peers

▶ Level two, where a technical speaker is talking about a technical subject to a technically naive or less sophisticated audience

You may also, on occasion, face an audience composed of a mix of levels one and two.

Mary Frances Buehler, whose research perspective was more informed by the needs of written technical communication than by the needs of technical speaking, advises that technical discourse should adhere to the elements of fidelity, use of complex verbal systems, completeness, and conciseness.

Here are some definitions of those terms.

Fidelity refers to the accuracy of the information being communicated.

In technical subjects there is often involved a *complex verbal system,* which was earlier referred to as a notational system at least one step removed from a natural language. The complex verbal system—or notational system appropriate to a scientific, artistic, technical or professional subject—is not to be confused with the use of jargon that the philosopher S. Langer labeled as language more technical than the ideas it serves to represent. Jargon may—and often does-afflict politicians, administrators, or almost anyone lusting after the appearance of depth.

Completeness means that all the necessary information needed for a decision, whether pleasant or unpleasant, must be presented, This element may have a difference in impact in spoken technical communication since in a rather complete review of the literature on technical speaking one of the most recurrent admonitions to the technical speaker is "don't try to do too much in one speech."

Conciseness means that a speaker should communicate the technical concepts and information as succinctly, with as little excess verbiage or time wasted as possible. As Menzel notes, "Effective technical communication does not waste time, words, or page space in conveying information" (Menzel, 1992, p. 5). The element or rule of conciseness may be more appropriate to writing than to speaking, because there is a certain expansiveness available in the oral setting as well as the opportunity for dialogue through questions and answers. The oral way of knowing is not the same as the written way of knowing.

Kent Menzel, in his excellent study, contends that the main reason for technical speaking is the continuing refinement of scientific and technical conceptualization (Menzel, 1992). He is saying that although spoken language constructs, furnishes, and reveals the intellect, in scientific and technical pursuits the main challenge of spoken language is to assist in the continual refinement and development of the conceptual content.

While acknowledging Buehler's rules for technical discourse, Menzel goes further in suggesting elements specific to technical speaking. He lists clarity, allurement, command, impact, passion, and refinement as necessary for excellence in technical speaking. Anyone wishing to study technical speaking in detail should consult Menzel's work. For the basic needs in this text, it must suffice to simply list and define Menzel's six elements, as follows:

Clarity involves all actions and strategies designed to faithfully deliver the conceptual content.

Allurement includes all of the processes whereby a speaker learns what audience members require in order to give their attention, as well as all the processes whereby the speaker provides the audience with these requirements. Decentering is essential to allurement, and shoshin helps.

Command is the projection of having control over the skills of speaking and the speech subject.

Impact refers to the use or meaning of the speech's content for the audience. What does the speech's ideas have to offer to the audience members?

Passion is the commitment of the speaker to the subject and the audience.

Refinement is the use of the speaking occasion not only to communicate information but to sharpen conceptual clarity.

Speech Aids in Technical Speaking

Buehler notes that there are times in which a technical communication is of such importance to life and limb (how does one ensure that the boiler will not explode, where on the machine's control panel is the off switch, how does one correctly read the pressure gauge, how does one correctly assemble the parts of the apparatus) that rather detailed graphics may be required.

The requirements for speech aids in technical speaking may often go beyond the requirements for speech aids when technology is not involved. However, the excessive urging of speech aids for every business presentation or technical speech is deplored. Vendors of software graphics packages make unsupported assertions about the efficacy of visuals in presentations. As the computer periodical *Infoworld* reported, "Yet market studies show that as little as 10 percent of the content of the typical presentation consists of the data-generated graphs and charts we've come to call business graphs. Instead, text charts account for 70 to 80 percent of presentation content, with illustrations and diagrams filling in the gaps. (Text charts include title slides, bulleted lists, columnar tables, and organization charts.) A recent survey of our readers who use presentation packages supports the claim of high use of text materials" (*Infoworld*, April 3, 1989, pp. 55-74).

There are corporate and organizational cultures where overuse of visual aids is the order of the day. Such overuse does not equate to either need or appropriateness. In some of these corporate cultures, the polish and flash of visuals tends to obscure the essential message: the communication of thought and reason, in the technical or business venture. Thoughts, ideas, and beliefs provide the real currency spent by the technical speaker of technical mentation.

The basic rule for the use of speech aids applies in technical speaking: Use an aid where it does something that cannot be done as well with words alone or when the aid represents added value for the audience.

References

Menzel, Kent E. (1992). *Critical Factors of Excellent Technical Speaking.* Unpublished Ph.D. dissertation. Denver, Cob.: University of Denver, June, 1992. An evenhanded and comprehensive examination of technical speaking.

Buehler, Mary Frances. (1983). *Rhetorical Foundations of Technical Communication.* Unpublished Ph.D. dissertation. Los Angeles: University of Southern California, 1983.
A primary research study and insightful analysis based on extensive experience in written technical communication.

Infoworld, April 3, 1989, pp. 55-74. Product Comparison of presentational graphics programs, the top 10.

Steiner, George. (1975). *After Babel: Aspects of Language and Translation.* London: Oxford University Press.

Suzuki, Shunryu. (1970). *Zen Mind, Beginner's Mind.* New York: Weatherhill.

Travers, Robert MW. (1970). *Man's Information System: A Primer for Media Specialists and Educational Technologists.* Scranton, Penn.: Chandler Publishing Co.

Wrap It Up

Conversational sounding presentations can be achieved by, first, performing sound audience analysis and by knowing the context of the speaking engagement. Your presentation should be well organized, including a concisely developed introduction, a thoroughly argued body, complete with strong evidence and verbal and nonverbal transitions. You mustn't forget to construct a memorable conclusion. Your presentation will be much more effective if your audience can see and hear the speech. The hearing part generally comes if you are loud enough, but the seeing comes from your effectual use of gestures. Make sure that your delivery style is appropriate for the group that you are addressing. Poor grammar and extensive vocal pauses may tend to minimize the effectiveness of your informational presentation. Remember, your message is lost if the audience can't hear you.

Before you deliver a speech, think about:

- How thorough are you with the material?
  - ❑ Do you have researched evidence to support your thesis?
  - ❑ Is there a balance between logical appeals and emotional ones?
- How well did you organize your presentation?
  - ❑ Is there contiguous flow?
  - ❑ Do you have substantial transitions?
- How much do you incorporate the audience into the presentation?
  - ❑ Do you pause when you ask them a question, even if it is a rhetorical one?
  - ❑ Do you adjust for audience feedback?
- How interesting do you make the topic, i.e., how do you show relevance of the topic to the audience?
- How are you in your delivery? (language, gestures, etc.).
  - ❑ Do you speak loudly enough?
  - ❑ Is your pace usually appropriate?
  - ❑ Do you smack your lips when you speak?
  - ❑ Do you shift back and forth when you speak?
  - ❑ Is your language clear and concise?

Name _____   Date _____

Section _____

Think About It → Write About It

Reflect on what you've just read. Now write what you are thinking.

_____

_____

_____

_____

_____

_____

_____

_____

_____

_____

_____

_____

_____

_____

_____

_____

_____

_____

_____

_____

_____

_____

_____

_____

_____

Activity 2

Components of an Effective Speech

1. Divide the class into groups of five.
2. Ask each group to select a topic.
3. One person in each group will prepare the Introduction.
4. The second person in each group will prepare a transition from the Intro to the Body.
5. The third person in each group will prepare a Body with 2 or 3 points.
6. The fourth person in each group will prepare the transition from the Body to the Closing.
7. The fifth person in each group will prepare the Closing.
8. Then allow each group to present.

Chapter 14

Persuasive Presentations: Using What You've Got to Get What You Want

Key Terms

Rhetoric
Attention-Getter
Forensic
Epidemic
Deliberative
Rhetorical Discourse

Ethos
Pathos
Logos
Inductive Reasoning
Deductive Reasoning

The first time my rhetoric class was offered, students registered for it immediately. The class was full within a couple of days. Students were inquisitive and wanted to know what this course was about. I am amazed at how many of my students were unaware of what the term "rhetoric" meant and was even more amazed when a substantial percentage did not know how to pronounce it. The students were befuddled when I commented, "rhetoric impacts your everyday lives. It is using what you've got to get what you want." How soon we forget. It wasn't that long ago that I sat in a classroom just as bewildered as my students are about this thing called "rhetoric." I introduce the theoretical concept of rhetoric in this text so that I can draw a connection between rhetoric and the use of symbols as a means of expression. Most introductory texts do not discuss the connection between verbal expression and rhetorical theory.

A professor once told me that people cannot effectively evaluate their individual circumstances without theory. His comment bothered me initially. I first read him as saying that uneducated people could not effectively evaluate their circumstance. Hey, let's face it. I know a lot of people who don't have a college education that do pretty well at evaluating and transcending their circumstances. After weeks of pondering and several office visits with the professor, I realized what he was trying to say. I'll explain his claim as it relates to human communication. Humans cannot effectively evaluate the impact that information has on them without understanding the objective of that communication.

In the American culture, we are bombarded with information. There are several twenty-four-hour news channels. There are more daily newspapers than ever before. On-line sources allow us access to information at the touch of a button. Because free speech is a constitutionally protected right in America, we are inundated with public speakers that have sometimes multiple and competing messages.

I believe it would be a disservice if I did not at least introduce the concept of rhetoric as a basis for understanding public address as well as a basis for understanding how people use language. Remember, words or symbols are arbitrary and ambiguous. The meaning of symbols is in the person sending the message and the person receiving the message. Yet, language ultimately shapes our existence. The major objective here is to increase your competence as an information consumer.

Rhetoric Finally Defined

Rhetoric, pronounced (ret'-a-rick), is the fundamental way people use language to accomplish their ends. I have read many different definitions of rhetoric; they all tend to differ. Yet, most concur that rhetoric is about using language to achieve an objective. My students know that I am frustrated by the overabundance of rhetoric definitions. Do not mistake my frustration with the canon of definitions as a frustration with the entire canon of research. It is not. Rhetoric is like Shakespeare's rose analogy. Rhetoric by any other name would achieve the same end. If I must, I will develop a definition of rhetoric, too. For this text, rhetoric is the use of language to evaluate, sustain, or alter the reality of an audience. It is using what you've got to get what you want.

Woodward and Denton explain that, "Communication and persuasion are not interchangeable terms. Not all communicators have as their primary goal the listener's acceptance of the legitimacy and importance of their messages."[1] Yet, rhetoric and persuasion are very similar. The relationship is so intimate that they are often considered as one. Rhetoric, however, has its own set of theories, just as persuasion has its own. This paradox confused me in the very beginning, so I know that some of this information may be challenging. For now, let's define rhetoric and look at its origins. I'll frame this section as a question and answer. I rely heavily on the work of rhetorical theorist James Herrick. Herrick says that:

> Rhetoric as a systematic study, then, was developed by a group of orators, educators, and advocates called Sophists, a name derived from the Greek word 'sophos', meaning wise or skilled. Central to their course of study was rhetoric, the art (Greek: techne) of logos, which means both 'words' and arguments. The title "Sophistes" (pl. Sophistae) carried with it something of the modern meaning of professor—an authority, an expert, a teacher. On occasion, a Sophist might hire himself out as a professional speechwriter, or logoraphos. Others were teachers who ran schools in which public speaking was taught. A third group were professional orators who gave speeches for a fee, whether for entertainment or in a court or

legislature. Of course, any particular Sophist might provide all three services—speechwriting, teaching, or professional speaking. Sophists earned a reputation for 'extravagant displays of language' and for astonishing audiences with their 'brilliant styles . . . colorful appearances and flamboyant personalities.'

Many of the Sophists became both wealthy and famous in Greece, while at the same time, they were despised by some advocates of traditional Greek social values . . .

Herrick continues, "But it was principally the study and mastery of persuasive discourse (or rhetoric) that brought the Sophists both fame and controversy. Sophists claimed that their courses of instruction would, provided enough money changed hands, teach the student to gain mastery over other people through speech.[2]

One of the more influential discussions of rhetoric is attributed to Plato. Plato develops numerous works that address the impact of rhetoric on the citizens of Greece. In the book, *Gorgias,* Plato's main character essentially claims that the type of rhetoric being taught in Athens only allowed "naturally clever" people to flatter their unsuspecting listeners into agreement.

Partly in response to Plato's negative views of rhetoric, Aristotle writes the *Rhetoric.* The book's main focus is the art of persuasive oratory (persuasive public speaking). Aristotle is credited for giving structure to this thing that everyone was calling rhetoric. The *Rhetoric* offers a systematic, philosophical approach to giving speeches: forensic, epideictic, and deliberative. The following diagram lays out Aristotle's system.

Forensic (Judicial)—Oratory of the Law Courts

1. Time province—the past
2. End or objective—the establishment of justice and injustice
3. Procedural mean—accusation and defense

Epideictic (Demonstrative)—Ceremonial Occasions

1. Time province—the present
2. End or objective—the establishment of honor and dishonor
3. Procedural means—praise and blame

Deliberative (Political)—Public Forum

1. Time province—the future
2. End or objective—the establishment of the expediency of the harmfulness of a proposed course of action.
3. Procedural means—exhortation and dehortation

Source: Corbett, E. B. J. Aristotle: "Introduction". In Aristotle, The Rhetoric and the Poetics of Aristotle. New York: Random House, 1984: xiii–xiv.

Sample Forensic (Judicial) Speech

Closing Argument of Johnnie Cochran (Excerpts)

Read through the sample excerpts. See if you can answer the questions in the margins.

MR. COCHRAN: The Defendant, Mr. Orenthal James Simpson, is now afforded an opportunity to argue the case, if you will, but I'm not going to argue with you, ladies and gentlemen. What I'm going to do is to try and discuss the reasonable inferences which I feel can be drawn from this evidence.

******

Ultimately, it's what you determine to be the facts is what's going to be important, and all of us can live with that. You are empowered to do justice. You are empowered to ensure that this great system of ours works. Listen for a moment, will you, please. One of my favorite people in history is the great Frederick Douglas. He said shortly after the slaves were freed, quote, "In a composite nation like ours as before the law, there should be no rich, no poor, no high, no low, no White, no Black, but common country, common citizenship, equal rights and a common destiny." This marvelous statement was made more than 100 years ago. It's an ideal worth striving for and one that we still strive for. We haven't reached this goal yet, but certainly in this great country of ours, we're trying. With a jury such as this, we hope we can do that in this particular case.

******

I'd like to comment and to compliment Miss Clark and Mr. Darden on what I thought were fine arguments yesterday. I don't agree with much of what they said, but I listened intently, as I hope you'll do with me. And together, hopefully these discussions are going to be helpful to you in trying to arrive at a decision in this case where you don't compromise, where you don't do violence to your conscious (sic), but you do the right thing. And you are the ones who are empowered to determine what is the right thing. Let me ask each of you a question. Have you ever in your life been falsely accused of something? Have you ever been falsely accused? Ever had to sit there and take it and watch the proceedings and wait and wait and wait, all the while knowing that you didn't do it? All you could do during such a process is to really maintain your dignity; isn't that correct? Knowing that you were innocent, but maintaining your dignity and remembering always that all you're left with after a crisis is your conduct during. So that's another reason why we are proud to represent this man who's maintained his innocence and who has conducted himself with dignity throughout these proceedings. Now, last night, as I thought about the arguments of my colleagues, two

How Does Cochran Use Language in His Defense of Simpson?

words came to mind. And I want to—I asked my wife this morning to get the dictionary out and look up two words. The two words were "Speculative" and "Cynical." Let me see if I can get those words that she got for me.

And I want you to tell me what does it mean to speculate, what does it mean to be cynical, as I thought about my colleagues' arguments and their approach to this case and their view of this case. "Cynical" is described as contemptuously distrustful of human nature and motives, gloomy distrustful view of life. And to speculate—to speculate, to engage in conjecture and to surmise or—is to take to be the truth on the basis of insufficient evidence. I mention those two definitions to you because I felt that much of what we heard yesterday and again this morning was mere speculation.

******

People see things that are totally cynical. Maybe that's their view of the world. Not everybody shares that view. Now, in this case—and this is a homicide case and a very, very, very serious case. And of course, it's important for us to understand that. It is a sad fact that in American society, a large number of people are murdered each year. Violence unfortunately has become a way of life in America. And so when this sort of tragedy does in fact happen, it becomes the business of the police to step up and step in and to take charge of the matter. A good efficient, competent, noncorrupt police department will carefully set about the business of investigating homicides. They won't rush to judgment. They won't be bound by an obsession to win at all costs. They will set about trying to apprehend the killer or killers and trying to protect the innocent from suspicion.

In this case, the victims' families had an absolute right to demand exactly just that in this case. But it was clear unfortunately that in this case, there was another agenda. From the very first orders issued by the LAPD so-called brass, they were more concerned with their own images, the publicity that might be generated from this case than they were in doing professional police work. That's why this case has become such a hallmark and that's why Mr. Simpson is the one on trial. But your verdict in this case will go far beyond the walls of Department 103 because your verdict talks about justice in America and it talks about the police and whether they're above the law and it looks at the police perhaps as though they haven't been looked at very recently. Remember, I told you this is not for the naive, the faint of heart or the timid. So it seems to us that the evidence shows that professional police work took a backseat right at the beginning. Untrained officers trampled—remember, I used the word in opening statement—they traipsed through the evidence.

******

Because of their bungling, they ignored the obvious clues. They didn't pick up paper at the scene with prints on it. Because of their vanity, they very soon pretended to solve this crime and we think implicated an innocent man, and they never, they never ever looked for anyone else. We think if they had done their job as we have done, Mr. Simpson would have been eliminated early on.

******

It took all four detectives, all four LAPD experienced detectives to leave the bodies. They had to notify the Coroner. They didn't have a criminalist to go over to notify O.J. Simpson. Who's fooling who here? This is preposterous. They're lying, trying to get over that wall to get in that house. You don't believe so? You're talking about saving lives. Remember what Arnelle said. First of all, they all make this big mistake. They forget and they say, "Well, when we leave from the back, we go right in that back door of the house there, go right in the back door." But they forgot. Arnelle Simpson comes in here and testifies you can't go in the back door because remember, Kato had put on the alarm. You had to go around the house to the front. Arnelle had to open the keypad to let them in, remember? You think who knows better? You'd think she knows better or they know better? She had to let them in. So they're worried about dead bodies and people being in that house and saving lives? Who goes in first? Arnelle Simpson goes in first. These big, brave police officers, and the young lady just walks in there first. They don't go upstairs looking. They just want to be inside that house and make her leave to give Fuhrman a chance to start what he's doing, strolling around the premises and doing what he's doing there.

******

Then we come, before we end the day, to Detective Mark Fuhrman. This man is an unspeakable disgrace. He's been unmasked for the whole world for what he is, and that's hopefully positive.

******

And they put him on the stand and you saw it. You saw it. It was sickening. And then my colleague, Lee Bailey, who can't be with us today, but God bless him, wherever he is, did his cross-examination of this individual and he asked some interesting questions. Some of you probably wondered, "I wonder why he's asking that." He asked this man whether or not he ever met Kathleen Bell. Of course, he lied about that.

******

Then Bailey says: "Have you used that word, referring to the 'n' word, in the past 10 years? "Not that I recall, no. "You mean, if you call someone a Nigger, you had forgotten it?

"I'm not sure I can answer the question the way it's phrased, sir." And they go on. He says, "Well—" And then pins him down. "I want you to assume that perhaps at some time since 1985 or '86, you addressed a member of the African American race as a Nigger. Is it possible that you have forgotten that act on your part? "Answer: No, it is not possible. "Are you, therefore, saying that you have not used that word in the past 10 years, Detective Fuhrman?

"Answer: Yes. That is what I'm saying. "Question: And you say under oath that you have not addressed any Black person as a Nigger or spoken about Black people as niggers in the past 10 years, Detective Fuhrman? "That's

How Does Conflicting Memory Play Out in Cochran's Arguments?

what I'm saying, sir. "So that anyone who comes to this court and quotes you as using that word in dealing with African Americans would be a liar; would they not, Detective Fuhrman? "Yes, they would."

* * * * * *

Why did they then all try to cover for this man Fuhrman? Why would this man who is not only Los Angeles' worst nightmare, but America's worse nightmare, why would they all turn their heads and try to cover for them? Why would you do that if you are sworn to uphold the law? There is something about corruption. There is something about a rotten apple that will ultimately infect the entire barrel, because if the others don't have the courage that we have asked you to have in this case, people sit sadly by. We live in a society where many people are apathetic, they don't want to get involved, and that is why all of us, to a person, in this courtroom, have thanked you from the bottom of our hearts. Because you know what? You haven't been apathetic. You are the ones who made a commitment, a commitment toward justice, and it is a painful commitment, but you've got to see it through. Your commitment, your courage, is much greater than these police officers. This man could have been off the force long ago if they had done their job, but they didn't do their job. People looked the other way. People didn't have the courage. One of the things that has made this country so great is people's willingness to stand up and say that is wrong. I'm not going to be part of it. I'm not going to be part of the cover-up. That is what I'm asking you to do. Stop this cover-up. Stop this cover-up. If you don't stop it, then who? Do you think the police department is going to stop it? Do you think the D.A.'s office is going to stop it? Do you think we can stop it by ourselves? It has to be stopped by you.

Justice or Injustice? Why?

* * * * * *

But the capper was finding those tapes, something that you could hear. Lest there be any doubt in anybody's mind, Laura McKinny came in here, and I can imagine the frustration of the Prosecutors, they've had the glove demonstration, they have seen all these other things go wrong and now they got to face these tapes.

* * * * * *

We owe a debt of gratitude to this lady that ultimately and finally she came forward. And she tells us that this man over the time of these interviews uses the "N" word 42 times is what she says.

And so-called Fuhrman tapes. And you of course had an opportunity to listen to this man and espouse this evil, this personification of evil. And so I'm going to ask Mr. Harris to play exhibit 1368 one more time. It was a transcript. This was not on tape. The tape had been erased where he said, "We have no niggers where I grew up." These are two of 42, if you recall. Then this was his actual voice.

(At 10:00 A.M., Defense exhibit 1368, a videotape, was played.)

This is the word text for what he then says on the tape. Now, you heard that voice. No question whose voice that is. Mr. Darden concedes whose voice that is. They don't do anything. Talking about women. Doesn't like them any better than he likes African Americans. They don't go out and initiate contact with some six foot five inch Nigger who has been in prison pumping weights. This is how he sees this world. That is this man's cynical view of the world. This is this man who is out there protecting and serving. That is Mark Fuhrman.

What Would You Decide after Hearing this Argument?

Sample Epideictic (Demonstrative) Speech, Antony's Speech at Caesar's Funeral (Shakespeare's *Julius Caesar*)

ANTONY

Friends, Romans, countrymen, lend me your ears;
I come to bury Caesar, not to praise him.
The evil that men do lives after them;
The good is oft interred with their bones;
So let it be with Caesar. The noble Brutus
Hath told you Caesar was ambitious:
If it were so, it was a grievous fault,
And grievously hath Caesar answer'd it.
Here, under leave of Brutus and the rest—
For Brutus is an honourable man;
So are they all, all honourable men—
Come I to speak in Caesar's funeral.
He was my friend, faithful and just to me:
But Brutus says he was ambitious;
And Brutus is an honourable man.
He hath brought many captives home to Rome
Whose ransoms did the general coffers fill:
Did this in Caesar seem ambitious?
When that the poor have cried, Caesar hath wept:
Ambition should be made of sterner stuff:
Yet Brutus says he was ambitious;
And Brutus is an honourable man.
You all did see that on the Lupercal
I thrice presented him a kingly crown,
Which he did thrice refuse: was this ambition?
Yet Brutus says he was ambitious;

What Is the Occasion?

And, sure, he is an honourable man.
I speak not to disprove what Brutus spoke,
But here I am to speak what I do know.
You all did love him once, not without cause:
What cause withholds you then, to mourn for him?
O judgment! thou art fled to brutish beasts,
And men have lost their reason. Bear with me;
My heart is in the coffin there with Caesar,
And I must pause till it come back to me.

Sample Deliberative (Political) Address

For Immediate Release
Office of the Press Secretary
October 7, 2002

President Bush Explaining Urgency of Iraqi Invasion

President Bush Outlines Iraqi Threat

Remarks by the President on Iraq
Cincinnati Museum Center—Cincinnati Union Terminal

Cincinnati, Ohio 8:02 P.M. EDT

THE PRESIDENT: Thank you all. Thank you for that very gracious and warm Cincinnati welcome. I'm honored to be here tonight; I appreciate you all coming.

What Is the Objective of this Speech?

Tonight I want to take a few minutes to discuss a grave threat to peace, and America's determination to lead the world in confronting that threat.

The threat comes from Iraq. It arises directly from the Iraqi regime's own actions—its history of aggression, and its drive toward an arsenal of terror. Eleven years ago, as a condition for ending the Persian Gulf War, the Iraqi regime was required to destroy its weapons of mass destruction, to cease all development of such weapons, and to stop all support for terrorist groups. The Iraqi regime has violated all of those obligations. It possesses and produces chemical and biological weapons. It is seeking nuclear weapons. It has given shelter and support to terrorism, and practices terror against its own people. The entire world has witnessed Iraq's eleven-year history of defiance, deception and bad faith.

We also must never forget the most vivid events of recent history. On September the 11th, 2001, America felt its vulnerability—even to threats that gather on the other side of the earth. We resolved then, and we are resolved today, to confront every threat, from any source, that could bring sudden terror and suffering to America.

How Does the President Go About Achieving His Objective?

Members of the Congress of both political parties, and members of the United Nations Security Council, agree that Saddam Hussein is a threat to peace and must disarm. We agree that the Iraqi dictator must not be permitted to threaten America and the world with horrible poisons and diseases and gases and atomic weapons. Since we all agree on this goal, the issues is: how can we best achieve it?

Many Americans have raised legitimate questions: about the nature of the threat; about the urgency of action—why be concerned now; about the link between Iraq developing weapons of terror, and the wider war on terror. These are all issues we've discussed broadly and fully within my administration. And tonight, I want to share those discussions with you.

First, some ask why Iraq is different from other countries or regimes that also have terrible weapons. While there are many dangers in the world, the threat from Iraq stands alone—because it gathers the most serious dangers of our age in one place. Iraq's weapons of mass destruction are controlled by a murderous tyrant who has already used chemical weapons to kill thousands of people. This same tyrant has tried to dominate the Middle East, has invaded and brutally occupied a small neighbor, has struck other nations without warning, and holds an unrelenting hostility toward the United States.

By its past and present actions, by its technological capabilities, by the merciless nature of its regime, Iraq is unique. As a former chief weapons inspector of the U.N. has said, "The fundamental problem with Iraq remains the nature of the regime, itself. Saddam Hussein is a homicidal dictator who is addicted to weapons of mass destruction."

Some ask how urgent this danger is to America and the world. The danger is already significant, and it only grows worse with time. If we know Saddam Hussein has dangerous weapons today—and we do—does it make any sense for the world to wait to confront him as he grows even stronger and develops even more dangerous weapons?

In 1995, after several years of deceit by the Iraqi regime, the head of Iraq's military industries defected. It was then that the regime was forced to admit that it had produced more than 30,000 liters of anthrax and other deadly biological agents. The inspectors, however, concluded that Iraq had likely produced two to four times that amount. This is a massive stockpile of biological weapons that has never been accounted for, and capable of killing millions.

What Role Does "Time/Timing" Play?

We know that the regime has produced thousands of tons of chemical agents, including mustard gas, sarin nerve gas, VX nerve gas. Saddam Hussein also has experience in using chemical weapons. He has ordered chemical attacks on Iran, and on more than forty villages in his own country. These actions killed or injured at least 20,000 people, more than six times the number of people who died in the attacks of September the 11th.

And surveillance photos reveal that the regime is rebuilding facilities that it had used to produce chemical and biological weapons. Every chemical and biological weapon that Iraq has or makes is a direct violation of the truce that ended the Persian Gulf War in 1991. Yet, Saddam Hussein has chosen to build and keep these weapons despite international sanctions, U.N. demands, and isolation from the civilized world.

Iraq possesses ballistic missiles with a likely range of hundreds of miles—far enough to strike Saudi Arabia, Israel, Turkey, and other nations—in a region where more than 135,000 American civilians and service members live and work. We've also discovered through intelligence that Iraq has a growing fleet of manned and unmanned aerial vehicles that could be used to disperse chemical or biological weapons across broad areas. We're concerned that Iraq is exploring ways of using these UAVS for missions targeting the United States. And, of course, sophisticated delivery systems aren't required for a chemical or biological attack; all that might be required are a small container and one terrorist or Iraqi intelligence operative to deliver it.

And that is the source of our urgent concern about Saddam Hussein's links to international terrorist groups. Over the years, Iraq has provided safe haven to terrorists such as Abu Nidal, whose terror organization carried out more than 90 terrorist attacks in 20 countries that killed or injured nearly 900 people, including 12 Americans. Iraq has also provided safe haven to Abu Abbas, who was responsible for seizing the Achille Lauro and killing an American passenger. And we know that Iraq is continuing to finance terror and gives assistance to groups that use terrorism to undermine Middle East peace.

We know that Iraq and the al Qaeda terrorist network share a common enemy—the United States of America. We know that Iraq and al Qaeda have had high-level contacts that go back a decade. Some al Qaeda leaders who fled Afghanistan went to Iraq. These include one very senior al Qaeda leader who received medical treatment in Baghdad this year, and who has been associated with planning for chemical and biological attacks. We've learned that Iraq has trained al Qaeda members in bomb-making and poisons and deadly gases. And we know that after September the 11th, Saddam Hussein's regime gleefully celebrated the terrorist attacks on America.

Iraq could decide on any given day to provide a biological or chemical weapon to a terrorist group or individual terrorists. Alliance with terrorists could allow the Iraqi regime to attack America without leaving any fingerprints.

Some have argued that confronting the threat from Iraq could detract from the war against terror. To the contrary; confronting the threat posed by Iraq is crucial to winning the war on terror. When I spoke to Congress more than a year ago, I said that those who harbor terrorists are as guilty as the terrorists themselves. Saddam Hussein is harboring terrorists and the instruments of terror, the instruments of mass death and destruction. And he cannot be trusted. The risk is simply too great that he will use them, or provide them to a terror network.

Terror cells and outlaw regimes building weapons of mass destruction are different faces of the same evil. Our security requires that we confront both. And the United States military is capable of confronting both.

Many people have asked how close Saddam Hussein is to developing a nuclear weapon. Well, we don't know exactly, and that's the problem. Before the Gulf War, the best intelligence indicated that Iraq was eight to ten years away from developing a nuclear weapon. After the war, international inspectors learned that the regime has been much closer—the regime in Iraq would likely have possessed a nuclear weapon no later than 1993. The inspectors discovered that Iraq had an advanced nuclear weapons development program, had a design for a workable nuclear weapon, and was pursuing several different methods of enriching uranium for a bomb.

Before being barred from Iraq in 1998, the International Atomic Energy Agency dismantled extensive nuclear weapons-related facilities, including three uranium enrichment sites. That same year, information from a high-ranking Iraqi nuclear engineer who had defected revealed that despite his public promises, Saddam Hussein had ordered his nuclear program to continue.

The evidence indicates that Iraq is reconstituting its nuclear weapons program. Saddam Hussein has held numerous meetings with Iraqi nuclear scientists, a group he calls his "nuclear mujahideen"—his nuclear holy warriors. Satellite photographs reveal that Iraq is rebuilding facilities at sites that have been part of its nuclear program in the past. Iraq has attempted to purchase high-strength aluminum tubes and other equipment needed for gas centrifuges, which are used to enrich uranium for nuclear weapons.

If the Iraqi regime is able to produce, buy, or steal an amount of highly enriched uranium a little larger than a single softball, it could have a nuclear weapon in less than a year. And if we allow that to happen, a terrible line would be crossed. Saddam Hussein would be in a position to Blackmail anyone who opposes his aggression. He would be in a position to dominate the Middle East. He would be in a position to threaten America. And Saddam Hussein would be in a position to pass nuclear technology to terrorists.

Some citizens wonder, after 11 years of living with this problem, why do we need to confront it now? And there's a reason. We've experienced the horror of September the 11th. We have seen that those who hate America are willing to crash airplanes into buildings full of innocent people. Our enemies would be no less willing, in fact, they would be eager, to use biological or chemical, or a nuclear weapon.

Knowing these realities, America must not ignore the threat gathering against us. Facing clear evidence of peril, we cannot wait for the final proof—the smoking gun—that could come in the form of a mushroom cloud. As President Kennedy said in October of 1962, "Neither the United States of America, nor the world community of nations can tolerate deliberate deception and offensive threats on the part of any nation, large or small. We no longer live in a world," he said, "where only the actual firing of weapons represents a sufficient challenge to a nations security to constitute maximum peril."

Understanding the threats of our time, knowing the designs and deceptions of the Iraqi regime, we have every reason to assume the worst, and we have an urgent duty to prevent the worst from occurring.

Some believe we can address this danger by simply resuming the old approach to inspections, and applying diplomatic and economic pressure. Yet this is precisely what the world has tried to do since 1991. The U.N. inspections program was met with systematic deception. The Iraqi regime bugged hotel rooms and offices of inspectors to find where they were going next; they forged documents, destroyed evidence, and developed mobile weapons facilities to keep a step ahead of inspectors. Eight so-called presidential palaces were declared off-limits to unfettered inspections. These sites actually encompass twelve square miles, with hundreds of structures, both above and below the ground, where sensitive materials could be hidden.

The world has also tried economic sanctions—and watched Iraq use billions of dollars in illegal oil revenues to fund more weapons purchases, rather than providing for the needs of the Iraqi people.

The world has tried limited military strikes to destroy Iraq's weapons of mass destruction capabilities—only to see them openly rebuilt, while the regime again denies they even exist.

The world has tried no-fly zones to keep Saddam from terrorizing his own people—and in the last year alone, the Iraqi military has fired upon American and British pilots more than 750 times.

After eleven years during which we have tried containment, sanctions, inspections, even selected military action, the end result is that Saddam Hussein still has chemical and biological weapons and is increasing his capabilities to make more. And he is moving ever closer to developing a nuclear weapon.

Clearly, to actually work, any new inspections, sanctions or enforcement mechanisms will have to be very different. America wants the U.N. to be an effective organization that helps keep the peace. And that is why we are urging the Security Council to adopt a new resolution setting out tough, immediate requirements. Among those requirements: the Iraqi regime must reveal and destroy, under U.N. supervision, all existing weapons of mass destruction. To ensure that we learn the truth, the regime must allow witnesses to its illegal activities to be interviewed outside the country—and these witnesses must be free to bring their families with them so they all beyond the reach of Saddam Hussein's terror and murder. And inspectors must have access to any site, at any time, without pre-clearance, without delay, without exceptions.

The time for denying, deceiving, and delaying has come to an end. Saddam Hussein must disarm himself—or, for the sake of peace, we will lead a coalition to disarm him.

Many nations are joining us in insisting that Saddam Hussein's regime be held accountable. They are committed to defending the international security that protects the lives of both our citizens and theirs. And that's why America is challenging all nations to take the resolutions of the U.N. Security Council seriously.

And these resolutions are clear. In addition to declaring and destroying all of its weapons of mass destruction, Iraq must end its support for terrorism. It must cease the persecution of its civilian population. It must stop all illicit trade outside the Oil For Food program. It must release or account for all Gulf War personnel, including an American pilot, whose fate is still unknown.

By taking these steps, and by only taking these steps, the Iraqi regime has an opportunity to avoid conflict. Taking these steps would also change the nature of the Iraqi regime itself. America hopes the regime will make that choice. Unfortunately, at least so far, we have little reason to expect it. And that's why two administrations—mine and President Clinton's—have stated that regime change in Iraq is the only certain means of removing a great danger to our nation.

I hope this will not require military action, but it may. And military conflict could be difficult. An Iraqi regime faced with its own demise may attempt cruel and desperate measures. If Saddam Hussein orders such measures, his generals would be well advised to refuse those orders. If they do not refuse, they must understand that all war criminals will be pursued and punished. If we have to act, we will take every precaution that is possible. We will plan carefully; we will act with the full power of the United States military; we will act with allies at our side, and we will prevail. (Applause.)

There is no easy or risk-free course of action. Some have argued we should wait—and that's an option. In my view, it's the riskiest of all options, because the longer we wait, the stronger and bolder Saddam Hussein will become. We could wait and hope that Saddam does not give weapons to terrorists, or develop a nuclear weapon to Blackmail the world. But I'm convinced that is a hope against all evidence. As Americans, we want peace—we work and sacrifice for peace. But there can be no peace if our security depends on the will and whims of a ruthless and aggressive dictator. I'm not willing to stake one American life on trusting Saddam Hussein.

Failure to act would embolden other tyrants, allow terrorists access to new weapons and new resources, and make Blackmail a permanent feature of world events. The United Nations would betray the purpose of its founding, and prove irrelevant to the problems of our time. And through its inaction, the United States would resign itself to a future of fear.

That is not the America I know. That is not the America I serve. We refuse to live in fear. (Applause.) This nation, in world war and in Cold War, has never permitted the brutal and lawless to set history's course. Now, as before, we will secure our nation, protect our freedom, and help others to find freedom of their own.

Some worry that a change of leadership in Iraq could create instability and make the situation worse. The situation could hardly get worse, for world security and for the people of Iraq. The lives of Iraqi citizens would improve dramatically if Saddam Hussein were no longer in power, just as the lives of Afghanistan's citizens improved after the Taliban. The dictator of Iraq is a student of Stalin, using murder as a tool of terror and control, within his own cabinet, within his own army, and even within his own family.

On Saddam Hussein's orders, opponents have been decapitated, wives and mothers of political opponents have been systematically raped as a method of intimidation, and political prisoners have been forced to watch their own children being tortured.

America believes that all people are entitled to hope and human rights, to the non-negotiable demands of human dignity. People everywhere prefer freedom to slavery; prosperity to squalor; self-government to the rule of terror and torture. America is a friend to the people of Iraq. Our demands are directed only at the regime that enslaves them and threatens us. When these demands are met, the first and greatest benefit will come to Iraqi men, women and children. The oppression of Kurds, Assyrians, Turkomans, Shi'a, Sunnis and others will be lifted. The long captivity of Iraq will end, and an era of new hope will begin.

Iraq is a land rich in culture, resources, and talent. Freed from the weight of oppression, Iraq's people will be able to share in the progress and prosperity of our time. If military action is necessary, the United States and our allies will help the Iraqi people rebuild their economy, and create the institutions of liberty in a unified Iraq at peace with its neighbors.

Later this week, the United States Congress will vote on this matter. I have asked Congress to authorize the use of America's military, if it proves necessary, to enforce U.N. Security Council demands. Approving this resolution does not mean that military action is imminent or unavoidable. The resolution will tell the United Nations, and all nations, that America speaks with one voice and is determined to make the demands of the civilized world mean something. Congress will also be sending a message to the dictator in Iraq: that his only chance—his only choice is full compliance, and the time remaining for that choice is limited.

Members of Congress are nearing an historic vote. I'm confident they will fully consider the facts, and their duties.

The attacks of September the 11th showed our country that vast oceans no longer protect us from danger. Before that tragic date, we had only hints of al Qaeda's plans and designs. Today in Iraq, we see a threat whose outlines are far more clearly defined, and whose consequences could be far more deadly. Saddam Hussein's actions have put us on notice, and there is no refuge from our responsibilities.

We did not ask for this present challenge, but we accept it. Like other generations of Americans, we will meet the responsibility of defending human liberty against violence and aggression. By our resolve, we will give strength to others. By our courage, we will give hope to others. And by our actions, we will secure the peace, and lead the world to a better day.

May God bless America. (Applause.)

END 8:31 P.M. EDT

http://www.whitehouse.gov/news/releases/2002/10/20021007-8.html: Retrieved January 4, 2005.

Rhetoric and the Everyday Speech

Think of rhetoric in terms of developing a speech. As we discussed in the previous chapter, you must do in-depth audience analysis to develop a good speech. You also have to work to ensure that your vocabulary is neither too lofty nor too base for your audience. You must pay close attention to how you structure the speech. Certain information is more effective if it is presented at the beginning; other information is more powerful in the ending. It is important that you organize and structure your speech in a way that is going to knock the audience onto their collective booties. What do you see happening in this speech prep scenario that I have just presented? Ultimately, preparing a strong public address requires that we get into the minds of our audience members. Now let's consider rhetoric as the study of how we effectively organize speeches and how we effectively use language based on the attitudes, values, and beliefs of the audience.

We use rhetoric to transmit emotions and thoughts through a system of symbols so that we can influence other people's decisions or actions.

Symbols are arbitrary. Meaning is in the individual. Yet we do have communal meaning based on social agreement. For example, during the Black power movement, the clenched raised fist was a symbol of Black power. What system do we rely on for communicating with others on a daily basis? The answer is language or verbal expression. Congratulations, you are not the weakest link! Other arts use symbols. Musicians, for instance, have notes, bars, clefs, etc.

How Do I Identify Rhetorical Discourse?

There are a couple of basic ways to identify rhetorical discourse; rhetoric is planned, and it is adapted to an audience.

Rhetoric Is Planned

The rhetor (re-tor), the person who uses rhetoric, plans her address by questioning: Which arguments will I advance? Which evidence best supports my point? How will I order and arrange my arguments and evidence? What aesthetic resources are available to me, given my topic and my audience?

Early rhetorical theorists introduced what they considered as elaborate "systems" that would assist speakers. Cicero, the Roman writer, introduced "inventio" (invention) to describe the process of discovering the arguments and evidence for a persuasive case. Cicero also discussed the effective ordering of arguments and appeals, "dispositio" (arrangement). "Elecutio" describes and explains the process of finding the right linguistic style for the message. Elecutio, then, refers to delivery. Aristotle's systematic rhetoric emphasizes the importance of the audience.

Rhetoric Is Adapted to an Audience

Rhetorical discourse forges a connection between the views of the speaker and audience. Remember, the rhetor must attend to an audience's values, experiences, beliefs, social status, and aspirations. Rhetoric relies on the commonality between the rhetor and an audience. The speaker or rhetor tries to identify with the audience by tailoring the speech to the audience. When the speaker or rhetor modifies a speech to make sure that the values, beliefs, and needs of the audience are a primary focus, audience adaptation has taken place. The audience determines the type of argument and the behavior of the speaker. Critics of rhetoric claim that rhetors base what they say or write on what their audiences believe or prefer. Yet, I don't see any form of behavioral or attitudinal modification that does not take into account the needs, values, beliefs, and motivations of the audience. One simply has to watch a television commercial, read a billboard, or listen to the lyrics of today's pop music to see that the needs and motivations of the audience dictate how messages are packaged.

Social Functions of Rhetoric

Rhetoric plays an important social role. Herrick explains that the social function of rhetoric is to test ideas, assist advocacy, discover facts, shape knowledge, and build community. Rhetoric is essential to understanding the world around us.

Rhetoric Tests Ideas

When students prepare for debates, they test their arguments and counter-arguments on their teammates. They put their information into the universe for public scrutiny. They are cross-examined as if on trial for their lives.

I faced one of my greatest challenges the day that I defended my doctoral dissertation. I had to plead my case as to why I chose my subject, mentoring Black men. I had to argue my rationale for theorists and theories that I used as support. I also found myself defending the language I chose. Although I was a little shaky after the whole ordeal, I felt more confident than ever before. My ideas withstood this dialectical encounter, this test of my ideas.

Rhetoric Assists Advocacy

Herrick says that, "the art of rhetoric is the method by which we advocate ideas we believe to be important. Rhetoric gives our private ideas a public voice, thus directing attention to them."[3] In the mid to late 1990s, I lobbied before Senate and House leaders in the nation's Capitol. I used rhetoric everyday to advance my cause. Before I started my day, I chose the arguments that I was going to advance. I knew the audience. I knew the language that the audience was more amenable to hearing. I knew that I had to get my audience in the right state of mind (pathos), present my best arguments (logos), and have the right kind of character (ethos). Ultimately, I used rhetoric to assist my advocacy.

Rhetoric Discovers Facts

We investigate to learn more about the subject under the social microscope. We read to find new ways of experiencing phenomena. We think critically about the evidence we have before us. We critically examine our facts against possible inferences. Once we compile all of our data, we have information that helps us to learn about ourselves in relation to the outside world. This information also helps us to interact in the world with a more global understanding. The discovery of knowledge is a means to social growth.

Rhetoric Builds Community

What is community and how can it be built using rhetoric? D. E. Proctor states that symbolic events which become the center of community identity are "dynamic spectacles."

These spectacles provide a "rhetorical framework through which to examine the symbolic process of community building."[4] Proctor further states:

The dynamic spectacle works to build community by 1. casting the material event into a symbol of communal past, 2. converting the event into a rhetoric of the community's ideology, and 3. transforming the event into a motive for community action.[5]

Let's look at the community that developed around the dream of Dr. Martin Luther King, Jr. During the 1950s and 1960s, Dr. King was shown brightly as one of the nation's more charismatic and rhetorically savvy public figures. He and the many, many people in the background of the civil rights movement created a community of activism. King's "dream" became accepted language in a community poised for change. Herrick writes:

As Dr. King spoke and wrote, his ideas were expressed, tested, and either embraced or rejected; those who embraced his ideas became part of a larger community that King was gradually building. Through his rhetorical efforts, King built a "community of discourse" that enabled people to think and act with unity to address a wide range of serious social problems. He developed an active community around certain very powerful ideas to which he gave voice rhetorically. Rhetorical processes were central to his work of community building.[6]

Developing Persuasive Presentations

Now let's draw from the rhetorical discussion and prepare to develop persuasive presentations. Let's first begin by defining persuasion in terms of it's rhetorical objective. **Persuasion is the process of preparing and presenting verbal and nonverbal messages with the purpose of evaluating, sustaining, or altering the reality of an audience.**

Persuasive speeches generally have two aims and arise out of three primary questions. *Persuasive presentations, generally, aim to either convince or to motivate.* Presentations developed with the purpose of convincing seek an informed and intellectual agreement from listeners. The presentations developed with purpose of motivating seeks both an informed and intellectual agreement from listeners, as well as action.

Persuasive presentations usually arise out of a speaker's desire to question facts, values, or policies. **Presentations/speeches questioning fact deal with whether something is believed to be true or to what degree something is factual.** All questions of fact cannot be answered with an absolute response, so the speaker makes a prediction. "Will the economy get better under a Republican administration?" Democratic pundits would probably argue, "no." While Republican ones would argue as fervently, "yes."

Persuasive speeches that question values assess the worth of an idea, object or individual. Many speeches during the 2004 election hit on the hotbed topic, same-sex marriages. These speeches begged audience's to make value judgments on this issue.

President George W. Bush, in his State of the Union Address on January 20, 2004, made the very persuasive statements regarding the value of marriage.

A Strong America Must Also Value the Institution of Marriage

I believe we should respect individuals as we take a principled stand for one of the most fundamental, enduring institutions of our civilization. Congress has already taken a stand on this issue by passing the Defense of Marriage Act, signed in 1996 by President Clinton. That statute protects marriage under federal law as the union of a man and a woman, and declares that one state may not redefine marriage for other states.

Activist judges, however, have begun redefining marriage by court order, without regard for the will of the people and their elected representatives. On an issue of such great consequence, the people's voice must be heard. If judges insist on forcing their arbitrary will upon the people, the only alternative left to the people would be the constitutional process. Our nation must defend the sanctity of marriage.

The outcome of this debate is important, and so is the way we conduct it. The same moral tradition that defines marriage also teaches that each individual has dignity and value in God's sight.

President George W. Bush, State of the Union Address on January 20, 2004.

http://www.cnn.com/2004/ALLPOLITICS/01/20/sotu.transcript.6/index.html

Speeches that question policy deal with how things "should" or "ought" to be. You may want your audience to agree with you that a particular policy ought to be in place, or you may want them to get busy. You may call for action. Ultimately in any persuasive speech, you want some type of action, whether it be passive agreement or vigorous activity.

When you deal with questions of policy, it is important to consider the need for the policy, to determine the plan to implement the policy, and to determine the practicality of the plan. If you don't have a practical plan to present to your audience, expect to bomb. If a plan has flaws and will not work, the audience will probably pick on that and will shut down on you.

Persuasive Presentations in Business

The types of persuasive presentations in business and what they are called vary from company to company. Some companies label the persuasive presentation a 'pitch,' others a 'proposal,' and still others a 'presentation'. Because the differences among these types are subtle, we will simply use the term *persuasive presentation.*

Many persuasive presentations are informal and are given within the organization by supervisors to their employees or by employees to their supervisors. Topics might include convincing employees of the need for a new reorganization plan, urging compliance with a company regulation, or advocating a new piece of machinery, policy change, or postponement of a deadline. (Hamilton, p. 409)

Persuasive presentations may also be given by company representatives to groups of individuals that represent interests outside of the company. These outside groups could range from international business moguls to congressional leaders to the general public. Persuasive presentations to outside groups are usually more formal than the intra-company presentations. Companies often make persuasive presentations in an attempt to create goodwill or to create a better image for the companies.

Use Laura Link Maggio's press release to develop a brief persuasive presentation aimed at creating a better image of Martha Stewart, the person. Think about the things you've read so far about how presentations are developed. What are the major concerns? Will you try to convince or motivate? Do these circumstances question fact, value, or policy?

Martha Stewart—Doing "A Good Thing"

Although there have been arguments that Martha Stewart as a brand was not working anymore, I disagree. She turned her indictment and sentencing into an opportunity.

(PRWEB) September 16, 2004—"While there are pros and cons on each side, I think Martha Stewart's request for 'finality' is brilliant from a public relations standpoint. She is remaining true to her brand no matter what," says Laura L. Maggio, APR, an eighteen-year accredited national leader and author in the field of public relations. "When a brand is working, there is usually no reason to change it. Although there have been arguments that Martha Stewart as a brand was not working anymore, I disagree. She turned her indictment and sentencing into an opportunity to tell the world that they can still count on Martha Stewart. She even brought the viewer through pictures of the holidays she would be missing, (the unstated being that we will miss her homemaking advice during these holidays) and verbally 'showed' us the garden she hopes to be out of prison in time to plant."

Laura L. Link earned her APR accreditation by PRSA in 1997, and holds a national office as 2004 National Assembly Delegate at Large for the Public Relations Society of America's International Conference. Laura L. Link is the author of *45 Days to Power Publicity: Learn the Insider Secrets to Getting the Word Out http://www.prweb.com/releases/2004/9/prweb 158847.php*: Retrieved 1/3/04.

Now that you have finished trying to persuade your classmates how wonderful Martha Stewart is, think about what you said. How did you go about preparing your presentation?

Earlier in this text, we discussed what the classical rhetoricians called **stasis** or the "status of the case." As you may recall, we determine the status of the case by asking questions such as: whether a thing is, what it is, and of what kind it is. You can further clarify the stasis by determining if the case questions facts, values, or policies.

Carefully assess the case by determining the needs of the audience. Is your audience well informed on the issue? Do they need a brief overview or an extensive historical oral report? Will this audience be swayed more by emotional appeals or by hard core statistical evidence?

Aristotle says that rhetoric or in this case its colleague, persuasion, exists to "affect the giving of decisions." (Aristotle, p. 90). Remember, we try to persuade by evaluating, sustaining, or altering the reality of an audience. But just how do you sustain or even alter someone's reality. I'm glad that you asked. Of course if you are to do anything to another's reality, you must first know what that reality is. How does your audience feel about the topic? How does the audience feel about being in this place, at your presentation? How does your audience feel about you?

Ethos/Ethical Appeal

Speakers with good character (ethos) that are able to state strong logical arguments (logos) and that are able to put the audience in the right frame of mind are inarguably much more likely achieve their suasory goals.

Many texts speak in terms of ethos of the speaker or the ethical appeal of a speaker. **The ethical appeal of a speaker mainly reflects his character and how the audience perceives his character.** Aristotle says, "the orator must not only try to make the argument of his speech demonstrative and worthy of belief; he must also make his own character look right and put his hearers, who are to decide, into the right frame of mind. . . . It adds much to an orator's influence that his own character should look right and that he should be thought to entertain the right feelings towards his hearers; and also that his hearers themselves should be in just the right frame of mind. (Aristotle, p. 91).

Aristotle further explains that when people or an audience is angry, they think about an issue in one way. But when they are friendly and conciliatory, they probably will respond to the same issue in a much different manner. These audience members' states of mind can be modified when the individual members of the audience have confidence in the orator's own character. Think about how you feel when you are sitting in your place of worship; you are listening to a sermon or religious ceremony. Is your opinion of the message altered by how you feel about the person who is leading the ceremony? If you know that the pastor is sleeping with every sister in the choir, are you as likely to concede to his hell and brimstone sermon that implores you to turn from your evil ways.

Logos/Logical Appeal

Certainly, if you have heard the term ethos, you have probably heard the term logos. **Logos usually refers to the orderly thinking of sequencing and relating one thought or idea to another.** Remember this analytic argument:

1. If A then B.
2. A.

   Therefore,

   B.

Logical arguments assert a claim and support that claim with premises. **A claim is a statement or declaration that we want others to accept.** In order to get others to accept our claims, we offer premises or good reasons that are common knowledge. Do not become confused with the terms premise, good reasons, and evidence. They all function to support your claim or thesis statement. These terms are used interchangeably in this text. When speaking specifically about persuasive presentations, theorists tend to use the terms good reasons and premises.

Let's look at how you might construct a logical argument.

Premise: If Jack wins the Pulitzer Prize, he will buy Ann a new Rolex.
Premise: Jack wins the Pulitzer.
                  (Therefore)
Claim: Ann will get a new Rolex.

This is an example of deductive or syllogistic reasoning. The first premise (if Jack wins the Pulitzer Prize, he will buy Ann a new Rolex) lays the foundation for the reasoning sequence that leads to an irrefutable claim. Understand, however, that your claims are vulnerable and will be tested. One of my friends tends to test syllogism and uses this one as her evidence:

Premise: God is love.
Premise: Love is blind.
                  (Therefore)
Claim: Stevie Wonder is God.

Based on my friend's reasoning because God is love, love is blind, and then God must be blind. And because Stevie Wonder is blind, he must be God. Pretty absurd assumption in some ways, but it goes to show that we cannot jump to conclusions in developing syllogisms. We are guilty of faulty reasoning when we jump to conclusions. Our discussion on rhetoric dealt in terms of its ability to test ideas. Think of persuasive presentations from that same perspective.

Arguments that assert a claim and then support that claim with premises are examples of inductive reasoning. According to Woodward and Denton (2000, p. 100), good reasons "provide explanations for arguable judgments which the persuader believes will probably elicit widespread agreement from an audience. The anticipated agreement is based on the fact that good reasons frequently summarize what members of a society already accept as true or right."

You appear more convincing and credible as a speaker when you provide your audience with logical arguments supported by credible evidence.

Claim:	CEOs that steal retirement money from their companies' employees should not be allowed to head Fortune 500 companies.
Reason:	Employees expect company leaders to provide the agreed upon benefits.
Reason:	Fortune 500 CEOs control the retirement funds for hundreds of thousands of workers who cannot afford for their leader to steal their retirement funds and to renege on the agreed upon benefits plan.

Absent Fathers' Effects on Children

James Majors was born with a debilitating disease that affected his ability to articulate words. His lack of dexterity would not allow him to hold a writing utensil. He used a wheelchair to come to class, although he could stand and walk for short periods of time. He was aware that his illness caused a speech impediment to a degree that most people would not be able to comprehend what he said. Therefore, when he delivered his final exam speech, a persuasive speech, he typed the entire script on PowerPoint. I insisted that my students select a topic they felt passionately about. I also wanted them to clearly use the **Forms of Persuasion . . . (Aristotle)** Pathos: A form of persuasion based on emotion. (How it feels . . .) Logos: Logical reasoning, thought plus action. (What makes sense is. . . .) Ethos: Ethical appeal (What is right & what is wrong . . .). After James Majors completed his presentation, a student asked James why he selected his topic. James responded by sharing the fact that his own father left his mother when he discovered they gave birth to a child with a debilitating disease.

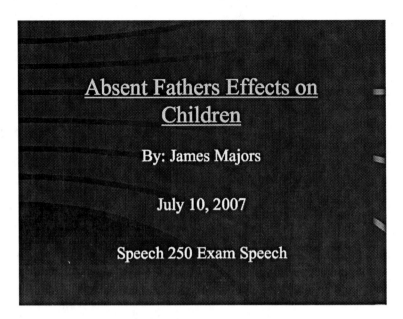

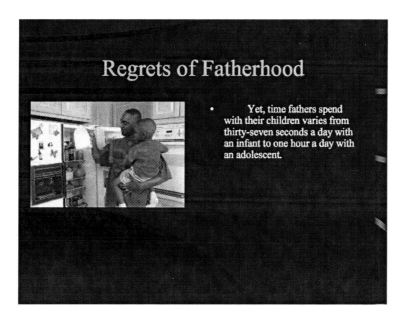

Being A Single Parent

- Single-parent households don't do as well when it comes to raising children because less income is an issue, so the single parents have to work twice as hard to try to provide for their children and to pay the necessary bills.

Babies

- From a baby's first crawl to being potty trained, the first years are very important to be a part of your child's life. Having an absent father can be painful for little children around birthdays and important holidays, like Christmas and Easter.

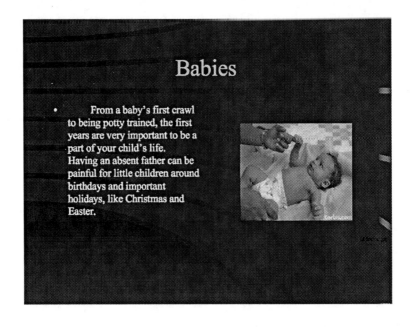

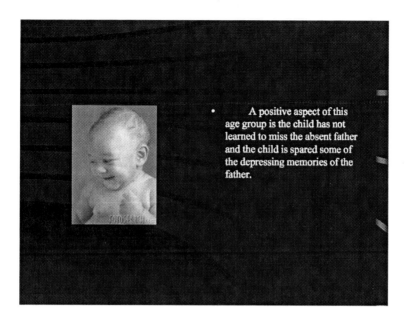

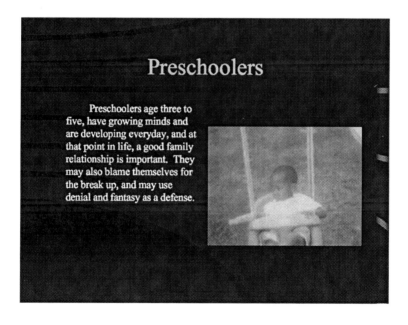

Older Children

For a child age six to eight, living without a father can be more of a painful sadness. Unlike small children that use denial, these children are on the brink of tears.

Preteen & Teenagers

For a preteen, age nine to twelve, they are going through many changes mentally, physically, and socially, and need to be around positive people, such as parents and friends.

Teenagers need good guidance and advice from their parents in order to make decisions that affect their future. They encounter a deep sense of loss and have more responsibilities at home if they have younger brothers or sisters.

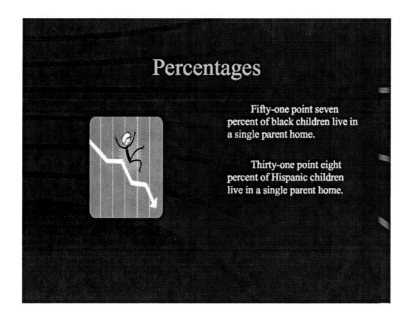

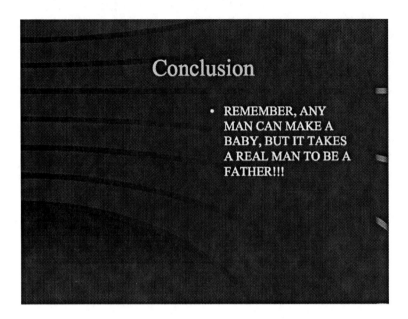

You're Gonna Need Support

Evidence is the foundation of any persuasive argument or presentation. Consider **evidence as support for your claim—as the facts that make your argument believable.** Evidence for persuasive presentations can take the form of **statistics, examples, comparisons, quotes, or expert testimony,** and **visual aids.** Refer to page 338 in Chapter 13.

Putting It All Together

Certainly, you have thought about your intended audience. You know whether or not you want to convince or motivate. You also should know whether your argument questions fact, value, or policy. As well, you probably have done all of the research and have your evidence to support your claim. Now what's next.

Let's think about ways to organize persuasive presentations. In this section we'll look at five different methods: topical/claim, cause/effect/solution or action, problem/solution/benefit or action, comparative advantages, and Monroe's motivated sequence.

Topical/Claim Pattern

The topical method allows you to present several categories or areas of focus to support your claim. In the introduction, you state the problem. You provide your reasons for believing/not believing a fact (questions of fact), for having/not having a particular value (questions of value), or for advocating/not advocating for a particular policy. Persuasive speeches organized in the topical method may make use of **inductive** or **deductive** reasoning. Many persuasive speakers that question facts or values usually organize their speeches topically.

I.   Claim #1
II. Claim #2
III. Claim #3

Cause/Effect/Solution or Action Pattern

The cause-effect method, of course, uses cause and effect reasoning. Unlike with informative speeches, persuasive speeches organized in this format should propose either a solution or should call for action. Make sure the audience can clearly see the relationship between one thing being the cause and the other being the effect.

I.   Cause   I.   Cause
II. Effect   II. Effect
III. Solution   III. Action

Problem/Solution/Benefit or Action Pattern

The problem-solution pattern begins with a detailed discussion of the problem in the introduction. As the speaker, you may need to define the problem, and discuss the effects of the problem. Remember you determine how in depth you need to be with this discussion by determining how much the audience knows and what it already thinks the problem.

The next piece to this pattern is the solution. Your place here is to provide the audience with a viable solution to the problem that you have just presented. Then you must convince the audience of either the benefits of your solution or recommend a particular action that you want the audience to take. This pattern is used frequently in questions of policy.

Comparative Advantages Pattern

The comparative advantage pattern is most likely used when the audience agrees that a problem exists. Although they may agree that a problem exists, they may not agree on the solution. Therefore, as the speaker, you want to spend your time comparing the advantages of your plan to an alternative plan. In each main point that you present, you will want to argue how superior your plan is to other possible choices. You want to make the alternative plan seem like an inferior choice. This pattern works well in presentations that question policy.

I.   Plan A does not work
II. Plan B does work
     (or)
I.   Plan A works, but not that well.
II. Plan B works much better.

Monroe's Motivated Sequence

Monroe's motivated sequence is perfect for persuasive presentations designed to motivate your audience to immediate action, such as when you question policy. This pattern is very similar to the problem-solution pattern, but is more detailed. The motivated sequence, developed by Alan Monroe in the mid-1930s, involves five steps: attention, need, satisfaction, visualization, and action.

1. **Attention.** You gain the attention of the audience in manners similar to what we discussed in Chapter 12 on informative speaking. You may capture the attention of the audience by stating a startling statistic or fact, by relating a powerful example or illustration, or by asking a rhetorical question.

2. **Need.** After you have the audience's attention. You paint a picture that clearly illustrates the problem. Use ethos, logos, and pathos to amplify the significance of the problem. Provide strong evidence. Offer sound arguments. You want your audience to be drawn in by this time. You want them to see the need.

3. **Satisfaction.** Once the audience sees the need, you hit them with the solution to the problem. Like in the comparative advantage and problem solution/benefit patterns, you show the audience your plan; show them how your plan works; and then show them how your plan is superior to any other. During this step, make sure you answer any objections that your audience may have.

4. **Visualization.** With your most vivid language, you lead the audience through life with your plan in place. You show, through colorful imagery, life if your plan were in place. Show the audience how much better life would be if your plan were in place.

5. **Action.** Now is the time to ask for the money. Your audience should be putty in your hands now, so call for action. Tell the audience what you want them to do. Finally, give them a rousing appeal that will get a personal commitment from them.

   1. Attention
   2. Need
   3. Satisfaction
   4. Visualization
   5. Action

Working Example of Monroe's Motivated Sequence

Attention: I'm sure all of you are familiar with the death penalty, but did you know that among the 683 executions carried out since 1977, 518 were by lethal injection, 149 by electrocution, 11 by lethal gas, 3 by hanging (two in Washington State and one in Delaware) and 2 by firing squad (both in Utah)?

http://usgovinfo.about.com/library/weekly/aa122001.htm

Need: Imagine you are convicted of killing your spouse. You did it in self defense, but the prosecution proves otherwise. You are sentenced to death. Not only do you lose your freedom and your family, but you have to lose your life. The judge says you will be executed by way of electrocution. Now let's all think of what it means to send electric current through a person's body. Have you ever been shocked from static electricity? That's minor, but we all know that it hurts. What if you had the amount of current that it takes to run the appliances in your household running through your body for up to thirty seconds, and in some rare cases a minute?

And what about your children? Heaven forbid they should ever commit a malicious crime. Don't think that if they are under the age of 18, that they are exempt from being sentenced to death. According to Amnesty International, the United States has executed 22 children since 1977 and over 70 children are currently under a death sentence. 1977 is not that long ago.

Overall there is too much uncertainty to sentence people to death. Death sentences are mandated by human beings, who are essentially flawed and without a doubt fallible. Even though death would be the surest way to keep convicted people from committing further crimes, it's not fair to take the lives of people based on man-produced evidence. People have the power to create whatever stories they want to create, and in a trial, the lawyer with the best story wins. Many people who are sentenced to death are mentally handicapped (and I don't mean just a claim of insanity) or completely innocent.

Satisfaction: But you don't have to let the fate of people that you know be determined by whether they can afford a good story. The death penalty could be abolished. The United States is leading in economics, yet 117 countries have surpassed us in abolishing the death penalty, including Canada, Hong Kong, and South Africa. We could join these countries and take a humane step to get rid of the death penalty.

Visualization: If we abolish the death penalty, it would not be possible for children to be sentenced to death. Innocent lives would be spared.

Action: So now you may be wondering what you can do. Write letters to your senators. Don't feel like your concerns are insignificant in time of war. No citizen complaint is insignificant. You could also get involved with international organizations like Amnesty International. Hold rallies, not riots, that will put pressure on your state governments. Whatever you do, don't stand around and watch people die because they don't have a good enough story. That is senseless.

Rhetoric Discourse: Persuasive Presentations

Example . . .
Topic: *"Vegetarianism is for everyone"*

Preplanning:
[I want my audience to consider that eating meat is not necessary.]

My attention-getter is:

> *"Ever eat a dead dog? How about a dead puppy? How does one determine which animals killed and eaten are or are not okay?"* (ethos)

[The evidence I have to support vegetarianism is:]

> *"According to the US Department of Agriculture the new food pyramid reflects recommended food servings are more aligned with a vegetarian diet:*
> *Grains, Vegetables, Fruits, Calcium-rich foods, Protein (beans, nuts, seeds, peas, small portions of lean meat)"*

[Provide at least one metaphor:]

> *A vegetarianism lifestyle is a healthy eating lifestyle."*

[Provide reasons to support your position: Reason A]

> *"Many people became vegetarians because they did not morally approve of the way animals were trapped, treated, and killed. (ethos)*
> *A dead pig's belly is your bacon, chopped up cow is your hamburger, and waste scraps from these murdered animals are your hot dogs."* (pathos)

"The thought of slashing open a calf's belly with a knife, wading through the blood and guts to carve out your favorite portion, then disposing of the carcass before it rots and stinks is not appetizing for most people, even though they pay others to do it. (pathos)

If we were really predisposed to eating flesh, we would not be bothered by killing ANY animal for food." (logos)

[Provide reasons to support your position: Reason B]

"Nutritional awareness is key! Not only do people object to the way animals are murdered, there is a growing awareness that healthy foods are considered an abundance of fruits and vegetables, not meat. Why be cruel and KILL animals when we can GROW all of the food we NEED to eat? (ethos/logos)

Why are we the only species that chooses to drink the milk of another species? Every other species is nourished from their mother's milk from birth until weaned. (logos)

[Provide reasons to support your position: Reason C]

"Consider the appropriate use of land and food resources. Why receive nutrients second-hand; eating a dead animal that absorbed their nutrition directly from plants when you can obtain the nutrients directly yourself?

We are the only species on earth not eating our food in it's natural state. (logos)

Concern about the environment is another factor as people become more aware about wasting world food resources by using land to raise animals for killing instead of growing crops that can directly feed more people" (ethos).

[Provide a conclusion to summarize your position and leave the audience with a memorable thought:]

"As I conclude, I hope you consider the idea of murdering selected animals, nutritional awareness and appropriate use of land a food resources when you are preparing your future meals. Contrary to popular opinion, we do not live to eat. We eat to live a full life . . . why can't animals eat and live their full lives?

"Thank you!"

Wrap It Up

Rhetoric is the use of language to evaluate, sustain, or alter the reality of an audience. Rhetoric, as a systematic study, was developed by a group of orators, educators, and advocates called Sophists. We use rhetoric to transmit emotions and thoughts through a system of symbols so that we can influence other people's decisions or actions. Rhetoric is planned, and it is adapted to the audience. Rhetoric functions in a social role.

It functions to test ideas, assist advocacy, discover facts, shape knowledge, and build community. Rhetoric is essential in shaping our understanding of the world around us.

I have addressed the idea of rhetoric in this chapter so that you can see the link between rhetorical theory, persuasion, and language. There are five different organizational patterns that you can use to arrange your persuasive message: topical, cause/effect/solution or action, problem/solution benefit, comparative advantages, and Monroe's motivated sequence.

Notes

1. Woodward, G. and R. Denton, *Persuasion and Influence in American Life (4th ed.)* Prospect Heights, Ill.: Waveland Press, Inc, 2000: 22.

2. Herrick, J. A. *The History and Theory of Rhetoric: An Introduction,* (2nd ed.) Needham Heights, Mass.: Allyn & Bacon, 2001: 34.

3. Ibid, p. 17.

4. Proctor, D. E. "The Dynamic Spectacle: Transforming Experience into Social Forms of Community." *The Quarterly Journal of Speech* 76 (1990): 120.

5. Ibid.

6. Herrick, J. A. The History and Theory of Rhetoric: An Introduction, (2nd ed.) Needham Heights, Mass.: Allyn & Bacon, 2001: 23.

References

Aristotle. *Rhetoric.* (W Rhys Roberts, Trans.). New York: The Modern Library, 1954. (Original work published 350 BCE)

Hamilton C. and C. Parker *Communicating for Results: A Guide for Business and the Professions,* (5th ed.) New York: Wadsworth Publishing Company, 1997.

Name _____   Date _____

Section _____

Think About It → Write About It

Reflect on what you've just read. Now write what you are thinking.

_____

_____

_____

_____

_____

_____

_____

_____

_____

_____

_____

_____

_____

_____

_____

_____

_____

_____

_____

_____

_____

_____

_____

Activity

Persuasive Power

1. Ask each student to find a partner.
2. Ask each pair to decide which one will be A or B.
3. Ask the "A" students to close one of their hands like a fist.
4. Remind the "A" students they may open their hand when they choose to do so.
5. Ask the "B" students to persuade the "A" students to open their hand.
6. After a few minutes, or when you see a few students open their hands, abruptly stop the conversations, ask the "B" students to close one of their hands like a fist.
7. Ask the "A" students to persuade the "B" students to open their hand.
8. After a few minutes or when you see a few students open their hands, abruptly stop the conversations and ask the following questions:
   a. Why did some of you refuse to open your hand?
   b. What motivated you to open your hand, those of you that did?
   c. How difficult was it to get your partner to open their hand?
   d. How would you connect this exercise to power?
      Persuasion? Choice?

Chapter 15

Special Occasion Speeches

Key Terms

Acceptance Speech
After Dinner Speech
Commemorative Speech

Presentation Speech
Outlining
Special Occasion Speech

Have you ever received an award or scholarship from a local church, club or sorority? Were you asked to give an acceptance speech at the club's next meeting? Have you ever given the welcoming remarks at school or social function? How about presenting an award—have you ever done that? If you answered yes to any of these questions, you have already given at least one special occasion speech. The general purpose of a special occasion speech is to entertain. Consider that entertainment does not always equate to Chris Rock funny. Entertain special occasion terms generally translates to inspire or to create enthusiasm.

There are numerous occasions that might require presentations. The specific purposes of these occasions may differ. Yet, they all may require you to give some type of special speech. There are several types of speeches that might be required at special occasions. You may welcome an audience to the occasion, may introduce the speaker, may accept or present an award, or may present an inspirational speech.

Welcome Speeches

Welcoming addresses are not as simple some may think. Yes, I know that it seems you should just be able to get up in front of an audience and say, "Welcome, and that's all I have to say about that." Well, Forest, that's not going to work. In this speech, **you welcome the audience to the event, state the purpose of the event, and create enthusiasm about the event.**

What Is the Purpose of the Public Speaking Event?

As the person delivering the welcome, it is important to know the exact purpose of the event. Be able to tell the audience that purpose. You also need to know the sponsors of the event and should acknowledge the leaders of the sponsoring group during your speech. The welcome should make the sponsors as well as the audience feel good. You achieve this esteem-building by mentioning something about the history and goals of the sponsoring group. Then link those goals to the goals of the audience. Also consider if the event is formal or informal. This information will inform your decisions on delivery. Your general purpose is to create enthusiasm about the event.

Who Are the Others/Audience in the Public Speaking Event?

Any time you get up in front of a group of people, you should know who they are. Remember: never address an audience you can conceive of only in vague and general terms. In mama's words, "Never talk to strangers." Address a specific audience that you are aware of and that you know. Think about what they expect of you. What kind of delivery do they expect? Certainly the type of event will inform your delivery decisions. It will also inform the way you decide to package your message.

What Are My Expectations of the Audience?

You always have a motive. What do you want from your audience? You want them to feel welcomed. This is the message that you want to convey. You want the audience to pay attention to your message. So, how do you arrange the speech to get your the intended message across to your audience? Be creative, but not so creative that it is inappropriate for the context of the speech.

Tips for Welcome Speeches

1. Know the purpose of the event during your presentation.
2. Know the audience.
3. Know the sponsors of the event and acknowledge the leadership of the sponsoring group.
4. Know the history and goals of the sponsoring group and link those goals back to the audience.
5. Enthuse the audience—most importantly, *Welcome Them!*

Sample Welcome Speech

Nagatha Tonkins

Ghandi once said, "Every worthwhile accomplishment, big or little, has its stages of drudgery and triumph; a beginning, a struggle and a victory."

Today's presenters have learned about the drudgery of getting started on a project, and they have persevered through the struggle. This afternoon they get to celebrate their victory. And, we are delighted that you have joined us for this occasion when our graduating seniors present to you the culmination of countless hours of hard work and research. This is excellent preparation for our seniors, many of whom will continue to make presentations in graduate school, at professional conferences, and in the workplace. The opportunity to share their learning experiences, research methods, and ideas can serve to enrich their future work and presentations. The College of Arts and Sciences is very excited about this program, and we ask that you stay for its entirety. It's an opportunity for students to showcase their talents in research and for us to commend them for their work. We hope you will continue to encourage others to participate in future programs, and that you will, also. Enjoy the program!

Enthusiastically delivered by Professor Nagatha Tonkins at North Carolina Agricultural and Technical State University College of Arts and Sciences Senior Symposium, December 1, 2004.

Introductory Speeches

Many events have keynote speakers. Those are the speakers who give the major address for the function. At my high school graduation, I was charged with the task of introducing our keynote speaker. I'm sure you had a featured speaker also. If yours was anything like mine, he stayed up there much too long. But back to the issue at hand, the introductory speech. My purpose in giving the introductory speech was to enthuse the audience about the speaker. I hyped the speaker's character and accomplishments. **Introductory speeches create enthusiasm about the upcoming speaker.** Hence, the general purpose is to enthuse.

My introductory speech was exciting. In some cases, speakers will send you a biographical statement that sounds more like an obituary than a pump'em up statement. Your job is to take the keynote speaker's boring fact sheet and turn it into a powerful introductory speech.

What Is the Purpose of the Public Speaking Event?

As the person introducing the speaker, it is important to know the exact purpose of event. It is just as important that you know your purpose. In this case, you are expected to build enthusiasm for the keynote speaker and his or her message. Your general purpose is to create enthusiasm about the person whom you are introducing.

Who Are the Others/Audience in the Public Speaking Event?

Any time you get up in front of a group of people, you should know who they are. Remember, never address an audience you can conceive of only in vague and general terms. Address a specific audience that you are aware of and that you know. Is this a formal or informal affair? Think about what the audience might expect of you. Use these answers to help you make your decisions on delivery. What kind of delivery do they expect? What type of message do they expect? Why are they here?

What Are My Expectations of the Audience?

You always have a motive. Why are you there introducing this speaker? You need know why the person you are introducing has been invited as the keynote speaker. Make sure that you are current on the speaker's background. You are responsible for conveying to the audience why the speaker is "so all that" that she has been invited to speak at this event. How do you arrange the speech to get your intended message across to your audience? How do you gain the audience's attention?

Tips for Introductory Speeches

1. Know the purpose of the event and why this speaker has been selected as the keynote. If the speaker is chosen because of philanthropic contributions, you will want to relate primarily to her philanthropic achievements. On the other hand, if the speaker is chosen because of academic achievements, you will want to relate primarily to her academic ones.
2. Know the audience. It is important that you find a way to link the speaker to the audience. What's the hook? Determine what your speaker and audience have in common and play on it. Your audience may desire to be like your speaker and is looking for inspiration. Inspire them.
3. Know the person that you are introducing. Make sure you gather current, accurate information about the speaker. If you are lucky, you can get a fact sheet about the person. If not, you need to make time to interview the featured speaker.
4. Stress ideas that will make the person you are introducing seem as credible as possible. Remember your general purpose is to create enthusiasm about the person you are introducing.
5. Don't read the boring chronological biography. Make it exciting.
6. Have an interesting opening and a creative body, and end with a statement that begs for applause.
7. Keep it brief. One to three minutes is usually enough. However, more accomplished keynote speakers may deserve a little longer introduction.
8. Talk about the person you are introducing—not yourself. And make sure you don't play the person up so highly that they can never live up to their introduction. That is, *minimize the superfluous listing of glorifying adjectives.*

Sample Introductory Speech
Marrissa R. Dick

Good evening distinguished guests, faculty, and colleagues. My name is Marrissa Dick, and I am a graduate student in the school of education here at North Carolina A&T State University. I have the privilege this evening of introducing one of the most dynamic and phenomenal scholars in the field of adult education. Her research and scholarship focus primarily on culturally grounded community based programming and the impact of racism on adult education theory and practice. Dr. Scipio A. J. Collin, III is an associate professor of Adult and Continuing Education at National-Louis University. She came to NLU from North Carolina State University where she was an assistant professor. She has also served on the faculty at Indiana University—Northwest, and Malcolm X College. Dr. Collin received her B.A. degree from Roosevelt University in Sociology and her M.A. in Urban Studies from Northeastern Illinois University. Following postgraduate studies at the University of Chicago, Dr. Collin earned an Ed.D. in Adult and Continuing Education from Northern Illinois University.

Last summer I had the honor of interviewing Dr. Collin when I attended the Adult Education Research Conference. AERC is the premier conference for adult education scholars to gather and share their research findings. Dr. Collin is an active member of the AERC Steering Committee. She serves in a variety of leadership positions in the field of adult education, including the Executive Committee of the Commission of Professors of Adult Education, the Adult Basic Education Section Chair, and the Urban Education Section Chair of the Illinois Association of Adult and Continuing Educators. She also serves on the Adult Learning Editorial Board and has been a Consulting Editor for the *Adult Education Quarterly,* the major journal for theory and practice in the field of adult education.

I was in awe to meet Dr. Collin who is the author of such profound works as 1. *Racism and Sexism in the United States: Fundamental Issues,* and 2. *African Ameripean Adult Education: A Historic Overview of Selected Activities.* When I approached Dr. Collin for an interview she agreed to meet with me the following morning at ten o'clock. When I showed up, little did I know that she was going to reverse the interviewing process. Before I knew it she was asking me why did I want to be an adult educator? Upon my response she could figure out that I didn't know what I wanted to do in adult education. She could tell that I was searching to find myself. While Dr. Collin imparted words of wisdom—like a child I became emotional which caused people to stare at us. Her response to me was to *"forget about them because this is an "A/B" conversation and in a minute I'm going to tell them to "C" their way out of it."* This is the type of progressive adult educator that we have with us tonight. Upon reflection, I have to tell you, Dr. Collin, that this was my first real experience with progressive learning and for that I thank you.

It is with great pride and pleasure that I present to you a woman who has been recognized by the African American Association of Continuing Educators for Meritorious Service. She has also been recognized internationally for her contributions to the Profession of Teaching and the Field of Educational History. Ladies and gentlemen, Dr. Scipio A. J. Collin, III.

Presentation Speeches

Have you ever watched the *Grammys* or any other video awards show? Almost always, there is some type of lifetime achievement award. Sometimes these presentations include a video montage with someone actually giving a speech of presentation. Then, other times, there is a celebrity saying a few words.

In a presentation speech, you acknowledge the recipient of an award. Your general purpose is to create enthusiasm about the award recipient. Tell what makes the recipient "so all that." Somewhat like the introductory speech, you will want to acknowledge achievements that relate to the award and obviously, to the event.

What Is the Purpose of the Public Speaking Event?

As the person giving the presentation speech, it is important to know the exact purpose of event. It is just as important that you know your purpose. In this case, you are expected to build enthusiasm about the person receiving the award. Also consider if the event is formal or informal. This information will inform your decisions on delivery. Your general purpose is to create enthusiasm about the person you are introducing.

Who Are the Others/Audience in the Public Speaking Event?

Any time you get up in front of a group of people, you should know who they are. Remember; "never talk to strangers." Think about what they expect of you. What kind of delivery do they expect? If this is a formal event, the audience may not be quiet as laid back. The type of message that the audience expects is determined by the purpose of the event. Know why your audience members are at this event. Are they here because of the recipient, or are they here because it's where all of the cool people are? Either way, you will want to draw parallels between the recipient and the audience.

What Are My Expectations of the Audience?

You always have a motive. Why are you here making this presentation speech? To enthuse the audience, right? You will want to arrange your presentation speech in a way that will be enthusiastic as well as informative. You want to grab the audience's attention. You may use the information about the speaker to wow them, or you may wow them with your delivery style. Analyze the situation and make your organizational and delivery decisions based on that analysis.

Tips for Presentation Speeches

1. Know the purpose of the event and why this person is receiving the award. Focus on achievements that have led to the recognition or award.
2. Know the audience. It is important that you find a way to link the recipient and the audience. What's the hook? Determine what your recipient and audience have in common and play on it.
3. Strive to gain audience agreement. Stress ideas that will make the person you are introducing seem as credible as possible. You want to make the audience agree with you that this person should receive the award. Remember: your general purpose is to create enthusiasm about the person who is receiving the award.
4. Don't read the boring chronological biography. Make it exciting.
5. Have an interesting opening, and a creative body, and end with a statement that begs for applause.
6. Keep it brief. Presentation speeches can range from the "and the winner is" one-liners to five minutes. One to three minutes is usually enough.

Sample Presentation Speech
Jackson Jordan

Good evening to you all and welcome to the Broke Celebrity Foundation's First Annual Celebrity Benefit Banquet. Oftentimes, we hear about the lives of the celebrities before us, such as MC Hammer, Mike Tyson, Vanilla Ice, Red Foxx, etc., who have lived beyond what their personal finances could allow. Now they are in need of our help so they can live like regular US citizens. Tonight, we will present all of the money our foundation has raised this year to a deserving celebrity, who will be announced later tonight.

From this year forward, we will attempt to increase the number of recipients and fulfill our organization's purpose, helping broke celebrities. Some of us here tonight are celebrities of high status; others of us are on the rise.

As a member of the BCF, I thank you all for coming out, donating, and volunteering. To everyone here, keep your pennies safe, pay your taxes, and have prosperous careers. But tonight, don't worry about any of that. Just sit back and enjoy the Broke Celebrity Foundation's First Annual Celebrity Benefit Banquet.

Presentation Speech
Ashley Harris

On behalf of the The American Physical Therapy Association, I would like to present this award to Ms. Ashley Lenora Harris for being the first Hispanic woman to start a chain of four Outpatient Rehabilitation facilities in the United States. This award has been well earned and achieved starting back when Ms. Harris attended T. Wingate High Point Andrews. She was in the Vocational Honors Society and completed Parts I and II of medical careers training, She then went on to receive her CNA license. She worked in a Presbyterian Nursing Home for a year.

In 2007 she received her bachelors in Biology of the Arts and Sciences program at Salem State University. During her last year, Ms. Harris was able to shadow several Physical Therapists with diverse backgrounds and settings. Unlike other volunteers, Ms. Harris not only observed the PT's administering therapy to the patients; she observed her surroundings. Ms. Harris noticed how she felt as soon as she walked in each facility, the cleanliness, the attitudes of the patients and employees, and how each facility was operated.

She then took this into consideration and started making plans for her own. After she received her degree, she then attended The University of North Carolina at Chapel Hill. There she received her Doctorate in Physical Therapy and started working for Moses Cone Hospital Acute Care in Greensboro, North Carolina. Ms. Harris stayed with Moses Cone for five years and the following year she opened up her first Outpatient Rehabilitation facility in High Point.

With three PT's working under her, 2 receptionists and 2 PT assistants, Ms. Harris ran the facility for 7 years and was able to open another in Augusta, Georgia. She hired PT's fresh out of college and trained them accordingly. Ms. Harris believed her facilities were the best. Harris also hired an Administrator from Augusta to run the facility because she continued to reside in North Carolina.

After 8 more years, Ms. Harris still had both facilities open and had managed to save enough money to open up her third facility in Chester, Pennsylvania. Once again she hired the majority of her therapists right out of college.

Today Ms. Harris has four facilities open on the east coast from Georgia to New York. She is well known for her hard work and for the talent that she places in each facility. Her patients say, "She has the most intelligent, caring, positive staff." Ms. Harris has retained most of the original employees in each of the clinics. Each facility caters to the young, the old, and the English and Spanish speaking populations. I am honored to be able to present this award to her. Put your hands together for Ms. Ashley Harris.

Acceptance Speeches

In my opinion, acceptance speeches are one of the most abused forms. I know that you have heard those long lists of shout-outs from award show recipients. Fortunately for us, network television has the ability to cut those speakers off. They play that ambient ghost music that signals the speaker to sit down. Some times those accepting the awards obey and sit down. Other times, they just keep right on talking.

Acceptance speeches should give credit where credit is due. Honestly most of us don't know or care about your "people from around the way" or your "fifth-grade teacher"—these are just some of the folks that commonly receive shout outs. But you can help us know those people and care about them. Know that I only want to hear about these people if you show the role they played in your winning this award or deserving this recognition. **In an acceptance speech, you give credit where credit is due—thank the appropriate people, tell what the award means to you, and how you got to where you are today.** Your general purpose in an acceptance speech is to inspire the audience.

What Is the Purpose of the Public Speaking Event?

You are receiving an award. Why? Don't you think it would be a pretty good idea to know the exact purpose of the event? Make sure you know the sponsors of the event. Know why and how they chose you to be acknowledged. Someone is recognizing you for your achievements. Don't be rude. Thank the sponsors. With all of that background in mind, you are to inspire the audience and convince them that you are worthy of the recognition. Always know whether the event is formal or informal.

Who Are the Others/Audience in the Public Speaking Event?

Any time you get up in front of a group of people, you should know who they are. Remember, never address an audience you can conceive of only in vague and general terms. Address a specific audience that you are aware of and that you know. Are you tired of hearing that yet? Maybe you are. But, I must keep reminding you that the audience is the center of every public speaking event. Think about what the audience expects of you. They want to hear about stuff that can get them in the exalted place that you are in on this occasion. Give the audience a message that will inspire them and help them believe that they to can achieve what you have achieved.

What Are My Expectations of the Audience?

You want the audience to believe that you are worthy of this recognition. You want to leave them inspired. How do you arrange the speech to get your intended message across to your audience? Think of creative ways to gain the audience's attention. Let the audience members know that they, too, can achieve what you have achieved. Remember to inspire.

Tips for Acceptance Speeches

1. Know the purpose of the event and why you are receiving the award.
2. Know the audience. It is important that you find a link between yourself and the audience. Find the hook. What do you have in common with the audience? Find that something and play on it. Inspire them.
3. Tell the audience what winning the award means to you.
4. Tell your "how I got over" story. Let the audience know how you got to where you are now. Focus on the path that led to your receiving this recognition.
5. Don't read the boring chronological biography. Make it exciting. Tell us a story about that fifth-grade teacher that was so inspirational in your getting to this place. The message here is to give life to the facts and faces to the names.
6. Have an interesting opening and a creative body, and end with a statement that begs for applause.
7. Stay within your time limit. Acceptance speeches can range from the "thank you" one-liners to an hour. I have heard Maya Angelou and John Hope Franklin give acceptance speeches that have a combined time of more than three hours. That's long. Just as you don't want to go over time, you definitely don't want to come up short either. Please, ask the sponsors prior to the program to make sure of your time limitations.

How Not to Do an Acceptance Speech

Wow, Athlete of The Year, I mean I really did not expect this!!!!!, especially with all of these great names I was put against, like Kobe, LeBraun, and the rest of the fellas. But first and foremost, I want to give praises to my Lord and Savior because without him wouldn't none of this be possible. I don't want to stand up here real long, but there are a couple of people I would like to, I want to thank my parents because I really and truly do not believe that I would not have been able to make it this far without them. They always kept me humble and on track. I want to also thank my beautiful fiancée, Alicia Keyes, in the first row, "I love you baby." You know what they say, "behind every successful man there is a strong black woman."

Man, I would just like to show some love to the whole New Jersey Nets Organization, especially my teammates, they are really the ones who are making everything happen. I want to also thank BET for honoring me with this award. And of course I had to save the best for last, I want to thank all of my fans out there, it is you who made this award possible. So I see this trophy as our together. . . . I am just going to keep it at my house . . . Thank you.

Acceptance Speech
Jennifer Harris

I am honored and extremely satisfied to know that the hard work and struggle of American's beautiful people does not go unnoticed. This is honestly why this award means so much for me.

First, I would like to honor God and thank Him for the strength and stability he has bestowed upon me throughout the years. It has been a long journey. A special and humble thank you to North Carolina Agricultural and Technical State University, Winston Salem State University, The University of Georgia, Grady Memorial Hospital, and the American Cancer Association for all of their dedicated research, long days, long nights, time and patience.

No one person can take credit for this research. I am here because of all of the beautiful minds from each of the institutions that I've named. They stood behind me 110% of the way. They are why I am able to stand before you today and accept this Nobel Peace Prize for developing a cure for cancer. Had it not been for those significant individuals and the experiences that God guided and pushed us through, this occasion would be nonexistent for me.

Today, I leave here honored and overjoyed; still, I cry internally. The fight and struggle does not stop here. There are so many lives to be saved and I challenge you all to help. Work toward the common goal of preserving life, not destroying it. Thank you and God bless.

Master of Ceremonies Speeches

Most special occasion events require someone to "run the show." That person is the Master of Ceremonies. Sometimes you hear the female serving as the Master of Ceremonies referred to as Mistress of Ceremonies. For our purposes here, we will alternate between masculine and feminine references, but will use Master of Ceremonies. "So, on with the show" as you might say if you are serving as the Master of Ceremonies or MC. **The MC carries the program. He sets the tone of the program, introduces the participants, and keeps the program flowing smoothly.**

At first glance, this might sound like an easy task that requires little to no preparation. WRONG. With that attitude, as the MC, you will be the weakest link. It is your responsibility to carry the program. The only way you can successfully do this is to know the entire program from top to bottom and from side to side. That takes preparation.

The general purpose of the MC is to entertain. Entertain in this case also means to create enthusiasm. You are to gain and retain the attention of the audience. Your opening remarks should be treated like any other introductory statement. You should gain the attention of the audience, introduce yourself, and briefly state the purpose of the event. Let's just hope that the rest of the program runs smoothly. It should, right? All you have to do is to announce the names of the people listed on the program, right? No, that's not right at all. Your responsibilities are much greater.

You must know the role of each participant. Before you get up in front of your audience, know who is and who is not present. Say it's three minutes to four and the person responsible for doing the welcome has not arrived. As the Mistress of Ceremonies, it is your responsibility to either give the welcome or find someone to replace the absent person. Again, you must know the role or job description of each participant.

Your responsibility does not end with simply knowing the role of each participant and making sure each participant's spot is covered in the program. You are the thread that weaves the entire program together. As the MC, you are to keep the audience enthused about the program, or, at the bare minimum, interested in the program. If the fill-in guy gives a boring welcome—a real sleeper—then you need to wake the audience up again. Keep'em hyped.

Tips for Master of Ceremonies Speeches

1. Know the purpose of the event.
2. Know the audience.
3. Know the entire program. You should not only know the program, but you should also convey specifics about the program to all the participants. Prior to the beginning of the program, let all the participants know where they are supposed to be and at what time. Make sure everyone participating in the program knows his or her responsibilities. For you to know all of this information, you should probably develop a script with an accompanying timeline and staging notes.
4. Know the participants in the event. Please be able to pronounce the names of the people that you introduce. Don't say things like, "I hope I get this right, but is it pronounced Jah breeva?" Know how it is pronounced before you go in front of your audience.
5. Don't just read the boring chronological agenda. Make it exciting. Keep the audience enthused throughout the program.

Inspirational Speeches

Let's say the local Order of the Eastern Star's Worthy Matron calls you and asks you to speak at their monthly luncheon. She asks that you speak on behalf of last year's scholarship winners. You agree! One big catch, you don't know how to plan for this type of speech. You say to yourself, "Self, I know how to do a welcome, an introductory speech, speeches of presentation, and acceptance. I even know how to MC the program. But what do I do if I am a featured speaker." The simple answer is, "you inspire."

There is a broad category of speeches that are actually called inspirational speeches. Guess the general purpose of this broad category. You got it. It is to inspire. **Inspirational speeches may aim to pay tribute to an idea, a person, or group.** All inspirational speeches appeal to human emotion. As the speaker, you arouse the emotions of the audience during your inspirational speeches. The audiences listening to your speeches are looking for a little entertainment. Again, not necessarily Chris Rock entertainment, but the kind that yields enthusiasm and inspiration. Let's look at inspirational speeches in some more specific sub-categories: the after-dinner and the commemorative.

After-Dinner Speeches

Let's say you do give the speech at the Eastern Star Chapter luncheon. Your speech would be considered an after-dinner speech. I know you're not really giving the speech after dinner, but any speech that is given before, during, or after any meal is considered an after-dinner speech. **After-dinner speakers use a light-hearted tone to make a specific point about a specific subject.**

You don't want to be too technical with an after-dinner audience. Think about how you feel around mealtime. I know I don't want to hear a speech about the micro-physical molecular atomic energy emissions of cell phones. Is that really possible? Anyway, I know I don't want a heavily visually illustrated presentation about the Tsunami and Sri Lanka. Either of these can be the topic, but neither of them can be discussed in a weighty tone. Your general purpose is to inspire. You may have an ulterior motive, such as informing or persuading your after-dinner audience, but you must not abandon the general purpose—to inspire.

Are you saying, "how do I inspire someone and discuss cell phones?" If you are, here is the answer. CREATIVITY. Find a novel way to discuss the old. You want to find the most exciting and creative way that you can to talk about cell phones. You want to organize your speech in a way that creates energy. Visualize this speech as a snowball rolling down the side of the hill. The speech, like the snowball, must grow in intensity, excitement, and inspiration as you move toward the conclusion. These speeches require you, as the speaker, to closely interact with your audience. Find a method that gains and retains the audience's attention.

After-dinner speakers sometimes use lots of humor. If you are the speaker, you might not want to try humor unless you are really funny. Some of us think that we are funny, but we really are not. Stick to what you know to be true and don't use a public event such as this one to try out jokes that you have not tried out on those who love you. If your people, your loved ones, didn't laugh, it's possible that strangers might not either. Remember, you have to find what works best for you.

What Is the Purpose of the Public Speaking Event?

Like always, it is important to know the exact purpose of event. You also need to know your purpose. What do the sponsors want you to do? Are you simply giving a motivational speech or a testimonial of some sort, or are you trying to drum up support for AIDS fund. Your general purpose is to inspire, but you may have ulterior motives.

Who Are the Others/Audience in the Public Speaking Event?

Any time you get up in front of a group of people, you should know who they are. Remember, "never talk to strangers." Think about what they expect of you. What kind of delivery do they expect? You know that this is an after-dinner or meal related event. You also know that people often get sleepy after they eat; especially after they eat lunch. That alone tells you that you need to pump up the delivery. You cannot give a monotone dry-language speech. Use vivid language. Have an exciting and energetic delivery. Don't be too animated. People sometimes shy away from that which appears artificial and over done.

Think about the type of message the audience expects? They want something light hearted. Find a way to tie your message to the organization, the event, and the audience.

What Are My Expectations of the Audience?

Most after-dinner speakers have an ulterior motive, even if that motive is as innocuous as building goodwill. Because we always have a motive, we need to ask, "Why am I here delivering this after-dinner address?" To inspire the audience, right? You might realize that you also need to inform them about how they can make contributions to the AIDS fund. Certainly, you will not miss out on the opportunity to persuade them to make contributions. So then, you will arrange your speech in a way that will be inspirational as well as informative. You want to gain and retain the audience's attention. Always analyze the situation and make your organizational and delivery decisions based on that knowledge.

Tips for After-Dinner Speeches

1. Know the purpose of the event and why you have been chosen to give this speech.
2. Know the audience. Relate your topic to the audience. Use examples and illustrations that involve them or that relate to them.
3. Don't read an after-dinner speech. You might read a poem, quote, etc. But do not read the speech. Make it exciting.
4. Have an interesting opening and a creative body, and end with a statement that begs for applause. Find a novel way of treating the old.
5. Know your time. Consult with the sponsors to determine the desired length of your presentation. You will also want to know whether the sponsors want you to speak prior

to the meal or after. Groups generally stay away from having speakers address the audience during the meal. If you do find a group that is insistent upon you speaking at that time, try to dissuade them. It is incredibly difficult to speak during a meal. For the most part, people don't pay attention. The internal and external noises are too great.

This speech could be delivered in a way that is motivating. Serious subjects are often addressed in creative manners that create enthusiasm.

Black Power
Ashley Smith

We're only good for playing sports. We aren't smart enough to compete educationally and we are definitely too ignorant to run this country! Black people are the worst! The men are lazy and are only good for smoking weed and riding around with their speakers blasting so loud that everybody in a three mile radius can hear them. And the women, don't get me started! The only thing they're good for is lying down on their backs and shaking their asses in music videos . . .

Do you want me to stop or should I keep going? I don't know if it's just me, but I'm tired of being subject to all the negative stereotypes society places on Blacks, especially the youth. We can help change and eliminate these stereotypes if we just step up to the plate and do something about it. Don't get me wrong; there are many successful Black figures in our society that are doing great things and setting the right example. We just need more.

We need to stop aspiring to be the things we see in gangster movies and rap videos and work towards improving our communities and educating our people about the things going on in the world. We need to end all the violence amongst our people. We should be helping each other on our quests for success, not killing each other. We should take our education more seriously and not settle for less than par facilities in our schools. We can do everything this society says we can't. We can excel and not just be considered average. We are a beautiful people; we just need to stop grasping on to excuses and live up to our potential. I want to once again be able to hold my fist up with pride, not hang my head low with shame, wishing we would just get it together. Are you up to the challenge? I know I am. Thank you.

Commemorative Speeches

Commemorative speeches are celebration speeches. They are the hallelujah hand-clapping spiritual kind of speeches. Okay, they may not be all of that. But **commemorative speeches do celebrate and praise an event, person, or group.** When people deliver eulogies, they celebrate and praise the life of a person. When people deliver commencement addresses, they celebrate and praise the graduates. **Commemorative speakers arouse the emotions of the audience by using powerful language—language that evokes vivid images.**

In some ways the commemorative speech is like the speech of presentation. In both, you create enthusiasm about your subject. Although the subjects differ, the aims are the same. In addition to enthusing the audience, the commemorative speaker seeks to inspire.

What Is the Purpose of the Public Speaking Event?

Know the exact purpose of the event. Know that your purpose is to inspire. I mean that "shake the earth" kind of inspiration. Okay, so maybe it does not need to be "shake the earth" inspirational. It does, however, need to be moving. You are at this event to celebrate or praise something. Is this event formal or informal? Is it appropriate to yell like Howard Dean after he lost the Iowa Caucus? You need to know what is and what is not acceptable. This information will inform your decisions on delivery. You may need to inform the audience about the person or event that you are commemorating. Yet, you want to focus on increasing the audience's admiration, excitement, and the respect of your subject.

Who Are the Others/Audience in the Public Speaking Event?

Any time you get up in front of a group of people, you should know who they are. Remember: "never talk to strangers." Think about what they expect of you. What kind of delivery do they expect? Is this event formal or informal? Your message at a gathering celebrating the anniversary of the February 1, 1960 sit-ins will differ from the message that you deliver at a memorial or funeral service. *Yes, eulogies are commemorative speeches.* Know why your audience members are at the event. Also remember that audiences generally expect to be moved when they hear commemorative speeches. Praise and celebration connote movement.

What Are My Expectations of the Audience?

I want my audience to walk away inspired. If you are delivering a commemorative speech, your aim should also be to have an inspired audience at the conclusion of your speech. Arrange your commemorative speech in a way that will be inspirational as well as informative. Use language that creates vivid images and that appeals to human emotion. Think about the situation and make your organizational and delivery decisions based on that analysis.

Tips for Commemorative Speeches

1. Know the purpose of the event and why you are giving the commemorative address.
2. Know the audience. Find and draw some parallels between the audience and the subject.
3. Don't read lists. Make it exciting. PRAISE & CELEBRATE.
4. Have an interesting opening and a creative body, and end with a statement that begs for applause.
5. Use vivid language that appeals to human emotion.
6. Stay within your time limit. Contact the sponsoring group to determine your time constraints.

Eulogy
Kenneth Flowers Jr.

Family, close relatives, and friends, we are gathered here today to celebrate the life of one of the most extraordinary women God has ever created. Born in the small town of Lillington, TX, Mrs. Henrietta Lula Thompson was destined for fame from an early age. The youngest of seven brothers and sisters born to the late Alfred Thompson and the former Lucille Crawford, Henrietta knew she had to stand out to be noticed. Never turning down an opportunity, Mrs. Thompson got her first commercial gig at the age of 16 and like the critics say, "the rest is history." Starring in numerous films over her 40-year career, Mrs. Thompson was best known for her remake of the film *Deep Waters* and the original *Connie and Slyde*. But what most do not know about Henrietta is how big her heart was. Always a giver, she donated millions of dollars over her lifetime for the less privileged, stating, "I remember growing up and not having much, and I just want to give others hope for a better life." She was also a very religious person, citing the church as the light that made her a star.

Having known Mrs. Thompson personally, I can truly say that I will miss her, but this is not a time for mourning, rather a time of celebration. We celebrate because we know this woman lived her life in a way that will result in her eternal happiness. Let us all stand and acknowledge the life of the late, but always great, Henrietta Lula Thompson.

Graduation Speech
Mikia Shaw

Good morning distinguished faculty, fellow classmates, family, and friends. I come before you as senior class president to say my final farewell to the class of 2010. I never like to say goodbye, so I will address it as I will see you later on in life. I will see you later on as our future president of the United States, as future CEO on the cover of "Black Enterprise" or "Time," or whatever successful path your future follows. We entered North Carolina A&T as underdeveloped boys and girls, but today we are leaving as mature, prestigious young men and women. The four years that we have endured at A&T have been full of so many emotions: laughter, cries, stress, and even relief. We have developed lasting relationships with people from all over the country; some have found best friends or even future mates, who will continue to be a part of their lives in the many years to come.

We started a new chapter of our lives upon entering, but the journey does not end here. As Newton Baker said, "The man who graduates today and stops learning tomorrow is uneducated the day after." We must take the experiences learned here at North Carolina A&T and start another chapter in our lives: adulthood. As we leave our prestigious university, let us remember the meaning of a real Aggie . . . Achieving Great Goals In Everything Producing Renowned Individuals Dedicated to Excellence . . . AGGIE PRIDE!

Retirement Speech
Sarah Marshall

Good morning. Thank you for joining us in celebrating the retirement of Patricia Mickley. Patricia or Pat as we call her, graduated from nursing school in 1964. She came to the Wesley Long Intensive Care Unit in 1983, with 19 years of experience. From the beginning Pat was different; she was special. She had a passion for her profession and for sharing her knowledge with others. Most of us fondly call her "Momma Pat." She is always looking out for everyone. When she is in charge, she has a plan and a backup plan to follow that one. She has taken on leadership roles in our department being a preceptor and orienting our new graduate nurses. Pat takes a special interest in our new graduates. She tries to help them learn and she tries to help them to be the best they can be. She may even give them homework to do! One of the nurses Pat oriented said Pat made her enjoy nursing again after going through some rough times. Pat received the National Preceptor Award at the National Teaching Institute in 2005. Pat is a natural teacher, teaching everyday by example. She always has the patient's best interest at heart. She also teachers CPR and Advanced Cardiac Life Support for the hospital.

Pat is a Centurion. For those of you who don't know, that is someone whose age and years of service equals to 100 years or more. Pat is a role model to those of us who work with her. Her enthusiasm and passion for her profession are an inspiration to all of us. Join us as we celebrate Pat's retirement after 42 years of nursing, 23 of those years with us here at Wesley Long. We will miss the guidance, stability, and friendship that Momma Pat has shown us. Pat, we thank you and we wish you well!

Wrap It Up

The general purpose of a special occasion speech is to entertain. Consider that entertainment does not always equate to Chris Rock funny. Entertain in terms of special occasion speeches generally means to inspire or to create enthusiasm.

There are numerous occasions that require special occasion presentations. The specific purposes of these occasions may differ. Yet, they all require you to either create enthusiasm or to inspire. There are several types of speeches that might be required at special occasions. You may welcome an audience to the occasion, introduce the speaker, accept or present an award, or present an inspirational speech.

In the welcome speech, you welcome the audience to event, state the purpose of the event, and create enthusiasm about the event. Introductory speeches create enthusiasm about the upcoming speaker. In a presentation speech, you acknowledge the recipient of an award. Your general purpose is to create enthusiasm about the award recipient. In an acceptance speech, you give credit where credit is due—thank the appropriate people, tell what the award means to you, and how you got to where you are today. The MC carries the program, i.e., sets the tone of the program, introduces the participants, and keeps the program flowing smoothly.

Inspirational speeches may aim to pay tribute to an idea, a person, or group. Inspirational speeches appeal to human emotion. These speeches can be broken into some more specific sub-categories: the after-dinner and the commemorative speeches. After-dinner speakers use a light-hearted tone to make a specific point about a specific subject. Commemorative speakers arouse the emotions of the audience by using powerful language that evokes vivid images.

Think About It → Write About It

Reflect on what you've just read. Now write what you are thinking.

_____

_____

_____

_____

_____

_____

_____

_____

_____

_____

_____

_____

_____

_____

_____

_____

_____

_____

_____

_____

_____

_____

_____

Activity

"We Welcome You!"

1. Divide the class into four groups (at least 6 students per group)
2. Ask each group to decide on which group member will do the
    a. "Welcome Speech"
    b. "Introductory Speech"
    c. "Presentation Speech"
    d. "Acceptance Speech"
    e. "After-dinner Speech"
    f. "Master of Ceremonies"
3. Allow each group to select their own special occasion for which they will be preparing speeches. Some suggestions are:
    a. Church or Pastoral Anniversary
    b. Graduating Senior Dinner
    c. National Honor Society Induction Ceremony
    d. Dedication of New Community Center
4. Allow the groups to prepare for their speeches to be shared at the next class session.

Chapter 16

Understanding the Copyright Law—
At Least an Awareness of the Law

Sheila M. Whitley, Ph.D.

Key Terms

Copyright   Trademarks
Copyright Protect   Patents
Fair-Use   Intellectual Property
Plagiarism

Yes, I've Heard the Term "Copyright"

We all have heard the term "copyright" and probably know it is a law, but may not give it much consideration. You may think you have nothing worth copyrighting, or your copyright violations are negligible to the owner. Perhaps you don't know if you are in violation of the copyright law. Whatever your understanding of the copyright law, we need to periodically look at this law so we will know, or be reminded of, the consequences when and if we violate the law, and how it protects our work. Let's begin with a look at some copyright infringement scenarios.

Some people willingly admit to infringing upon copyright and are able to justify their violation. Here is an example. You are a *broke college student*. Your favorite group just released a new CD. You ask your willing friend, who purchased the CD and has a CD recorder on her computer, to make a copy of it for you. You really like the group, but you're not going to buy the CD—you're broke and the CD is too pricey. You reason, this so-called violation hurts no one. The artist makes plenty of money from all the "legal" sales, including your friend's purchase. Isn't the recording the property of your friend, and isn't she free do to with her property as she wishes? If she wishes to make you a copy for you, what's the problem?

According to the copyright law, there is a problem. Yes, she owns a legal copy of the CD, and it is her property to give away or sell, but not to copy. You must understand what your friend owns and does not own to grasp why this is copyright infringement. She only owns the physical copy of the CD, which is the tangible property she legally purchased and is in her possession. She is not the copyright owner, and the purchase of a copy of the CD did not give her copyright owner privileges. The copyright most likely belongs to the recording company that released the CD. The copyright is attached to the intangible or intellectual property protected by the Copyright Act of 1976, which gives the owner in part the right to copy and distribute their property. Therefore, your friend cannot legally give you permission to make a copy or give you a copy she made. She is free to give you or sell you her property (transfer of ownership) which is the "legal" copy she purchased (United States Copyright Office, 2002).

I know many believe this infringement does not cost the recording industry much money. It is only one copy of the recording, and they make a lot of money from all the other sells. The Recording Industry Association of America (RIAA) takes this infringement very seriously, and this violation has burgeoned in recent years with the development of high-quality recording devices and the Internet. The RIAA reports the industry loses about $300 million domestically and about $4.2 billion worldwide a year to illegal recordings (Pember, 2000; Recording Industry Association of America, 2003).

If you set aside the domestic and worldwide money lost each year to illegal copying, including bootleg selling, you still might think the recording industry and all artists make a lot of money and neither will feel a financial impact from one pirated copy. This argument only focuses on the recordings that make money. According to RIAA, 85 percent of the recordings don't make enough money to cover their costs. The highly profitable 15 percent of recordings that make money support the industry and allow for new artists and others to produce material that is unprofitable. Most pirated copies are from the highly profitable 15 percent of the industry that supports 100 percent of the industry. Therefore, the financial loss to the recording industry and profit-making artists is tremendous (Recording Industry Association of America, 2003).

The second scenario is guilty by association or coercion. Maybe you don't want or intend to violate the copyright law, but you work for someone who has no regard for copyright, no fear of getting caught, or no knowledge that he is breaking the law. Let's say you are a videotape producer at an educational institution with a small production budget. Your boss asks you to use all or a piece of popular music on the videotape you are producing. Popular music is copyrighted—no ifs, ands, or buts. In addition to copying and distributing rights, the copyright laws gives the owner exclusive rights to publicly exhibit or display their work (United States Copyright Office, 2002). You are about to copy, distribute, and perform publicly a piece of copyrighted music. That's three strikes and a blatant violation of the copyright law.

The only way you can legally use copyrighted music is to obtain written permission from the copyright owner or pay for the right to use the music for a specified purpose (needle drop fee). Your boss is not willing to do either. The copyright owner may give you permission to use the piece without any financial compensation. Never hurts to ask. You are not likely to get free-use permission if it is a popular piece. Keep in mind, the copyright owner supports a business from the selling of the CD to individuals and the needle drop fees paid for public use of the music. Your small production budget cannot pay the fee to legally obtain the right to use the piece. Your boss argues the owner will never come after you, because they will never know their music was used without permission or financial compensation. Maybe 100 people will see the tape. The tape is not for worldwide distribution. It is a small piece for training. Your boss also argues he owns a "legal" copy of the piece so he can use the music anyway he wants (this rationale if from our first scenario—busted here too). His final justification is in the name of education, and who would sue an educational institution for a little copyright violation?

This is infringement, and the copyright owner can sue. Yes, the owner will have to know you used its piece of music before they can bring legal action. Maybe you're thinking the likelihood of the owner seeing the piece is so remote you consider yourself safe. You never know who will see your videotape once it is produced. The owner might never see it, but what about his/her cousin, brother-in-law, business manager, attorney, and so on. You better believe they will tell the owner. The recording artist is not the only person making money from a hit song. In addition to the artist, the songwriter, business manager, attorneys, musicians, and so forth have a vested interest in protecting the copyright. Is it worth the risk? If you're caught, you're sued, and you lose.

Still don't think they care or you'll get caught? One of my colleagues tells a story from his mid-1970s college days. A classmate used, without permission, a song by a popular 1960s folk singer in a student film. She didn't see the film, but someone who knew her did see the film and told her. Ergo, the student got caught using copyrighted material without permission or paying the needle drop fee. The recording artist was NOT happy and took action. You can't say they will never know or care about these so-called minor infringements. They might find out and take legal action.

How can producers with a small production budget afford to use music in their tapes? Without a doubt, music enhances the message or adds interest. Although purchasing the right to use popular music in a videotape is very expensive, you can't afford the risk of having illegal music on your tapes. There are many reasonably priced music libraries for purchase or lease. Music libraries are designed to be used in productions and typically work better as foreground and background music than most popular pieces.

The third scenario for violating the copyright law is that you are unaware something is protected. These violations fall under the "innocent infringer," meaning infringement was not intentional and the violator may be protected by the copyright law from liability for infringement (Pember, 2000). Beware, ignorance is not an excuse to violate the law. It may mitigate your guilt but not release you from all consequences. If there is a visible copyright notice on the product and you copy it, you just lost your plea of "innocent infringer" (United States Copyright Office, 2002).

Do you or someone you know fall into any of the above categories? Or maybe you know of a scenario not mentioned? Do you fully understand the copyright law—what is protected, how you get something protected, what is fair-use, and what is infringement? The term copyright may seem straightforward. If you don't own the copyright—don't copy it. Is there more? As we saw in our scenarios, the law gives the copyright owner the right to copy and distribute the work. Additionally, the copyright owner has the right to make a byproduct or deviation, and publicly display or exhibit the original work. If the original work is a sound recording, the owner has the right to publicly perform the work via digital audio transmission (United States Copyright Office, 2002).

Maybe the law isn't that simple. A meager search will reveal a long list of pending, active, and settled court cases alleging copyright infringement. If you use copyrighted material, you need to understand the amount of material you may use—if allowed—before you cross into infringement. If you create original works, you need to understand what your rights are as the creator and how to protect your property.

Not a New Concept

If you dislike history, you might be tempted to skip this part. Please stay with me. I love to hear the history of how and why things came to be. A little history lesson helps us understand the context for our current copyright law. If we don't know where we've been and how we got here, we may be at risk of losing a vital area of protection or may be allowing an outdated law that needs revising to continue or hold us to a law that serves no function in our society today.

Written expression has been with mankind almost since the beginning of time. Archeologists discovered libraries dating back to the third millennium B.C. in the ancient Near East (Casson, 2001). The old saying, "knowledge is power," is very true. Until literacy became common in recent times, to possess a book meant power and wealth. You had to have power and wealth to own a book. They were expensive, and very few people could read. Those with the power and wealth cherished their position in society and weren't willing to let the peasants and other less fortunates in on their good thing (Folkerts & Lacy, 2001).

By medieval times, the Catholic Church restricted the reproduction of books. Most books were duplicated in monasteries by scribes. Monks copied these books by hand and one at a time. This was a long and laborious process (Folkerts & Lacy, 2001). Needless to say, there weren't a lot of "illegal" copies due to the limited number of people who could read and write and the amount of time it took to copy a book.

In the mid 1400s, Gutenberg changed the world when he invented the first working movable type printing press. This press enabled the printed word to be reproduced more easily, quickly, and the price of a publication started to drop, making printed material more affordable. At this time, the common man was still illiterate, but the door of knowledge and opportunity for a better life was cracked open, allowing all who desired to enter. The literacy rate increased over time as books become more affordable and plentiful. As the literacy rate increased, so did income. Therefore, the more literate a person, the greater potential for income (Folkerts & Lacy, 2001).

Slowly but surely, the printing press allowed common people to enter the literary world, and this threatened the elite's power and control they had over the common man. This was a major step in the evolution of democratizing mankind and power shifting. The ability to read and purchase books changed the world we live in. We take reading, writing, and owning books as trivial. Children are given thick-paged books to drool and chew on before they can crawl. Even today—as in the past—not all people are in favor of the common person reading and writing. Prior to the ability to read and own books, the elite told the common people what to think and how to act. For example, the new printing press ushered in mass production of *The Holy Bible*. Prior to the common person's ability to own a copy of *The Holy Bible* and read it, the clergy told the people what *The Holy Bible* said and the common people believed what the clergy told them. They didn't have access to a copy of *The Holy Bible*, and, if they did, they couldn't read and check for accuracy. The people trusted the clergy. Unfortunately, not all clergy of the day accurately relayed what they read, but instead used their position to guarantee that people remained subjugated (Folkerts & Lacy, 2001).

Clergy weren't the only ones who wanted to control all the power, knowledge, or truth. At some point in time, almost all governments have tried to restrict what was printed. This type of restriction is known as prior restraint. Do not confuse prior restraint with censorship. Censorship happens *after* a book or other material is produced. Prior restraint is a government prohibition of printing specified material. The printer must have a license issued by the government prior to printing government approved and endorsed material. Prior restraint is the method the monarchs in England used to control all printing from the early 1500s to the end of the 1600s (Folkerts & Lacy, 2001).

In 1518, King Henry VIII issued printing privileges to the printers loyal to the crown. This was an effort to squelch anti-government writers and publishers. In 1710, the British Parliament passed the country's first copyright law, which gave rights to the authors instead of the printers. The law, "An Act for the Encouragement of Learning, by Vesting the Copies of Printed Books in the Authors or Purchasers of Such Copies, during the Time Therein Mentioned," was passed during Queen Anne's eight years of rule and became known as the "Statute of Eight Anne." The idea behind this law was to promote the creative mood and allow authors to financially benefit from their work. This was accomplished by giving ownership of literary property to the person who created the work or to the person the author gave ownership (Pember, 2000).

The "Statute of Eight Anne" was applied as law to Colonial America until the Revolutionary War when Article 1, Section 8 of the United States Constitution provided a foundation for our copyright law (Pember, 2000).

The Congress shall have Power . . . To promote the progress of science and useful arts, by securing for limited times to authors and inventors the exclusive right to their respective writings and discoveries.

In 1790, Congress passed a copyright law which was similar to the "Statute of Eight Anne." The law gave authors, who were citizens of United States, the right to protect books, maps, and charts for twenty-eight years, two fourteen-year terms (Pember, 2000).

The copyright law does not work in isolation. As mentioned earlier, prior restraint is a method for the government to control the message given to the people. Almost all governments have practiced prior restraint at one time or another. The founding fathers of this country included an amendment to the Constitution to guarantee the citizens the right to print without government inference. The First Amendment of the United States Constitution prohibits prior restraint by giving us freedom of the press. More broadly, the First Amendment gives us the freedom of expression (Dennis & Merrill, 2002). The First Amendment states:

> "Congress shall make no law respecting an establishment of religion, or prohibiting the free exercise thereof; or abridging the freedom of speech, or of the press; or the right of the people peaceably to assemble, and to petition the government for redress of grievances."

I'm going to digress for a moment. I feel the First Amendment needs a little discussion. There is debate if we truly have a free press or not. Granted, the First Amendment has a few limitations and must work in conjunction with other amendments and laws. For example, libel is not protected by the First Amendment. If you print it—there is nothing to prevent you from printing it except an editor who knows the law—you may be held accountable in a court of law (Dennis & Merrill, 2002). The government has the right to restrict the flow of information during times of war or for reasons of national security. This is for the good of the people and nation. Our enemies read our newspapers and watch our television. They could use the information for combat strategies, thereby putting all of us at physical risk (Folkerts & Lacy, 2001). I think it is important that we understand the First Amendment gives us radical rights. Our First Amendment is not understood by most people around the world. Currently, and certainly historically, most people in other countries have no rights equal to our First Amendment (Dennis & Merrill, 2002).

Now, back to point. Today, we understand writers and creators of original works hope they will make money from their art, and many do make a living from selling their creative works. Writers have not always felt they should financially benefit from their work. Many Renaissance writers—including Martin Luther—felt their words were divinely received. They believed they were a vessel for God. Therefore, as His messenger they should give their divine revelation to the people (Bucy, 2002).

By the eighteenth century, the book industry had grown, and some writers began wanting to make livings as writers. The image of the vessel writer changed into an artist who uses inspiration to create wonderful original prose from ordinary words (Bucy, 2002).

What is the reality? Do authors create original works, or do they adapt other works into a new perspective? Ecclesiastes 1:9-10 in the Old Testament of *The Holy Bible* says,

"What has been will be again, what has been done will be done again; there is nothing new under the sun. Is there anything of which one can say, 'Look! This is something new'? It was here already, long ago; it was here before our time" (New York International Bible Society, 1978).

Maybe you are asking yourself, "How do the ancient words from the Old Testament apply to copyright?" Copyright assumes originality, but is anything original? What comes to mind when I say, "whodunit?" What type of story am I talking about? You quickly reply, "murder mystery." A whodunit always starts out with a murder, and the rest of the story is in search of the guilty party as the author drops little clues that lead you to whodunit. We also know to suspect the butler. Well, maybe not today. That is an old joke with whodunits—the butler did it. Where is the originality?

If I said I'm going to write a love story, you already have formed the basic plot in your mind. You may not know the particulars, but you know I'm talking about "boy meets girl, boy wins girl, and they live happily ever after." That's the classic definition of a love story, and you never have to say your sorry. I tell you I'm writing a love story. In my love story the boy lives in one town, the girl in another town, and they never meet or have any contact with each other. Don't you think that is an original plot for a love story? After your-deer-caught-in-the-headlights stare, you reply, "That's not a love story—they must meet and fall in love." Distant unconnected lives don't even make for a good whodunit—no murder.

Maybe you are thinking, this is the twenty-first century and we just ran out of originality, but what about one, two, three, four hundred, or a thousand years ago? Did they have original stories? Let's consider one of the most studied playwrights by every high school and college student, William Shakespeare. Many scholars believe Shakespeare borrowed heavily from other works while creating his masterpieces like *Julius Caesar* and *Henry V* (Bucy, 2002).

Shakespeare wrote tragedies, comedies, and love stories. Did he create the idea of a love story? No. What would you say if I ask you to tell me history's greatest love stories? Maybe you immediately think of Shakespeare's *Romeo and Juliet*. They didn't live happily ever after, but still a great love story. What about Old Testament love stories like Sampson and Delilah, Isaac and Rebekah, or Adam and Eve? Get the idea? Stories about romance have been around since the beginning of time. Love story authors borrow from a similar plot—one that is a reflection of life. Borrowing doesn't just occur in literature. What about visual artists and painters? American pop artist Andy Warhol painted Campbell's Soup cans. Go to any grocery store and you can buy a can of soup a lot cheaper than one of Warhol's paintings (Bucy, 2002). Warhol was known for imitated life in his culture—that is a pop artist by definition.

Some artists look to other art movements for inspiration. Vincent Van Gogh is one of my favorite artists. He was a Post-Impressionist artist along with Paul Cezanne and Paul Gauguin. The Post-Impressionist were influenced by the Impressionists—Claude Monet and Edger Degas—but their work had more emotion and was a bit more formal (Artcyclopedia, 2003).

If there is nothing new under the sun, how can anyone claim copyright as an original creator? Keep the spirit of the law in mind. Without a doubt, certain artists and writers make an impact on their society and many transcend time and touch future generations. Shakespeare wrote *Julius Caesar* in the late 1590s and it is still studied today, albeit to the chagrin of many high school and college students. The Impressionist movement occurred from the 1860s to the 1890s and the Post-Impressionist from 1880s to 1900. Andy Warhol painted soup cans found in every American grocery store in 1968. Are they guilty of duplication and void of originality? No. Every culture and generation has a different or unique spin on life and their surroundings. Copyright is not intended to stifle an artist's interpretation of his/her environment. Copyright is intended to encourage proliferation of the arts and sciences within specified guidelines (Bucy, 2002).

Our copyright law tries to keep the spirit of the law and changes with technological advancements and as our definition of intellectual property expands. In 1802, the copyright law included protection for print, and in 1831 the length of time for protection increased an additional fourteen years, and musical compositions gained protection. In 1865, photographs were given protection. Protection was provided for works of fine art and translations in 1870. The copyright law underwent a major revision in 1909 which expanded the length of protection and attempted to balance public interest and the rights of the copyright owner (Pember, 2000 and Masciola, 2002). The last major revision of the copyright law was in 1976. This revision attempted to address technological developments, and to bring the United States into compliance with the international copyright laws as specified in the Berne Convention (Masciola, 2002). The Berne Convention is an international copyright agreement enacted in 1887 and today is administered by the World Intellectual Property Organization (WIPO). In 1989, the United States joined the Berne Convention (Bucy, 2002).

So, What Is Copyright?

Hopefully, a look at the history of copyright helps you understand how the law started and evolved. We haven't talked about what copyright is and what it protects. The concept of copyright deals with intangible and intellectual property—property you can't see or touch. For example, if I write a song and only have it in my head, it is intangible and intellectual property. You can't see or touch it and you don't know I have that property unless I tell you. Nevertheless, it exists.

Once I write the song down on a piece of paper, it becomes tangible and is in a fixed format, but it is still my intellectual property. You can handle and see the song on the piece of paper. What if you saw the paper with the song and from memory wrote my song down, note for note and word for word, and claimed it as your song? You own and possess the paper with the copied song. I created the song and my intellectual property cannot be taken away from me, regardless of the tangible form of the song you own. Keep in mind, intangible property is not to be confused with physical property where possession may indicate ownership (Zelezny, 2001).

The copyright law specifies eight copyrightable categories: (1) literary works; (2) musical works, including any accompanying words; (3) dramatic works, including any accompanying words; (4) pantomimes and choreographic works; (5) pictorial, graphic, and sculptural works; (6) motion pictures and other audiovisual works; (7) sound recordings; and (8) architectural works for a limited time. These categories should be viewed broadly, because changing and new technology adds ways of creating original works almost daily. For example, literary works include computer programs and compilations. Pictorial graphics and sculptural works may include maps and architectural plans (United States Copyright Office, 2002).

Fair-Use—Exception to Copyright

Many people have heard the term "fair-use" and know it allows some relaxation of the copyright law. This exception intends to alleviate copyright restrictions to educators and researchers in some incidences so their work will not be stifled by the law and to encourage art and science. Broadly speaking, fair-use allows a certain amount of copying and distributing without the copyright owner's permission or compensation (Pember, 2000).

Be careful. A little bit of knowledge is dangerous, and you may stray into infringement in the name of education and research. My students try to apply this argument as justification for using popular music on videotapes—this is not fair-use and a no-no. At the university, some faculty use this concept for unlimited copying of protected material. There are limitations to fair-use, and it is not the great loophole for unrestricted copying or distribution of copyrighted material in the name of education or self use.

Some photocopying of copyrighted material in the name of education is infringement. An example of this type of violation is to photocopy a custom-made anthology for class distribution. Let's say a professor wants to compile an anthology for a class with several pieces of copyrighted material, but did not obtain permission from the copyright holder. The professor may be under the impression this type of photocopying is for fair-use or educational purposes, but that may not be the case. Many publishers do not view this as fair-use, and will ask the courts for restitution (Wagner, 1991).

Kinko's Graphics got caught in the middle of "in the name of education." Through its Professor Publishing Service, Kinko's produced custom-made anthologies for college professors that were identical to what a university print shop might compile. Kinko's believed they were exempt from copyright violations based on educational fair-use. Basic Books sued Kinko's Graphics for violating the copyright law because they did not obtain permission from the publisher prior to duplicating the anthologies. In March 1991, a New York federal district judge ruled that Kinko's had to pay $510,000 plus attorneys' fees in the case *Basic Books v. Kinko's* (Wagner, 1991).

Why did Kinko's get sued, and what happened to the fair-use argument? Kinko's is a profit company, and thereby was found in violation of the classroom guidelines. The impact of the Kinko's decision is that universities' print shops printing custom-made analogies may also be violating the law (Wagner, 1991). Therefore, obtaining permission from the copyright owner is crucial for faculty and print shops prior to mass duplication of copyrighted material. The more likely scenario is the professor sends you to the library to read the article out of the journal.

Fair-use is using copyrighted work for a legitimate purpose such as research, scholarship, criticism, news reporting, teaching, and the like. It is considered fair after examination of four open-ended set of factors: 1. the purpose and character of the use; 2. the nature of the work; 3. the amount used; and 4. the impact (actual or potential) on the market for, or value of, the work (Burke, 1993 and Burgunder, 2004).

A literary critic utilizes the concept of fair-use. The critic may cite certain segments of a copyrighted work within the context of criticizing the work. If the critic did not have this right, the author could withhold consent, and the critic would not be allowed to express an opinion (Burke, 1993).

Another example of a fair-use violation is if a library photocopies an expensive and arcane academic journal for distribution in an effort not to purchase additional copies of the journal. The excuse is usually that the coping is for research and teaching. Usually, the real motive is not buying additional journals instead of fair-use behind this type of violation. The Fair-Use Doctrine is not a license for piracy (Burke, 1993).

The Fair-Use Doctrine has some flexibility with copyright restrictions, but fair-use does not have a set test or definition of what constitutes fair-use. Educational fair-use has been a case-by-case test. Historically, the incentive to sue educators has been low. The courts have not provided much guidance to offset misinterpretation or understanding of the law (Wagner, 1991).

Many universities, libraries, and copy centers have or should have a fair-use policy posted near every copier. Whether or not you see a fair-use policy, understand you can only copy a small amount of material in the name of advancing the sciences, arts, criticism, and so forth.

Maybe you can't identify with mass photocopying of material, or think only libraries and college professors exercise fair-use. Fair-use is not a simple concept, and it can be difficult to define violations. New technologies have created a plethora of confusion over what a copyright violation is, resulting in lawsuits that test the law.

In January 2000, MP3.com launched a new Internet subscription service. This service intended to relieve subscribers from transporting their legally purchased CDs by allowing them to access the CDs via their web site. MP3.com purchased tens of thousands of popular CDs and converted them into MP3 files. The MP3 files were copied, without the copyright owners' permission, onto their computer servers. The owners of MP3.com felt they were free to provide this service under fair-use. After all, the company purchased the CDs, and the subscribers had to prove they legally owned a copy of the CD before they could access the CD via the Internet (Burgunder, 2004).

UMG Recording and other major recording studios sued MP3.com for copyright infringement. The District Court for the Southern District of New York examined the four factors for fair-use to determine if there was a violation. The court determined the purpose of use was commercial. The amount of usage was they replayed the entirety of the copyrighted material. Since MP3.com was a commercial entity, it had an adverse market effect on the recording industry. Therefore, MP3.com lost the suit and was found guilty of infringing on plaintiffs' copyrights. The court ruled the appropriate amount of statutory damages was $25,000 per CD. It was estimated that MP3.com had about 4,700 CDs. The damages translated into about $118 million. The total amount will be determined at the final phase of the trial (Burgunder, 2004). Ouch. That's a hefty penalty for not understanding fair-use and not getting the proper consent.

Who Owns the Copyright?
Maybe Not the Creator—Works Made for Hire

Who owns the copyright? As we saw earlier, the copyright law refers to the creator of original works as the copyright owner. The creator is not always the copyright owner. If you create a work in the scope of your employment or are hired as a freelancer to create something, the work may fall under the concept of works made for hire. In that case, the copyright belongs to the employer or the one who commissioned the work (Burgunder, 2004). For example, many newspaper writers and photographers hired as freelancers and full-time employees fall under works made for hire, and the employer has all legal rights to that work (Sinofsky, 1995).

This concept has an impact in academic publishing. Often in academic publishing, the author must sign away copyrights on a release form to get published, and the author may be granted free reprint rights. The logic behind this concept is the authors are publishing within the context of their work, and therefore it is works made for hire (Sinofsky, 1995).

There is not a clear consensus on whether works made for hire apply to the faculty or not. One argument is that an institution employs the faculty and that institution requires the faculty to publish works in their discipline to keep their jobs. On the other hand, scholars are supposed to have freedom to expand the boundaries of knowledge. Therefore, universities do not necessarily control or supervise scholarly work (Kilby, 1995). Once again, it is an example of a concept under the copyright law that is not easily defined or understood. When ownership is in dispute, the courts decide.

Several court cases upheld faculty members' ownership of their work, for example *William v. Weisser* (1969), *Hays v. Sony* (1988), and *Weinstein v. University of Illinois* (1987). On the other hand court, cases have given the employer the copyright. In 1995, *Colorado Foundation v. American Cyanamid* accepted the premise that academic articles written by professors fall within the scope of their employment and were works made for hire. As a result, many faculty members are reevaluating their intellectual property rights (Sinofsky, 1995).

Faculty members argue that applying the works made for hire to faculty would be devastating. If the university could claim the copyright of everything created by faculty members, they could also claim—instead of the creator—the rewards from the sale of computer programs, textbooks, semiconductor chips, and even the sale of artwork (Kilby, 1995).

There have been several alternative attempts to clarify copyright ownership. One alternative is a "shop right" amendment. This would allow the employee-author to be the legal author and copyright owner of works created within the scope of employment, and the employer would have the right to use the works for its own business purposes (Kilby, 1995).

Another option is to exempt "professional" employees from works made for hire. It is not likely Congress would consider a law that only effects one class of citizen (Kilby, 1995).

A likely workable situation for professors, freelancers, and employees is to include a clause in their contract stating they own the copyright (Kilby, 1995). As you can see, the concept of works made for hire is a major issue at colleges and universities, especially since there is not a consensus on whether the faculty falls under this concept.

Works made for hire affect every profession where copyrightable material is created by an employee or freelancer. If you create copyrightable material as an employee or freelancer, you need a written statement defining who owns the copyright. Do you own the copyright, or does your employer because it is a work made for hire?

What About the Internet and All the Free Stuff?

Has technology hurt the copyright owner? Has it taken income from the artists? Has it stifled creativity or the desire of artists and scientists to create original works? There are two sides to this argument. One side says technology has hurt the copyright owner, and there is a need for stronger laws and greater enforcement. The other side says technology promotes new work with no financial loss, and might increase financial gain.

The Internet is wonderful. I spend a lot of time using the Internet for research, e-mail, and so forth. The Internet has made my life easier—that is, after I got past the aggravation of using the technology. I can access any library in the world and search comprehensive databases for relevant material. Often, I legally download an abstract or full-text article I can read at my leisure. I don't have to physically go the library, find some big old book, look up citations for my topic, go to the card catalog to see if my library holds that source, retrieve the journal, read it in the library, and take notes in the library or check it out to do likewise at home. Oh happy days—technology makes research easy compared to the past.

Want to find out the current population of the world? Go to <http://www.census.gov/> and you will find all kinds of statistics on population, economics, business, and on and on. Need to find out who your congressional representative is? Go to your state's home Web page. Want to grow azaleas and don't know if you can? Go to the United States Department of Agriculture <*www.usda.gov*> and search for azaleas. The first hit is "Azalea Questions and Answers," a site maintained by the United States National Arboretum. Want to buy a bicycle? Visit the bicycle manufacturers' Web sites for specs and other Web sites for independent reviews. Get the idea? You literally have a world of information at your fingertips. Much of the information is free.

The Internet also gives you shopping opportunities with the convenience of never leaving home. I'm not a shopper and I don't enjoy shopping. Shopping via the Internet works well for me. I avoid the stores, and I can easily find the best price with just a few keystrokes.

A quick warning about using the Internet: it's a wonderful tool, but buyer beware. Not all information on the Internet is reliable, so you might get bogus or false information since anyone can post on the Internet. Not all e-commerce sites are legitimate businesses. Some are in the business of taking your money in exchange for inferior or no merchandise. Know where and from whom you are getting your information, and who is selling you a product. Know you can trust them.

The Internet also poses major problems for copyright owners. Can you quickly think of an industry that complained about the negative impact on profits due to the Internet? I only need to say Napster, a peer-to-peer music file sharing Web site. In December 1999, the Recording Industry Association of America (RIAA) brought suit against Napster for copyright infringement (Recording Industry Association of America, 2003).

A little information about RIAA gives us a context as to why they felt they should sue Napster. RIAA is a trade association. Ninety percent of all legitimate sound recordings produced and sold in the United States are created, manufactured and/or distributed by RIAA members. The mission statement for RIAA specifies they work "to protect intellectual property rights worldwide and the First Amendment rights of artists; conduct consumer industry and technical research; and monitor and review state and federal laws, regulations and polices" (Recording Industry Association of America, 2003).

As we saw earlier, RIAA claims a substantial loss in annual revenue due to bootlegging and illegal coping. They do not see file sharing as harmless MP3 file sharing among friends, and the courts agreed. In September 2003, RIAA extended their litigation to include individuals sharing music files via peer-to-peer sites as copyright infringers (Ahrens, 2003).

Many peer-to-peer users claim they file share because CDs are too expensive or they only want one or two songs from a CD. Technology (peer-to-peer Web sites) allowed consumers to select the songs they wanted and for a better price (free). The abuse and capabilities of new technology inspired the recording industry to offer alternatives to consumers. Universal Music Group (UMG) plans on dropping the price of CDs and is urging retailers to sell most CDs for $12.98. UMG hopes other music companies will also drop prices (Ahrens, 2003). Over the last year, many legal music distribution Internet sites, such as Apple's iTunes, emerged. These sites allow the customer to listen, select, and buy quality copies of their favorite songs.

The RIAA suits against Napster and peer-to-peer file sharers bring up many questions about copyright and new technologies. Our current copyright law underwent the last major revision in 1976. That was before the Internet and digital technology. There are major gaps in the copyright law concerning new technologies. In 1998, Congress passed the Digital Millennium Copyright Act (DMCA) which clarified many of these new issues. Companies and individuals posting original works on the Web received protection. This material cannot be downloaded for commercial purposes. Fair-use rules also applies for Web material. The online providers are exempted from liability for copyright violations by their subscribers (Vivian, 2001).

Is the Internet site solely accountable to the law for file sharing, or are individuals trading via the Internet at risk? The No Electronic Theft (NET) Act is an amendment to Section 506 of the Copyright Act, and directly addresses Internet file sharing, including not for profit. The individual may also face civil liability for file sharing. The statutory damages may be as great as $150,000 per copyright infringement. As you can see, file sharing is punishable under the law for the Internet site and individuals. If found guilty, the penalty may be hefty (United States Copyright Office, 2002; Recording Industry Association of America, 2003). These are a few of the laws intended to protect copyright owners in cyberspace. Will they? Can they?

The new technologies and Internet fuel the opponents' argument that the copyright law is outdated because their existence make it impossible to enforce the law. These opponents also argue that copying and distributing copyrighted material does not effect sales, but instead pushes that product into the mainstream and increases sales (Bucy, 2002).

The Grateful Dead did not take kindly to fans copying their commercially produced albums. However, years ago they discovered allowing their fans to make "illegal" tapes of their concerts and freely distribute them among themselves actually drew people to their concerts. They primarily made their money from the sale of concert tickets (Bucy, 2002). Did the Grateful Dead's strategy work? Did the illegal copying of concerts increase concert ticket sells? I've never been a Dead Head and don't know much about the group, except they had gobs of loyal fans who traveled the country to see them in concert night after night in city after city.

I witnessed the Grateful Dead concert phenomena firsthand. I never attended a concert or kept up with their schedule, but I always knew when they were in town. They came to town every year and typically performed two shows over a two-day period. You couldn't get near the coliseum for days surrounding the concerts. The Dead Heads followed the group to town and camped in the coliseum parking lot until time to travel to the next concert location. That's a loyal fan. They didn't have just a few loyal fans, they had thousands. The Grateful Dead had no problems selling every seat for every show. Did the illegal copies of their concerts ultimately benefit the group? The Grateful Dead never tried to stop it and even encouraged it.

Is there another example of illegal copying benefitting an industry? In the early days of the software revolution, software companies copy-protected their software, which prohibited the legal owner from making a backup copy, much less a copy for a friend.

This was an effort to prevent illegal copying, and it did. Illegal copying began when the software companies stopped copy protection. The result of illegal copies flooding the market created a possibility that the pirated software would become a standard. Why? The consumer using the illegal copy soon found it more convenient to purchase a legal copy since that was the only way to get technical support and some documentation (Bucy, 2002).

Does music file sharing really hurt the recording industry? Critics of the copyright laws argue that CD sales increased by 20 percent since the appearance of MP3 music on the Internet (Bucy, 2002). RIAA attributes the increase to a healthy economy during the period prior to litigation and argue sales would have been even higher without music file sharing (Recording Industry Association of America, 2003).

Some people believe copyright is an outdated concept. Proponents of the law argue there is a need for copyright protection. If the author or creator was not guaranteed some type of legal protection, anyone could take their original idea, copy it as their own idea, sell it, and get the financial and other benefits that rightly belong to the author or creator. The argument continues that it wouldn't take long before the creative stopped creating because they wouldn't get the benefit or reward for their work (Pember, 2000 & Zelezny, 2001).

Does copyright violation discourage people from creating original works? Was creativity stifled prior to the copyright law? How many of us studied the ancient story *Oedipus*? How many of us know anything about Socrates, da Vinci, Michelangelo, Shakespeare, Bach, and scores of other philosophers, artists, writers, musicians, and the list goes on? They were prolific in their science or art, and all created works before copyright laws existed. Their works are still studied, performed, exhibited, and adaptations appear daily. We still give them credit for their work and we can identify an adaptation of their work (Bucy, 2002).

Regardless of the benefit or harm, the Internet and new technologies are here to stay. The digital age spurred new laws to protect copyright ownership. People and industries file lawsuits when their copyright is infringed via the Internet or new technology.

What Is Not Protected by the Law?

Not everything is eligible for copyright protection. The law specifies four areas that are not protected by copyright law: 1. Works that have **not** been fixed in a tangible form of expression—for example, choreographic works that have not been notated or recorded, or improvisational speeches or performances that have not been written or recorded, 2. Titles, names, short phrases, and slogans; familiar symbols or designs; mere variations of typographic ornamentation, lettering, or coloring; mere listings of ingredients or contents, 3. Ideas, procedures, methods, systems, processes, concepts, principles, discoveries, or devices, as distinguished from a descriptive, explanation, or illustration, and 4. Works consisting **entirely** of information that is common property and containing no original authorship—for example: standard calendars, height and weight charts, tape measures and rulers, and lists or tables taken from public documents or other common sources (United States Copyright Office, 2002).

Let's look at my the song in my head and if it is copyrightable. As we saw above, my ideas or intangible material can not be copyrighted. Therefore, the song in my head is not copyrightable. I must put my idea in a fixed or tangible form of expression before it is protected by the copyright law. If I write the song on paper or make a recording of the song, it comes under protection, because the law protects works that are written or displayed via the aid of a machine or device (Pember, 2000).

Facts cannot be copyrighted. The person who discovers a fact may not be able to claim ownership for that fact. There is some protection for gathering the facts. This is known as "sweat of the brow" doctrine. The idea behind this concept is if you spent time finding the facts and arranging them, you should have some limited protection and reap the financial benefits (Pember, 2000).

News events also fall under noncopyrightable material. We hope news events are based on facts. Facts can't be copyrighted. The style or way the story is presented may have limited protection. The newscaster cannot prevent other media outlets from reporting their facts (Pember, 2000).

How Is Copyright Obtained, and Do I Have to Do Anything?

The author automatically gains copyright and ownership when the work is created and fixed in a copy or phonorecord for the first time. No additional action is required by law to secure copyright (United States Copyright Office, 2002). Note of warning: remember, ideas cannot be copyrighted. If you discuss an idea you have for a story or original work with someone, and they take your idea and write it down, they have the copyright because they put it in a fixed format. You cannot claim ownership even though you had the idea first.

According to the law, work created under the 1976 Copyright Act no longer needs to include a copyright notice due to the United States participation on March 1, 1989 with the Berne Convention. Works created prior to 1978 must contain the copyright notice. The United States' Copyright Office advises it may be important to include a notice of copyright on all works. The notice informs the public the work is protected, and identifies the owner and the year first published. If a published copy or copies has a copyright right notice and is infringed, the defendant cannot claim innocent infringement. Innocent infringement is when the infringer did not realize the work was copyrighted (United States Copyright Office, 2002).

The copyright notice must be visually perceptible on copies and should contain three elements: (1) The symbol: © (the letter C in a circle), or the word "Copyright," or the abbreviation "Copr.," (2) the year of first publication of the work, and (3) the name of the copyright owner. Therefore, the copyright notice needs to contain the following information: Copyright © 2003 by Name of Author (United States Copyright Office, 2002).

Certain types of work like musicals, dramatic, and literary works may not be in fixed copies; therefore it is difficult to place a visible copyright notice. These works may have an audible notice of copyright such as an audio recording (United States Copyright Office, 2002).

Keep in mind, copyright takes effect when the work is put in a fixed format. Registration with the United States Copyright Office is separate from copyright and is not automatic. The copyright holder must register the work with the United States Copyright Office. Why would you want to register a copyright if the rights are automatic? Registration is not necessary for protection, but gives the copyright owner more legal power if there is an infringement. Registration is a legal formality which makes a public record of the copyright claim. For works created in the United States, you cannot file for an infringement suit if the work is not registered. Registration may be made anytime during the life of the copyright (United States Copyright Office, 2002).

To register a copyright, the owner must send three elements in the same envelop or package to Library of Congress, Copyright Office, 101 Independence Ave., SE, Washington, DC 20559-6000. The package must have a completed copy of the proper application form (available through the US Copyright Office), a nonrefundable filing fee, and a nonreturnable copy of the work being registered (United States Copyright Office, 2002). Check with the US Copyright Office at <http://www.copyright.gov/> for the current filing fee and appropriate application form.

How Long Is Copyright Binding?

The length of copyright protection is one of those nuances in the law. Depending on when the work was published or created depends on how long it is protected. All work created (put in a tangible form) after January 1, 1978 is protected from the moment of creation for the lifetime of the author plus an additional 70 years. If there is more than one author, then protection is 70 years after the last surviving author's death (United States Copyright Office, 2002).

Protection for works made for hire and anonymous and pseudonymous works (unless the Copyright Office is given the identity of the author) is 95 years from publication or 120 years from creation, whichever is shorter (United States Copyright Office, 2002).

If a work was created before January 1, 1978 but never published or registered with the Copyright Office, it is automatically brought under the same duration as works created after January 1, 1978 (United States Copyright Office, 2002).

Copyright protection for works originally created and published or registered before January 1, 1978, and under the Copyright Act of 1909 initially last for 28 years and may be renewed for an additional 28 years. The copyright holder must renew the copyright to gain the additional 28 years. The 1976 Copyright Act extended the renewal term from 28 years to 47 years for a total of 75 years of protection (United States Copyright Office, 2002).

The terms of protection may not be as simple as when the work was created and if the copyright was registered. In 1984, the CBS documentary "The 20th Century with Mike Wallace" used about sixty percent of Dr. Martin Luther King, Jr.'s 1963 *I Have a Dream* speech. CBS thought the speech was in public domain and did not pay royalties or request permission from the King estate to use the speech. The estate sued CBS for copyright infringement (*Estate of Martin Luther King, Jr. v. CBS*, 1998).

Was the speech protected? Dr. King delivered the *I Have a Dream* speech in a Washington, D.C. march on August 28, 1963. Dr. King applied for copyright protection of the speech under the Copyright Act of 1909, on September 30, 1963. The Copyright Office issued a certificate of registration on October 2, 1963. The King Estate took full advantage of copyright protection for 20 years, until the suit against CBS (*Estate of Martin Luther King, Jr. v. CBS*, 1998).

The court reviewed the case and made a decision based on the Copyright Act of 1909 (the law when the copyright was issued). The court decided the widespread and unlimited use of the speech during the Washington march pushed it into a general publication of the speech which basically made it public domain. The district court granted summary judgment to CBS (*Estate of Martin Luther King, Jr. v. CBS*, 1998).

The King estate appealed the decision, and on July 12, 2000 a press release from the King Center announced CBS and the estate had reached an agreement. CBS retained the right to use the footage of the *I Have a Dream* and other speeches, while providing the estate's claim to intellectual property rights. Additionally, CBS, in an effort to promote Dr. King's work and struggle for civil rights, made a contribution to the Martin Luther King, Jr., Center for Nonviolent Social Change (Vickers, 2000).

Public domain is not an open and shut case. Even if material is in public domain or considered pushed into public domain, you may be at risk of infringement if you use it. The estate of Martin Luther King, Jr. thought the *I Have a Dream* speech was copyrighted. They were right. Copyright registration was issued to Dr. King in October 1963, and the copyright was properly renewed as specified by the law. Additionally, the Copyright Act of 1976 should have extended the copyright from a total of 56 to 75 years.

CBS thought the *I Have a Dream* speech was public domain. The court agreed with CBS. There were other factors surrounding the speech that made some of the judges reviewing the case question if the speech was truly in public domain. The judges had to use the 1909 law for their decision, since that was the law King copyrighted his speech under. As we saw, CBS and the Estate came to an agreement. Ultimately, the Estate gave CBS permission with stipulations to use the *I Have a Dream* and other speeches by Dr. King.

You may think you are not infringing on copyright because you presume the material is in public domain. Beware, some of the material may be in public domain, but some aspect of it is protected by copyright law. For example, Mozart's music is in public domain, but a recording of his music may not be in public domain. Look for the copyright symbol and see when and if the recording was copyrighted. Just because the material is old, don't presume it is in public domain. Find out if any aspect of the material is under copyright. Be safe and not in court.

Plagiarism, Trademarks, and Patents

I will briefly discuss copyright's three intangible property relatives: plagiarism, trademarks, and patents. Plagiarism is passing off someone else's ideas, words, or thoughts as your own (Pember, 2000). Plagiarism is a big problem in most high schools, universities, and in the work world. This is another area where the Internet has created great opportunity for misuse. For example, a number of Internet sites sell term papers for a few dollars a page. Most students see this as a legitimate way to "write" a term paper. This is not a legitimate paper—it is a plagiarized paper. The student has taken someone else's work, put their name on the paper, and turn it in as their own research and writing. Yes, the student may have the required parenthetical citations and a works cited page, but they didn't do the work. It is someone else's work and author's permission to plagiarize their work does not mitigate the offense.

A trademark is used to identify a person or company's goods and services from the competition's products and services. It is the trademark that tells the consumer you are getting the product you think you are purchasing. Trademarks eliminates consumer confusion and clearly identifies a product or service with a company (Pember, 2000).

Many brand names are protected by trademark, for example Q-Tips and Black & Decker, to name a few. Some companies trademark other identifying marks such as the hourglass shape of the Coca-Cola bottle. Slogans can have a registered trademark. When we hear the slogan "Don't Leave Home Without It" we think of American Express. This is not by accident. American Express registered the slogan as a trademark (Pember, 2000).

Trademarks must be registered with the Patent and Trademark Office and then renewed five years later. After the first renewal, sequential renewals must be made every ten years. A trademark can remain indefinitely as long as the owner renews the trademark at proper intervals. If the trademark is not renewed, the owner can lose the trademark (Pember, 2000).

In 1996, Congress passed the Federal Dilution Trademark Act. This law gives trademark owners additional protection by giving them legal recourse if theirs or a similar trademark is used on a dissimilar products'. For example, prior to this act, Sony couldn't stop an appliance company from using one of their electronic products' trademark from being used on a washing machine. Now, Sony can stop a company from using any of their trademarks on any electronic or non-electronic product (Pember, 2000; Zelezny, 2001).

Patent law is a federal statute, the Patent Act. There are two types of patents: utility and design (Radcliffe, 2001). Patents rights may only be claimed after the United States government issues the patent (Pember, 2000).

Utility patents apply to any new and useful process, machine, manufacture, or composition of matter, and they may be electrical, mechanical, or chemical. The microwave oven is an example of a device that can be patented. A new chemical that cleans up an oil spill may be patented. Many new technology inventions are protected as utility patents, for example data compression techniques, information storage, and retrieval devices (Radcliffe, 2001).

The second type of patent is a design patent, which is an ornamental design for articles of manufacture. The sole of a new running shoe applies for this type of patent. To get a design patent, the design must be new, original, and ornamental. Therefore, this type of patent is not suitable for any invention that is considered intellectual property (Radcliffe, 2001).

Obtaining a trademark or patent is not automatic, and cannot be registered as easily or cheaply as copyright. If you want a trademark or patent, you must hire a patent attorney and pay higher registration fees. To take advantage of trademark or patent protection, you must have a valid registered trademark or patent.

Why Should I Care about Copyright?

Maybe you think copyright law is necessary to protect and encourage creators of original works, or you might not agree with the law and see it as useless and inhibiting. Regardless of your position, copyright is a law, and violations trigger lawsuits.

The electronic technologies and new media have created new copyright concerns, and these concerns will grow in the future. We are in a Renaissance stage where we are merging technology and imagination, and this convergence is redefining how cultures create and represent knowledge (Lyman, 1995).

The debate is not whether we need copyright laws, but if the existing laws are too narrow to protect or include the new electronic methods of dissemination. The law was revised to include electronic dissemination, but the law may not be clear or complete concerning violations of the copyright law and the electronic media (Lyman, 1995).

To ensure the copyright law is understood, corporations and universities should adopt a copyright policy. A copyright policy is developed for several reasons. A policy helps protect the company, university, employees, or students from possible litigation. An informed end user is less likely to infringe on the law by making better informed decisions, and thereby not get involved in litigation (Vlcek, 1993).

The policy gives end users direction. They will understand their legal responsibilities according to the law, it will give them the power to refuse to perform functions that may infringe on the law, and will help prevent expensive litigation (Vlcek, 1993). A loss infringement suit means the violator pays actual and statutory damages, that can be as high as $150,000 per infringement, and all legal and court fees (Burgunder, 2004).

The copyright policy needs to include the following elements: a statement that administrators intend to abide by the copyright law, and they expect the end users to do similarly; prohibits copying except what is acceptable in the fair-use guidelines, license agreements, or proprietor's permission; details that the person who infringes on the law is the one legally responsible; creates the position of copyright officer who is responsible for overseeing copyright issues; requires the development of a copyright manual which explains how to handle copyrighted materials; requires placement of copyright warning labels around all copiers and other types of copying equipment to advise what is unlawful copying; creates a single office to house all copyright records to eliminate duplication of securing copyrights to books, software, etc. (Vlcek, 1993).

Wrap It Up

From the beginning, the copyright law intended to regulate "proprietary rights in the marketplace for information and the public interest in knowledge as a keystone for an informed and free society" (Bennett, 1993). The solid intent behind the copyright law was to provide information to a free society. Therefore, the copyright law should be viewed as a tool to procreate or enhance creativity instead of an attempt to stunt dissemination.

The world is changing—the first desktop computer started a revolution into a new age, and that age does not make the copyright law a relic of another time. Most people do not know how the copyright law affects them directly or indirectly. Understand that the law is important, and it is the responsibility of everyone to uphold this law. In an attempt to understand the law, many questions need answering. Who owns the copyright? How does one obtain a copyright? What are the rights of the copyright owner? How long is a copyright valid? What are the penalties for violating the law?

Copyright is automatically given when the work is created and fixed in a copy or phonorecord for the first time. No additional action is required by law to secure copyright (United States Copyright Office, 2002). The copyright law only protects the expression of the work. The underlying ideas, principles, systems, or concepts of the work are placed in the public domain. Since the United States joined the Berne Convention, the copyright holder does not need a copyright notice or to register for a copyright (Burke, 1993).

Copyrighted works are not just protected in the United States. The Berne Convention protects materials copyrighted in the United States against violation in other countries participating in the Berne Convention (Burke, 1993). The Berne Convention is an international copyright agreement enacted in 1887, and today is administered by the World Intellectual Property Organization (WIPO). In 1989, the United States joined the Berne Convention (Bucy, 2002).

Typically, the creator of an original work is the copyright owner. The concept of works made for hire may apply if you create a work in the scope of your employment or are hired as a freelancer to create something. In that case, the copyright belongs to the employer or person who commissioned the work (Burgunder, 2004).

Fair-use allows reproducing or using copyrighted works for a legitimate purpose such as research, scholarship, criticism, news reporting, teaching, and the like. Fair-use is frequently used by educators and critics, but it is not a license for unlimited copying and distribution rights (Burke, 1993 and Burgunder, 2004). A set test for fair-use violation does not exist, and traditionally this claim has been tested in the courts on a case-by-case basis.

The duration of the copyright depends on several factors, such as, when the work was published or created, and if it is a works made for hire. All work created (put in a tangible form) after January 1, 1978 is protected from the moment of creation for the lifetime of the author plus an additional 70 years. If there is more than one author, then protection is 70 years after the last surviving author's death (United States Copyright Office, 2002).

Copyright infringement is a crime. The infringer may receive an injunction prohibiting any further unauthorized use, pay actual and statutory damages that resulted from the copyright infringement, and be obligated to pay all attorney fees (Burke, 1993).

Is copyright a simple concept? It gives the author the right to copy, right? Yes, no, maybe . . . The copyright law is anything but simple. As we have discussed, there are many nuances to the law. You may think you are totally protected by the law, and then you may find out you aren't. You may think the material you want to use is fair-use or public domain, and it might not be.

Keep the law in mind when dealing with copyrighted material, and abide by it. Remember, infringement is punishable under the law. A copyright infringer is caught holding the proverbial smoking gun—you have the evidence in hand with your name attached. Therefore, copyright infringers don't win many lawsuits.

References

Ahrens, F. "Music Industry Sues On-line Song Swappers; Trade Group Says First Batch of Lawsuits Targets 261 Major Offenders," *The Washington Post* (2003, September 9): A.01.

Artcyclopedia (2003). *Artist by Movement: Impressionism.* [On-line]. Available: <http://www.artcyclopedia.com/history/impressionism.html>

Artcyclopedia (2003). *Andy Warhol.* [On-line]. Available: <http://www.artcyclopedia.com/artists/warhol_andy.html>

Bennett, S. (1993). Copyright and innovation in electronic publishing: A commentary. *Journal of Academic Librarianship,* 19 (2), 87–91.

Bucy, E. P. *Living in the Information Age: A New Media Reader.* Belmont, Calif.: Wadsworth, 2002.

Burgunder, L. *Legal Aspects of Managing Technology,* (3rd ed.). Ohio: Thomson, 2004.

Burke, E. B. "Copyright Catechism," *EDUCOM Review,* 28 (5), (1993): 46–49.

Casson, L. *Libraries in the Ancient World.* New Haven: Yale University Press, 2001.

Dennis, E. E. and J. C. Merrill, J. C. *Media Debates: Great Issues for the Digital Age,* (3rd ed.). Belmont, Calif.: Wadsworth, 2002.

Estate of Martin Luther King, Jr., Inc. v. *CBS, Inc.*, 13F. Supp 1347 (11th Cir. 1998).

Folkerts, J. and S. Lacy. *The Media in Your Life: An Introduction to Mass Communications* (2nd ed.). Boston: Allyn and Bacon, 2001.

Hunter, K. "The Changing Business of Scholarly Publishing," *Journal of Library Administration*, 19 (3–4), (1993): 23–38.

Kasunic, R. "Fair Use and the Educator's Right to Photocopy Copyrighted Material for Classroom Use," *Journal of College and University Law*, 19 (3), (1993): 271–93.

Kilby, P. A. "The Discouragement of Learning: Scholarship Made for Hire," *Journal of College and University Law*, 21 (3), (1995): 455–88.

Lyman, P. "Copyright and Fair Use in the Digital Age: Q and A with Peter Lyman," *Educom Review*, 30 (1), (1995): 32–35.

Masciola, A. (2002). *Timeline: A History of the Copyright Law*. Association of Research Libraries. [On-line]. Available: <*http://arl.cni.org/info/frn/copy/timeline.html#18C*>.

New York International Bible Society. *The Holy Bible*. Grand Rapids: Zondervan, 1978.

Parrish, D. "Scientific Misconduct and the Plagiarism Cases," *Journal of College and University Law*, 21 (3), (1995): 517–54.

Pember, D. R. *Mass Media Law: 2000 Edition*. Boston: McGraw Hill, 2000.

Radcliffe, M. Gray Cary Ware & Freidenrich LLP, and D. Brinson. *The Multimedia Law and Business Handbook*. TOWN: Ladera Press, 2001.

Recording Industry Association of America (2003) *What is copyright?* [On-line]. Available: <*http://www.riaa.org/Copyright-What.cfm*>

Sinofsky, E. R. "The Water's Not Safe Yet!" *TechTrends*, 40 (6), (1995): 12–14.

United States Copyright Office. *Circular 1: Copyright Basics*. Washington, D.C.: Library of Congress/Copyright Office, 2002.

Vickers, R. (2000). *CBS news and the estate of Martin Luther King, Jr. reach agreement on use of footage of Dr. King's speeches*. [On-line]. Available: <*http://thekingcenter.com/news/press_release/07-12-2000.htm*>

Vivian, J. *The Media of Mass Communication*. Needham Heights, Mass.: Allyn & Bacon, 2001.

Vlcek, C. "Copyright Policy Development," *TechTrends*, 38 (2), (1993): 13–14, 46.

Wagner, E. N. "Beware the Custom-Made Anthology: Academic Photocopying and Basic Books v. Kinko's Graphics." *West's Education Law Reporter*, 68 (1), (1991): 1-20.

Wertz, S. L. and M. E. Chase. "Media Directors and Copyright Issues: How Much Do We Really Know?" *TechTrends*, 39 (3), (1994): 7–8.

Zelezny, J. D. *Communications Law: Liberties, Restraints, and the Modern Media* (3rd ed.). Belmont, Calif.: Wadsworth, 2001.

Name _____   Date _____

Section _____

Think About It → Write About It

Reflect on what you've just read. Now write what you are thinking.

_____

_____

_____

_____

_____

_____

_____

_____

_____

_____

_____

_____

_____

_____

_____

_____

_____

_____

_____

_____

_____

_____

_____

Activity 1

Ask the class to express their thoughts about copyrights, music downloads, bootlegged videos. Ask how different they would feel if they were the artist and their work was copied to avoid paying for the music.

Activity 2

1. Divide the class into three groups.
2. Assign Group A to "Believe technology has hurt the copyright owner and we need stronger laws and enforcement."
3. Assign Group B to "Believe technology promotes new works with no financial loss, and may increase financial gain."
4. Request Group C to assess which group made the most persuasive argument. (Be sure there is an odd number of students in Group C.)
5. Ask each group to prepare an argument to support their position.
6. Give each group equal time to speak.
7. Allow for at least three rounds.
8. Have Group C determine the winners.

Appendix

Business Communication

Materials provided by Dr. Lisa Gueldenzoph

Throughout this text, I and the other contributors have spoken in our honest voices. At times, others and I have used slang and cultural idioms. There is a time and place for everything. For this learning situation and for my teaching philosophy, our relaxed language and laid-back presentation are fine. In the business arena, however, the norms are somewhat different. This section of the text is dedicated to business communication. It is designed to help you gain more effective professional communication skills. The lessons taught here give you the basics needed for developing cover letters, resumes, and thank you notes, effectively conducting yourself in job interviews, and networking situations. Dr. Lisa Gueldenzoph, provides:

▶ Techniques for Effective Business Writing
▶ Business Correspondence Examples
▶ A Checklist for Making Persuasive Requests
▶ A Business Etiquette Workshop
▶ An Employment Workshop

Techniques for Effective Business Writing

Business Writing Is ...

▶ Purposeful
  —Solves Problems & Conveys Info
▶ Economical
  —Concise
▶ Reader-Oriented
  —Focus on Receiver, Not Sender

3-x-3 Writing Process

▶ Pre-Writing
—Analyzing, Anticipating, Adapting
▶ Writing
—Researching, Organizing, Composing
▶ Revising
—Revising, Proofreading, Evaluating

Use the "YOU" View

(when wanting to personalize the communication. This method is best used for positive messages. Use caution with this method when communicating a negative message.)

▶ The warranty starts working immediately.
▶ Your warranty starts working for you immediately.
▶ We just sent the order.
▶ You will receive your order.

"You" View ... What's Wrong?

▶ To prevent us from possibly losing large sums of money, our bank now requires verification of any large check presented for immediate payment.

Emphasize the "You" View

▶ To prevent us from possibly losing large sums of money, our bank now requires verification of any large check presented for immediate payment.

The "You" View

▶ To ensure you have access to your funds, your identity will be verified when you present a large check for payment.

Emphasize the "You" View

▶ We take pride in announcing a new schedule of low-cost flights to Hawaii.
▶ You can enjoy a new schedule of low-cost flights to Hawaii.

Emphasize the "You" View

▶ We want you to complete the enclosed card so that we may bring our customer records up to date.

▶ If you complete the enclosed card, your information will be up to date.

Emphasize the "You" View

▶ For just $300 per person, we have arranged a three-day trip to Las Vegas.

▶ For just $300 per person, you can enjoy a three-day trip to Las Vegas.

Emphasize the "You" View

▶ I give my permission for you to attend the two-day workshop.

▶ You may attend the two-day workshop.

Eliminate Language Bias

What's Wrong ... ?

▶ Any applicant for the position of fireman must submit a medical report signed by his physician.

Eliminate Language Bias

What's Wrong ... ?

▶ Any applicant for the position of fireman must submit a medical report signed by his physician.

Eliminate Language Bias

▶ Any applicant for the position of firefighter must submit a medical report signed by his or her physician.

▶ OR ...

Eliminate Language Bias

▶ All applicants for the position of firefighter must submit a medical report signed by their physicians.

Eliminate Language Bias

▶ Some restaurants have a special menu for old people.

Eliminate Language Bias

▶ Some restaurants have a special menu for old people.
▶ Some restaurants have a special menu for senior citizens.

Eliminate Language Bias

▶ How many man-hours will the project require?

Eliminate Language Bias

▶ How many man-hours will the project require?
▶ How many hours will the project requires?

Eliminate Language Bias

▶ James is afflicted with arthritis, but his crippling rarely interferes with his work.

Eliminate Language Bias

▶ James is afflicted with arthritis, but his crippling rarely interferes with his work.
▶ James has arthritis, but it rarely affects his work.

Eliminate Language Bias

▶ All conference participants and their wives are invited to the banquet.

Eliminate Language Bias

▶ All conference participants and their wives are invited to the banquet.
▶ All conference participants and their guests are invited to the banquet.

Eliminate Language Bias

▶ Our company encourages the employment of handicapped people.

Eliminate Language Bias

▶ Our company encourages the employment of handicapped people.

▶ Our company encourages the employment of physically challenged people.

Focus on the Positive

▶ What's wrong? ...

▶ If you fail to pass the examination, you will not qualify.

Focus on the Positive

▶ What's wrong? ...

▶ If you fail to pass the examination, you will not qualify.

Focus on the Positive

▶ If you fail to pass the examination, you will not qualify.

▶ When you pass the exam, you will qualify.

Focus on the Positive

▶ In the message you left at our Web site, you claim that you returned a defective headset.

Focus on the Positive

▶ In the message you left at our Web site, you claim that you returned a defective headset.

▶ In the message you left at our Web site, you said you returned a headset.

Focus on the Positive

▶ We can't process your application because you neglected to include your social security number.

Focus on the Positive

▶ We can't process your application because you neglected to include your social security number.

▶ We will process your application when you provide your social security number.

Focus on the Positive

▶ Construction cannot begin until the building plans are approved.

Focus on the Positive

▶ Construction cannot begin until the building plans are approved.
▶ Construction will begin when the building plans are approved.

Focus on the Positive

▶ In response to your email complaint, we are investigating our agent's poor behavior.

Focus on the Positive

▶ In response to your email complaint, we are investigating our agent's poor behavior.
▶ In response to your email, we are investigating our agent's behavior.

Focus on the Positive

▶ It is impossible to move forward without community support.

Focus on the Positive

▶ It is impossible to move forward without community support.
▶ We will move forward with community support.

Focus on the Positive

▶ Customers are ineligible for the 10% discount unless they show their membership cards.

Focus on the Positive

▶ Customers are ineligible for the 10% discount unless they show their membership cards.
▶ Customers are eligible for the 10% discount when they show their membership cards.

Business Correspondence Examples
What's wrong with this memo ... ?

MEMORANDUM

DATE: January 1, 2000

TO: Mr. Melton Smith

FROM: Harry Jones

Attached are the list of names you requested. Please review them at your convenience and reply with your comments via email. These are the issues I'd like you to address:

- · Gender equity
- · Diversity should be balanced
- · Age discrimination

I'm looking forward to your response, before the end of the weak.

Sincerely,

Harry Jones

The problems are ...

- ▶ The heading format is wrong
- ▶ Subject line is missing
- ▶ Need to be consistent with the use of titles (Mr./Ms.)
- ▶ Subject/verb agreements ("Attached are)
- ▶ The names were requested for what?
- ▶ Comma missing for the compound sentence
- ▶ Bulleted list is not parallel in its construction
- ▶ Delete the comma after "response"
- ▶ Spelling problem (weak s/b week)
- ▶ Don't use a signature block for memos
- ▶ Missing attachment notation

Improved Example ...

MEMO TO: Mr. Melton Smith

FROM: Mr. Harry Jones

DATE: January 1, 2000

SUBJECT: Names for Accounting Position

Attached is the list of names you requested for the accounting position. Please review them at your convenience, and reply with your comments via email (*hjones@aol.com*).

- · Gender equity
- · Diversity balance
- · Age discrimination

I'm looking forward to your response before the end of the week.

Attachment: Names for Accounting Position

What's wrong with this memo ... ?

MEMO TO;   TAMIKA PARKER

FROM;   OGDEN MARTIN

DATE;   JANUARY 1, 2000

SUBJECT; NOTES

Hi. My name is Ogden Martin. On Tuesday at 9am, I am hold a meeting of all the sales associates to discuss our new marketing strategy. Would you be available to take notes at the meeting. I will be to busy to do it myself and would value you're expertise.

Please call me as soon as possible. I look forward to hearing from you.

The problems are ...

- · Heading (colons, not semi-colons)
- · Heading info NOT all caps
- · Spacing problems
- · Delete "Hi"—tone/style
- · Delete "My name is Ogden Martin."
- · "hold" s/b/ "holding"
- · "Would you ..." needs a question mark
- · "to busy" s/b "too busy"
- · "you're expertise" s/b "your expertise"
- · Need phone number

Improved Example ...

MEMO TO: Tamika Parker

FROM: Ogden Martin

DATE: January 1, 2000

SUBJECT: Taking Notes at Meeting

On Tuesday at 9am, I am holding a meeting of all the sales associates to discuss our new marketing strategy. Would you be available to take notes at the meeting? I will be too busy to do it myself and would value your expertise.

Please call me at 555-1234 as soon as possible. I look forward to hearing from you.

What's wrong with this memo ... ?

MEMO TO: Mrs. Phyllis Stahl, Sales Director

FROM: Jerry Koble, Human Resources Director

DATE: January 1, 2000

SUBJECT: Interviews for sales position

At 3 on Friday the 5th we will be interviewing 3 candidates for the sales position at our Main street branch. As you will be working very closely with whomever is chosen for this position I am requesting that you attend the interviews to help us decide who to select.

Matthew Barnes will be interviewed first. He has no experience but he has a bachelors degree in business. The 4pm interview is with Sarina Hicks. She has three years of sales experience and a bachelor's degree in marketing she was also the president of her marketing club in college. The final candidate at 5pm is Tyler Thomas who has know sales experience, but holds a MBA as well as five years of military service.

All of the interviews will be held in Conference Room C. If you are unable to attend, please send your assistant. If you have questions or concerns about the interviews, contact me at 555-1234.

The problems are ...

- Personal title missing for Jerry
- Subject line s/b initial caps
- "At 3" s/b "At 3pm"
- Need a comma after 5th
- "3 candidates" s/b "three"
- "street" s/b "Street"
- Need a comma after "position"
- Need a comma after "experience"
- "bachelors" s/b "bachelor's"
- Need a semi-colon after "marketing"
- "know" s/b "no"
- "a MBA" s/b "an MBA"

Improved Example ...

MEMO TO: Mrs. Phyllis Stahl, Sales Director

FROM: Mr. Jerry Koble, Human Resources Director

DATE: January 1, 2000

SUBJECT: Interviews for Sales Position

At 3pm on Friday the 5th, we will be interviewing three candidates for the sales position at our Main Street branch. As you will be working very closely with whomever is chosen for this position, I am requesting that you attend the interviews to help us decide who to select.

Matthew Barnes will be interviewed first. He has no experience, but he has a bachelor's degree in business. The 4pm interview is with Sarina Hicks. She has three years of sales experience and a bachelor's degree in marketing; she was also the president of her marketing club in college. The final candidate at 5pm is Tyler Thomas who has no sales experience, but holds an MBA as well as five years of military service.

All of the interviews will be held in Conference Room C. If you are unable to attend, please send your assistant. If you have questions or concerns about the interviews, contact me at 555-1234.

BUSINESS COMMUNICATION CASE STUDY: DANGEROUS COMPANY CAR PHONE PRACTICES

As one of the managers at Genre, a hair care and skin products company, you are alarmed by a newspaper article you read. A stockbroker for Smith Barney was making cold calls on his personal phone while driving. His car hit and killed a motorcyclist. The stockbroker's firm was later accused of contributing to an accident by encouraging employees to use cellular telephones while driving and eventually sued. To avoid the risk of having to pay huge damages that might be awarded by an "emotional" jury, the brokerage firm offered the victim's family a $500,000 settlement.

You begin to worry, knowing that your company has provided its 75 sales representatives with wireless phones that will help them keep in touch with home base while they are in the field. At a management meeting, it is agreed that you should draft a memo detailing some wireless phone safety rules for your company sales representatives.

Following up on the Web, you find a number of relevant recommendations. For example, wireless phone users should get to know all the features of their phones, including speed dial, automatic memory, and redial. Another suggestion involves a hands-free device. (Management members consequently decide to purchase one for every sales representative; the devices will be available within a month.) In addition, a wireless phone in a car should be within easy reach. It should be where you can grab it without taking your eyes off the road. If you get a call at an inconvenient time, you should allow your voice mail to pick up the call. You should never, of course, talk on a wireless phone during driving conditions made hazardous by rain, sleet, snow, or ice.

Taking notes during wireless phone conversations and looking up phone numbers before making wireless phone calls are also dangerous activities when driving. You want to warn sales representatives not to involve themselves in such activities. The more you think about it, the more you are sure that sales representatives should not even use their wireless phones at all while they are driving. They really should pull over to make and receive calls. You know, however, that getting them to do so will be a difficult proposition.

YOUR TASK: Playing the role of Operations Manager, write a memo to the Genre sales representatives outlining company suggestions (or rules?) for safe wireless phone use in cars. Analyze your audience and shape your message accordingly. Try to suggest some receiver benefits in your message. (How will the suggested driving and phoning practices potentially benefit the reader?)

Checklist for Making Persuasive Requests

✔ Gain Attention—Open with a compliment, statement of agreement, stimulating question, reader benefit, or a candid plea for help. End with your request. (1st ¶)
✔ Build Interest—Prove the accuracy and merit of your request with solid evidence including facts, examples, and details. Suggest direct and indirect benefits for the receiver. Avoid sounding high-pressured, angry, or emotional. (2nd ¶)

✔ Reduce Resistance—Identify what factors will be obstacles to the receiver; offer coun-terarguments. Show how the receiver or others will benefit. (2nd ¶)

✔ Motivate Action—Confidently ask for specific action. Include an end date and try to repeat a key benefit without being redundant. (3rd ¶)

YOUR TASK: Assume you are in charge of organizing a campus fundraising event to raise money to build a new student parking garage at A&T. You decide to hold an auction with items donated from area businesses. Write a letter to your favorite celebrity requesting his/her attendance at the Aggie Auction to benefit the university's fundraising campaign. You would like the celebrity to emcee the event to ensure a large audience turn out. In addition, You'd like the "big" auction item to be something the celebrity will donate. The auction will begin at 7pm on Saturday, November 23, 2002. Make up any additional information you feel is necessary to persuasively make your request.

DO NOT USE ANY OF THE ASSIGNMENT TEXT VERBATIM!

Business Etiquette Workshop

True or False ...

    1. The following is an appropriate business introduction of a client to your boss: *"Ms. Mathews, this is our new client, Mr. Smith."*

FALSE
> ▶ Introduce person of importance first.
> ▶ Gender or age is not the deciding factor.
> ▶ Include both first and last names.

True or False ...

    2. If someone forgets to introduce you, it's appropriate to move on with the con-versation without saying anything.

FALSE
> ▶ Introduce yourself.
> ▶ "My name is John Doe; I don't believe we've met."

True or False ...

    3. If you forget someone's name, don't worry about it. Keep talking.

FALSE
> ▶ It's okay to admit you don't remember.
> ▶ I'm sorry, my mind just went blank, your name is?"

True or False ...

    4. When shaking hands, a man should wait for a woman to extend her hand.

FALSE

       ▶ Business etiquette has become gender neutral.

       ▶ Women don't have to hesitate to offer their hands first.

True or False ...

    5. When leaving your office to take a client to lunch, you should let her go through the revolving door first.

FALSE

       ▶ The host should be ready on the other side to direct the guest.

True or False ...

    6. It's okay to hold private conversations in office bathrooms and elevators.

FALSE

       ▶ You never know who's listening!

What do you think ...

    7. What percentage of the message you communicate is conveyed through your visual appearance?

75–93%

       ▶ Verbal message filtered by nonverbal cues.

       ▶ Wardrobe should be appropriate.

       ▶ Know your body language.

       ▶ Don't forget to smile!

What do you think ...

    8. When two business people talk face-to-face, how far apart should they stand?

THREE FEET

       ▶ Avoid a colleague's personal space.

       ▶ Don't yell across the room.

       ▶ Understand cultural differences.

True or False ...

    9. It's okay to tell a business associate if his zipper is open.

TRUE

       ▶ Don't prolong the embarrassment.

       ▶ Applies to lipstick on teeth, etc.

       ▶ Be subtle.

True or False ...

10. The host—the one who does the inviting—pays for the client's lunch.

TRUE

> ▶ Know your company's policy.
> ▶ Make sure restaurant is in budget.

True or False ...

11. When using a speakerphone, announce if anyone else is present before the conversation begins.

TRUE

> ▶ Identify everyone in the room.

True or False ...

12. If you're out of the office, it's important to change your voice mail message.

TRUE

> ▶ Indicate when you'll return.
> ▶ Provide information to contact a "real" person, if possible.

True or False ...

13. It's okay to send confidential information and large attachments by email.

FALSE

> ▶ Private email does NOT exist.
> ▶ Deleted messages can be retrieved.
> ▶ Consider traditional mail methods.

True or False ...

14. During a meeting, it's okay to leave a cell phone on if you're expecting a call.

FALSE

> ▶ It's VERY rude!
> ▶ Turn it OFF - use voice mail.

True or False ...

15. If you overhear a colleague's conversation in a cubicle, it's OK to comment on what you just heard.

FALSE

> ▶ Use discretion.
> ▶ Try not to eavesdrop.

Social Business Gatherings

- ▶ You're NOT there to eat!
- ▶ Talk to people you don't know.
- ▶ Shake hands (keep right hand free)
- ▶ Learn small talk (focus on other person).
- ▶ Listen before talking.
- ▶ Make eye contact. Introduce yourself.
- ▶ Avoid taboo topics.
- ▶ Close conversations and circulate.

Business Dinners

- ▶ Never put used silverware on the table.
- ▶ Butter your plate, use that for bread.
- ▶ Butter each piece as you eat it.
- ▶ Take small bite-sized pieces.
- ▶ When done, use 4 o'clock position.
- ▶ Don't ask for a doggie bag.
- ▶ Be discreet; follow lead of host.

Business Netiquette

- ▶ Never send personal email at work.
- ▶ Always use a subject line.
- ▶ Begin message with a greeting.
- ▶ Don't use emoticons.
- ▶ Use proper spelling, grammar, etc.
- ▶ NEVER TYPE IN ALL CAPS!
- ▶ Announce attachments.
- ▶ Close with your name (signature block).

International P's and Q's

- ▶ Men should be gentlemen.
- ▶ Women should dress conservatively.
- ▶ Avoid gesturing.
- ▶ Keep hands OUT of pockets.
- ▶ Don't slouch or lean against things.
- ▶ Don't blow your nose in public.
- ▶ Avoid clichés.

Wrap-Up Quiz

1. In the business arena:
    A. Only men should stand for handshaking and all introductions.
    B. Only women should stand for handshaking and all introductions.
    C. It is not necessary for men or women to stand for handshaking or intro-
        ductions.
    D. Both men and women should stand for handshaking and introductions.

2. In the business arena:
    A. Only men should stand for handshaking and all introductions.
    B. Only women should stand for handshaking and all introductions.
    C. It is not necessary for men or women to stand for handshaking or intro-
        ductions.
    D. Both men and women should stand for handshaking and introductions.

3. To show confidence, authority during a handshake, use:
    A. The bone crusher.
    B. The limp fish.
    C. The glove.
    D. The fingertip holder.
    E. The web-to-web.

4. To show confidence, authority during a handshake, use:
    A. The bone crusher.
    B. The limp fish.
    C. The glove.
    D. The fingertip holder.
    E. The web-to-web.

5. For easy reading, one's name badge should be worn:
    A. On the left shoulder.
    B. On the right shoulder.
    C. On the left hip.
    D. Around one's neck.

6. For easy reading, one's name badge should be worn:
    A. On the left shoulder.
    B. On the right shoulder.
    C. On the left hip.
    D. Around one's neck.

7. If you accidentally drop your fork on the floor in a restaurant
   A. Pick it up, wipe it off, and use it.
   B. Pick it up, give it to the server, and ask him/her to bring you another one.
   C. Leave it on the floor and ask the server to bring you another one.
   D. Leave it on the floor and use your neighbor's fork when he's not looking.

8. If you accidentally drop your fork on the floor in a restaurant
   A. Pick it up, wipe it off, and use it.
   B. Pick it up, give it to the server, and ask him/her to bring you another one.
   C. Leave it on the floor and ask the server to bring you another one.
   D. Leave it on the floor and use your neighbor's fork when he's not looking.

9. If someone mistakenly uses your bread plate, you
   A. Tell him he made a mistake and ask for your plate back.
   B. Don't say anything and eat from your other neighbor's plate.
   C. Don't say anything and convince yourself you don't need bread.
   D. Ask the server for another roll and use the side of your dinner plate.

10. If someone mistakenly uses your bread plate, you
    A. Tell him he made a mistake and ask for your plate back.
    B. Don't say anything and eat from your other neighbor's plate.
    C. Don't say anything and convince yourself you don't need bread.
    D. Ask the server for another roll and use the side of your dinner plate.

11. A woman's handbag, if it's small, can be placed on
    A. A desk.
    B. A boardroom table.
    C. A restaurant table.
    D. All of the above.
    E. None of the above.

12. A woman's handbag, if it's small, can be placed on
    A. A desk.
    B. A boardroom table.
    C. A restaurant table.
    D. All of the above.
    E. None of the above.

13. If you want to remove something in your teeth,
    A. Use your knife when no one is looking.
    B. Raise your napkin to your mouth and be discreet.
    C. Use your business card.
    D. Politely ask your server for a toothpick.
    E. Excuse yourself and go to the bathroom.

14. If you want to remove something in your teeth,
    A. Use your knife when no one is looking.
    B. Raise your napkin to your mouth and be discreet.
    C. Use your business card.
    D. Politely ask your server for a toothpick.
    E. Excuse yourself and go to the bathroom.

15. If you bite into a piece of tough meat that is hard to chew,
    A. Pretend to wipe your mouth and deposit it into your napkin.
    B. Use two fingers or your fork to remove it and place it on the edge of your plate.
    C. Swallow it and hope you don't choke.
    D. None of the above.

16. If you bite into a piece of tough meat that is hard to chew,
    A. Pretend to wipe your mouth and deposit it into your napkin.
    B. Use two fingers or your fork to remove it and place it on the edge of your plate.
    C. Swallow it and hope you don't choke.
    D. None of the above.

17. The best way to meet people and "work a room" is to
    A. Head for the bar or buffet upon arrival.
    B. Introduce yourself to two people who are deep in conversation.
    C. Look confident, stand in the center of the room and wait.
    D. Introduce yourself to groups of three or more.
    E. Stick close to only those you know.

18. The best way to meet people and "work a room" is to
    A. Head for the bar or buffet upon arrival.
    B. Introduce yourself to two people who are deep in conversation.
    C. Look confident, stand in the center of the room and wait.
    D. Introduce yourself to groups of three or more.
    E. Stick close to only those you know.

19. When you are finished eating, your napkin should be
    A. Folded loosely and placed on the right side of your plate.
    B. Folded loosely and placed on the left side of the plate.
    C. Folded loosely and placed in the center of the plate.
    D. Folded like a dove and placed on the seat of your chair.

20. When you are finished eating, your napkin should be
    A. Folded loosely and placed on the right side of your plate.
    B. Folded loosely and placed on the left side of the plate.
    C. Folded loosely and placed in the center of the plate.
    D. Folded like a dove and placed on the seat of your chair.

Employment Workshop

What Do You Want?

▶ What Do You Want to DO With Your Major?
  - What Are Your Talents & Strengths?
  - Work With People (Customers, Clients)?
  - Creative Position or Procedural Job?
  - Big or Small Company?
  - Travel Frequently?

▶ Identify Your Interests & Goals
  - Evaluate Your Qualifications
  - Choose a Career Path
  - Plan Your Future (What's Next?)
  - Search the Open Job Market

The Perfect Resume

▶ Choose a Style That Fits YOU:
  - Chronological

▶ Focuses on Education & Work Experience
  - Functional

▶ Focuses on Skills Rather Than Employment
  - Combination

▶ Profiles What You Can Do for the Employer

Resume Contents

- ▶ Length—One or Two Pages?
- ▶ Heading—ALL Contact Information
- ▶ Career Objective—Be Unique, Skip Mundane
- ▶ Education—College Only; GPA; Graduation
- ▶ Work Experience—Quantify Achievements
- ▶ Capabilities & Skills—Emphasize Job Skills
- ▶ Awards, Honors, Activities
- ▶ References—Provide on Separate Sheet

Resume Samples

- ▶ Find a Format/Style That Fits YOU
- ▶ Focus on Employer Needs
- ▶ Be Unique ... But Professional
- ▶ Use GOOD Paper
- ▶ Don't Mass Copy

Cover Letters

- ▶ Create Uniquely Worded Template
  - Gain Attention in First Paragraph
- ▶ Identify Recipient's Name & Indicate Job Ad
  - Build Interest in Body
- ▶ Relate Reader Benefits & Reduce Resistance
  - Motivate Action in the Closing
- ▶ Ask for Interview & Include Contact Info
- ▶ ALSO ... Reduce "I" Strain!

Interviewing Skills

- ▶ Before the Interview...
  - Do Your Homework—Research the Company
  - Prepare a List of Questions for Them
  - Plan to Sell Yourself (Know Frequently Asked Questions)
  - Bring an Additional Resume
  - Arrive Early & Dress Appropriately (Hanger Rule)
- ▶ After The Interview...
  - Make Notes (Pros, Cons, Additional Questions)
  - Write a Thank You Letter

Interviewing Meals

▶ Follow Your Host (Simon Says)
- Don't Order First
- Napkins on Your Lap or Chair
- Socialize Before Reading Menu
- Know Small Talk (Current Events)
- Know Your Silverware
- Dinner is a Social Occasion w/an Agenda

Know HOW to Order

▶ Arugala ...
▶ Bouillabaise ...
▶ Capers ...
▶ Carpaccio ...
▶ Caviar ...
▶ Ceviche ...
▶ Escargot ...
▶ Foie Gras ...
▶ Fricassee ...
▶ Gnochi ...
▶ Salad Greens
▶ Stew
▶ Flower Bud
▶ Raw Beef
▶ Fish Eggs
▶ Raw Fish
▶ Snails
▶ Goose Liver
▶ Stew
▶ Potato Dumplings

Know HOW to Order

▶ Leeks ...
▶ Morels ...
▶ Parsnips ...
▶ Red Mullet ...
▶ Rhubarb ...
▶ Tartare ...
▶ Truffle ...
▶ Turbot ...

- Venison ...
- Vermicelli ...
- Onions
- Mushroom
- Root
- Fish
- Plant (Tart Pie Filling)
- Raw
- Mushroom
- Fish
- Bambi
- Thin Spaghetti

Follow-Up Letters

- IMMEDIATELY AFTER INTERVIEW...
- Show Gratitude for Opportunity to Interview
- Include Position & Date of Interview
- Indicate What You Learned About the Job
- Emphasize Strengths & Willingness to Learn

Other Tips ...

- Get Permission from References
  - Use PROFESSIONAL References

Application Forms

  - Type or Neatly Print (Handwriting Analysis)
- Send Rejection Follow-Up Letters
  - Opportunity to Maintain on File
  - Emphasize Continued Interest in Company

Know Your Job Market

- Find an Job Posting Online
  - Summer Internship   OR   Real Job
- Assignment:
  - Job Advertisement
  - Cover Letter
  - Resume

Quiz Review

What Three Things Should You Know To Find Your Dream Job?
▶ Know Yourself
▶ Know the Job Market
▶ Know the Employment Process

How Many Jobs Can You Expect to Work During Your Career?
▶ 12–15

What Are the Two Typical Resume Styles?
▶ Chronological—Employment
▶ Functional—Focus on Skills

What Are the Advantages & Disadvantages of Focused Resume Objectives?
▶ Helps the Recruiter
▶ Limits Your Opportunities

How Should Work Experience Be Listed?
▶ Most Recent Jobs First

How Do Large Companies Process Resumes?
▶ Scan w/ Tracking Programs

What Are the Three Purposes of a Letter of Application?
▶ Introduce Your Resume
▶ Highlight Your Strengths
▶ Obtain an Interview

Communicating Across Cultures
Team Activity

In small groups, come up with three unique examples for each of the ambiguous word uses shown below in red. Your team will need one example in each category for each group member. Each group member should be prepared to make an oral presentation such as this:

▶ Avoid **IDIOMS** such as "once in a blue moon," which means something that does not happen very often.
▶ Don't use **SLANG** like "my presentation really bombed," which means it failed.
▶ Spell out **ACRONYMS** like "ASAP"—use "as soon as possible" instead.
▶ Similarly **ABBREVIATIONS** like "DBA," which means "doing business as" should be avoided.
▶ Also stay away from **JARGON** such as "bottom line" when you really mean the main idea.
▶ And finally, do not use **SPORT REFERENCES** like "ballpark figure" because some people my not realize you mean an approximae figure.

Glossary

Accommodation   Rejecting one's goals for those of the other party.

Ad Hoc Committees   Committees that form and carry out a specific task within a given time.

Aesthetics   Environmental factors and how they are manipulated to influence our feelings and emotions. Environmental factors include colors, lighting, spatial arrangement, and sounds.

Audience Analysis   The information gathered regarding the audience that a speaker plans to address. The information includes demographic, situational, and dispositional characteristics of the audience.

Avoidance   Failing to take a position in a conflict.

Artifacts   Objects that we use to express our identities.

Attribution   The process of understanding the reasons for our own as well as other's behaviors.

Attribution Error   When we overestimate dispositional causes and underestimate situational causes of others' actions.

Authoritarian Leaders   strive to have the greatest control over the group and its members.

Beliefs   Those things that we consider as truth.

Brainstorming   A way to solicit alternatives ideas when problem solving.

Causative Influences   Impetuses or forces which have continued to produce a specific speech situation.

Certainty/Superiority Language   Absolute communication that does not allow for further discussion and creates a defensive communication climate.

Chronemics   Refers to how we use and handle time to communicate messages.

Claim   A statement or declaration that we want others to accept.

Circumstantial Influences   Context and environment that shape a specific speech situation.

Codes   Methods used to transport messages: vocal, verbal, visual.

Collaboration   Meeting both parties' needs. It is concerned with finding new options and joint problem solving.

Collectivistic Cultures   Cultures that focus on the collective or group rather than the individual person.

Collectivistic Worldview   Perspective of life where the focus is on the good of the collective regardless of the expense to the individual.

Cohesion   A commitment and attraction to the collective identity of the group.

Combination Method (of generating alternatives)   A combination of the oral style of brainstorming and the silent method of recording that is characteristic of the nominal group technique to generate ideas.

Committees   Work groups that form as a result of the needs of a larger group or the needs of an individual in power.

Communication   A systematic process in which we share ideas and create meaning through human symbolic action.

Competition   Winning at the expense of others.

Compromise   Only partially meeting both parties' needs. Both parties give in.

Conflict   The situation that results when the needs, ideas, and/or opinions of one or more group members are incongruent.

Contemporaneous Influences   The events, norms, and feel of a time period or era that shape a specific speech situation.

Control Language   attempts to manipulate the listener into accepting the speaker's point of view. Defensive communication.

Cultural Competence   The ability to communicate effectively with people from a cultural background that is different from your own.

Democratic Leaders   value the input of members in the group.

Descriptive Language   Describes behaviors without evaluating whether they are good or bad, right or wrong. Supportive communication.

Differentiation   Raising the conflict issue, spending time and energy clarifying the positions, pursuing reasons behind the positions, and acknowledging the severity of the differences. A substantive conflict process.

Direct Definitions   Communicate to us who our parents and society see us as.

Egocentrism   The belief that everything centers around "me" and my way of doing and being.

Emotional Expressiveness   The use of inflection, vocal range, rhythm, emphasis, and tone when speaking.

Empathetic Speech   Communicates to the listener that he or she is worthwhile. Creates a supportive communication climate.

Ethics   Moral principles for living and making decisions inclusive of, beliefs, norms, and values that societies use to determine right from wrong.

Ethos/Ethical Appeal   The character of a speaker and how the audience perceives the speaker's character.

Ethnocentrism   The belief that everything centers around our culture's way of doing and being in our interpersonal relationships.

Evaluative Language   Illustrates us as good or bad, right or wrong.

Equality Language   Communicates congruency. Creates a supportive communication climate.

Explicit Norms   Rules of behavior that are expressed verbally or that may be put in writing.

Extemporaneous Speaking   Speaking from an outline or notes.

Fact   A statement that can be demonstrated as true or false, regardless of our own personal beliefs.

Feedback   The receiver's response to the sender's message

Feng Shui (pronounced fung shway)   A 3,000-year-old Chinese method of using space to maximize the flow of energy.

Formal Roles   Specifically assigned roles by the group that often carry a title.

Frame of Reference   Refers to our background and our personal experiences.

General Purpose   The general rationale behind giving a speech. There are three purposes: (1) to entertain, (2) to inform, and (3) to persuade.

Generalized Other   The faceless group of rules and roles accepted by our social community. The generalized other represents society's concerted views.

Gesture   A movement of the body or limbs that expresses or emphasizes an idea.

Groupthink   A status that results when groups are unable to rationally make decisions because individual group members are too close to each other.

Haptics   Nonverbal communication that involves physical touch.

Heterogeneous Groups   Small groups whose members have little or no demographic commonalties.

Homogeneous Groups   Groups whose members share common interests, attitudes, levels of knowledge, and other demographics.

Implicit Norms   The understood and expected behaviors of the group.

Impromptu Speaking   is free-style speaking. It is strictly off the cuff.

Individualistic Cultures   Cultures that place greater emphasis on the individual person rather than the group.

Individualistic Worldview   Perspective of life in which the focus is on the individual advancing, regardless of the cost to the collective.

Inferences   Statements based on personal preferences and opinions.

Informal Roles   Naturally occurring roles and are based more on function (accomplishing a specific task) than position (overall governing of the group).

Informative Speech   Enlightens the audience and provides them with information that they probably did not already know.

Interpersonal Communication   Moving beyond yourself to consider another person's needs, perspectives, and interpretations of your words and actions in the context of your relationship. (one-to-one communication)

Interpersonal Communication Climate   The way people feel when they interact with each other. Concerned with the feel of closeness and warmth continuums.

Kinesics   Form of nonverbal communication that deals with how we use body movements to communicate.

Laissez Faire   Leaders don't lead much at all; they sit back and let the group self-direct. This leader may call the group together, but that's about it. The group and individual members are left to set their own direction.

Learning Groups   Groups that enable individuals to enhance their knowledge and skills in a particular area.

Logos/Logical Appeal   Refers to the orderly thinking of sequencing and relating one thought or idea to another.

Material Components of Culture   Objects that rise out of our way of life and that have been physically created by humans.

Neutral Speech   Communicates a lack of concern about the listener. Creates defensive communication climate.

Nominal Group Technique   A method of generating ideas that lets individuals generate ideas silently and then have their ideas recorded on the board, the overhead, or a flipchart.

Nonmaterial Components of Culture   Intangible constructions that impact how we behave and think.

Nonverbal Communication   The process of transporting messages through behaviors, physical characteristics, and objects.

Nonverbal Transitions   Physical behaviors that signal to your audience that you are introducing new points or that you are moving on from the present point.

Norms   Informal rules that govern our social and personal conduct.

Norms (group)   Informal rules that govern how members are expected to communicate and behave within the group context.

Oculesics   Form of nonverbal communication that refers to eye behavior.

Olfactics   Form of nonverbal communication that relates to the perception of scents and smells.

Paralanguage (Vocalics)   The way we use our voices to emphasize our messages. Rate, volume, pitch, and inflection.

Particular Others   The people most important to us when we are infants. These are the people that initially communicate to us who we are and what is expected of us.

Perception   How we select, organize, and interpret information so that we can understand our surroundings.

Persuasion   Process of preparing and presenting verbal and nonverbal messages with the purpose of evaluating, sustaining, or altering the reality of an audience.

Persuasive Speech   Seeks some type of behavioral or attitudinal modification.

Physical Appearance   An individual's physical qualities.

Proxemics   A form of nonverbal communication concerned with how we use space to communicate.

Problem-Oriented Language   Solicits collaborative decision-making. Supportive communication climate.

Provisional Language   Communicates a willingness to listen and hear other perspectives and criticisms. Creates a supportive communication climate.

Question of Fact   A type of question asked and answered in a persuasive speech that deals with whether something is believed to be true or to what degree something is factual.

Question of Policy   A type of question asked and answered in a persuasive speech that deals with how things "should" or "ought" to be.

Role   The part that an individual plays within a group.

Self   The multidimensional product that results from the complex process of internalizing and acting from direct definitions that we receive as we communicate.

Self Disclosure   The process of providing others with information about the self.

Self-Help Groups   Groups that provide support to individuals who need help dealing with some aspect of their personal lives.

Self-Fulfilling Prophecy   When we act in ways that bring about expectations or judgments of ourselves, i.e., fulfilling the prophecy of the haters.

Self-Sabotage   Arises out of negative self-talk. We talk ourselves into negative situations.

Self-Serving Bias   A distorted perception of our worth in relation to others in the world. We develop an unrealistic image of ourselves and our abilities when we perceive ourselves as invincible and omnipotent.

Self-talk (Intrapersonal Communication)   The inner conversations we have with ourselves that greatly influences our emotional well-being.

Service Groups provide their members with the opportunity to show goodwill.

Small Groups   Three to five interdependent individuals who communicate with one another to accomplish a common goal.

Social Groups Seek to accomplish a recreational or social end. Essentially these groups want to have fun.

Speaking from a Manuscript entails writing out your entire speech on paper and reading it to an audience.

Speaking from Memory entails writing the speech on paper, memorizing the speech, and, from memory, delivering the speech to the audience.

Specific Purpose The general purpose plus one main aspect of your topic. The specific purpose narrows your topic so that you can focus on accomplishing one specific goal.

Speech Communication (Communication Studies) A humanistic and scientific discipline that focuses on how, why, and what effects communication has on people.

Spontaneous Speech Instantaneous speech, not contrived, not manipulative and does not have a hidden agenda. Supportive communication climate.

Standing Committees Committees formed so that they can routinely carry out a specific function.

Stasis Status of the case.

Strategy Language Planned message with hidden motives that intends to dupe or manipulate listeners.

Symbolic Action The usage of verbal, as well as nonverbal symbols to create meaning.

Task Force Ad hoc committees that are appointed to investigate specific issues and that are expected to make recommendations based upon their findings.

Team Special kind of work group whose success is based on the resources contributed by the individual members.

Thesis Statement Tells exactly what you plan to do in the speech.

Turn-taking Refers to who speaks (and when) and who listens (and when) in a one-on-one or group conversation.

Verbal Codes (language) The means of transporting our messages using the spoken word.

Verbal Transitions Words or sentences that connect ideas and the parts of your speech.

Visual Codes (nonverbal) Behaviors that we use to communicate messages, such as facial expressions, gestures, posture, appearance and so on.

Vocal Codes (paralanguage) The vocal elements that accompany the spoken word. These codes include the volume, pitch, rate and inflections of the voice.

Work Groups Focus on accomplishing specific goals or tasks for associations, companies, organizations, faith groups and institutions.

Worldview Your vantage point, how you see the world.

Outlines

Cause–Effect

Organize this speech arguing that one situation is directly caused by another.

I. **Introduction**

    A. **Attention Gaining Device:** *Choose a startling statistic or fact, a powerful example or illustration, or rhetorical question to capture your audience's attention.*

    _____

    _____

    _____

    _____

    _____

    B. **Audience Motivation:** *Explain to the audience how your subject directly impacts them. Give them a reason why they should listen.*

    _____

    _____

    _____

    _____

    _____

    C. **Establish Credibility:** *Tell the audience what makes you an expert on the topic.*

    _____

    _____

    _____

    _____

    _____

D. **Specific Purpose and Thesis:** *Tell the audience in a concise sentence the overall theme of the speech and your purpose for making the speech. Do you know your purpose? Are you informing, persuading, or entertaining?*

_____

_____

_____

_____

_____

E. **Preview Main Points:** *Tell the audience the main points of your speech.*

_____

_____

_____

_____

_____

II. **Body** (Present the issues that you talk about in your thesis statement and in your preview.)

A. **Main Point #1** *(The Cause)*

_____

_____

_____

_____

_____

1. Supporting Evidence for Main Point #1
   ❏ Statistic
   ❏ Example
   ❏ Illustration
   ❏ Comparison
   ❏ Quote/Expert Testimony
   ❏ Visual Aid

_____

_____

_____

_____

_____

2. Supporting Evidence for Main Point #1
   - ❏ Statistic
   - ❏ Example
   - ❏ Illustration
   - ❏ Comparison
   - ❏ Quote/Expert Testimony
   - ❏ Visual Aid

   _____

   _____

   _____

   _____

   _____

3. Supporting Evidence for Main Point #1
   - ❏ Statistic
   - ❏ Example
   - ❏ Illustration
   - ❏ Comparison
   - ❏ Quote/Expert Testimony
   - ❏ Visual Aid

   _____

   _____

   _____

   _____

   _____

[Transition]

B. **Main Point #2** _(The Effect.)_

_____

_____

_____

_____

_____

1. Supporting Evidence for Main Point #2
   - ❏ Statistic
   - ❏ Example
   - ❏ Illustration
   - ❏ Comparison
   - ❏ Quote/Expert Testimony
   - ❏ Visual Aid

   _____

   _____

   _____

   _____

2. Supporting Evidence for Main Point #2
   - ❏ Statistic
   - ❏ Example
   - ❏ Illustration
   - ❏ Comparison
   - ❏ Quote/Expert Testimony
   - ❏ Visual Aid

   _____

   _____

   _____

   _____

3. Supporting Evidence for Main Point #2
   - ❏ Statistic
   - ❏ Example
   - ❏ Illustration
   - ❏ Comparison
   - ❏ Quote/Expert Testimony
   - ❏ Visual Aid

[Transition]

   _____

   _____

   _____

   _____

   _____

III. **Conclusion**

    A. **Review Main Points:** *Remind the audience of the main points that you have just discussed.*

_____

_____

_____

_____

_____

    B. **Memorable Statement:** *Put the cherry on top. Choose a startling statistic or fact, a powerful example or illustration, or rhetorical question to conclude your presentation. You may also want to make reference to something that you said in the introduction.*

_____

_____

_____

_____

_____

Chronological

Organize this speech based on time relationships.

I. **Introduction**
   A. **Attention Gaining Device:** *Choose a startling statistic or fact, a powerful example or illustration, or rhetorical question to capture your audience's attention.*

   _____

   _____

   _____

   _____

   _____

   B. **Audience Motivation:** *Explain to the audience how your subject directly impacts them. Give them a reason why they should listen.*

   _____

   _____

   _____

   _____

   _____

   C. **Establish Credibility:** *Tell the audience what makes you an expert on the topic.*

   _____

   _____

   _____

   _____

   _____

   D. **Specific Purpose and Thesis:** *Tell the audience in a concise sentence the overall theme of the speech and your purpose for making the speech. Do you know your purpose? Are you informing, persuading, or entertaining?*

   _____

   _____

   _____

   _____

   _____

E. **Preview Main Points:** *Tell the audience the main points of your speech.*

_____

_____

_____

_____

_____

II. **Body** (Present the issues that you talk about in your thesis statement and in your preview.)

A. **Main Point #1** *(The first or last item of a chronological sequence)*

_____

_____

_____

_____

1. Supporting Evidence for Main Point #1
    ❑ Statistic
    ❑ Example
    ❑ Illustration
    ❑ Comparison
    ❑ Quote/Expert Testimony
    ❑ Visual Aid

_____

_____

_____

_____

2. **Supporting Evidence for Main Point #1**
    ❑ Statistic
    ❑ Example
    ❑ Illustration
    ❑ Comparison
    ❑ Quote/Expert Testimony
    ❑ Visual Aid

_____

_____

_____

_____

   3. **Supporting Evidence for Main Point #1**
- ❏ Statistic
- ❏ Example
- ❏ Illustration
- ❏ Comparison
- ❏ Quote/Expert Testimony
- ❏ Visual Aid

[Transition]

_____

_____

_____

B. **Main Point #2** *(The second or next to the last item of a chronological sequence)*

_____

_____

_____

_____

   1. Supporting Evidence for Main Point #2
- ❏ Statistic
- ❏ Example
- ❏ Illustration
- ❏ Comparison
- ❏ Quote/Expert Testimony
- ❏ Visual Aid

_____

_____

_____

_____

2. Supporting Evidence for Main Point #2
   - ❏ Statistic
   - ❏ Example
   - ❏ Illustration
   - ❏ Comparison
   - ❏ Quote/Expert Testimony
   - ❏ Visual Aid

_____

_____

_____

_____

3. Supporting Evidence for Main Point #2
   - ❏ Statistic
   - ❏ Example
   - ❏ Illustration
   - ❏ Comparison
   - ❏ Quote/Expert Testimony
   - ❏ Visual Aid

[Transition]

_____

_____

_____

_____

_____

_____

C. **Main Point # 3** *(The third item of a chronological sequence)*

_____

_____

_____

_____

_____

1. Supporting Evidence for Main Point #3
    - ❏ Statistic
    - ❏ Example
    - ❏ Illustration
    - ❏ Comparison
    - ❏ Quote/Expert Testimony
    - ❏ Visual Aid

    _____

    _____

    _____

    _____

    _____

2. Supporting Evidence for Main Point #3
    - ❏ Statistic
    - ❏ Example
    - ❏ Illustration
    - ❏ Comparison
    - ❏ Quote/Expert Testimony
    - ❏ Visual Aid

    _____

    _____

    _____

    _____

    _____

3. Supporting Evidence for Main Point #3
    - ❏ Statistic
    - ❏ Example
    - ❏ Illustration
    - ❏ Comparison
    - ❏ Quote/Expert Testimony
    - ❏ Visual Aid

    _____

    _____

    _____

    _____

    _____

III. **Conclusion**

    A. **Review Main Points:** *Remind the audience of the main points that you have just discussed.*

_____

_____

_____

_____

_____

    B. **Memorable Statement:** Put the cherry on top. *Choose a startling statistic or fact, a powerful example or illustration, or rhetorical question to conclude your presentation. You may also want to make reference to something that you said in the introduction.*

_____

_____

_____

_____

Comparison

Organize this speech by comparing two or more situations, emphasizing their differences and similarities.

I. **Introduction**
    A. **Attention Gaining Device:** *Choose a startling statistic or fact, a powerful example or illustration, or rhetorical question to capture your audience's attention.*

    _____

    _____

    _____

    _____

    B. **Audience Motivation:** *Explain to the audience how your subject directly impacts them. Give them a reason why they should listen.*

    _____

    _____

    _____

    _____

    C. **Establish Credibility:** *Tell the audience what makes you an expert on the topic.*

    _____

    _____

    _____

    _____

    D. **Specific Purpose and Thesis:** *Tell the audience in a concise sentence the overall theme of the speech and your purpose for making the speech. Do you know your purpose? Are you informing, persuading, or entertaining?*

    _____

    _____

    _____

    _____

E. **Preview Main Points:** *Tell the audience the main points of your speech.*

_____

_____

_____

_____

_____

II. **Body** (Present the issues that you talk about in your thesis statement and in your preview.)

_____

_____

_____

_____

_____

A. **Main Point #1** *(The first item to be compared)*

_____

_____

_____

_____

_____

    1. Supporting Evidence for Main Point #1
- ❏ Statistic
- ❏ Example
- ❏ Illustration
- ❏ Comparison
- ❏ Quote/Expert Testimony
- ❏ Visual Aid

_____

_____

_____

_____

_____

2. Supporting Evidence for Main Point #1
   - ❏ Statistic
   - ❏ Example
   - ❏ Illustration
   - ❏ Comparison
   - ❏ Quote/Expert Testimony
   - ❏ Visual Aid

_____

_____

_____

_____

_____

3. Supporting Evidence for Main Point #1
   - ❏ Statistic
   - ❏ Example
   - ❏ Illustration
   - ❏ Comparison
   - ❏ Quote/Expert Testimony
   - ❏ Visual Aid

[Transition]

_____

_____

_____

_____

_____

B. **Main Point #2** *(The second item to be compared)*

_____

_____

_____

_____

_____

1. Supporting Evidence for Main Point #2
    - ❑ Statistic
    - ❑ Example
    - ❑ Illustration
    - ❑ Comparison
    - ❑ Quote/Expert Testimony
    - ❑ Visual Aid

    _____

    _____

    _____

    _____

    _____

2. Supporting Evidence for Main Point #2
    - ❑ Statistic
    - ❑ Example
    - ❑ Illustration
    - ❑ Comparison
    - ❑ Quote/Expert Testimony
    - ❑ Visual Aid

    _____

    _____

    _____

    _____

    _____

3. Supporting Evidence for Main Point #2
    - ❑ Statistic
    - ❑ Example
    - ❑ Illustration
    - ❑ Comparison
    - ❑ Quote/Expert Testimony
    - ❑ Visual Aid

[Transition]

_____

_____

_____

_____

C. **Main Point # 3** *(The third item to be compared)*

_____

_____

_____

_____

_____

1. Supporting Evidence for Main Point #3
   ❑ Statistic
   ❑ Example
   ❑ Illustration
   ❑ Comparison
   ❑ Quote/Expert Testimony
   ❑ Visual Aid

_____

_____

_____

_____

_____

2. Supporting Evidence for Main Point #3
   ❑ Statistic
   ❑ Example
   ❑ Illustration
   ❑ Comparison
   ❑ Quote/Expert Testimony
   ❑ Visual Aid

_____

_____

_____

_____

_____

3. Supporting Evidence for Main Point #3
    ❏ Statistic
    ❏ Example
    ❏ Illustration
    ❏ Comparison
    ❏ Quote/Expert Testimony
    ❏ Visual Aid

[Transition]

_____
_____
_____
_____
_____

III. **Conclusion**
  A. **Review Main Points:** _Remind the audience of the main points that you have just discussed._

_____
_____
_____
_____
_____

  B. **Memorable Statement:** Put the cherry on top. _Choose a startling statistic or fact, a powerful example or illustration, or rhetorical question to conclude your presentation. You may also want to make reference to something that you said in the introduction._

_____
_____
_____
_____
_____

Problem–Solution

Organize this speech into a discussion of a problem and solution.

I.   **Introduction**
   A.   **Attention Gaining Device:** *Choose a startling statistic or fact, a powerful example or illustration, or rhetorical question to capture your audience's attention.*

   _____

   _____

   _____

   _____

   B.   **Audience Motivation:** *Explain to the audience how your subject directly impacts them. Give them a reason why they should listen.*

   _____

   _____

   _____

   _____

   _____

   C.   **Establish Credibility:** *Tell the audience what makes you an expert on the topic.*

   _____

   _____

   _____

   _____

   _____

   D.   **Specific Purpose and Thesis:** *Tell the audience in a concise sentence the overall theme of the speech and your purpose for making the speech. Do you know your purpose? Are you informing, persuading, or entertaining?*

   _____

   _____

   _____

   _____

   _____

E.   **Preview Main Points:** *Tell the audience the main points of your speech.*

_____

_____

_____

_____

_____

II.   **Body** (Present the issues that you talk about in your thesis statement and in your preview.)

A.   **Main Point #1** *(The Problem)*

_____

_____

_____

_____

1.   Supporting Evidence for Main Point #1
- ❑   Statistic
- ❑   Example
- ❑   Illustration
- ❑   Comparison
- ❑   Quote/Expert Testimony
- ❑   Visual Aid

_____

_____

_____

_____

2.   Supporting Evidence for Main Point #1
- ❑   Statistic
- ❑   Example
- ❑   Illustration
- ❑   Comparison
- ❑   Quote/Expert Testimony
- ❑   Visual Aid

_____

_____

_____

_____

3. Supporting Evidence for Main Point #1
    - ❏ Statistic
    - ❏ Example
    - ❏ Illustration
    - ❏ Comparison
    - ❏ Quote/Expert Testimony
    - ❏ Visual Aid

[Transition]

_____

_____

_____

_____

_____

B. **Main Point #2** *(The Solution)*

_____

_____

_____

_____

1. Supporting Evidence for Main Point #2
    - ❏ Statistic
    - ❏ Example
    - ❏ Illustration
    - ❏ Comparison
    - ❏ Quote/Expert Testimony
    - ❏ Visual Aid

_____

_____

_____

_____

2. Supporting Evidence for Main Point #2
   - ❏ Statistic
   - ❏ Example
   - ❏ Illustration
   - ❏ Comparison
   - ❏ Quote/Expert Testimony
   - ❏ Visual Aid

_____

_____

_____

_____

_____

3. Supporting Evidence for Main Point #2
   - ❏ Statistic
   - ❏ Example
   - ❏ Illustration
   - ❏ Comparison
   - ❏ Quote/Expert Testimony
   - ❏ Visual Aid

[Transition]

_____

_____

_____

_____

_____

III. **Conclusion**
   A. **Review Main Points:** _Remind the audience of the main points that you have just dis-cussed._

_____

_____

_____

_____

_____

B. **Memorable Statement:** Put the cherry on top. *Choose a startling statistic or fact, a powerful example or illustration, or rhetorical question to conclude your presentation. You may also want to make reference to something that you said in the introduction.*

_____

_____

_____

_____

_____

Topical

Organize this speech into several categories or areas of focus.

I. **Introduction**
    A. **Attention Gaining Device:** *Choose a startling statistic or fact, a powerful example or illustration, or rhetorical question to capture your audience's attention.*

    _____

    _____

    _____

    _____

    _____

    B. **Audience Motivation:** *Explain to the audience how your subject directly impacts them. Give them a reason why they should listen.*

    _____

    _____

    _____

    _____

    _____

    C. **Establish Credibility:** *Tell the audience what makes you an expert on the topic.*

    _____

    _____

    _____

    _____

    _____

    D. **Specific Purpose and Thesis:** *Tell the audience in a concise sentence the overall theme of the speech and your purpose for making the speech. Do you know your purpose? Are you informing, persuading, or entertaining?*

    _____

    _____

    _____

    _____

    _____

E. **Preview Main Points:** *Tell the audience the main points of your speech.*

_____

_____

_____

_____

_____

II. **Body** (Present the issues that you talk about in your thesis statement and in your preview.)

A. **Main Point #1** *(The first topic to be discussed)*

_____

_____

_____

_____

_____

1. Supporting Evidence for Main Point #1
    - ❏ Statistic
    - ❏ Example
    - ❏ Illustration
    - ❏ Comparison
    - ❏ Quote/Expert Testimony
    - ❏ Visual Aid

_____

_____

_____

_____

_____

2. Supporting Evidence for Main Point #1
   - ❑ Statistic
   - ❑ Example
   - ❑ Illustration
   - ❑ Comparison
   - ❑ Quote/Expert Testimony
   - ❑ Visual Aid

_____

_____

_____

_____

_____

3. Supporting Evidence for Main Point #1
   - ❑ Statistic
   - ❑ Example
   - ❑ Illustration
   - ❑ Comparison
   - ❑ Quote/Expert Testimony
   - ❑ Visual Aid

[Transition]

_____

_____

_____

_____

_____

B. **Main Point #2** *(The second topic to be discussed)*

_____

_____

_____

_____

_____

1. Supporting Evidence for Main Point #2
   - ❑ Statistic
   - ❑ Example
   - ❑ Illustration
   - ❑ Comparison
   - ❑ Quote/Expert Testimony
   - ❑ Visual Aid

   _____

   _____

   _____

   _____

   _____

2. Supporting Evidence for Main Point #2
   - ❑ Statistic
   - ❑ Example
   - ❑ Illustration
   - ❑ Comparison
   - ❑ Quote/Expert Testimony
   - ❑ Visual Aid

   _____

   _____

   _____

   _____

   _____

3. Supporting Evidence for Main Point #2
   - ❑ Statistic
   - ❑ Example
   - ❑ Illustration
   - ❑ Comparison
   - ❑ Quote/Expert Testimony
   - ❑ Visual Aid

[Transition]

_____

_____

_____

_____

C. **Main Point # 3** *(The third topic to be discussed)*

_____

_____

_____

_____

_____

1. Supporting Evidence for Main Point #3
    ❏ Statistic
    ❏ Example
    ❏ Illustration
    ❏ Comparison
    ❏ Quote/Expert Testimony
    ❏ Visual Aid

_____

_____

_____

_____

_____

2. Supporting Evidence for Main Point #3
    ❏ Statistic
    ❏ Example
    ❏ Illustration
    ❏ Comparison
    ❏ Quote/Expert Testimony
    ❏ Visual Aid

_____

_____

_____

_____

_____

    3. Supporting Evidence for Main Point #3
- ❏ Statistic
- ❏ Example
- ❏ Illustration
- ❏ Comparison
- ❏ Quote/Expert Testimony
- ❏ Visual Aid

[Transition]

_____

_____

_____

_____

_____

III. **Conclusion**
   A. **Review Main Points:** *Remind the audience of the main points that you have just discussed.*

_____

_____

_____

_____

_____

   B. **Memorable Statement:** Put the cherry on top. *Choose a startling statistic or fact, a powerful example or illustration, or rhetorical question to conclude your presentation. You may also want to make reference to something that you said in the introduction.*

_____

_____

_____

_____

_____

Index